Education among
Indigenous Palestinians in Israel

Education among Indigenous Palestinians in Israel

Inequality, Cultural Hegemony, and Social Change

MAJID AL-HAJ

SUNY
PRESS

Published by State University of New York Press, Albany

For information, contact State University of New York Press, Albany, NY
www.sunypress.edu

Library of Congress Cataloging-in-Publication Data

Name: Al-Haj, Majid, author.
Title: Education among indigenous Palestinians in Israel : inequality, cultural
  hegemony, and social change / Majid Al-Haj.
Description: Albany : State University of New York Press, [2024] | Series:
  SUNY series, Intersections: Philosophy and Critical Theory | Includes
  bibliographical references and index.
Identifiers: ISBN 9781438498546 (hardcover : alk. paper) | ISBN 9781438498560
  (ebook) | ISBN 9781438498553 (pbk. : alk. paper)
Further information is available at the Library of Congress.

To my grandchildren, Majid Jr., Omar, and Aya,
who symbolize the hope for a better future!

Contents

List of Illustrations

Figures

Tables

Acknowledgments

I am indebted to many people for their help and encouragement while this book was in the making. First and foremost, I wish to thank my wife, Ibtisam, and my children—Ibrahim, Hassan, Moataz, and Nadine. Without their unfailing support, understanding, and constant encouragement, this book would not have been possible. Special thanks go to my son Moataz, who devotedly offered his outstanding technological skills in response to my relevant queries throughout my work on this monograph.

The longitudinal research on which this monograph is based covers a period spanning more than 70 years and is grounded in qualitative and quantitative data I accumulated over 30 years of fieldwork. Throughout this long process, a large number of people participated in the detailed interviews, focus group discussions, field observations, field studies, surveys, and more. My sincere thanks go to all of them, including students, teachers, school principals, superintendents, professionals, facilitators, field workers, and community representatives. Special thanks to the volunteers and professional staff of INSANN and to the leaders of the formerly non-recognized Palestinian villages. I have been fortunate to witness the successful outcome of the long and persistent struggle of the inhabitants of these villages for official recognition and the wonderful ways they are now reaping the fruits of the seeds planted by INSANN in the fields of education and culture.

Thanks to the head and administrative staff of the Research Authority at the University of Haifa, which provided generous funds for preparing this manuscript for publication. Thanks to Donna Bossin, who I found to be a most congenial editor. My thanks furthermore go to Carly Miller, the copyeditor, for her effective and diligent work. Special thanks go to Dr. Rebecca Colesworthy, senior acquisitions editor at SUNY. I very much enjoyed Rebecca's enthusiasm, understanding, support, and efficient work throughout the various stages of preparing this monograph for publication. The cooperation of Ryan Morris, Aimee Harrison, Julia Cosacchi, and Kate R. Seburyamo at SUNY Press was most helpful. The remarks and suggestions of the three anonymous readers proved very useful, and I extend my sincere thanks to all of them.

Majid Al-Haj

Introduction

This monograph traces the education system among the Palestinian Arabs in Israel since the establishment of the state, with a brief background on the pre-state period. It seeks to examine the complex relationship between education and social change among an indigenous "involuntary" minority living in an ethnonational state, which, despite its pluralistic structure and formal democracy, lacks multicultural ideology. The monograph discusses historical changes along with educational policies, formal programs, and local initiatives for empowerment originating in the Arab community. Using a comparative approach, the study juxtaposes the Arab and Hebrew education systems from early childhood through higher education in terms of administration, resources, curriculum content, and returns. The monograph offers a detailed analysis of the impact of the ongoing Israeli-Palestinian conflict on the goals and content of Arab and Hebrew education, with special focus on the narratives and official knowledge conveyed to Jewish and Arab students through the history curriculum. Changes in education are analyzed together with contextual, demographic, economic, and sociopolitical changes at the local, national, and regional levels.

This monograph represents the only comprehensive and current social science account of contemporary Palestinian Arab education in Israel to date. Moreover, it is the only detailed analysis of Arab education that is based on longitudinal research, thus providing an important opportunity to examine trends in formal policy, school content, educational attainment, and outcomes and other important issues, with the added perspective afforded by the passage of time. No less significant, it simultaneously addresses formal policies of control versus efforts for self-empowerment initiated by the indigenous Palestinian community. In this context, the monograph represents the first systematic examination of an authentic model for social change and educational empowerment initiated by the Palestinian Arabs in Israel through a civil society organization. Throughout this monograph I use the terms Palestinian Arabs in Israel, Palestinian Arabs, the Palestinian/Arab minority, Arabs, and Arab population interchangeably.

Methodology

The analysis incorporates a broad variety of qualitative and quantitative methods to provide a thorough examination of the education system. The qualitative methods include the use of pertinent documents from the State Archives, in addition to specific reports obtained from the Ministry of Education and the minutes of the Follow-Up Committee on Arab Education in Israel. Until recently, a large portion of the documents obtained from the State Archives were classified as "secret" or "top secret." They provide an outstanding opportunity to examine the foundations of the official policy toward the Arab population in general, and toward the education system in particular, during the first decade of statehood, a policy that was crucial in determining the structure and goals of Arab education.

The qualitative research also entailed a content analysis of the history curricula in the Arab and Hebrew schools over a period of 70 years, from 1950 through 2020, as well as analysis of pertinent reports in Israeli newspapers and periodicals published in Arabic, Hebrew, and English. The Hebrew publications included *Al-Hamishmar, Davar, Haaretz, Leket, Lemerchav, Maariv*, and *Yisrael Hayoum*. The Arabic publications were *Al-Gadid, Al-Hadaf, Al-Ittihad, Al-Mujtama', Kul el-Arab, Al-Sinnarah*, and *Fasl el-Makal*. The analysis also included the English-language newspaper *The Jerusalem Post*.

In addition, the qualitative methods included conducting three focus groups: a focus group of 14 Arab students from different faculties at the University of Haifa (November 2019) and two focus groups of Arab teachers (January 2020), one that included 10 Arab elementary school teachers and another that included 12 Arab teachers from secondary and middle schools.

The focus group technique was used as a *supplementary* data source and a follow-up data collection method to further explore the meaning of the survey data and obtain a sense of recent trends. Focus groups offer several advantages. They provide an opportunity to observe a large number of interactions on a topic within a limited period of time. Moreover, they facilitate the exploration of controversial issues and complex and sensitive subjects. Focus group discussions enable group members to react and build on the responses of other group members. In addition, the results of focus groups are easy to understand and interpret since the researchers can ask respondents to elaborate and further explain their statements. (For reviews on the focus group technique, see Morgan 1998; Litosseliti 2003; Tadajewski 2016.)

By nature, focus groups do not constitute representative samples and have several other limitations (for limitations of focus groups, see Litosseliti 2003, 21). Nevertheless, we sought to select groups that represented a wide spectrum of experiences and attitudes. In addition, we made sure that the participants selected were affiliated with the main categories of the studied groups.

The focus groups were moderated by professional moderators, who were informed of the study's aims, content, and the main principles to be sought in the group discussion (for the skills required of moderators, see Litosseliti 2003, 42). Every effort was made to maintain a comfortable, flexible, and open atmosphere during the discussions and to enable all participants to contribute. The research team ensured participants that their identities would remain anonymous. Consequently, the names used in the text are pseudonyms, unless otherwise indicated.

The questions formulated for the focus groups were unstructured open-ended questions according to specific topics. The analysis of the discussions was based on strictly qualitative methods that entailed examination of direct quotations from the discussions and relevant statements from the one-to-one interview data. In the analysis, these statements were used as illustrative quotations without losing sight of the specific context within which the material was generated (e.g., Wilkinson 1998, 196).

The qualitative research also entailed systematic observations conducted at a number of elementary, middle, and secondary Arab schools in the Galilee (northern Israel) and the Little Triangle region (central Israel) during the months of January and February 2020. These school visits also provided opportunities to conduct a number of unstructured interviews with teachers, principals, and superintendents. Yet in the wake of the COVID-19 pandemic and the consequent school closures, efforts to continue this systematic observation through 2021 were very difficult and in many cases impossible.

The quantitative methods entailed two major surveys. The first survey, conducted in November 1993, was the first representative nationwide survey of Arab teachers in Israel. Based on a representative sample of 852 teachers, the survey examined the status, attitudes, and orientation of Arab teachers in Israel. The sample was selected in three stages. First, 26 localities were randomly selected to represent the different categories of Arab localities: (a) geographical area (Galilee-north, Triangle-center, Negev–Naqab-south); (b) religion (Muslim, Christian, Druze, mixed communities); and (c) size, as determined by municipal status (town, local authority, regional authority, none). Second, a sample of schools was selected from each chosen locality according to a predetermined quota based on population data regarding school level, type, and affiliation. Third, a random sample of teachers was selected from the schools included in the sample in accordance with the predetermined quota based on school size. The research tool was a multiple-choice questionnaire that was distributed to the participants, who filled it out individually and anonymously.

The second survey focused on problems and adjustment patterns among Arab and Jewish students. It was conducted in May 2001 among a representative sample of Arab and Jewish students at the University of Haifa, which was chosen because it has the largest concentration of Arab students among Israeli universities. Moreover, the Arab students at the University of Haifa constitute a cross-section of Arab students in Israel in terms of religious affiliation, residential locality, gender, and other pertinent characteristics. The sample of Jewish students was aimed at placing the findings within a comparative perspective.

This survey used three-step sampling: (1) selecting the main faculties in which Arab students enroll—humanities, social sciences, healthcare, natural sciences, education, and law; (2) randomly selecting one department from each faculty; (3) selecting one compulsory course for each year of undergraduate studies and one course from the first year of graduate studies. A total of 410 Jewish and 193 Arab students were interviewed. Arab students were overrepresented in the sample (32 percent in the sample compared to 18 percent of the student body) to ensure that the different subgroups among the Arab students were represented and to have enough cases for statistical analysis.

In addition, the quantitative analysis examined available pertinent statistics and reports from the Israel Central Bureau of Statistics over the course of more than 70 years, from 1949 through 2022. These include all the annual Statistical Abstracts of Israel and special press reports up to 2022. National Institute for Testing and Evaluation (NITE) reports for the period 1991–2020 were used to analyze the Psychometric Entrance Test (PET), which is required for admission to Israeli universities and academic colleges. In addition, the analysis utilized relevant data about local school tests (Meitzav) provided by RAMA–the National Authority for Measurement and Evaluation under the auspices of the Ministry of Education, together with data from international tests, including the Programme for International Student Assessment (PISA) (2006–2018) and Trends in International Mathematics and Science Study (TIMSS) (1999–2019).

Chapter Descriptions

The monograph contains seven chapters and a conclusion, as follows:

Chapter 1 stipulates a general theoretical framework on education, multiculturalism, and social change among minorities in contemporary societies. The framework is based upon an eclectic approach that combines elements from a number of theoretical perspectives, among them critical multicultural education, Freirean critical-transformative pedagogy, and Gramscian theory of cultural hegemony. Based on these elements, I propose a critical model of *empowering multicultural education.*

Chapter 2 provides background on the status and characteristics of the Palestinian Arabs in Israel and discusses their identity formation. I begin by outlining theories pertaining to multicultural democracy and the rights of indigenous groups and national minorities. I then summarize developments among the Palestinian Arabs in the wake of their transition from a majority into an "involuntary minority" after Israel was established. Next, I discuss the main factors that affected their social, economic, and political development as well as their complex status as a "double periphery" simultaneously situated at the margins both of Israeli society and of the Palestinian national movement. I conclude with a detailed analysis of the major barriers to multicultural democracy in Israel, especially Israel's ethnonational character, the securitization of state-minority relations, and the blurring of majority-minority boundaries.

Chapters 3 to 6 cover the educational system for the Arabs since the establishment of the state of Israel, from elementary school through higher education.

Chapter 3 traces the main developments in formal education for the Palestinian Arabs in Israel since the establishment of the state, including a brief summary covering the pre-state period. First, I provide some background about the administrative structure of Arab education and describe the policy considerations that have led to this structure. Next, I point out the main trends in the expansion of education among the Palestinian Arab minority, as reflected in the increase in the number of Arab students and the growing educational attainment of Arab female students, from early childhood through the end of high school. The second part of this chapter focuses on qualitative changes and inequalities vis-à-vis Hebrew education. After outlining a brief theoretical framework, I examine the achievements of Arab students compared to those of their Jewish counterparts based on scores on local Israeli tests (Meitzav and Bagrut) and a series of international tests (PISA and TIMSS). I also examine trends that reflect educational inequalities between Jews and Arabs as well as inequalities within each group based on gender and socioeconomic background, and I discuss the factors contributing to these inequalities. I conclude this chapter with a brief discussion of the implications of the COVID-19 pandemic on educational gaps between Arab and Jewish schools.

Chapter 4 is devoted to the goals and content of Arab education compared to Hebrew education. It discusses how the majority manipulates the education system as a mechanism of control and cultural hegemony. More specifically, the chapter examines how rival histories and competing narratives are taught in the shadow of the Israeli-Palestinian conflict. After proposing a theoretical framework, I give some background on the goals of Arab and Hebrew education that were introduced when Israel was established and discuss how these goals have changed over time. The major part of this chapter constitutes a content analysis of the history curriculum over 70 years, from the establishment of the state until the present. The critical multicultural perspective used to examine the findings sheds light on the limits of the education system and the repercussions of the lack of multicultural ideology on the possibility of enhancing diversity and mutual acceptance of rival narratives in a deeply divided society.

Chapter 5 examines the status and attitudes of Arab teachers in Israel. After a brief theoretical discussion, I outline the foundations of the policy of control and the culture of silence imposed upon Arab teachers immediately after the state was established. I then focus on the findings of a nationwide survey that examined the characteristics of Arab teachers and their attitudes toward cardinal issues within the school system and in society at large. A special section is devoted to burnout among Arab teachers and the impact of individual, institutional, and societal factors on burnout rates. Recent local and global trends are discussed, including the impact of the COVID-19 pandemic on the status and conduct of Arab teachers.

Chapter 6 examines higher education among the Palestinian Arabs in Israel. In this chapter, I trace the main trends in the expansion of tertiary education among the Arab population from the establishment of the state until the present period and compare these trends to the Jewish population. First, I outline the factors that have made education in general, and higher education in particular, top priorities for the Arabs. Along with the impressive expansion of higher education among the Arabs in Israel, I discuss factors that have retarded their educational attainment. More specifically, I discuss the role of the PET as a gatekeeper that has negatively affected not only Arabs' access to higher education but also their chances of being admitted to prestigious areas of study. Next, I outline the main adaptation problems of Arab students during their academic studies, with special emphasis on cultural adaptation and its implications for identity and political social-ization. I conclude this chapter with a detailed discussion of employment opportunities for Arab college and university graduates and the relationship between educational expansion and socioeconomic mobility.

Chapters 7 focuses on empowerment through local initiatives among the Palestinian Arabs in Israel. I begin with a brief theoretical introduction to empowerment in general, and among indigenous minorities in particular, and then discuss the role of nongovernmental organizations (NGOs). After that, I briefly summarize the obstacles to the development of civil society organizations among the Palestinian Arabs in Israel.

The major part of this chapter is devoted to an analysis of the unique experience of INSANN, which was established in 1991 as the first nationwide Palestinian NGO in Israel in the field of education and culture. I provide a detailed analysis of INSANN's strategy of empowerment and social change, as reflected in its various community projects and initiatives. I conclude by discussing the significance of civil society organizations among minorities and the lessons to be learned from this specific experience.

In the conclusion of this monograph, I summarize and further consider the central theoretical questions raised throughout. In particular, I discuss the policy implications of the major findings of this comprehensive study. I examine the significance of these implications in understanding the role of education among indigenous minorities and disadvantaged groups in deeply divided societies in the context of social change, multiculturalism, ethnic stratification, cultural hegemony, and strategies for self-empowerment.

Chapter 1

Theoretical Framework

Multiculturalism, Hegemony, and Social Change

Abstract

The theoretical framework I propose here forms the basis of my examination of education and social change among the Palestinian Arabs in Israel. I begin by placing education within a general multicultural framework and then draw upon an eclectic theoretical approach that combines a number of theoretical perspectives. Together these perspectives comprise my critical model of *empowering multicultural education*. This eclectic theoretical approach—also known as theoretical eclecticism, the integrative approach, and meta-theory—integrates several complementary theories. It is often used in the fields of social science, education, culture, and economics as it provides a broad understanding of complex processes and developments, especially in studies of a comprehensive nature and scope (for examples of the use of the eclectic theoretical approach in various disciplines, see Hermessi 2022; Karppinen, Moe, and Svensson 2008; Jenks, Lee, and Kanpol 2001). In addition to proposing this general model, in each chapter I also provide a specific theoretical framework for the particular topic under discussion.

Multiculturalism—A Background

Issues related to minority claims, cultural pluralism, and differentiated group rights began to gain momentum after the Second World War, when the world's attention shifted to internal ethnic conflicts (Kymlicka 2018). Indeed, in many societies such internal conflicts intensified during the postwar period, primarily due to competition over the local stratification system as well as to attempts on the part of disadvantaged groups to improve their status. The 1960s civil rights movement in the United States lent further impetus to disputes over issues related to multiculturalism. Black Americans began demanding community control of schools and called for revising the curriculum to accommodate their history and unique culture. Other ethnic groups subsequently began demanding similar steps toward advancing multi-ethnic education (Banks 1981, 2001a). During the 1970s and 1980s, interest in multiculturalism continued to rise, both as a general concept and as a strategy for legitimizing diversity, empowering minorities and disadvantaged groups, and handling issues of equality and equity (see, for example, Banks 1981, 2001b; Sleeter 1996; Kymlicka 1995, 2007a, 2010, 2018).

What, in fact, is multiculturalism? Goodstein (1994) refers to two types of cultural diversity: diversity as "variety" and diversity as a "critical perspective." The first type espouses a literal definition of diversity as reflecting the existence of numerous cultures that contribute to the richness of the national or global community. In this type of multiculturalism those who hold the power are the ones who define the term "diversity" and its contents. Thus, disadvantaged groups, minorities, and women who engage in multicultural discourse usually use the language of multiculturalism without taking part in its formation (Estrada and McLaren 1993).

Unlike this mainstream form of multiculturalism, critical multiculturalism does not consider diversity per se to be its goal. Instead, it maintains that diversity should be framed "within a politics of cultural criticism and commitment to social justice." Hence, "multiculturalism without a transformative political agenda can just be another form of accommodation to the larger society" (Estrada and McLaren 1993, 31).

Even though multicultural models differ from place to place, they share some important basic components. In his book *Theories of Multiculturalism*, Crowder (2013) identifies the principle of *recognition* as a cornerstone of multiculturalism. He claims that most contemporary societies are diverse and encompass multiple cultures that are normatively approved and given positive recognition in public policy and public institutions (see review by Law 2014, 1964). Therefore, in order for a state to be considered multicultural democracy, it should first and foremost be regarded as belonging to all its citizens. Hence, all policies that seek to assimilate or exclude members of nondominant groups must be abolished. At the same time, members of these groups should have equal access to all national institutions while still being able to express their ethnocultural identity. The state for its part must recognize its obligation to accommodate and recognize the history, language, and culture of nondominant groups. To be multicultural, the state must also acknowledge any injustice done to nondominant groups through the aforementioned policies of assimilation and exclusion and must offer some sort of remedy for these historical injustices (Kymlicka 2007a, 66–67). Thus, critical multiculturalism represents a political undertaking that attempts to redefine the relationship between ethnocultural minorities and the state through the adoption of new multicultural policies that empower minorities and safeguard their individual and group-differentiated rights (e.g., Nieto and Bode 2008; Kymlicka 2007a, 2018).

Retreat from the Multicultural Model

Whereas the 1970s and 1980s signaled the advancement of multicultural policies in various Western democracies, since the mid-1990s multiculturalism in both North America and Europe has been the target of growing criticism. In fact, multiculturalism had never been deeply entrenched in Europe, and new waves of Muslim immigrants sent the continent into a period of deep crisis (see Chin 2017, reviewed by Moussa 2018). In an atmosphere marked by the perceived threat posed by these Muslim migrants, the extreme right in Europe began lobbying against multicultural policies and has become much more vocal in the wake of 9/11 and other terrorist acts. This atmosphere has undoubtedly affected policymakers in various European countries, as noted by Kymlicka (2007b, 55): "Fears that Muslim immigrants will seek to use multiculturalism to perpetuate illiberal cultural practices within the country are now combined with fears that multiculturalism will be used to shelter the local nodes of militant international political movements that seek to overthrow liberal democracy. Thus, we see the 'securitization' of relations between Western states and their immigrant Muslim communities." Most critiques of multiculturalism contend that such policies tend to foster separate communities and encourage them to maintain nondemocratic values and lifestyles that clash with those of society at large. The claim is that these policies prevent minority groups from identifying with broader society and lead to hostility and radicalization (Ryan 2010), hence deepening the distrust between minority groups and the majority (see Heath and Demireva 2014, 162).

Focusing on European countries that had previously adopted various forms of multiculturalism, Joppke (2004) identifies three main factors responsible for the steady retreat from multiculturalism in Europe: (1) the longstanding liberal critique of multiculturalism; (2) the failure of multicultural policies, especially in promoting socioeconomic mobility among minority groups; and (3) the new assertiveness on the part of liberal states in imposing centrist policies of civic integration. All these arguments apply to immigrants in general and to Muslim immigrants in particular. They do not apply to national minorities and indigenous groups that have traditionally been the focus of multicultural policies (Joppke 2004). May (2021) similarly examines perceptions of multiculturalism in Canadian newspapers between 2010 and 2020. His findings reveal a sharp ideological divide between the left and the right, with the left largely in favor of multiculturalism and the right clearly hostile to it. Moreover, May's study shows that rejection of multiculturalism is mainly directed against immigrants and reflects widespread concerns about Muslim political extremism (May 2021, 1952–53).

In light of the above summary, I contend that democratic countries today do not question whether multiculturalism is indeed necessary. Rather, they challenge its contents, its depth, and the conditions of its implementation. This claim gains support from different field studies conducted in various countries. In a study examining the relationship between ethnonational identity, endorsement of multiculturalism, and supportive attitudes toward equal rights for ethnic minorities in Japan, Nagayoshi (2011) concludes that "ethno-national identity has positive effects on the endorsement of multiculturalism, while having negative effects on the endorsement of equal rights between ethnic majorities and ethnic minorities." This conclusion implies that the Japanese do not see multiculturalism as antithetical to maintaining ethnic homogeneity within the nation. Rather, their endorsement of multiculturalism stems from their belief in the uniqueness of "Japaneseness" (561).

Based on an extensive literature review and an analysis of public opinion survey data from Canada, Donnelly reaches a similar conclusion, pointing to a gap between public attitudes and actual behavior. The public feels comfortable supporting multiculturalism as an abstract value. Yet when faced with more complex decisions, the public also exhibits support for discrimination against minorities. A comparison with the United States shows that Canadian and American respondents exhibit similar rates of discrimination (Donnelly 2021, 166).

This brief review of the literature shows that in examining the state of multiculturalism in the world today, what matters are not the general public's attitudes toward multiculturalism but rather people's actual behavior, alongside official policies regarding diversity and multicultural democracy. Also, as Kymlicka claims, of the three familiar patterns of multiculturalism (i.e., indigenous peoples, national minorities, and immigrant groups), the main retreat from multiculturalism is associated with immigrant groups, especially in the case of Muslim immigrants. In contrast, commitment to new models of multicultural citizenship for indigenous peoples has increased, as can be seen in international human rights organizations' growing recognition of indigenous rights and as reaffirmed by the UN General Assembly's adoption of the Declaration of the Rights of Indigenous Peoples in 2007. Moreover, commitment to new models of multicultural citizenship for national minorities persists (Kymlicka 2018, 139; see also chapter 2).

How does multiculturalism find expression in the field of education? Is there a unified concept of multicultural education, or rather do various concepts emerge from the positivist and critical multicultural approaches? Can multicultural education be combined with other models of critical education, namely critical-transformative pedagogy and cultural hegemony? In the following section I attempt to answer these questions. After examining multicultural education, I describe the critical-transformative pedagogy approach and the Gramscian hegemonic theory. I then propose an eclectic model of empowering multicultural education.

Multicultural Education: Concepts and Development

The education system is one of the most prominent domains in which multiculturalism is designed, practiced, and evaluated. Multiculturalism is reflected in the degree of equity and equality in the structure, administration, and content of education, as well as in the teaching methods, the allocation of resources, and the educational outcomes. The extent of multiculturalism in the education system is measured through the state's official policies toward minorities and ethnocultural groups, as mirrored by the *vertical* relations between these groups and the state and by the *horizontal* relations among majority and minority groups within the education system.

Multicultural education, a byproduct of multicultural ideology, first emerged as a response to the ethnic revitalization movements of the 1960s (Banks 1981), when it was known as "multiethnic education." As part of its demand for equal civil rights, the Black protest movement called for serious reform of the education system, including rewriting school textbooks to reflect Black history and narratives (Banks 1981, 19). Thus, from the outset multicultural education has been closely tied to issues of minority and ethnic civil rights and to the ways such groups are treated in the school curriculum and by society at large (Sleeter and McLaren 1995, 11; Gay 1983, 560).

The concepts of multicultural education, multiethnic education, and education for diversity that have developed in Western societies emerged from the debate over what ideology should prevail in treating immigrant groups. Philosophers who supported the ideology of multiculturalism argued that in view of the failure of the melting pot ideology, political democracy should be accompanied by cultural democracy that recognizes the right of ethnic-immigrant groups to express their own cultures. Indeed, multicultural reforms emerged against the backdrop of competing assimilationist and cultural pluralistic ideologies, forming the basis for multicultural education (Banks 1981, 77).

Positivist versus Critical Multiculturalism

For a long time, positivist multiculturalism was the dominant form of multicultural education (see Nesterova 2019; Nieto 2000). This type of multiculturalism seeks to preserve the diversity of existing cultures and to educate members of all groups to live together peacefully. Nevertheless, positivist multiculturalism does not attempt to confront issues of domination, oppression, discrimination, or racism. As such, it never sought to abolish the oppressive structures faced by disadvantaged and marginalized minority groups (Nesterova 2019, 256).

Critics of positivist multiculturalism contend that mainstream multicultural education is nothing more than another form of social and cultural control used by dominant groups to avoid the real debate over racism and discrimination (see Sleeter 1992, 3). For example, Olneck (1990) claims that multiculturalism in the United States is constructed around individual differences, "advances a political and fragmented model of culture, and presumes an attitudinal explanation of ethnic conflict" but does not devote any serious attention to collective identities and claims (147). Olneck concludes that "both intercultural and multicultural education symbolically represent authoritative meanings having to do with components, organization, dynamics, and identity of American society." Hence, these symbolic representations function as instruments of social control (66).

Mainstream positivist multiculturalism has been also criticized for not reflecting the indigenous voices of ethnic and cultural minorities (Phillips 1995, 372). This state of affairs derives from the fact that official school curricula, particularly history texts, usually reflect dominant narratives and stories (Sleeter 1996).

The failure of traditional positivist multiculturalism led to the emergence of critical multiculturalism. Numerous researchers and critical thinkers contend that multicultural education per se is insufficient and cannot be effective unless it replaces the existing cultural hegemony and challenges the dominant narrative in the school curriculum. Indeed, genuine multiculturalism should first acknowledge the inherent hegemony and historical fallacies of the curricula and then make room for multiple perspectives and narratives, including those of disadvantaged groups (see Nieto and Bode 2008).

Based on the critical approach, Banks and Banks (2001) contend that multicultural education must encompass the major referent groups in the education system. They further claim that equality should be an integral part of this type of education: "Multicultural education is an idea, an educational reform movement, and a process whose major goal is to change the structure of educational institutions so that male and female students, exceptional students, and students who are members of diverse racial, ethnic, language, and cultural groups will have an equal chance to achieve academically in school" (1). Banks further states that multicultural education requires an empowering social structure. This form of education should encourage a school culture that empowers students from diverse racial, ethnic, cultural, and social backgrounds (Banks 2001b).

Nieto and Bode define seven basic characteristics of multicultural education: it is anti-racist; it provides basic education; it is important for all students, not only for students of color and disadvantaged students; it is pervasive in that it offers a "philosophy or way of looking at the world"; it educates for social justice; it is a process; and it is based on critical pedagogy. In explaining these characteristics, Nieto and Bode (2008) stress that multicultural education should be explicitly anti-racist and anti-discriminatory, for if schools do not adhere to these two basic principles, they are liable to turn multicultural education into a "celebration of ethnic festivals" or in the worst case may even "perpetuate stereotypes" (44–45).

Multicultural Education and Critical-Transformative Pedagogy

Several concepts emerging from critical-transformative pedagogy can be integrated into multicultural education. Indeed, these concepts can be used to advance multicultural education by exploring how pedagogy functions as a cultural practice that *produces* rather than merely *transmits* knowledge within the asymmetrical relations of power that shape teacher-student relations (Giroux 1992, 98).

According to Sleeter and Dilgado Bernal (2004, 241), critical pedagogy emerged from at least two sources. One is critical theory and the Frankfurt school; the other is the work of Paulo Freire and the Latin American liberation movements. Critical perspectives (mainly critical pedagogy, critical race theory, and anti-racist education) complement one another in that they attempt to address various forms of oppression and social change and to propose oppositional discourses in mainstream schools (254).

In their review of critical pedagogy, Sleeter and Delgado Bernal (2004) describe four ways in which this theory can contribute to multicultural education. First, it provides tools for examining the meaning of culture, thus offering a broad definition of culture rather than the simplistic conceptions often used in multicultural education. Hence, instead of the emphasis on otherness found in multicultural education, critical pedagogy places culture within a historical context of colonialism, oppression, and power relations (see Giroux and Simon 1989).

Second, critical pedagogy challenges existing structural and cultural power relations and assigns special importance to the analysis of social class. Thus, whereas multicultural education emerged mainly from racial and ethnic struggles, critical pedagogy grew primarily out of class struggle (Sleeter and Delgado Bernal 2004, 243). Consequently, instead of discussing educational *reform*, critical pedagogy highlights the importance of educational *revolution* (see McLaren 2000).

Third, according to Apple (2000), critical pedagogy offers tools for examining ideology in terms of "who produces what kinds of ideologies, why some ideologies prevail, and whose interests they serve" (cited by Sleeter and Delgado Bernal 2004, 243). Critical pedagogy also examines the associated issue of power in the classroom and what is needed to empower students. Therefore, whereas multicultural education focuses on developing transformative curricula as an important strategy in supporting high achievements for all students, critical pedagogy connects "student-generated knowledge with student empowerment" (Sleeter and Delgado Bernal 2004). Paulo Freire (1972) further stresses that teachers must shift from the "banking method" to a "dialogical process" in which they act as students' partners.

Fourth, according to Sleeter and Delgado Bernal (2004), critical pedagogy for multicultural education entails analysis of language and literacy. Indeed, critical pedagogy recognizes a close connection between language and culture. Paulo Freire further distinguishes between technical and critical approaches to literacy. The technical approach focuses on language as "words emptied of the reality they (students) are meant to represent" (Freire 1973, 37). In contrast, critical literacy begins with words from the students' experience and then positions them historically, thus helping students learn to question their world by using language as a tool of critical analysis (cited by Sleeter and Delgado Bernal 2004, 244). Hence, critical pedagogy emphasizes the importance of language as a tool for shaping identity and consciousness and as a means of control and of liberation as well (Giroux 1997).

Throughout his work, Freire (e.g., 1972, 1973, 1985, 1998a) emphasized the importance of learning and teaching as an integral part of critical pedagogy. He contended that education is not merely the transference of knowledge. Rather, it is a form of communication and dialogue. Indeed, students gain practice through education by seeking knowledge rather than merely receiving it passively (Freire 1973). Thus, according to Freire, "the class is not a class in the traditional sense, but a meeting place where knowledge is sought and not where it is transmitted" (Freire, 1973, 150).

Critics of Critical Pedagogy

Some scholars have criticized critical pedagogy, arguing that because it is class-based and shaped by neo-Marxist critique of capitalism it has overlooked other forms of oppression. In addition, they claimed that the critical approach offers a paradigm that is difficult to implement (see Kincheloe 2007; Weiner 2007; Stanley 2007). For example, Weiner (2007) contends that critical race theories and postcolonial theories constitute a challenge to critical pedagogy theory. He claims that critical pedagogy is chiefly a class-oriented theory of reproduction that emphasizes the universal experience of oppression/liberation as opposed to offering a more localized critique of difference (57). Weiner concludes that critical pedagogy is marred by what he refers to as "imaginative inertia," which, if not remedied, will prevent critical pedagogy from attracting educators and students (58).

Rather than invalidating critical theory, this criticism suggests that critical theory should be revitalized, updated, and expanded to deal with new questions emerging from rapid economic, social, political, and cultural changes and from the diversification of contemporary societies. According to Weiner, critical theory should not focus only on class-based forms of oppression. Rather, it should consider and investigate all forms of oppression.

Moreover, critical pedagogy should be driven by "public intellectuals, not academics and theoreticians, even though a public intellectual might also be both of these things" (Weiner 2007, 76).

The Gramscian Theory of Cultural Hegemony

The theory of cultural hegemony serves as a perfect complement to critical multicultural education and critical-transformative pedagogy. As noted by Sleeter and Delgado Bernal (2004), multicultural education emerged mainly from racial and ethnic struggle, whereas critical pedagogy grew primarily out of class struggle (243). The theory of cultural hegemony grew out of the cultural struggle of subordinate classes and the subsequent analysis of their strife in terms of counter-hegemonic discourse. Cultural hegemony also adds an important dimension in that it highlights the importance of civil society in counterbalancing the hegemonic policies imposed by the ruling political entity or state. In this section I briefly review the theory of cultural hegemony and show how it is related to multiculturalism and critical-transformative pedagogy.

Based on the neo-Marxist sociology of education, Gramsci sought to develop a suitable theory of modern states and societies in which cultural hegemony serves as the major component of dominance and control. Note that Gramsci does not disregard the importance of the economic factor. Nevertheless, he asserts that in modern societies, hegemony is not primarily economic but rather mainly cultural and educational (Pagano 2017).

Gramsci describes striving for hegemony on the part of the state as an ongoing project in which the efforts of the dominant groups are constantly directed toward maintaining the status quo in order to preserve their interests. Yet although these interests usually prevail, they are continually challenged by counter-hegemonic forces that represent diverse conceptions: "The life of the state is conceived of as a continuous process of formation and superseding of unstable equilibria (on the juridical plane) between the interests of the fundamental [i.e., dominant, 'hegemonic'] group and those of the subordinate groups—equilibria in which the interests of the dominant group prevail, but only up to a certain point" (Gramsci 1971, 182, cited by Bilton and Soltero 2020, 683). This notion of hegemony is central to Gramsci's neo-Marxist social theory. He views literacy both as a concept and as a social practice that should be linked historically to configurations of knowledge and power. For Gramsci, literacy is a "double-edged sword;

it could be wielded for the purpose of self and social empowerment or for perpetuation of relations of repression and domination" (cited by Giroux 1987, 1–3).

Gramsci contends that education and culture are inseparably linked. It cannot be otherwise, for education is also a vision of the world, a way of being, a system of ethical and civic behavior: "Culture and education exist in a continuum, blending into and feeding each other. Culture and education are bearing structures (or, as Marx says, superstructures), cornerstones of our society that need to be supported and diffused by intellectuals and the school" (Pagano 2017, 57). Therefore, Gramsci considers culture and education to be the central pillars of every society and believes that government policies should be evaluated accordingly: "Gramsci suggests that one could assess the character of a government from its cultural and educational policies. If it builds its cultural policy from the bottom to the top, then the government is progressive because it aims to raise the cultural development of the common people, and to form intellectuals, not by drawing on the privileged only but on an extensive and widespread basis. To the contrary, if the direction of the cultural policy is from the top to the bottom, the government is repressive" (Gramsci 1971, Q6 §170, PN3 126–27, cited by Pagano 2017, 58).

The notion of "common sense" lies at the core of Gramscian theory of cultural hegemony. He describes common sense as "a collective noun . . . a product of history and a part of the historical process" (Gramsci 1971, 325–26). He sees common sense as "the folklore of philosophy" since, like philosophy, it is a way of thinking about the world that is grounded in material realities. Unlike philosophy, however, common sense is unsystematic, heterogenous, spontaneous, incoherent, and inconsequential, "a chaotic aggregate of disparate conceptions" (Gramsci 1971, 324, cited by Jones 2006, 54; see also Bilton and Soltero 2020, 683). Gramsci further points out that every social group, and even society as a whole, has its own "common sense," which is "continually transforming itself, enriching itself with scientific ideas and with philosophical opinions which have entered ordinary life" (Gramsci 1971, 326, cited by Jones 2006, 54).

As noted, the theory of cultural hegemony goes hand in hand with critical multiculturalism and critical-transformative pedagogy. Indeed, Tarlau classifies Gramscian theory among social transformation theories that emphasize the role of education as a control system but that at the same time point to the possibilities of utilizing education as a mechanism of social change. Despite the complexity of her analysis, Tarlau determines that Gramsci also maintains a form of Freirean optimism by emphasizing how educational practices can enhance students' critical reflection ability and make them agents of social change (see Tarlau 2017, 119–20; for theories of social reproduction, see Apple 1979, 1982, 2000, 2004; Bourdieu and Passeron 1990).

Indeed, both Gramscian theory and critical-transformative pedagogy maintain that despite serving as a mechanism of control and domination, the school system also contains the seeds of social change and liberation. As in the transformative model of pedagogy, Gramsci contends that the education system also encompasses counter-hegemonic forces that, through the mechanism of conscious teachers and pupils, act to counterbalance the state's hegemonic policy. Hence, Gramscian hegemonic theory intersects with Freire's transformative pedagogy in that both see education not only as a system for knowledge transfer but also as a place of knowledge production. Students cannot be passive. They are not mere knowledge recipients but are knowledge producers as well (see Freire 1973, 1985; for the Gramscian conception, see Tarlau 2017, 119–20).

Eclectic Model of Empowering Multicultural Education

Based on the eclectic theoretical approach described above, I now outline the main principles of the proposed model of empowering multicultural education. The proposed model incorporates the following elements of critical multiculturalism, critical-transformative pedagogy, and Gramscian theory of cultural hegemony:

1. *Critical multiculturalism.* Multicultural education should be for all students, whether from the majority or from the minority. It also should be comprehensive, embracing the overt curriculum, the hidden curriculum, and the atmosphere at the school (see Nieto and Bode 2008; Banks and Banks 2001a). School curricula should be based on three principles. First, they should acknowledge diversity and the right to be different, together with mutual recognition of the life experiences, the culture, and the historical narratives of both majority and minority students (see Nieto and Bod 2008). This diversity must go beyond mere recognition of variety. It should also challenge issues of domination, oppression, discrimination, and racism, and it should place the concept of otherness within a historical context of oppression and domination (e.g., Nesterova 2019; Sleeter and Delgado Bernal 2004). Second, school curricula should reflect a strong commitment to

the human right to equity and equality. For indigenous national and other distinct groups, these rights should also include group-differentiated rights as an integral part of recognized equality (see Kymlicka 2007a, 2018). Third, school curricula should acknowledge the importance of creating a shared circle of civil activity in the form of active citizenship (for active citizenship, see Banks 2017) that reflects the aforementioned equality.

2. *Holistic Cultural Competence.* Alongside the principle of critical multicultural education, the proposed model of empowering multicultural education places cultural competence as a central component. Yet this notion of cultural competence differs from the traditional narrow definition that sees cultural competence as "knowledge, understanding and practice in the other culture" while overlooking the individual's "own culture" (see review by Alizadeh and Chavan 2016, e121–22). Hence, the proposed model adopts an expanded and holistic form of cultural competence comprising two complementary and inseparable components: knowledge of one's own culture, narrative, and identity, alongside knowledge of the cultures of others. This expanded notion of cultural competence is especially important for minorities and disadvantaged groups subject to cultural denial by the dominant majority (see Freire 1998a, 1998b; Giroux 2001; Resnik 2006; Wiggan and Watson-Vandiver 2019).

3. *Encompassing Transformative Pedagogy.* Education must be empowering for students and teachers alike. That is, education should be centered simultaneously on both students and teachers (i.e., student-teacher centered and not merely student centered). This principle should be reflected in school curricula and teaching methods, which should be based on creativity and critical thinking. Students should become teachers' partners by acting as knowledge producers and not merely knowledge receivers. Hence, students and teachers alike can play an active role in turning the school into a place that mirrors students' life experiences, identity, and historical narrative and also a venue of empowerment for teachers (see Giroux 1992, 1997, 2001; Freire 1973, 1985, 1998a).

4. *Complementary School-Community Relationships.* Both Gramscian theory and critical-transformative pedagogy contend that challenging the official knowledge conveyed by the school system requires bridging the gap between school and society and giving a voice to the unofficial knowledge of society at large. I adopt this conclusion as a central component of the suggested eclectic model of empowering education. Yet I also acknowledge that for this to happen, alternative educational methods must be developed that challenge the conservative methods currently used in the schools (see

Gramsci 1971, 35–36, cited by Entwistle 1979, 26; Freire 1973). Moreover, I contend that school-community relationships should be complementary rather than contradictory. I believe that any type of empowerment that is hostile to the school system and overlooks teachers will only serve to increase the animosity and alienation of both students and teachers and widen the gap between school and society, eventually becoming yet another source of disempowerment.

5. *Combating Various Forms of Oppression and Control.* I contend that the above critique of critical pedagogy also applies to the Gramscian theory of hegemony in that both are class-based models and thus serve to emphasize class-based forms of oppression. Hence, empowering education should combat all forms of oppression and control, whether based on class, gender, ethnicity, nationality, or social background. This expanded conception is vital, especially in view of the resurgence of ethnic, religious, and other types of local identities in the era of globalization and the growing internal conflicts marking the 21st century.

Summary

In this chapter, I proposed a general theoretical framework for discussing education and social change in contemporary societies. I used an eclectic approach to combine elements from a number of theoretical perspectives that together form a critical model of empowering multicultural education. This eclectic theoretical approach seems perfectly suited to this examination of education among the Palestinian Arabs in Israel as an indigenous minority in a deeply divided society, which, despite its pervasive multicultural social structure, has never adopted a multicultural ideology. Hence, an eclectic approach is essential for discussing wide-ranging issues of educational development, domination and cultural hegemony, identity formation, inequality, self-empowerment, and social change that cannot be covered by any single theoretical approach.

The next chapter provides background on the Palestinian Arabs in Israel as an indigenous group within an ethnonational state. It describes their transition from a majority into an involuntary minority after the establishment of Israel, together with the main developments in Arab society and the Arabs' relationships with the state and the Jewish majority. It also addresses the barriers to the development of a multicultural democracy in Israel.

Chapter 2

Background

The Palestinian Arabs in Israel

Abstract

This chapter serves as a background discussion of the condition, characteristics, and identity formation of the Palestinian Arabs in Israel and of
their relationships with the Jewish majority. It delineates the main factors
that have affected social, economic, and political developments among the
indigenous Palestinian Arabs. Moreover, it discusses their complex status
as a "double periphery" simultaneously situated at the margins of Israeli
society and of the Palestinian national movement (see Al-Haj 1989b, 1993,
1997). Unlike the conventional state-centered approach that positions Arabs
along one axis only—Arabs versus the state—I examine their status using
a multidimensional model that concurrently combines three dimensions: a
local dimension that includes internal demographic, social, and economic
developments within the Arab population; a national dimension that encompasses official state policy toward the Arabs in Israel and the implications
of the lack of official recognition of their status as an indigenous national
minority; and a regional dimension that is affected by the relationships of
the Arab population in Israel with the Palestinian people as a whole and
with the entire Arab world, under conditions of ongoing conflict and the
transition to conflict resolution since the 1990s.

I begin by offering a theoretical framework for understanding multicultural democracy and the rights of indigenous groups and national
minorities. Then I outline the major developments among the Palestinian

Arabs as they shifted from a majority to an involuntary minority after the establishment of Israel. I conclude the chapter with a detailed analysis of the major barriers to developing multicultural democracy in Israel, including Israel's ethnonational character, the securitization of state-minority relations, and the blurring of majority-minority boundaries.

Theoretical Framework: Multicultural Democracy, National Minorities, and Indigenous Groups

In his discussion of minorities and multicultural democracy, Kymlicka (2007a) differentiates between three types of minority groups: indigenous peoples, national minorities, and immigrant groups. He refers to the first two groups as *old minorities* in that they were already living in their territories before said country became independent. In contrast, he calls the third group *new minorities* in that they arrived in the region as immigrants (77). This classification of minority groups is in line with the differing levels of needs and rights assigned to these groups by multicultural democracies. Moreover, the nation-state's demands and expectations of these groups differ considerably. Hence, while rights of immigrants are often limited to the individual level, national and indigenous minorities also involve group-differentiated rights (Kymlicka 2007a).

Similarly, Ogbu (1991) offers a detailed classification of minorities by dividing them into two main categories: *voluntary* and *involuntary*. According to this classification, immigrant minorities are voluntary minorities because they left their homes with the hope of improving their economic well-being and standard of living and/or of achieving greater political freedom. Involuntary minorities, in contrast, are "people who were brought into their present society through slavery, conquest or colonization. They usually resent the loss of their former freedom, and they perceive the social, political and economic barriers against them as part of their undeserved oppression" (9). Immigrant minorities perceive whatever barriers they face as a temporary problem stemming from the fact that they are "foreigners" and do not know the language. Thus, they believe they can overcome these barriers through education and hard work. At the same time, they have a dual frame of reference: their home country and the host society. Involuntary minorities, on the other hand, perceive discrimination against them as an ongoing reality associated with their status as outsiders and as a subordinate group. They have only one reference group: the members of the dominant group. Involuntary minorities develop a survival strategy that is not limited to individual efforts but rather is also based on collective efforts and group mobilization.

One of the major differences between voluntary and involuntary minorities is related to types of identity. Voluntary immigrants bring their social identity and culture with them, which will most likely be maintained, at least by the first generation. Thus, an immigrant's social identity does not develop as a response to that of the dominant group in the host society. Involuntary minorities, in contrast, develop a new sense of peoplehood or social identity after having been involuntarily incorporated into the society in which they currently live. Because they perceive discrimination and exclusion as collective and enduring, involuntary minorities adopt an "oppositional identity" that engenders ongoing distrust between them and the dominant group (Ogbu 1991, 15–16).

The following analysis of multicultural policies focuses on involuntary minorities (according to Ogbu 1991) or those Kymlicka categorized as *old minorities* (see Kymlicka 2007b). I begin with national minorities. I then shift to indigenous minorities and provide a detailed analysis of international conventions on the rights of indigenous groups.

National Minorities

National minorities are found in countries across the globe, including in Western countries such as Canada (the Quebecois) and Spain (the Catalans). These groups are concentrated in specific geographical regions and recognize themselves as nations within a larger state. In the past, the states in which such groups lived made every effort to erode any sense of nationhood and suppress any expression of substate nationalism, which they perceived as a threat (see Brubaker 1996). Over time these policies have changed, particularly in Western democracies, which have begun incorporating the nationalist aspirations of these groups in one way or another, usually in the form of multinational and multilingual federalism. In addition, in most cases the languages of these groups are recognized as official state languages within the region or in the country as a whole (see Kymlicka 2007a, 69).

New forms of multicultural citizenship for national minorities typically include some combination of the following six elements: federal or quasi-federal territorial autonomy; official language status, either in the region or nationally; guaranteed representation in the central government and on constitutional courts; public funding of minority language universities, schools, and media; constitutional or parliamentary affirmation of multinationalism;

and international representation (e.g., allowing the substate region to be represented on international bodies) (Kymlicka 2018, 137).

INDIGENOUS GROUPS

According to the World Bank, there are an estimated 476 million indigenous peoples with distinct social, cultural, and collective identities across the globe, constituting 6 percent of the world's population (World Bank 2023; also see Zinsser 2004; Ojong 2020). These indigenous peoples are thought to speak more than 4,000 of the world's 7,000 languages (World Bank 2023).

The report submitted by José Martinez Cobo in 1986 to the UN Sub-Commission on Prevention of Discrimination and the Protection of Minorities posits the following working definition of indigenous communities:

> Indigenous communities, peoples and nations are those which, having a historical continuity with pre-invasion and pre-colonial societies that developed on their territories, consider themselves distinct from other sectors of the societies now prevailing in those territories, or parts of them. They form at present non-dominant sectors of society and are determined to preserve, develop and transmit to future generations their ancestral territories, and their ethnic identity, as the basis of their continued existence as peoples, in accordance with their own cultural patterns, social institutions and legal systems. (Cobo 1986, cited by Franke 2007, 362)

In his detailed report, Cobo emphasized two additional elements that should be taken into consideration when defining indigenous populations. First, the classification of a group as indigenous is not necessarily based on, or limited to, the formal-legal recognition of the authorities of the state in which these groups reside. According to Cobo (1986): "Several governments have stated explicitly that there are no legal definitions of indigenous populations in their countries. Several others have not furnished information on this subject. . . . In some countries legal definitions exist in the statute books but there are wide variations in the scope of application and purposes of these definitions" (44). Second, when defining a group as indigenous, the group's self-definition should be considered. Accordingly, under the heading of group consciousness Cobo noted: "The use of this criterion emphasizes the fact that the individual or group considers himself or itself as indigenous, or that the community in which the individual or group lives considers him or it indigenous—or alternatively that there is a combination of personal and communal considerations which make him or it an indigenous person or group. In other words, the subjective criterion of the person, group or community in question is taken into consideration" (37).

INTERNATIONAL RECOGNITION OF INDIGENOUS RIGHTS

The long journey of indigenous peoples to the UN began in the 1920s, when the indigenous nations of Great Turtle Island in Canada (then a colony of Great Britain) made an attempt to speak at the League of Nations in Geneva (see Venne 2011, 558). Yet it is only recently that indigenous rights have emerged as a distinct body of rights that are internationally distinguished from minority rights, including in UN organizations (Sargent 2012). Zinsser notes that nongovernmental organizations played a key role in bringing the concerns of indigenous peoples to the attention of the UN and its agencies. Already in the late 1960s and the early 1970s, groups of anthropologists, first in Denmark, then in the United Kingdom, and finally in the United States, founded three of the earliest and most effective advocacy groups for indigenous peoples (Zinsser 2004, 79).

Mobilized by these international advocacy networks, in 1969 the UN empowered the Sub-Commission on Prevention of Discrimination and the Protection of Minorities to study the issue of indigenous rights. José Martinez Cobo was nominated to undertake the study (see Venne 2011, 561). Cobo submitted the aforementioned report in stages, beginning in 1983. The third and final part, *Special Rapporteur of the Sub-Commission on Prevention of Discrimination and Protection of Minorities*, which was submitted in 1986, provided the conceptual framework for addressing the rights of indigenous people (Cobo 1986).

Since then, the international community has become increasingly aware of indigenous and minority human rights (Hatzikidi, Lennox, and Xanthaki 2021). These international efforts peaked with the United Nations Declaration on the Rights of Indigenous Peoples (UNDRIP), issued by the UN General Assembly on September 13, 2007. The declaration sets out the individual and collective rights of indigenous peoples, including their right to self-determination; to preserve their identity, language, cultures, and traditions; and to maintain their own institutions, especially in the field of education (Lightfoot 2010, 86).

The first five articles of this declaration are most significant in that they convey the essence of the rights of indigenous peoples, which are linked to international human rights. These rights recognize indigenous peoples as distinct groups entitled to equality at both the individual and collective levels, including the right to self-determination and especially the right to determine their political status and all issues connected to their development in various fields. The declaration also underscores that in addition to the right of self-determination, indigenous people also have the right to participate fully in all arenas of life in the state (UNDRIP 2007).

Even though this declaration is not an international treaty and is therefore not legally binding, it has become part of the human rights consensus regarding protection of the rights of indigenous peoples. According to Burger, who for more than 20 years headed the indigenous peoples and minorities program at the Office of the UN High Commissioner for Human Rights, the UNDRIP was a historical turning point in putting forward the case and rights of indigenous peoples. In addition, the declaration enhanced claims made by indigenous peoples that states had strongly resisted in the early 1980s, such as rights to self-determination, land, and resources. Furthermore, the participation, diversity, and experiences of indigenous peoples differed markedly from their situation in the 1980s and 1990s. Representatives of indigenous peoples have become much more active and involved in national and international forums dealing with their rights and claims (Burger 2019, 29–30). Some experts even claim: "The UN Declaration is gradually establishing itself as legally binding through its association with existing UN treaties. It is also used by experts of UN treaty bodies and regional human rights courts as well as domestic courts as a reference and a means of determining rights and corresponding state responsibilities" (Burger 2019, 23).

Nevertheless, the very principle of self-determination, which is positioned at the center of the UNDRIP, evoked fears among UN Member States that had indigenous groups within their jurisdictions. These states were worried that the notion of indigenous self-determination would undermine the principles of state sovereignty and would potentially lead to secessionist movements (Franke 2007, 360; see also Barsh 1996).

According to Franke (2007), these states had difficulty accepting the notion that "indigenous peoples are socially and culturally equal to the nation state communities in which they live and that states now have the responsibility to provide the conditions under which self-determination is possible" (360). Franke adds that "such fears are the result of very poor understandings of the ethical principles under which the relations between indigenous peoples and nation states already have been formed under centuries of European colonialism." Franke goes on to explain that in seeking self-determination, indigenous people were not seeking statehood but rather the "right to first determine the nature of self for themselves" (359). Similarly, Marion Young (2009) contends that in claiming greater self-determination, indigenous peoples seek *nondomination and noninterference* rather than sovereign independence (176). Anaya (2008) further explains that self-determination for indigenous peoples does not entail secession or separate statehood, but rather non-domination and full participation in the governing institutional apparatus connected to indigenous groups (cited by Kosko 2013, 295).

Indeed, article 46 (1) of the UN Declaration clearly states that the right to self-determination of indigenous people should go hand in hand with preservation of the territorial integrity of independent nation-states (UNDRIP 2007).

Educational Rights of Minorities and Indigenous Groups

The educational rights of indigenous groups should be viewed both as an integral part of the universal human right to education and as an outcome of international recognition of the unique status, needs, and rights of indigenous peoples. The human right to education is widely recognized by international law and applies to all indigenous as well as minority groups (for a review of UN declarations on educational and cultural human rights, see Saaresranta 2014).

Numerous international declarations consider the right to education to be a basic human right for individuals and groups. Yet education defined as a human right goes beyond the traditional meaning of mere formal schooling and differs significantly from the right to education as often defined by governments (see review by Saaresranta 2014, 343–55). The Human Rights-Based Approach to Education document issued by UNICEF and UNESCO (UNICEF and UNESCO 2007, chap. 1, 10–11) elaborates extensively on this issue, particularly in discussing two important principles connected to educational rights: (1) *participation and inclusion* and (2) *empowerment.* The document defines *participation* as follows: "Every person and all peoples are entitled to active, free and meaningful participation in, contribution to and enjoyment of civil, economic, social, cultural and political development, through which human rights and fundamental freedoms can be enjoyed." Participation must be accompanied by *empowerment,* defined as follows: "Empowerment is the process by which people's capabilities to demand and use their human rights grow. They are empowered to claim their rights rather than simply wait for policies, legislation or the provision of services. Initiatives should be focused on building the capacities of individuals and communities to hold those responsible to account. The goal is to give people the power and capabilities to change their own lives, improve their own communities and influence their own destinies" (UNICEF and UNESCO 2007, chap. 1, 10–11).

International human rights declarations have devoted special attention to the right to education for indigenous peoples. The formulation of specific educational rights for indigenous groups stems from their unique needs, their underprivileged status, their harsh experiences, and their persistent inequalities in education as well as in other social and economic fields. Studies show that many indigenous groups have been subject to educational policies inherited from the colonial system, which used education as a mechanism of control, deprivation, and cultural hegemony. In many cases, formal education was designed to wipe out the identities, narratives, and core cultures of these groups and was used as a means of involuntary assimilation (see Bellino, Paulson, and Worden 2017). Moreover, mainstream educational systems usually overlook, and in many cases even suppress, the experiences and unofficial knowledge indigenous students bring to school (see overview by Khanolainen, Nesterova, and Semenova 2020, 4–5). Likewise, the achievements of indigenous students are often evaluated by non-indigenous standards that ultimately discriminate against them and reflect a distorted and misleading picture of their skills and capabilities (Aitken and Radford 2018).

International bodies and UN agencies treat the educational rights of indigenous groups as an issue of major importance and as an integral part of the human rights of indigenous peoples. Article 14 (1,2) of the UNDRIP (2007) strongly asserts that the right to education of indigenous groups is an integral part of their declared right to self-determination:

1. Indigenous peoples have the right to establish and control their educational systems and institutions providing education in their own languages, in a manner appropriate to their cultural methods of teaching and learning.

2. Indigenous individuals, particularly children, have the right to all levels and forms of education of the State without discrimination.

Further, article 15.114 asserts the rights of indigenous peoples to incorporate their indigenous culture and knowledge into the mainstream education system. Other parts of UNDRIP (e.g., article 8) affirm a clear connection between indigenous rights, development, and education. The article states that indigenous rights to education, language, and culture are parallel to indigenous rights to self-determination, land, resources, and sustainable development (Bellier and Préaud 2012, 478).

Issues concerning language and education constitute one of the most difficult areas in which indigenous groups face challenges in negotiating with nation-states. This is because nation-state building and political nationalism are often accompanied by linguistic and cultural homogenization (May 1998, 278–79). Evidence from different countries shows that educational efforts directed at indigenous peoples have largely focused on *access to education*, whereas states have generally not devoted enough attention to linguistic and cultural rights. Hence, the UN's 2005 *Special Rapporteur on the Situation of Human Rights and Fundamental Freedoms of Indigenous People* called education "a two-edged sword" for indigenous peoples: "While the school system enables the acquisition of knowledge and skills, simultaneously it often de facto forcibly changes and in some cases destroys indigenous cultures" (cited by Saaresranta 2014, 355).

Even contemporary state policies that focus on attempting to close the gap between indigenous groups and majority groups in effect reflect assimilationist policies that detach educational outcomes from the authentic knowledge, culture, and experience of indigenous peoples (cited by Bellier and Préaud 2012, 478, referring to Canadian Council on Learning 2009). According to several studies, education in the postcolonial era should serve as a mechanism for resisting and disrupting colonial policies of control and identity deprivation among indigenous peoples, as well as a tool for revitalizing their indigenous knowledge and cultural well-being (e.g., Khanolainen, Nesterova, and Semenova 2020).

Multicultural Democracy, Liberal Democracy, and Indigenous Rights

The above analysis shows that indigenous human rights can be realized only within a multicultural democracy framework that simultaneously recognizes individual as well as collective rights. Such rights cannot be realized through other subtypes of majoritarian democracy that focus solely on individual liberties (see also Marri 2003; Kymlicka 2007a).

In many contemporary democratic societies, including the United States and other Western countries, liberal majoritarian democracy is the dominant form of democracy. This type of democracy is characterized by free, fair, and frequent elections and by freedom of expression. Moreover, this type of democracy upholds inclusive citizenship, such that citizens have the right to form relatively independent associations or organizations, including independent political parties and interest groups. Nevertheless, this type of democracy has been incessantly criticized for its various deficiencies, in particular when it comes to safeguarding diversity and protecting the rights of minorities and other distinct social and cultural groups (e.g., Kymlicka 1995, 2007a, 2018; Parker 1996; Marri 2003; Conversi 2012).

Another criticism of contemporary liberal majoritarian democracy is that it is color-blind in terms of the specific rights of distinct minorities and national groups (Marri 2003, 265–67). Indeed, many critics contend that this form of democracy systematically gives the majority the advantage and reduces the political power and cultural viability of national minorities and indigenous groups (Kymlicka 1995). Unlike liberal majoritarian democracy, multicultural democracy is often thought to be a better form of democracy in terms of protecting minority rights, diversity, and democratic citizenship (Kymlicka 1995; Marri 2003; Gibson and Grant 2012). According to Marri, it overcomes the shortcomings of several subtypes of democracy, including liberal majoritarian democracy:

> Multicultural democracy minimizes the possible existence of a permanent underclass because a multicultural democracy strives to incorporate the cultural and socio-economic diversity of its citizens along with political diversity. Multicultural democracies better meet the needs of all citizens by making their diversity essential to their success and, thus, citizens may be more likely to participate in elections and the democratic process. Secondly, multicultural democracies do not minimize the freedoms and rights of their citizens, because such democracies hold diversity as a central tenet. When democracies incorporate a variety of opinions, opportunities for democratic engagement are increased. Citizens increase their participation beyond voting and minimize the chances for infringement of their rights by governments. (Marri 2003, 271)

Multicultural democracy is therefore seen as an extension and enhancement of liberal democracy in that it goes beyond political participation by advocating a multicultural society that provides space for all citizens, while emphasizing commitment to justice and equality at the individual and group levels (Gibson and Grant 2012). Kymlicka notes that liberal multicultural democracy entails a "citizenization" process aimed at remedying Western liberal democracies' long history of illiberal and undemocratic actions toward nondominant groups and religious and national minorities: "Liberal multiculturalism in the West can be understood as a process of 'citizenization,' in sociological jargon. . . . The task for all liberal democracies has been to turn this catalogue of uncivil relations into relationships of liberal-democratic citizenship, in terms of both the vertical relationship between the members of minorities and the state, and the horizontal relationships amongst the members of different groups" (Kymlicka 2007a, 96). The above analysis shows that liberal democracy that focuses solely on safeguarding universal citizenship and individual rights is insufficient for guaranteeing indigenous rights. According to Yashar, in recent decades indigenous movements have increasingly contested the foundations of liberal democracy (Yashar 1999). These movements have sparked fundamental political debates over territorial autonomy, legal pluralism, citizenship, representation, and multiculturalism. Indeed, indigenous groups have begun demanding multicultural recognition that cannot be reduced to individual rights. In this regard, Yashar (1999) concludes that "indigenous movements have posed a postliberal challenge, by demanding a different kind of political mapping, one that would secure individual rights but also accommodate more diverse identities, units of representation, and state structures" (88).

Even a cursory survey of the literature shows that since the turn of the twentieth century, demands to achieve individual and collective rights have always been interwoven into the struggles of indigenous groups. Indeed, the claims of indigenous peoples have always involved collective group-differentiated rights, including the right to self-determination (Cobo 1986; Lightfoot 2010); land (Cobo 1986; Lightfoot 2010; Fierro 2020); language, tradition, and culture (Hatzikidi, Lennox, and Xanthaki 2021); education (Bellino 2015, Levinson 2012; Aikman and King 2012); recognition of identity and historical narratives (Nash 2006; Gellman and Bellino 2019); and other related issues.

The Palestinian Arabs in Israel: An Involuntary Indigenous Minority

Toward the end of the British Mandate period (1947), the Arab population in Palestine numbered 1,294,000, constituting two-thirds of the population of Palestine, with Jews constituting the remaining one-third (Gilbar 1989, 3). By the end of 1948 and immediately after the Israeli-Arab war, the former Palestinian Arab majority in Palestine had become a small minority in Israel, numbering nearly 160,000 and representing 13.5 percent of the total population of 1,173,900 at the end of 1949 (Statistical Abstract of Israel [SAI] 1985, no. 36, 32).

The flight and expulsion of approximately 80 percent of the Arab population (nearly 700,000 people) from the land within the boundaries of the new State of Israel was a disaster for the Palestinian Arabs. The refugees left behind broken families, relatives, homes, and property. Those who remained were now confined to 100 villages and encampments, where previously there had been 434 Arab villages within the aforementioned boundaries (Al-Haj and Rosenfeld 1989, 206). Only around 6 percent of the Palestinian Arab urban middle and upper classes remained in Israel after the war (Lustick 1980). Some members of those classes who had not left before the outbreak of hostilities fled during the war, and many others were expelled (Al-Haj and Rosenfeld 1990, 24). Most of those who stayed behind were villagers, of whom approximately 80 percent lived in rural areas in the Galilee, the Little Triangle, and the Negev (Kanaana 1975). Moreover, approximately 20 percent of the Palestinian Arab population in Israel became "internal refugees" who were forcibly moved to new localities after their original villages were destroyed during and immediately after the war (Al-Haj 1988a; Saabneh 2019). The vast majority of Arabs who remained in Israel were placed under military rule, which continued until 1966.

The aforementioned radical changes suggest that what took place in 1947–1948 was not merely a break from the past for a fragmented Palestinian Arab population. By every imaginable personal and group criterion it was a total catastrophic breakdown: a *Nakba* (catastrophe, in Arabic) deeply rooted in the Palestinian collective memory. In the following sections, I briefly describe this dramatic transition of the Palestinians in Israel from the majority group to an involuntary minority. I discuss the gap between their status as an indigenous national minority—a status to which they are entitled according to historical facts and by their own self-definition—and their official status, according to which the state recognizes the Palestinians in Israel merely as a religious-cultural minority, or rather as a mix of cultural minorities. Next, I trace the factors and the main changes that have affected the national and citizenship identity of the Palestinian citizens since 1948, with special emphasis on demographic, economic, and social-political changes.

GAP BETWEEN REALITY AND OFFICIAL RECOGNITION OF ARABS AS AN INDIGENOUS GROUP

I begin this section by making the following claim: the Palestinian Arabs in Israel meet all the conditions for recognition as an indigenous people, as set out in the aforementioned report submitted by José Martinez Cobo in 1986 to the UN Sub-Commission on Prevention of Discrimination and the Protection of Minorities. Indeed, the Palestinian Arabs in Israel are the continuation of the Palestinian majority prior the establishment of the state and the colonial invasion. Palestinian Arabs differentiate themselves from other sectors of Israeli society. They form the nondominant part of this society and are determined to preserve, develop, and transmit their territorial claims, their culture, and their ethnic-national identity to future generations as the foundation of their existence as a distinct group with their own cultural patterns and social systems.

These basic elements derive from the very definition of the characteristics typifying other indigenous peoples and are reflected in the self-definition of the Arab leadership. In fact, already in the early 1950s the Palestinians in Israel campaigned for recognition of their status as an indigenous minority, as reflected in their struggle over issues of land, culture, and education. Yet under the military government rule imposed on Arabs until 1966, this campaign was sporadic and characterized by spontaneous efforts on the part of individuals or separate communities (see Al-Haj 1988a; Al-Haj and Rosenfeld 1989).

Since the early 1970s, the Arabs' intensive campaign for recognition of their status as an indigenous people and a national minority has become more conspicuous, under the influence of various factors: abolishment of the military government in 1966; the 1967 war, which enhanced Palestinian national identity; and as a side effect of Israeli authorities' nationalizing enterprise in an effort to Judaize the land and the social space. This campaign may have also been influenced by the aforementioned growing international movement to obtain the rights of indigenous peoples, which gained special impetus in the early 1970s.

As an indigenous group, the Palestinian Arabs in Israel attribute special meaning to land, a meaning that goes far beyond its economic significance. Indeed, land forms a central component of their political culture, identity, and collective memory. Land is a basic component of the historical narrative of the Palestinians, who lived on this land for many generations, long before the region was conquered by the State of Israel (see Khalidi 1997). Defending the land also forms one of the central components of the national struggle of the Palestinians in Israel. To this end, in 1975 the Palestinian leadership in Israel established a national committee known as the Committee for the Defense of Arab Lands.

One of the most prominent landmarks of the political struggle of the Palestinian citizens in Israel is *Yom el-Ard* (Land Day), which was launched on March 30, 1976, in protest against plans by Israeli authorities to expropriate Arab lands as part of a national project to Judaize the Galilee. In various declarations prior to and following Land Day, Arab leaders employed several slogans. One was *Nahno Ashab el-Ard* (We Are the Landowners). Others reflected the native identity of a nation, not of a minority (e.g., Al-Haj 2019). The basic notion was of *al-Jamahir al-Arabiya* (the Arab Peoples) and never of an Arab minority (see the report on Land Day, Rekhess 1977). Land Day has become a national day for all Palestinians, including those living in the West Bank, in Gaza, and in the Palestinian diaspora.

Together with Henry Rosenfeld, I launched a comprehensive project to document the political struggle of Arab local authorities in the wake of Land Day. We emphasized the connection between this struggle and indigeneity, both in our book titled *Arab Local Government in Israel* (Al-Haj and Rosenfeld 1990) and in our article titled "The Emergence of an Indigenous Political Framework in Israel: The National Committee for the Heads of the Arab Local Authorities" (hereinafter we use the term National Committee, "al-Lajna al-Qutriyya" in Arabic, as often used among the Arab population) (see Al-Haj and Rosenfeld 1989, 206). In the next paragraphs I summarize the relevant parts of this article, beginning with the Arab leadership's self-definition of the Arabs as an indigenous national group and through the response of Yitzhak Rabin, then prime minister of Israel, which mirrors the reluctance of Israeli authorities to recognize this status and their attempts to relegate the Arabs' official standing to that of a mere cultural-religious minority.

Immediately after the events of the first Land Day (March 30, 1976), representatives of the National Committee (at the time part of the Israeli Center for Local Government) sent a memorandum to then prime minister Yitzhak Rabin. This memorandum was the Arabs' first demand for recognition of their collective rights with respect to Arab land and the Muslim Waqf, along with a demand to transfer administration of the Waqf to Muslims. The memorandum also raised the issue of the Middle East conflict while emphasizing the status of Arab citizens of Israel as part of the Palestinian people (Al-Haj and Rosenfeld 1989, 217).

In his reply, Prime Minister Rabin stressed that Israel is a Jewish state that is committed to granting the Arabs full rights as a unique cultural and religious entity. On June 17, 1976, the Arab leadership responded in a detailed letter, which the National Committee signed for the first time as an independent body. This letter consisted of three parts. The first and final sections are the most significant: for the first time since the establishment of the state, the Arab leadership issued a statement referring to the Arab citizens as an indigenous national minority whose status equals that of the Jewish majority. At the same time, the Arab leaders rejected the official ethnonational and Jewish-Zionist definition of the state, as can be seen in the following excerpt:

> Your Honor's (Prime Minister Rabin) clear response, that Israel is a Jewish state whose purpose and aims are the realization of Zionist yearnings while safeguarding the equal rights of the Arabs in the areas of culture and religion, leads us to fear that this declaration regarding our status as an Arab nation in Israel, this incomplete perception, will lead to treating the Arabs as subjects and not as citizens with equal rights. We feel, and we ask Your Honor to respect that feeling, that we are equal partners in the country, and that the Israeli-Arab conflict can in no way justify any lessening of the right of the Arabs to equality and the recognition of their national affiliation, which is a historic fact. (Al-Haj and Rosenfeld 1989, 218)

The final section of that letter clearly demands the right to self-determination as a means of realizing the collective rights of the Arabs in Israel in terms of land and development:

> We have great confidence in the victory of democracy and justice, and we believe that co-existence in peace and brotherhood in Israel between the **two nations** is a historical imperative and should be realized in such a way to serve the interests of peace. We should decrease existing points of conflict and find solutions to them. The major point of contention which is liable to lead to the danger of the two nations drawing further apart is the

denial of our **status as a national minority and the failure to recognize our right to keep the land on which our forefathers lived**, as well as the lack of concern for promoting the level of local services on the basis of equality, and the absence of coordination with the Arab local authorities regarding the subject of planning and development in our villages in the areas of agriculture, industry and housing. (Al-Haj and Rosenfeld 1989, 219)

Prime Minister Rabin never responded to this letter. Instead, Israel Keoning, northern district commissioner of the Ministry of Interior, published a document known as the Keoning Document, which emphasized the Jewish-Zionist nature of the state and the "reward and punishment" approach to dealing with and supervising the Arab population (Al-Haj and Rosenfeld 1989, 219; see also *Al-Hamishmar*, September 7, 1976).

This broad discrepancy between the official definition of the status of the Palestinian Arabs and their own perception of their status continues to this day. Israel has never recognized the status of its Arab citizens as an indigenous or national minority, and the Arabs have never relinquished their right to be defined as such.

The claim of the Palestinian Arabs in Israel for recognition as an indigenous group entitled to group-differentiated rights found expression in a series of documents known as the Future Vision Documents. These documents were initiated by the National Committee responsible for National Committee's document and two other civil society organizations: Adalah (responsible for Adalah's document) and Mada al-Carmel (responsible for the Haifa Declaration) (see National Committee for the Heads of the Arab Local Authorities 2006; Adalah 2007; Mada al-Carmel 2007).

The Vision Documents portray the Palestinian Arab citizens of Israel as an indigenous people with status and collective rights equal to those of the Jewish majority. This claim is reflected in all issues addressed by these documents, including self-identification, relationship to the State of Israel, relationship with the other parts of the Palestinian people, citizenship rights, and position regarding resolution of the Israeli-Palestinian conflict.

More specifically, all of these documents define the Palestinian Arabs as a homeland minority that was transformed from a majority into an involuntary minority as a result of the 1948 *Nakba*. Thus, Arabs are defined as a continuous majority with historic roots, culture, and rights to the land that has become the State of Israel. The Haifa Declaration states: "We, sons and daughters of the Palestinian Arab people who remained in our homeland despite the Nakba, who were forcibly made a minority in the State of Israel after its establishment in 1948 on the greater part of the Palestinian homeland" (Mada al-Carmel 2007, 7). Adalah's document similarly states: "The legal starting point of this constitutional proposal is: The Arab citizens in the State of Israel are a homeland minority. . . . [They] have lived in their homeland for innumerable generations. Here they were born, here their historic roots have grown, and here their national and cultural life has developed and flourished" (Adalah 2007, 4).

In reference to the self-definition of the Palestinian Arabs in Israel, the National Committee's document states: "We are the Palestinian Arabs in Israel, the **indigenous people**. . . . The war of 1948 resulted in the establishment of the Israeli state . . . and we were forced to become citizens of Israel. This has transformed us into a minority living in our historic homeland" (Adalah 2007, 5). In effect, the state's failure to recognize the Arabs in Israel as an indigenous national minority reflects the ethnonational nature of the state. This failure positions Israel far removed from Western countries and even countries in Latin America and elsewhere that have made serious progress in recognizing the collective rights of indigenous peoples within their jurisdictions, as shown earlier in this chapter. Furthermore, Israel's ethnonational character is reflected in its official policy toward Arabs, a policy that has exerted a major impact on changes and development among the Palestinian Arabs in various fields, as briefly discussed below.

CHANGES AMONG THE PALESTINIAN ARABS IN ISRAEL

Demographic Change

Since the establishment of the State of Israel, the Arab population has increased 12.5 times, reaching 1,622,000 by 2021 and constituting nearly 18 percent of the total population (SAI 2022, 2, table 2.1). This figure does not include the Palestinians living in East Jerusalem, who have been granted special status since 1967 and are beyond the scope of this study. Together with those living in East Jerusalem, the Palestinian Arabs in Israel number 1,997,000, constituting 21 percent of the total population. Whereas this demographic growth among the Arabs can be attributed almost solely to natural increase, 37.6 percent of the growth of the Jewish population has been the result of immigration (SAI 2021, 3). In 2020, the Arab population of Israel comprised 85.5 percent Muslims, 7.5 percent Druze, and 7 percent Christians (SAI 2021, 4–5, table 2.3).

Moreover, the Arab population has undergone conspicuous demographic changes over time. Until the mid-1960s, Arabs had extremely high fertility rates compared to Jews. Fertility was especially high among Muslims, with a fertility rate almost three times greater than that of Jews. Since the early 1970s, the Arab population has exhibited a steady, albeit gradual, decline in fertility rates, accompanied by family planning (Al-Haj 1987). Similar to the period of the British Mandate, the Arab population has remained heterogeneous in terms of demographic characteristics, with Muslims continuing to exhibit the highest fertility rates, followed by Druze and Christians (table 2.1).

The high rate of natural increase among the Arabs was a direct result of a marked decrease in mortality rates, in particular infant mortality (Gilbar 1989). Cultural-religious values coupled with the patriarchal system and the traditional division of labor between men and women also served as central factors in increasing fertility among Arabs (e.g., Al-Haj 1987). In addition, coercive contextual factors may have been at least partly responsible for the high fertility rates, as in the case of other ethnic minorities whose high rate of natural increase is closely associated with their economic marginalization, their residential segregation and social exclusion from the majority, and ultimately their lack of a sense of social security (see Goldscheider and Uhlenberg 1969; Goldscheider 2006; Martin 2020).

Until the mid-1960s, Palestinian Arabs in Israel were extremely localized. The military government that ruled Arab localities from 1949 through 1966 placed major restrictions on their movement. Through various measures and laws imposed by the military government apparatus, Israeli authorities suspended many of the citizenship rights and legal protections of the Arab

Table 2.1. Total Fertility Rates among Arabs in Israel by Religion vs. Jews (1960–2018)

	Muslims	Christians	Druze	Jews
1960–64	9.23	4.68	7.49	3.38
1970–74	8.47	3.65	7.25	3.28
1980–84	5.54	2.41	5.40	2.80
2000–4	4.57	2.35	2.87	2.67
2010–14	3.50	2.18	2.30	3.03
2018	3.17	2.06	2.18	3.20

Source: CBS, SAI 2019, table 2.41, 1–2.

population (Degani 2015, 84). Moreover, this system served to exercise a policy of close surveillance and control over the Arab citizens, thus ensuring their isolation from the country's economic, social, and political systems (Forman 2006, 338). In this sense, the Israeli government not only restricted the movement of Arabs and their economic and social relationships with the Jewish majority but also controlled the internal relationships among the Arab communities themselves (see Lustick 1980; Ozacky-Lazar 1996, 2002; Forman 2006).

Since the early 1970s, fertility rates among all Arab groups have steadily declined. The proportional decline among Muslims and Druze has been dramatic and conspicuous. In 2018, the overall fertility rate among Muslims was 3.17, even a bit lower than that year's fertility rate of 3.20 among Jews. As shown in table 2.1, Muslim fertility in 2018 was one-third of the rate in the early 1960s. The relative decline in fertility among the other Arab religious groups was also dramatic. In 2018, the fertility rates for both Druze and Christians were lower than the rate among Jews: 2.18 among the Druze population and 2.06 among the Christians. As opposed to the trend among the Arab population, the overall fertility rate among Jews has been on the rise in the last two decades.

The median age of the Arab population is conversely related to fertility rates and has continued to increase over time. In 1955, the median age was 17.4 years among Muslims, 17.2 among Druze, 20.4 among Christians, and 25.8 among Jews. By 2020, the median age was 22.9 years among Muslims, 29.0 among Druze, 33.3 among Christians, and 31.7 among Jews (see SAI 1986, 62; 1991, 58–59; 2021, 4, table 2.5). Yet, despite the drastic decrease in fertility rates, Muslims are still the youngest population group in Israel, followed respectively by Druze, Jews, and Christians.

One of the main consequences of this age structure is the growing number of school-aged children. As of 2020, school-aged children constitute around 38.6 percent of the Arab population (5–19), compared to 26.7 percent among Jews. Taking into consideration that children ages 3–4 are now eligible for compulsory education (by the 2015 Compulsory Education Law), potential pupils constitute as much as 50 percent of the Arab population in Israel (SAI 2021, table 2.5, 2–4).

Social Change

Conspicuous changes are evident among the Arabs in Israel in various spheres. The rise in their level of education is probably the most salient. In 1961, the median number of years of schooling among the adult Arab population (14 years and over) was 1.2. By 1999 this figure had risen to 10.8, and by 2018, to 12.0 years (table 2.2). Despite this significant increase in years of schooling among the Arabs since the 1990s, the gap with the Jewish population remains wide: the median number of years of schooling among Arabs in 2018 was equivalent to the number for Jews in 2006, such that the Arabs lag behind the Jews by 12 years (see tables 2.2a, 2.2b).

This across-the-board increase in educational level applies to all the Arab religious groups, to urban and rural populations, and to men as well as women. The expansion of higher education among women has been particularly meaningful. As of today (2023), women constitute the majority among Arab students across the various levels of undergraduate and graduate

Table 2.2a. Persons Aged 14 and Over by Group and Years of Schooling over Time (1961–2018) (Arabs)

Year	0	1–4	5–8	9–10	11–12	13–15	16+	Median
1961	49.5	13.9	27.5	–	–	–	1.5	1.2
1970	36.1	13.7	35.1	–	–	17.0	0.4	5.0
1980	18.9	10.0	33.9	16.0	13.5	5.5	2.2	7.5
1990	13.0	6.5	30.8	17.4	23.2	6.1	3.0	9.0
2006	6.1	3.9	19.3	18.8	32.7	10.3	8.9	11.0
2018	3.7	1.8	13.2	16.3	38.6	11.5	14.9	12.0

Source: SAI 1991, 604–5; 2020, table 4.80, 2–3.

Table 2.2b. Persons Aged 14 and Over by Group and Years of Schooling over Time (1961–2018) (Jews)

Year	0	1–4	5–8	9–10	11–12	13–15	16+	Median
1961	12.6	7.5	35.4	–	34.6	6.3	3.6	8.4
1970	9.3	6.3	31.7	–	39.7	10.7	7.0	10.3
1980	6.4	3.9	21.3	17.2	30.4	12.3	8.5	11.1
1990	4.2	2.4	13.7	13.5	38.0	16.0	12.2	11.9
2006	2.1	1.0	6.0	9.2	35.5	24.2	22.0	12.0
2018	1.0	0.4	3.2	7.2	32.1	24.1	31.9	14.0

Source: SAI 1991, 604–5; 2020, table 4.80, 2–3.

study in Israeli institutions of higher education (for a detailed analysis, see chapter 6).

A parallel transformation has taken place in family life. The large-scale transition from agricultural work on the family farm to hired labor outside the village weakened the typical extended Arab family and eroded the patriarchal regime within the family. At the level of the nuclear family, research shows that Arab parents, without exception, strongly aspire for their children to attain higher education (see Al-Haj 2006). The rise in the standard of living alongside major exposure to the influence of the Jewish population and the media have engendered a variety of new consumption patterns among the Arab population. The individual needs of family members have begun to play an important role in determining these patterns. Indeed, women and children, who in the past exerted limited and even marginal influence in this area, over time have become more central to family life (Al-Haj 1989a; Al-Krenawi and Graham 1998; Haj-Yahia and Lavee 2018; Meoded et al. 2021).

Parent-children relationships have also been affected by technological changes. As in other contemporary societies, among the Arabs in Israel one of the major changes in family lifestyle has to do with the growing number of families that have introduced internet-based media into their homes (e.g., Meoded et al. 2021). A 2014 study conducted by Tzischinsky and Haimov (2017) on internet use among Muslim and Jewish schoolchildren (7–11 years) in both urban and rural residential settings showed a rise in screen time among Muslim children, despite having fewer computers than Jewish children.

Within the Arab family as well, the division of labor between spouses has considerably changed. The younger generation is much more open to egalitarian attitudes and practices within the family. Nevertheless, the issue of family lifestyle is complex, encompassing both traditional and modern attitudes (Haj-Yahia and Lavee 2018). The principal factors promoting change are associated with women's education and employment outside home, as well as contact with the Jewish population and residential proximity to Jewish communities (Haj-Yahia and Lavee 2018, 29).

Along with a deep shift from local and traditional forms of identity to an identity that first and foremost is based on national consciousness, the Arabs in Israel have also undergone an extensive process of politicization, becoming profoundly aware of their status and rights as a national minority. The traditional Arab leadership is being replaced by a young, educated, and sophisticated leadership, as reflected in both local and national politics. Arab students and academics have assumed an active leadership role in processes of national consciousness and in establishing national and professional organizations as well as civil society organizations (Khalaily and Ghanem 2023).

Nevertheless, the aforementioned change among the Arab population has been restricted to the individual-local level and is much less noticeable on the national institutional level. Moreover, although social change among Arabs has raised aspirations for socioeconomic mobility, the ethnic stratification in Israel constitutes a clear mobility ceiling as far as Arab citizens are concerned (Lewin-Epstein and Semyonov 1986; Lewin-Epstein, Al-Haj, and Semyonov 1994).

Employment distress among the Arabs has only increased over time, further impeding the potential role of education in promoting women's status and decreasing Jewish-Arab inequalities. Based on national census data on education and employment among Muslim, Christian, and Druze spouses in Israel, Offer and Sabah (2011, 338–40) conclude that despite the radical economic and social changes among Arabs in Israel over time, the labor force participation of Arab women, in particular married women, has remained limited (see also chapter 6). Indeed, according to official statistics, in 2020 only 27.8 percent of Arab women aged 15 and over were part of the labor force, compared to 64.9 percent among Jewish women and 54 percent among Arab men (SAI 2021, tables 9.5, 9.10). As a result, in 2020 only 41 percent of Arabs were part of the labor force, compared to 66.4 percent of Jews (SAI 2021, tables 9.5, 9.10).

Social and Political Localization

Social changes and political structure among the Palestinian Arabs in Israel are characterized by social and political localization. The term *social localization* is used here to describe the almost absolute spatial and residential segregation between Arabs and Jews, together with closed social networks and primary social relationships that are for the most part restricted to the same group. Similarly, *political localization* refers to Arabs' constrained role in nationwide politics, such that the local municipal system has become the main arena of political mobilization among the Arab population.

The Arabs in Israel live in three geo-cultural areas: the Galilee, the Little Triangle, and the Negev. The vast majority (about 90 percent) live in separate Arab localities, with only around 10 percent residing in mixed Jewish-Arab localities. Even in these mixed localities, the Arabs live in segregated neighborhoods (Waterman 1987; Ben-Artzi 1980). The fact that the Arabs in Israel have not migrated to urban centers is contrary to the sociodemographic processes typical of developing societies across the globe. In most of those societies, proletarianization has resulted in mass migration from rural areas to urban centers. Yet despite broad proletarianization among the Arabs in Israel, movement to Jewish cities or to urban centers has been quite limited, such that most of the Arab labor force commutes from Arab villages and towns to Jewish industrial centers (Rosenfeld 1978; Schnell and Haj-Yahya 2014; Goldscheider, 2015; Haj-Yahia and Lavee 2018).

The only major migration among the Arabs has been the forced migration of internal refugees and Bedouins. The migration of the internal refugees was collective in nature: in most cases an entire original community, or large parts of it, moved together and settled in the same new locality. As mentioned earlier, the Palestinian internal refugees, comprising nearly 20 percent of the Palestinian population, were displaced from their original communities, which were demolished during or right after the 1948 war. Although these people remained in Israel and became Israeli citizens, they have been prevented from returning to their villages. These internal refugees faced grave problems of adjustment, locally and in Israeli society at large, and have actually been pushed to the status of a minority within the minority (for a detailed analysis of the internal refugees, see Al-Haj 1988a).

Moreover, the government initiated a sedentarization plan for the Bedouins as part of its ongoing policy of Judaization of land and space in the Negev and the North (Falah 1989; Rotem and Gordon 2017). This plan, which aimed at severely restricting the Bedouins' traditional nomadic movements, has resulted in the localization of almost the entire Bedouin population. The sudden transition from dry farming and cattle grazing to earning a living through paid labor seriously disrupted the Bedouins' traditional lifestyle. In addition, this localization has eradicated their historical economic base, thereby greatly increasing their dependency on the Jewish center (Falah 1989).

As residents of peripheral rural areas and small towns, Arabs are at a double disadvantage: first as Arabs and second as a rural population. Using national data from the 2005 Family Expenditure Survey in Israel, Kimhi (2010) reports that per capita household income in 2005 was more than 30 percent lower in rural communities and small towns than in the country as a whole. At the same time, the per capita income of the rural Arab population was more than 40 percent lower than that of the rural population as a whole (382).

In fact, there has always been a gap between Jews and Arabs in terms of standard of living, and this discrepancy has widened over time. As shown in the Central Bureau of Statistics (CBS) special report for 2021, the average gross monthly income in Jewish households was 1.6 times higher than in Arab households, and the average net per capita income (accepted as a measure of standard of living) in Jewish households was 1.9 times higher than in Arab households (CBS 2022, 11).

The social localization of the Arabs is coupled with political localization in that the Arabs' political power at the national Israeli level is very limited. Already in 1949, the Arabs, as citizens of Israel, were granted the right to vote in the first free and democratic elections for the Israeli parliament. Nevertheless, the Arabs have a restricted share of the national center of power. The circumstances that prevailed among the Arab population in the aftermath of Israeli statehood facilitated political localization of the Arab minority. The lack of national Arab leadership together with the Arabs' weak political consciousness at the time made it possible for the traditional *hamula* (clan/kinship group) leadership to exercise control over the entire population via a few key people. At the same time, the dominance of the *hamula* structure perpetuated internal divisions among the Arabs, thus preventing the formation of a collective national identity or any rapprochement with the left-wing parties (see Al-Haj and Rosenfeld 1990; Al-Haj 1995c).

As mentioned, since the early 1970s the increasing politicization of the Palestinians in Israel has been accompanied by a national awakening and a mounting struggle for civic equality as an indigenous national minority. Yet despite this politicization and the increasingly pragmatic orientation of the predominantly Arab parties, the Arabs have remained outside the borders of legitimacy in Israeli political culture and have been denied any access to the national power center. For a long time, no Arab party was allowed to be a full partner in a government coalition, including those based on Labor and the left wing. A good example is the case of the predominantly Arab parties during the period of the Rabin-Peres government (1992–1996). Even though the Arab parties' support for this government was a crucial component in its parliamentary majority, they were only permitted to support it from the outside as part of the blocking majority that made it impossible for the Likud to form a government. This situation actually transformed the predominantly Arab parties into a *blocked minority* that was permanently denied access to any share of the benefits of the exclusively Jewish power center (Al-Haj 1997). The Barak government is another example of the exclusion of Arabs from the power center in Israel. Although 95 percent of Arab voters supported Ehud Barak in the 1999 elections, when it came time to form his government, he ignored the Arab parties, which once again were relegated to the status of a *permanent opposition* (see Ghanem and Ozacky-Lazar 1999).

Since the events of the 2000 Al-Aqsa intifada, which further deepened the Jewish-Arab rift, the trend toward political localization among the Arabs has increased. That is, the Arabs focused their main political activity within their localities through local municipal elections, whereas their participation in Knesset parliamentary elections decreased drastically. Moreover, the Palestinian vote has become increasingly "Arabized," such that those who vote in Knesset elections for the most part support Arab parties.

Arab turnout in the 1999 Knesset elections reached 75 percent, resembling voter turnout in the Israeli population as a whole (78.7 percent). Since then, Arab voter turnout has decreased considerably. In most of the elections since 2000, only 50 percent of the Arabs voted. The elections in 2015 and in March 2020, in which the major Arab parties were unified in a single Joint Arab List, were an exception, with nearly two-thirds of the Arabs voting in these elections (see Rudnitzky 2016; Hitman 2021). In the March 2021 elections, the Arab voter turnout was only 44.6 percent, compared to 64.8 percent in the general population (Rudnitzky 2021).

Political localization is also reflected in Arab voters' massive support for Arab parties, whereas Jewish-Zionist parties have almost disappeared from the local Arab political scene. In the 1992 elections, Arab parties received only 47.7 percent of Arab votes. By the 2015 elections this figure had increased to 83.2 percent (Rudnitzky 2016, 686). In the March 2020 elections, 88 percent of Arab voters supported Arab parties, and in the March 2021 elections, nearly 80 percent voted for Arab parties (Rudnitzky 2021).

Yet this trend toward political localization does not mean that Arabs in Israel have lost interest in national politics and in parliamentary elections, as some researchers claim (e.g., Bligh 2013). On the contrary, this trend is the result of Arab voters' disappointment in their marginal impact on national politics and also of their dissatisfaction with the performance of Arab Knesset members. As mentioned, Arab voter turnout rose considerably in the 2015 and 2020 elections when the Arab parties formed a unified list, reflecting Arab voters' hopes that they might have a greater say in Israeli politics.

In the March 2021 elections, the United Arab List (commonly known by its Hebrew acronym Ra'am), broke off from the Joint List of Arab parties and ran alone on a platform of willingness to bring about change from the inside. Ra'am ultimately joined the coalition—the most diverse coalition since the establishment of the state for it included parties from the right, center, and left, together with an Arab party. Unlike the Arab parties' outside support for the Rabin government in 1992, for the first time an Arab party was part of the government coalition. Nevertheless, this government's composition and distribution of power, and the fact that Ra'am was part of the coalition but not of the government, reflected the asymmetric Jewish-Arab relations and the permanent marginal status of Arabs in Israeli politics. Two parties—Yamina (led by Naftali Bennett) and Ra'am (led by Mansour Abbas)—were considered crucial to the coalition's formation and survival. With only six Knesset seats, Naftali Bennett became prime minister and his party was awarded two additional ministerial positions: minister of the interior and minister of religious affairs. Nevertheless, even though Ra'am's four seats were crucial for forming the government, Ra'am was not represented in the government and did not receive any ministerial position or even a deputy minister position. In any event, this coalition was short-lived. On June 20, 2022, Prime Minister Bennett declared that this coalition had come to an end, leading the country into a fifth round of elections in less than four years (Weiss 2022).

These elections, held on November 1, 2022, produced the most extremist government in Israel's history. Led by Netanyahu, this new government is composed of 64 Knesset members, all of whom belong to Jewish right-wing and ultra-Orthodox parties. These include Otzma Yehudit (Jewish Power) led by Itamar Ben-Gvir—an ultra-right party often identified as Kahanist and anti-Arab—and the Religious Zionist party led by Bezalel Smotrich—an extreme rightist and ultra-nationalist anti-Arab party. Together these two parties have 14 seats in the Knesset. As a result, the Arab parties, including Ra'am, have been further marginalized and politically localized.

The above analysis reveals a wide gap between Arabs and Jews in Israel in every conceivable field. It also points to a controlled form of development that is restricted mainly to the individual level and very limited at the group-collective level. In this context, Arabs have not been able to build their own institutions, nor have they integrated into Jewish-controlled national institutions. Moreover, even though Arabs are entitled to the status of a national indigenous minority according to the definitions of international human rights conventions and the UNDRIP, the state does not officially recognize this status. Indeed, the state has downgraded their status to that of a mere religious-linguistic-cultural minority. As a result, Arabs do not enjoy any group-differentiated rights, not to speak about the right for self-determination, which constitutes the pillar of the UN Declaration of Indigenous Rights (see UNDRIP 2007).

Thus far, I have focused on two dimensions of the status and development of the Palestinian Arabs in Israel: the horizontal dimension connected to local-community developments among the Arab population and the vertical dimension associated with the nature of the state and its policy toward the Palestinian Arabs. On the vertical dimension I have addressed the impact of state policy, which has placed the Palestinian Arabs at the margins of Israeli society and opportunity structure. Yet the problematic identity of Arabs is not merely the byproduct of factors related to these dimensions. Regional-national factors also affect the marginal position of Arabs vis-à-vis the Arab world, and especially with respect to the Palestinian national movement (see Al-Haj 1989, 1993, 1997, 2005a). This complex status has far-reaching implications for the identity, political orientation, and patterns of mobilization among the Palestinian Arabs in Israel, as described in the next section.

Identity of the Palestinian Arabs in Israel: Situated within a Double Periphery

Most researchers who have examined the identity of Palestinian Arabs in Israel agree that this identity encompasses two key elements: the civic component stemming from the Arabs' status as citizens of the State of Israel and the national component referring to the affiliation of the Arabs in Israel to the Arab world and the Palestinian people (see, for example, Peres and Yuval-Davis 1969; Nakhleh 1975; Smooha 1989, 2010; Rouhana 1989, 1997; Amara 2016, 2019; Arar and Ibrahim 2016; Harpaz and Nassar 2021). Yet these researchers disagree on how to rank the importance of these components and how to reconcile the internal contradictions between them.

For quite some time, researchers focused mainly on the contradictions and complexities of the Israeli citizenship component and rarely addressed the complexity of the Palestinian national component (see, for example, Nakhleh 1975; Smooha 1989; Rekhess 1989; Rouhana 1997; Arar and Ibrahim 2016; Amara 2016, 2019). In fact, the literature reflects a latent assumption that the main contradiction for Palestinian Arabs in Israel in terms of their status and identity is primarily associated with the Israeli citizenship component, whereas their relationship to the Palestinian national component is straightforward and lacks any contradiction that needs to be addressed (e.g., Amara 2019, 275). Amara and Schnell attribute this to the "many Israeli Arab feelings of humiliation due to the fact that their citizenship is not tolerated in Israeli society. In this sense the Palestinian identity supplies them at least with some sense of pride" (Amara and Schnell 2004, 189).

Ostensibly, the contradiction inherent in the Israeli citizenship component of the identity of the Arabs in Israel is much larger than the contradiction in the national Palestinian component. Nevertheless, it is important to note that the Arabs in Israel have never enjoyed equal or full membership in terms of their national Palestinian affiliation. Al-Haj was the first to identify this double marginality of the Arabs in Israel with respect both to the Israeli citizenship component and to the Palestinian national component of their identity. Accordingly, he proposed the notion of a *double periphery* to express the Arabs' position at the margins both of Israeli society and of the Palestinian national movement (see Al-Haj 1989, 1993, 1997). This proposed notion emerged against the background of the first Palestinian intifada (1987–1992), which highlighted the complex identity of the Arabs in Israel. According to Al-Haj:

> The Arabs' unequivocal identification with, and support for, the intifada, although within the confines of law, were perceived by large segments of the Jewish Israeli population as being anti-Israeli action, since loyalty of the Arab citizens to the national cause is considered by most Jews as contradictory to their loyalty to Israel. Thus, the image of the Arab citizens as a 'hostile minority' has been strengthened, pushing them even further to the **periphery of Israeli society.** On the other hand, the political behavior of the Arabs highlighted their marginal role in the Israeli-Palestinian conflict and the fact that they are placed at the **periphery of the Palestinian National Movement**. (Al-Haj 1993, 73)

The peace process between Israel and the Palestinians and the signing of the Oslo Accords in September 1993 did nothing to change the disadvantaged status of the Palestinian citizens in Israel. Contrary to the common misconception, the peace process has not improved the status of the Arabs in Israel, nor has it significantly altered the ethnic-national culture of the Jewish majority. What is most conspicuous to date is that the Jewish majority's struggle for the state's Jewish-Zionist identity has intensified, thus further marginalizing the Palestinian Arabs in Israel (Al-Haj 2005a). Issues connected to the Palestinian population in Israel have been overlooked by the Palestinian national movement as well. For most Israelis the acceptance of the Palestine Liberation Organization (PLO) of the principle of "two states for two peoples" means acceptance of the principle of a Palestinian state alongside a Jewish state. This principle has been accepted by the PLO without concern for the status of the Palestinian citizens of Israel.

Indeed, the Oslo Accords deepened the status of the Palestinians in Israel as a double periphery, causing them to reassess their relationships both with the Palestinian national movement and with the State of Israel and ultimately to place citizenship issues at the center of their struggle (Al-Haj 2005a). Eli Rekhess (2007) aptly describes this trend as the "localization of the national struggle" of the Arabs in Israel (71), a trend that finds expression in the consolidation of particularistic national Palestinian patterns within Israel itself.

This trend toward national localization among the Palestinian Arabs in Israel was further strengthened in the wake of the Arab Spring, the name given to the mass demonstrations and actions that began in Tunisia in December 2010 and spread across much of the Arab world. The people who took part in these mass demonstrations were protesting against the ruling regimes. They demanded democracy, employment, civil rights and liberties, and an end to corruption, under the slogan *Ashaab Yurid Taghier el-Nitham* (the People Demand a Change in the Regime) (see Hassib 2013; Danahar 2015; Matar 2016).

The Arab Spring also affected the Palestinian Arab citizens in Israel. One could argue that these demonstrations and protests further reinforced the trend defined by Rekhess as the localization of the national struggle (Rekhess 2007). According to Khaizran, the Arab Spring heightened the public legitimacy of different patterns of localism and discourse among the Arabs in Israel. It also reinforced a form of civil discourse toward the state that acts as the antithesis of its Jewish character (Khaizran 2020, 284).

The Jewish majority, however, rejected the nationalization trend or the localization of the national struggle (Rekhess 2007) among the Palestinian Arab population, perceiving it as a threat to Israel's security and to its Jewish character (Ghanem and Khatib 2017). The political leaders on the Israeli right have also used this trend as an excuse to intensify their campaign to strengthen the ethnonational Jewish-Zionist character of Israel and to intensify the existing policy of exerting control over the Palestinian Arab population. As a result, since 2009 a series of bills have been proposed in the Knesset that are intended to undermine Israeli Arabs (Kremnitzer and Fuchs 2016, 189; Sagi 2016, 178).

This retreat from civil liberal features in favor of ethnonational aspects peaked with the Knesset's approval of the Basic Law: Israel as the nation-state of the Jewish people, otherwise known as the Nationality Law (July 2018). In practice, the Nationality Law further reinforces the ethnonational Jewish-Zionist character of the State of Israel, while totally overlooking its democratic character, even at the declarative level. The law completely disregards the existence of the Palestinian citizens of Israel and of other non-Jewish groups. It annuls the status of Arabic as an official language. Instead it declares that "the Arabic language has a special status in the state," though it does not define this special status (Knesset 2018).

The situation described above raises a number of questions: What are the barriers to creating an encompassing form of citizenship that would guarantee equality and equity for all groups, including the Palestinian Arab citizens? What are the barriers to instituting multiculturalism in Israel as a format that would guarantee the Arabs' right to be different and equal at the individual and collective levels? In general, is there any chance of instituting multicultural democracy in Israel? I attempt to answer these questions in the following section. After a short conceptual framework, I focus on Jewish-Arab relations in Israel.

Barriers to Multicultural Democracy and Jewish-Arab Relations

Brubaker (2011) provides a broad framework for understanding how nationalizing states construct a nationalist discourse after achieving their independence, thus further deepening their ethnonational character at the expense of diversity and multicultural democracy. He contends that achievement of independent statehood per se does not mark the end of nationalist politics but rather represents the transition to a new kind of nationalism that constitutes a stimulus for a policy of control over minority groups. It also serves as a legitimizing mechanism for instituting nondemocratic policies toward national minorities and for rejecting their demands for group-differentiated rights.

Brubaker (2011, 1786) mentions five characteristic motifs of nationalist discourse that are used to justify nationalizing policies and reject minority rights in a variety of domains: (1) the notion that the state contains a "core nation" or nationality, understood in ethnocultural terms and distinguished from the citizenry or permanent resident population of the state as a whole; (2) a claim to ownership or primacy: the state is understood as the state of and for the core nation; (3) the claim that the core nation is in a weak or unhealthy condition; (4) the claim that state action is needed to strengthen the core nation and promote its language, cultural flourishing, demographic robustness, economic welfare, or political hegemony; and (5) the claim that such action is remedial or compensatory, needed to redress previous discrimination or oppression suffered by the core nation.

Wars and ongoing conflicts have been identified as a hotbed for the proliferation of nationalist discourse and ethnonational political culture. In his article on war and ethnicity, Anthony Smith (1981) contends that ongoing conflicts and wars exert a powerful impact on state and society and on shaping ethnic community and nationhood. In this sense, prolonged wars both create and reinforce military elites, which become highly dominant relative to their security function and their mass participation in war (377). In addition, warfare is manipulated for ethnic mobilization and through intensive propaganda that constructs favorable self-images and negative enemy stereotypes. According to Smith: "In the modern ideological era, this trend is greatly enhanced, because ethnic sentiments and national cohesion can be strongly influenced by the propaganda of 'populist' ideologies and the impetus they provide for further wars, which in turn requires mass mobilization. . . . War propaganda furthers the community's ethnocentrism, the belief in the centrality and superiority of one's group and its culture. Ethnocentrism inevitably devalues outsiders and their cultures, breeding solipsism or in some cases hostility" (390–91). Kymlicka (2007a) similarly concludes: "Where states feel insecure in geo-political terms, fearful of neighbouring enemies, their treatment of minorities is heavily shaped by this sense of insecurity. In particular, states will never voluntarily accord rights and powers to minorities if they think this will increase the likelihood of minorities acting as potential collaborators with, or as a 'fifth column' for, a neighbouring enemy" (118). Here Kymlicka emphasizes that state-minority securitization factors constitute a key barrier to embracing a multicultural form of democracy that recognizes collective minority rights. Indeed, Kymlicka claims that in order to adopt a model of multicultural democracy, state-minority relationships should be "taken out of the 'security' box, and put in the 'democratic politics' box" (120).

This conceptual framework perfectly applies to Israel. To begin, Israel is a nationalizing state in which nation building is closely connected with the Jewish core nation, whereas the Arab minority is kept outside the state's national consensus and its borders of legitimacy. In this regard, Israel's nationalization project as a Jewish-Zionist state did not end with the establishment of the state but rather has been expanded and enhanced over time (Kimmerling 2004; Ghanem 2016). After the 1948 war, Israel fostered a nationalist-statist ideology that included transferring Arab-owned land and property to Israeli state ownership (Carmi and Rosenfeld 1989). This land takeover occurred during the first years of Israeli statehood, when Palestinians were under the strict control of the military government and were especially weak, few in number and demoralized (Al-Haj and Rosenfeld 1989).

The Israeli-Arab conflict, which has involved a chain of regional wars and a number of military operations with Gaza, has always been a stimulus for nationalizing Israeli society and a central factor in crystalizing Israel's national ethos and collective identity. Like nationalizing states elsewhere that are under ongoing conflict, Israel has used security considerations as a mechanism for legitimizing its policy of surveillance and control over the Palestinian Arabs. Note also that this principle of security considerations has ethnocentric significance and is intimately associated with the Jewish-Zionist character of the state. Thus, any attempt on the part of the Palestinian Arabs to question or challenge this character is placed under the security rubric and is ultimately considered a threat to Israel's very existence as a Jewish state (e.g., Ghanem and Khatib 2017).

The dominance of Israel's militaristic culture undoubtedly constitutes a major barrier to the development of a multicultural democracy. Despite the different opinions regarding militarism and its impact on civil society in Israel, the broad consensus is that Israel's militaristic culture comes at the expense of its democratic character (see Barzilai 1992; Ben-Eliezer 2003; Kimmerling 2016; Sheffer and Barak 2016). The fact that Israel was created as a result of war and remains in an ongoing state of emergency has generated the prevalent belief among the Jewish public at large that the state is facing existential threats that necessitate a strong military and ongoing preparation for the next war (Ben-Eliezer 2003; Kimmerling 2016). Many generals in the Israel Defense Forces (IDF) also continue to play a major role in political, social, and economic spheres of civilian life after they finish their military service (see Ben-Eliezer 1998; Sheffer and Barak 2016).

Immigration is another central pillar of this nationalizing project. Not only has immigration been the main source of demographic growth among the Jewish population in Palestine, and later in Israel, it is also a major source of strengthening its nationalization project and has affected every aspect of Israel's ethnic structure, collective identity, and political culture (Goldscheider 2015). In this context, the 1990s influx of immigrants from the former Soviet Union constitutes one of the most significant waves of immigration to Israel. This wave generated a radical change in the political map in that it strengthened the political right and further deepened the ethnonational character and ideological rift in Israel (see Al-Haj 2019).

Clearly, then, Israel's nationalizing project has contributed to the homogenization of Israeli society, while excluding the Arabs. Indeed, the Arabs are considered not only a barrier to this project but also a threat to its realization because Israel is affiliated with a core nation—the Jewish people—and because it was established by Jews to be the national home of the Jewish people, not a state for all its citizen (Kimmerling 2004; Smooha 2016; Ghanem 2016; Yiftachel 2016).

Indeed, the state's ethnonational character constitutes a major barrier to developing multicultural democracy and has resulted in a type of democracy that is inferior to that of other Western democracies. According to Smooha (2016): "The quality of Israel's liberal democracy is degraded by the absence of a constitution, the permanence of emergency regulations, religious coercion, and the pivotal idea that Israel belongs to all Jews in the world and not to its citizens and its nature as a Jewish state is a permanent and unchangeable system" (686).

Multicultural Democracy and the Blurred Majority-Minority Boundaries

Thus far, I have discussed the barriers that inhibit the creation of a multicultural democracy in Israel from the perspective of vertical state-minority relationships. In addition to these factors, another important aspect that is often overlooked is connected to horizontal Jewish-Arab relations. In particular, this aspect is related to the nature and clarity of majority-minority boundaries as perceived by each group. I contend that the *lack of definite majority-minority boundaries* in Israel constitutes a major barrier to creating a multicultural democracy.

As shown in the literature, in order to implement a policy of multiculturalism, clear and definite majority-minority boundaries are needed. Such boundaries are essential to defining the rights and responsibilities of each group—the majority as well as the minority—in forming a common civic treaty based on multicultural democracy and centered on the principles of "mutual recognition and acceptance, diversity, and equality" (see Crowder 2013, reviewed by Law 2014, 1964; Kymlicka 2007a, 66–67).

In the next sections I examine Jewish-Arab "majority-minority boundaries," not only in terms of demographic composition and actual power relationships, as I have done so far, but also in terms of how these boundaries are perceived by each group and of their implications for Jewish-Arab relations.

In a work published elsewhere, I defined the status of the Jewish majority and its deep and ongoing fear of becoming a demographic minority in terms of *a majority with a minority phobia* (see Al-Haj 2019, 56). According to official statistics, the majority status of the Jewish population within the Green Line (the pre-1967 borders) is guaranteed for the short and the long run. As indicated earlier, in 2018 fertility rates among all Arab groups (including Muslims, Christians, and Druze) were lower than those of the Jewish population. Hence, official CBS projections for the Israeli population show that through 2065 the 80:20 ratio of Jews to Arabs within the pre-1967 borders is not expected to change (SAI 2021, table 2.10, 1–9).

Despite these facts, the demographic threat is a topic of ongoing discourse among both the Jewish leadership and the public at large. Indeed, the demographic issue, and in particular the changing Arab-Jewish population ratio, has always had powerful political, economic, and ideological implications for the Israeli-Arab conflict and for the emerging Jewish state (see Soffer 1988, 2016; Rebhun and Malach 2012; Bystrov and Soffer 2013).

Since the 1967 war and the inclusion of Palestinians living in the West Bank and Gaza under Israeli occupation, this demographic issue has become even more crucial (see Goldscheider 2002, 67). Therefore, many important domestic and foreign policy issues in Israel are formulated and determined under pressure of demographic considerations (Cohen and Susser 2009, 57). Indeed, Jewish policymakers in Israel constantly emphasize the importance of taking all required measures to encourage Jewish fertility and immigration while reducing the numbers of Palestinians, with the aim of maintaining a clear Jewish majority in Israel (see Al-Haj 2019).

Another basic element that both creates and strengthens the perception of a *majority with a minority phobia* is connected to the belief of the Jewish population that Israel is under constant physical threat of destruction, or at least under the threat of being destroyed as a "polity" (Kimmerling 2004, 151). Psychology professor Yoram Yuval, a lecturer at the Hebrew University of Jerusalem, criticized this minority phobia among the Jewish population of Israel in his article titled "After a Hundred Years of Zionist Success Story, We Are Also Allowed to Be Free from Fear." The background for this article was the widespread protest among Israeli politicians and the public at large against the decision of the faculty of humanities at the Hebrew University not to sing the Israeli national anthem "Hatikva" at the faculty's graduation ceremony. Among other things, Yuval had this to say:

> One thing has not changed, in my opinion, since the terrifying days before the Six Day War (1967) to the present day: We still have a deep, almost exiled, frightening existential anxiety. It causes

many of us, encouraged by our agile politicians, to act and feel like a persecuted minority, not as a regional super power. . . . I think that after a hundred years of a Zionist success story, we are allowed to be a free people in our country—a people that is also free of fear. (Yuval 2017)

The existential anxiety that has become a central component of Israel's collective identity has been continuously used as an excuse for its militaristic policies and has further strengthened its *civilian militarism* and *military militarism*. According to Kimmerling (2001): "The existential anxiety built into Israeli collective identity and collective memory simultaneously fuels civilian militarism and reinforces 'military militarism' and the military-cultural complex, creating a vicious circle that always leads to self-fulfilling 'worst case' prophecies. Even the main motives for peace-making are driven either by xenophobic feelings of separateness or instrumental manipulation of improved control over 'the other side' and preservation of 'our' ultimate military might" (228). Kimmerling (2004) stresses that based on this perception, "the Holocaust is not only a traumatic event that crystallizes to a large extent the collective memory and consciousness, but an existential situation that could happen again" (151).

Magal, Bar-Tal, and Halperin (2016) further maintain that the Jewish majority's perception that Israel is under constant threat of destruction has far-reaching repercussions on Israel's political culture and holds the potential to develop an anti-democratic atmosphere. Under such circumstances, the Jewish public at large perceives the use of military force and even oppression against the Palestinians in the territories and the Palestinian citizens of Israel as necessary for survival. Thus, all of these means are perceived as "prudent, justified, and in accordance with moral standards" (1219). Furthermore, this perceived "existential fear" serves as an important factor in delegitimizing Arabs, especially Palestinians, who are stereotyped by large segments of the Israeli Jewish public as "violent" and "untrustworthy" with "continuous intention to harm Jews." These perceptions are a hotbed for the development and justification of anti-democratic and anti-multicultural values and practices among Israeli leaders and the greater public alike (1227–31).

Contrary to the aforementioned complex status of the Jewish population in Israel as a *majority with a minority phobia*, the Palestinian Arabs in Israel may be defined as a *minority with a sense of majority*. In other words, there is a discrepancy between the objective status of Arabs as a vulnerable marginalized minority and their subjective sense of being a majority, or at least a regional majority.

Already in the 1950s, Ben-Gurion, the first prime minister of Israel, acknowledged the unique status of the remaining Arabs in Israel as a minority with a sense of majority. For this reason, he recognized that a major factor in Arabs' estrangement from the State of Israel was related to their involuntary transition from a majority into a minority. In his autobiography, Ben-Gurion stated:

> Not all Israeli Arabs have come to terms with the State of Israel. They are the only Arabs in the entire region from southern Turkey and western Persia in Asia and all of North Africa from Egypt to Morocco, who do not stand on their own, but constitute a minority in a Jewish state, that did not exist throughout nearly 1300 years of their living on this land. They still remember that they were a majority here and they became a minority. (Ben-Gurion 1971, 363; translated from Hebrew [MA])

Al-Haj and Yaniv were the first researchers to recognize the unique identity of the remaining Palestinian Arabs as a *minority with a sense of majority* due to their cultural affinity with the regional Arab majority in the Middle East and their national and cultural connection to the entire territory of historic Palestine: "The Arabs in Israel constitute a special case insofar as they form a minority within the present international boundaries, but in feeling and culture they are also part of a regional majority for whom the entire territory of historic Palestine, and not only the part of it, which is inhabited by Arabs, is a part of their historic heritage" (Al-Haj and Yaniv 1983, 146).

Various regional developments since the late 1960s have reinforced this sense of being part of a regional majority among the Palestinians in Israel (see Reiter 2009). After Israel occupied the West Bank in 1967, their renewed contact with their Palestinian brethren strengthened their Palestinian identity and revived their sense of belonging to the Palestinian people. Moreover, the Jewish settlements in the West Bank obliterated the Green Line that up until 1967 had separated Israel and the Palestinian territories. Contact between the Palestinians in Israel and those in the territories became much stronger toward the late 1970s: both the October 1973 Israeli-Arab war (which Arabs perceived as a victory over Israel's superiority) and growing international recognition of the PLO revived Arab Palestinian pride (see Rekhess 1976), as did the peace with Egypt and later with Jordan and the silent normalization with a number of Arab countries, among them Morocco and several Gulf states. For the first time, in 1978, the Arab population of Israel was given the opportunity to make the pilgrimage (*hajj*) to Mecca, when Jordan began allowing Israeli Muslims to cross its border in order to travel to Saudi Arabia. For the Palestinians in Israel, all of these developments reinforced their sense of belonging to a large national and religious majority in the Middle East.

This complex status of the Palestinian citizens of Israel as a *minority with a sense of majority* incorporates some important elements that can potentially help promote multiculturalism by contributing to cultural openness among the Palestinian Arabs and reducing their fear of cultural assimilation (Al-Haj 2019). On the other hand, this status also raises Palestinian citizens' expectations regarding achievement of their collective cultural, linguistic, and national rights. This is clearly reflected in the aforementioned Arab Vision Documents, which call for changing the Jewish character of Israel into a binational, bilingual, multicultural democracy in which Jews and Arabs enjoy equal status (Adalah 2007, 8). Yet not only were state authorities not even willing to negotiate these demands, but, as mentioned earlier, they have accelerated official efforts toward reinforcing Israel's ethnonational and anti-multicultural character, a situation that has only served to strengthen the existing "oppositional identity" among the Palestinian Arabs in Israel vis-à-vis the state and its Jewish-Zionist identity (see Al-Haj 2019).

Summary

In this chapter I have provided background information about the Palestinian Arabs in Israel. I have discussed major developments and identity formation among the Arabs in Israel since the establishment of the state, including the dramatic change in their status from a longstanding majority into a vulnerable minority trapped within the margins of citizenship and nationality. I have examined the implications of this complex status on their identity, orientation, and political mobilization. I have also discussed the barriers to the development of multicultural democracy in Israel, including vertical minority-state factors and horizontal majority-minority group perceptions.

The insights emerging from this chapter can facilitate our understanding of the complex relationship between education and social change among the indigenous Palestinian Arabs throughout the education system, from early childhood through higher education. Moreover, these insights enrich our analysis of the relationship between education and inequalities as manifested in majority-minority relations as well as within each group as far as social inequalities are concerned. The complex status of the Palestinian Arabs in Israel also helps explain the profound alienation of Arab students because the official curriculum overlooks their narrative and transmits a type of knowledge that totally contradicts their nonofficial knowledge embodied in their self-perception as a *minority with a sense of majority*.

In the next chapter, I outline the main attributes of formal education among the Arabs in Israel from early childhood through the end of senior high school and discuss the foundations of the formal policy and administrative structure of Arab education. The major part of the chapter is devoted to tracing the major quantitative and qualitative changes in terms of educational access versus educational outcomes and school achievements.

Chapter 3

Trends in Elementary, Intermediate, and Secondary Education

Quantitative Expansion and Persistent Qualitative Gaps

Abstract

This chapter traces the main developments in formal education among the Palestinian Arabs in Israel from the establishment of the state until the present period and also briefly summarizes the pre-state period. The discussion focuses both on quantitative and on qualitative changes in Arab elementary, intermediate, and secondary education throughout this period. First, I describe the emergence of the administrative structure of Arab education, including the policy underlying the formation of this structure. I then discuss how the state created sectoral subdivisions within Arab education, among them distinctive Druze and Bedouin education categories that embody the notion of treating the Arabs as a "mix of cultural-religious minorities" rather than as a unique national minority. Next, I underscore the main trends in educational access and expansion among the Palestinian Arab minority, as reflected in the growing number of Arab students at all educational levels and greater access to education among female students. In the second part of this chapter, I examine qualitative changes and inequalities in the Arab education system compared to the Hebrew system. After outlining a brief theoretical framework, I examine the achievements of Arab students compared to those of their Jewish counterparts based on scores on local Israeli tests and a series of international tests. Moreover, I trace the emergence of educational inequalities between Jews and Arabs over time as well as gender inequality within each group, and I discuss the factors behind these inequalities. Finally, I briefly discuss the impact of the COVID-19 pandemic on educational inequalities.

Background

During the 27 years of the British Mandate for Palestine (1921 through 1948), the number of Palestinian students increased by 500 percent, reaching some 150,000 by the end of that period. The scope of this development becomes more impressive when considering that this growth was four times greater than the overall increase in the Palestinian population (Al-Haj 1995a, 43).

Private schools played a major role in the development of the Palestinian education system. Even though private schools represented only about one-third of the total number of schools, they constituted the most dominant player in secondary education. Indeed, by 1941/42 some 2,650 students were enrolled in private schools at the secondary level. And whereas in the public schools girls constituted only 18 percent of the student body, in the private schools female students comprised as much as 43 percent (Badran 1969, 132–33).

These private Arab schools can be divided into three main groups: Muslim schools, Christian schools administered from abroad, and locally administered Christian schools. The "millet" system in effect during the Ottoman period recognized Jews and Christians as "protected minorities" that were entitled to preserve their religious-ethnic autonomy and maintain their unique identity (Karpat 1988). As these rights also included education, both the Christian and the Jewish communities established their own educational institutions. In contrast, private education in the Muslim community lagged behind the Christian and Jewish communities up to the end of the Ottoman period. Within a short period after the British Mandate for Palestine went into effect, the Supreme Muslim Council began establishing private elementary, secondary, technical, and theological schools, whose numbers increased from 42 in 1921/22 to 181 in 1938/39 (Tibawi 1956, 183).

Hence, by the end of the Mandatory period diverse educational options were available to the Palestinians, with private schools serving as a central component. As in the Ottoman period, the local Palestinian communities autonomously administered these private schools and had full control of their educational content. In contrast, the Mandatory government took over the Ottoman public education system in its entirety, placing it under the authority of the governmental Department of Education (Nardi 1945, 22).

During the Mandatory period, access to education among the Palestinian population varied greatly, particularly between rural and urban residents. The Muslim population was mainly rural, placing Muslims at the greatest disadvantage. Yet the Arab villagers were rapidly becoming aware of the importance of education. By the early 1930s, they exhibited clear signs of seeking mobility in society at large, particularly by attaining government jobs. Education was naturally perceived as the main vehicle for achieving this goal (Badran 1969).

The Mandatory government failed to meet this increasing demand for education among the Palestinian villagers. In most cases, elementary school enrollment was dictated by school availability. Even toward the end of the Mandate, only 69 percent of Arab children who applied were able to secure a place at school, a fact that accelerated the development of private elementary schools, mainly among the Muslim communities (Badran 1969; Al-Haj 1995a).

In summary, by the end of the Mandatory period a diverse Palestinian education system had emerged, with autonomous private schools playing a major role, especially in secondary education. Moreover, during the second half of the Mandatory period, the Palestinian community, and particularly the rural Muslim population, had become increasingly aware of the importance of education. This awareness motivated mounting efforts to establish private elementary schools. In contrast to this relatively autonomous system of private education, the Mandatory government had absolute control over the public system, which remained somewhat backward, selective, and conservative, thus failing to meet the Palestinian community's growing demand for education.

When the state of Israel was established in 1948, the existing format of Palestinian education totally collapsed. One result was that the longstanding and autonomous private education systems in both the Christian and the Muslim communities were abolished and merged into the Israeli public education system. Hence their administration, curricula, and educational content were completely subjugated to the centralized Israeli education system. Moreover, as described later in this chapter, the state of Israel completely dismantled the private Muslim schools and confiscated the Muslim Waqf property. Under pressure from Western countries, Israel eventually allowed a form of "controlled continuity" for private Christian schools within the general school system (Al-Haj 1995a; Al-Haj 2006).

In contrast, immediately after the establishment of Israel, all streams of Hebrew education from the British Mandate period were unified into one state education system under the umbrella of the Israel Ministry of Education. Nevertheless, this unified system was actually a "two-stream" system, one for the secular population and the other for the religious population. The religious track was given complete internal autonomy over administration, curriculum, and teaching staff, all financially supported by the state (Katz 1999). Later, the ultra-Orthodox schools were also recognized as an autonomous stream in the Ministry of Education, with the ultra-Orthodox community given full responsibility over its own education, resources, and curricula. Today the formal education system in Israel encompasses four main subsystems: (1) general state education (mainly for secular Jews); (2) religious state education (for Jews affiliated with the religious Zionist stream); (3) independent ultra-Orthodox education (for ultra-Orthodox Jews known as Haredim); and (4) Arab education (which in the late 1970s was further divided into Arab, Druze, and Bedouin subsystems).

In the following sections, I describe the historical background underlying the development of the administrative structure of Arab education in Israel. Then, I discuss the dismantling of the Arab private school system and the creation of the Druze and Bedouin education subdivisions within the Arab education system, a step that further distorted the uniqueness of Arab education.

The Administrative Structure of Arab Education

Upon the UN's November 1947 decision regarding the partition of Palestine, the Jewish authorities formed a special committee charged with formulating a practical plan for educating those Arabs expected to be included in the areas designated as the Jewish state (Prime Minister's Office 1955, 12). Yet as a result of developments ensuing from the 1948 Israeli-Arab war, only a small Arab minority remained within the borders of the state of Israel (see chapter 2). In August 1948, a special committee comprising representatives of the Ministry of Minorities was formed to discuss education for the Arab population. Y. Blom, a Department of Education supervisor during the Mandatory government, was placed in charge of education for Arabs living in the "occupied areas" (Ministry of Minorities 1949, 23).

The policymakers charged with determining the fate of Arab education after the establishment of Israel first had to decide how to administer the system and how to deal with the cultural and national uniqueness of the remaining Arab population. Some strongly supported assimilating Arab schools into the general Israeli education system. Others insisted upon total segregation without any autonomy and with stringent state control over Arab educational administration and content.

Y. Blom, the appointed superintendent of Arab schools, pushed toward a policy of assimilation rather than one that emphasized the uniqueness of Arab culture. He delineated his conception in a "top secret" document addressed to the minister of education (no date indicated):

> I have already expressed my conception regarding the Arab problem and regarding its tackling in the field of education. I said that in my opinion it is possible to think that by abolishing the differences between us and them (the Arabs) or minimizing them to the minimum point, we can also decrease the contradictions originated in different orientations, and from here on the probabilities for a quiet and calm life would increase. In the field of education, this might be reflected in giving the Arab schools the same structure which exists in the Hebrew schools as far as possible, the same methods, the same class hours, the same atmosphere, and if possible, also similar curricula. . . . In this way we can hope not only to bring our Arabs closer to us but also to take them away from the Arab World surrounding us. (SA [State Archives] 145/1733/G)

This assimilation strategy led to an interesting discussion in the Ministry of Education regarding whether Arabic or Hebrew should be the medium of instruction in Arab schools. Some officials suggested hiring a large number of Jewish teachers in Arab schools in order to "teach Hebrew, assist in the administration of Arab schools in particular as liaisons with the establishment, be active among youngsters and spread Hebrew language and culture among adults outside of schools" (SA 145/1733/G).

The group supporting this assimilation strategy soon realized that in the absence of a general secular orientation to Israeli citizenship it would be quite difficult to educate Arabs to identify as Israelis. At the time, Israeli identity was strongly interwoven with Jewish-Zionist symbols, which naturally excluded Arabs. In addition, this group reached the conclusion that such a strategy would exact a high price as it would necessitate granting full and equal civil rights to the Arab minority.

Yehuda Ben-Or, one of the central policymakers for Arab education in the 1950s, expressed this clearly in an internal document distributed by the Office of the Prime Minister's Advisor for Arab Affairs (1957):

> The atmosphere in the Jewish schools is based mainly on two premises: religion, tradition or historical values on the one hand, and national values on the other. Not only are these elements dominant in school celebrations, meeting, trips and the like, they also penetrate the teaching materials themselves. Contrary to this situation, in the Arab schools we are confronted with a difficult problem which nobody could predict how it would be resolved. Because of the mixture of religious groups among both the teachers and the pupils, and because we have tried for the time being not to emphasize the national element. During the first years of statehood this fact was understandable, since the wounds were still unhealed. But it should be asked whether the time has come to change things. The difficulty stems from the fact that Jewish schools have not in fact separated between national-Jewish values and citizenship values. On the one hand, we should not copy the national Israeli-Jewish values to Arab schools; on the other hand, general Israeli citizenship values have not yet been developed. (SA 145/1292/GI)

The separation-control strategy was guided by the following principles: "To diminish the sense of deprivation (among Arabs) on the one hand and to intensify control over Arab education on the other" (SA 145/1292/GI). Therefore, policymakers were faced with the crucial question of "how to achieve the goal of educating the Arab young generation to be loyal to the state of Israel" (Ben-Or 1951, 8). Yet these policymakers clearly understood that loyalty to the state does not necessarily mean solidarity with it. Officials were aware that under the prevailing circumstances this goal was unachievable. Therefore, the director of Arab education stated: "Arab schools will not be required to take part in Israeli national activities, unless they frankly and consciously adopt them as personal initiatives. We did not want them to pretend. We did not encourage national celebrations, such as flag hoisting or saluting the flag, singing the national anthem Hatikva or celebrating national (Jewish) occasions, etc. If such activities were done it was without our knowledge or against our will. However, security considerations are first and foremost" (8). The *controlled segregation strategy* eventually gained the upper hand and has been systematically implemented in Arab education over time. As the following analysis shows, this strategy is reflected in all aspects of education, including goals, curricula, and textbooks. In fact, as shown throughout this book, this controlled segregation was merely another type of *assimilation* without the state having to pay the price of assimilation.

The Compulsory Education Law passed by the Israeli Parliament (Knesset) in 1949 divided responsibilities in the entire educational system between state and local authorities. This law dictated that the state, together with the local authorities, must guarantee free compulsory education for eight years of elementary schooling for all children between the ages of 5 and 13. The state was responsible for supplying, training, and paying teachers and for determining the curriculum, whereas the local authorities were in charge of the physical plant (i.e., buildings, furniture, and school maintenance) (Jiryis 1976, 204).

According to this law, the government and the local authorities had to share the cost of teachers' salaries, leaving the local authorities to cover all other expenditures. When the law was passed, however, only three Arab localities had been granted formal municipal status (Al-Haj and Rosenfeld 1990). Therefore, a special sub-section was added to the law proclaiming that:

> (a) The Minister of Education, in consultation with the Minister of Interior, may, by order published in the Israel Government Gazette, confer upon a recognized committee or a person appointed by the committee as a local education authority, the power to impose on and collect from the inhabitants of the area . . . a rate to cover the expenditure involved in carrying out the obligations imposed on that local education authority under this law. (Cited by Guttman and Hes 1960, 84)

In practice, application of this law discriminated against the disadvantaged Arab population. In Jewish localities the government paid the local authority its share of the teachers' salaries, with the local authority supplementing the remaining amount necessary to pay the teachers. In Arab villages, the government paid the teachers directly and then collected a cumbersome tax from the villagers in the form of an annual poll tax paid by every villager over the age of 18. Property owners also paid an additional amount equivalent to the poll tax (Guttman and Hes 1960, 84–85). Only Arabs had to pay this "education tax," whereas Jews who lived in localities without municipal status paid no education tax. In 1950, when the poll tax on education was first levied on the Arab population (according to regulation package No. 131 dated November 23, 1950), every person over the age of 18 paid IL 31 annually, which covered about 25 percent of teachers' salaries and almost all other expenses of the Arab schools. Over time, the amount of this poll tax rose, covering 44 percent of teachers' salaries in 1953 and 45 percent in 1954 (SA 1351/1616/GL; report of the Ministry of Education, September 22, 1955). Note that local authority participation in teachers' wages in the Jewish sector was abolished in April 1953, though it continued in the Arab sector (SA 1351/1616/GL).

Due to the relatively high cost of education for the Arab population, local Arab leaders were reluctant to open and maintain schools in their communities. According to a report by the director of the Arab division in the Ministry of Education (April 1955), dozens of kindergartens closed in many Arab localities because the local population was unable to pay for their children's education. This report also stated: "Many mukhtars and heads of villages negotiated the amount of the tax and the number of class hours and demanded that fewer teachers be employed" (SA 1351/1616/GL).

In effect, the education tax was a "poll tax" levied equally regardless of income, thus increasing the burden on poorer Arab families (SA 1351/1616/GL). Moreover, at that time most Arab families were large. Either they depended upon poor agriculture as a source of income or they were part of a disadvantaged labor force (Rosenfeld 1964). Hence, it is safe to assume that many parents did not send their children to school because they could not afford to pay the tax. Instead, these children joined the labor force to help their families (*The Jerusalem Post*, August 5, 1954).

The Compulsory Education Law (1949) formally guaranteed education to all pupils, but for a long time this law was not implemented among the Arabs due to a shortage in school buildings and facilities. For instance, in the 1955/56 school year, some 500 pupils in Um el-Fahm were not admitted to the local school due to lack of space (*Al-Ittihad*, September 20, 1955). That same year, only 250 pupils in Deir Hanna were admitted to the local school, which from the outset was in very poor condition (*Al-Ittihad*, October 2, 1955).

In the framework of this controlled segregation strategy, the Ministry of Education established the Section for Arab Education that had de facto responsibility over matters concerning administration, curriculum, and personnel. Yet because this section had no defined goals and no set structure, many important issues affecting Arab education were overlooked. This situation prevailed until 1958, when the Ministry of Education renamed this body the Division of Arab Education and clearly defined its status and goals.

Until the late 1950s, the division of authority between the Ministry of Education and the military government was vague (see chapter 2 for a discussion of the military government). In some regions, the military governors considerably intervened in the Arab schools, even against the will of the Ministry. The military government also intervened in Arab schools through local education committees. Although the members of these committees were nominated by the Ministry of Education, the military governors actively participated by selecting local people loyal to them to serve on these committees (SA 1528/1621/GI).

In the mid-1970s, the name of the Division of Arab Education was changed to the Department of Education and Culture for Arabs. Under this new structure, this department was relegated to coordinating among the different departments handling Arab education. All that was left to the Department of Arab Education was supervising the pedagogical work of the Arab school superintendents (Government Yearbook 1975, 153). The Department of Arab Education continued to function as an independent unit until 1987, when its director, Emanuel Kupileivitch, retired and for the first time an Arab educator, Ali Haidar, was appointed head of the department. This led to defining the Department of Arab Education as a unit in the Ministry of Education reporting to the Pedagogical Secretariat, further degrading its independent status.

The controlled segregation structure described above still exists until this day (2023). The segregated Arab school system is dispersed throughout the six districts of the Ministry of Education. Each district has an Arab District Superintendent who serves as a liaison between the Arab schools and the district director of the Ministry of Education. There is still a tiny education unit for Arabs under the name Division of Education for Arabs (not Arab education) headed by a symbolic Arab appointee who has no authority whatsoever. All matters pertaining to administration, budgets, or educational content are determined by a centralized system in the Ministry of Education. Moreover, there is not even one Arab director in all the Ministry of Education districts, even in the Northern district in which Arab students constitute the majority.

Private Christian Schools

As mentioned earlier in this chapter, the establishment of the state of Israel was accompanied by a sharp decline in the status of private Arab schools. This decline can be attributed to several factors: the sudden decrease in the number of Arab urban residents, most of whom had become refugees in Arab countries; Israel's abolishment of the Muslim Waqf as an autonomous institution, including confiscation of all Waqf property by the state authorities; and diminished European involvement in running the Christian schools after the end of the British Mandate (Al-Haj 2006).

At first, the state of Israel was ambivalent regarding the few remaining private schools for the Arab population, but by the mid-1950s the government had adopted a clearer stand. On several occasions officials declared they were not against reinstating the private (i.e., Christian) school system on condition that it complied with the following Ministry of Education demand: these schools were not to be involved in subversive actions and were to educate their pupils to be loyal to the state of Israel (SA 145/1292/GL).

Until 1957, no private Christian school was officially recognized, and in fact parents who sent their children to these schools were considered in violation of the law. Although no measures were taken against these parents, diplomas issued by private schools had no formal validity (SA 145/1292/ GL). In a detailed report released on August 28, 1957, Ben-Or, then deputy director general of the Ministry of Education, suggested adopting a clear policy toward Christian schools based on providing financial support for these schools to bring them under full Ministry of Education supervision (SA 145/1292/GL).

Subsequently, the government began partially supporting the Christian schools to accelerate their official recognition. This support implied that the Ministry of Education had control over curricula, textbooks, and teacher appointments (SA 1351/1616/GL). In this way, Israel abolished the autonomous status these private schools had enjoyed during the Ottoman and Mandatory periods.

Table 3.1 shows the decline in the status of private schools after the establishment of Israel compared to the Mandatory period. In 1945/46 about 35 percent of Arab pupils studied in private schools, whereas in 2020/21 only 6.2 percent of Arab pupils attended such schools (table 3.1).

Almost all private schools serving the Arab population today belong to the Christian community. Unlike the Christians, the Muslims were not allowed to keep their autonomous religious institutions (Layish 1966), and the Muslim private school system that had developed during the Mandatory period was dismantled after Israeli statehood. As noted, Israel's differential policy toward the Muslim and Christian communities was largely affected by diplomatic considerations connected to Israel's relationships with Western countries. This policy was clearly reflected in the 1993 agreement between

Table 3.1. Arab Pupils in Private and Public Schools in Selected Years (1945/46–2020/21)

Year	Public (%)	Private (%)	Total N	Total (%)
1945/46*	64.9	35.1	124,927	100.0
1956/57	75.6	24.4	38,682	100.0
1965/66	82.4	17.6	72,097	100.0
1973/74	88.8	11.2	140,719	100.0
1989/90	92.5	7.5	230,288	100.0
2020/21	93.8	6.2	562,134	100.0

Figures from 1948/49 upward are based on SAI 1967, table T/16, 535; 1974; SAI, 1990, 620

*Mandatory period. Cited by SA No. 145/1733/G. The number for 2020/21 is an estimation, based on CBS 2020. Media Release, December 23, 2020, and SAI 2021, taking into consideration that nearly one-third of students in Christian schools are non-Christian Arabs, mainly Muslims (see Al-Haj 2006).

Israel and the Vatican, in which Israel declared its unequivocal commitment to the Catholic schools, thus protecting Christian educational institutions from government interference (Al-Haj 2006).

Due to the low rate of natural increase among the Christian Arabs (see chapter 2), the number of Christian students steadily decreased over time and today they constitute a minute percentage of all Arab students. In 1996, Christian students constituted 9 percent of all Arab students; by 2016 this rate had decreased to 5 percent (Weisblai 2017, 2). In the 2019/20 school year, there were 26,858 Christian students in the Israeli school system, constituting 1.5 percent of the total number of students in Israel and only 4.7 percent of Arab students (CBS 2020a). It is estimated that nearly two-thirds of students in private schools are Christians, with the remaining third affiliated with other religious groups (Weisblai 2017, 2). Most of the non-Christian students attending private Arab schools are Muslims, who often transfer to these schools for senior high school. Hence, these schools play a major role at the secondary level and a lesser role at the elementary and intermediate levels (Al-Haj 2006).

Indeed, most of the private schools established or reinstated after Israeli statehood are secondary schools. The main reason for this is financial. During the Mandatory period, private schools were fully funded by the government regardless of level, but after the establishment of Israel the Arab elementary private school system received only negligible governmental support. Until 1978 all secondary schools, including private ones, received only a partial subsidy from the Ministry of Education, with most of the expenses covered by students' fees and other sources (municipalities in the case of public schools and informal organizations for private schools).

Since 1978, when the Free Secondary Education Law was passed, the financial situation of the secondary schools, public as well as private, has improved considerably due to growing financial support from the Ministry of Education. Today every secondary school receives a per capita allocation, though the amount differs from one school to another depending on the "level of services" provided by each school and the profile of its teachers (e.g., education, age). Although the government allocation is not sufficient to cover all the expenses involved, it remains vitally important for the maintenance and development of these schools (Al-Haj 2006).

In the case of private elementary schools, the Ministry of Education's financial involvement remained minor until the late 1980s. Thus, even though elementary education was supposed to be free and compulsory, students had to pay to attend these schools. In the early 1980s the Ministry of Education began extending its financial support to private elementary schools. Today most private Christian schools receive 80–90 percent of their budget for maintenance and teachers' salaries from the Ministry of Education. This support is conditioned, however, on complete Ministry of Education supervision. Accordingly, the private schools must use the same curriculum as the public schools and the Ministry of Education has the final say regarding teacher appointments. In 2015, the Christian private schools in Israel launched a campaign to attain equal budgets, which eventually led to signing an agreement with the Ministry of Education (Steinmetz and Ashkenazi 2015). The campaign was largely supported by the Christian community in Israel, which perceives Christian schools as an important pillar of its distinct Christian identity (Agbaria and Shehadeh 2022, 11–12).

The Christian community in Israel is considered an advantaged group. Most Christians live in urban communities in which selective private Christian schools are accessible. Muslims and Druze are disadvantaged compared to Christians with respect to socioeconomic background, educational attainment, and opportunities for attending a private school (Al-Haj 1995a, 2006). Indeed, statistics show that Christian students score higher on the matriculation exams than Muslim and Druze students (see CBS 2020a). Furthermore, Christian Arabs are somewhat more highly represented than Muslims and Druze in higher education and prestigious educational programs, despite being at a disadvantage compared to Jewish groups. Yet the small advantage that Christians have over Muslims and Druze disappears after socioeconomic background, high school major, and previous achievements are taken into account. Hence, Arabs—whether Muslims, Christians, or Druze—are at a disadvantage compared with Jews on both the vertical (access) and the horizontal (field of study) dimensions (Feniger, Mcdossi, and Ayalon 2014, 7–9).

Note that the Central Bureau of Statistics (CBS) does not provide systematic figures regarding the number of students attending private Christian schools in Israel or regarding their achievements. Such reports are often sporadic and their results are usually merged with those of all Muslim and Druze students. In addition, reports on psychometric exams and international tests (PISA and TIMSS) refer to the scores of Arab students as a whole, without internal religious divisions. The only systematically reported internal division among Arabs regarding educational attainment is that of gender. Therefore, unless otherwise indicated, the statistics below report gender differences while referring to Christian and Druze students as part of Arab students as a whole.

Druze Education

In 1957, the Israel Minister of Religious Affairs issued regulations that recognized the Druze as a separate religious community, after having been treated as part of the Muslim community for generations. Four years later, in October 1961, the religious leadership of the Druze people headed by Sheikh Amin Tarif was recognized as a Religious Council. In 1962, the Knesset completed the process by authorizing the Druze Religious Law Courts (Falah 1974; Standel 1973). Yet perhaps the most important move in this context came earlier, in 1956, when the Compulsory Army Service Law was applied to the Druze. Since then, Druze men have been conscripted into the army, theoretically entitling them to certain educational, social, and financial benefits denied to those who do not serve in the Israeli army. This cultivation of the Druze community as a separate religious and political entity found further expression when the nationality clause in their identity card was changed from Arab to Druze (Al-Haj 1996a, 57).

In the late 1950s, Israeli officials began promoting Druze particularism in the field of education. A joint committee comprising representatives of the prime minister's office and the Division of Arab Education that met on October 22, 1957, stressed the following point: "We should take the Druze element into consideration. More Druze teachers should be hired and awareness of the Druze people as a separate community should be reinforced" (SA 145/1292/GL). In fact, this separation of the Druze community is an attempt to turn the Arab minority in Israel into an assortment of tiny minorities to stress their religious and cultural identity rather than their national identity (Smooha 1980).

In the early 1970s, a new trend became apparent among the younger generation of the Druze population, one that cannot be divorced from the simultaneous overall nationalization apparent among the Arab population. Due to their high expectations from army service and the price they paid for the "Jewish-Druze alliance," the Druze community may have become even more frustrated than the overall Arab community (Oppenheimer 1978). In line with the emerging trend toward a "resurgent Arab national identity," a growing number of Druze youngsters refused to serve in the army. Indeed, some Druze intellectuals concluded that the Druze community had been harmed by the particularization process and began stressing that their community was an integral part of Arab nationality, culture, and language. This trend culminated in the formation of Lujnat al-Mubadara al-Durziyya (the Druze Initiative Committee) in 1972 (Nakhleh 1977).

Two steps were taken to counterbalance this emerging trend, one by the Druze community itself and the other by the government. In 1973, some Druze leaders in Daliat al-Carmel and other Druze localities established al-Halaka al-Durziyyah al-Sahioniyyah (the Druze Zionist Movement). This movement views the Druze community in Israel not only as a religious group but also as a separate national entity and emphasizes the "blood alliance" and brotherhood between the Jewish and Druze peoples. As such, it enthusiastically supports Druze military service as a means to "protect the Holy Land and reinforce the linkages with the Jewish brethren" (*Al-Hadaf*, May 1979).

The government formed two official committees to deal with the Druze situation: the Ben-Dor Committee, headed by Professor Gabriel Ben-Dor of the University of Haifa, and the Shechterman Committee, chaired by then chairman of the Knesset Education Committee (Falah 1977, 7). Both committees recommended that all Druze affairs be removed from Arab departments and integrated into the districts of the different ministries. The government adopted these recommendations in June 1975, and a committee of directors general was appointed to carry out the government's decision.

The Ministry of Education was the first to respond. Druze education was integrated into the Haifa and Northern districts, and a special Unit for Druze Education was established in 1975, with Salman Falah, a Druze educator, as chairman (Falah 1977). The formal goal of the Druze unit is to "designate policy for Druze education, plan pedagogical activity and distribute resources for the Druze schools in coordination with the several units of the Ministry and handle issues such as students, culture, sports, and youth" (Ministry of Education and Culture 1987, 64).

Both the authority and the activity framework granted to the Druze unit clearly go far beyond those granted to the Arab unit. The appointee for Arab education has no resources at his disposal and is not able to exert any influence on decision-making regarding budgets and planning. In contrast, the head of the Druze education unit has a relatively powerful position and a fair amount of influence over policy governing Druze education. Nevertheless, he remains totally dependent on the Ministry of Education and cannot act autonomously insofar as budgets or curriculum content for Druze schools are concerned.

The particularism granted to Druze education was not restricted to administrative matters. Indeed, the Ministry devoted major efforts to creating a new Druze identity among Druze pupils by highlighting the uniqueness of their people (Ministry of Education and Culture 1987, 6). To this end, the Peled Committee formulated the following special goal for Druze education:

> The goal of state education in the Druze sector in Israel is to base education on the foundations of Druze and Arab cultures; on the achievement of science, on the aspiration for peace between Israel and its neighbors, on love of the shared country by all citizens, and loyalty to the state of Israel, on partnership in the building and defense of Israel—through emphasizing the common and the unique interests of all citizens; on advancing the unique connections between Jews and Druze, on knowledge of Jewish culture, on fostering Druze-Israeli identity, on the grounding of young Druze in the heritage of their community and the shared fate of the members of the Druze communities in all countries. (Falah 1977, 8)

To meet this goal, the Druze education unit began changing the content of the Druze curricula by preparing new textbooks for Druze primary and high schools under the heading of Druze Heritage. To reinforce this trend, the Committee for Druze Education began organizing an annual celebration known as Druze Heritage Week.

Another means used to reinforce the separate nature of Druze education is the attempt to hire only Druze teachers, if available. Before the Druze unit was established, more than 50 percent of the teachers employed in Druze schools were Christians or Muslims. After the Gordon Teachers Seminary in Haifa began offering classes to train female Druze teachers, by 1987 about 70 percent of the teachers in these schools were of Druze origin. Today (2023) almost all teachers in the Druze schools are of Druze origin.

The Department of Druze Education was also expanded to include the Circassian schools. The Circassians are a small community of non-Arab Muslims who live in two homogenous villages in the north. Like the Druze, the Circassians serve in the Israeli army.

Note that the unique curriculum developed for the Druze schools is not confined to Druze heritage. Special textbooks were created for the Druze schools in subjects that presumably should be the same for all Arab schools, among them Hebrew, Arabic, and history. However, Arabic remains a core subject in Druze education and is defined as "the mother tongue and the language of instruction in Druze schools." Arabic occupies an important place for the Circassians as well because it is used for Muslim religious studies (Ministry of Education 2002). Yet, as in the case of Arab education, in the Druze and Circassian schools the curriculum of Arabic language and literature is completely controlled by the Ministry of Education (e.g., Al-Haj 2006).

Bedouin Education

Like the Druze, the Bedouin population is currently undergoing an officially oriented process of particularization, albeit with strong resistance from large segments of this community (Alafenish 1987; Abu-Sa'ad 2019). The authorities sought to use education as a means of creating a distinct Bedouin identity. In this regard, the Bedouin schools, both in the North and in the Negev, were the first to be separated from the rest of the Arab schools and administered directly by the respective districts in the Ministry of Education. Unlike the Druze schools, however, the Bedouin schools use the same curricula as the Arab schools.

One of the prime problems impeding the separation of Bedouin education from Arab education was the shortage of qualified Bedouin teachers, especially in the Negev, necessitating the recruitment of Arab teachers from the Little Triangle and the Galilee. In 1978, only one-third of the 276 teachers employed in the Negev were Bedouins. In addition, two-thirds of the Bedouin teachers were unqualified (Meir and Barnia 1987, 166).

Non-Bedouin teachers assigned to Bedouin schools in the Negev to some extent perceived this as a form of punishment, since they had to adjust to a new environment with a different social structure. Furthermore, officials were concerned that the presence of these Arab teachers might provoke nationalistic feelings among some segments of the Negev Bedouins (Meir and Barnia 1987, 166). In an attempt to accelerate the training of Bedouin teachers, the Ministry opened special classes for Bedouins at a teachers' seminary in Beersheba. As a result, by 1986 the proportion of Bedouin teachers had increased to 52 percent of the total number of teachers in Bedouin schools in the Negev (Meir and Barnia 1987).

Over time, an increasing percentage of teachers in Bedouin schools in the Negev have acquired academic education. For example, in 2020, 24.5 percent of the teachers in the Bedouin education system as a whole and 30.7 percent of the teachers in Bedouin middle schools held MA degrees, compared to 40.3 percent in the education system nationwide and 30.7 percent in the middle schools (Ben-Gurion University and Negev Center for Sustainability 2020).

Indeed, education is on the rise among the Arab Bedouin population in the Negev. In 2022, 97,544 Bedouin pupils were enrolled in schools up to the end of high school, constituting 5.3 percent of the total student body in Israel (Ministry of Education and Shkifut Bachinch 2022) and almost 50 percent of the total Bedouin population in the Negev. That is, every second citizen among the Arab Bedouin population is a student.

Yet Bedouin education has remained extremely disadvantaged compared to Hebrew education and to general Arab education in terms of conditions and achievements at the various levels (see Al-Haj 2006; Vergen and Lutan 2007; Abu-Sa'ad 2019; Ayalon et al. 2019). For example, in the 2020 school year, the dropout rate in the Bedouin education system was more than three times the general dropout rate in Israel (3.5 percent compared to 1 percent) (Ben-Gurion University and Negev Center for Sustainability 2020). This high dropout rate stems from the difficult life circumstances of the Bedouin population in the Negev: nearly 40 percent of Bedouins live in officially non-recognized villages and tribes (Vergen and Lutan 2007, 3) that lack even the most basic conditions and services, such as running water, electricity, and public transportation. Failure to recognize these villages is part of the state's attempt to evacuate them and transfer their inhabitants to centralized localities as part of the national project to Judaize the Negev and the attempt to gain control of Bedouin land and space (see Rotem and Gordon 2017; Reiter 2022).

In this context, the indigenous Bedouin Arabs' struggle for their right to education has become an integral part of their survival strategy and their broader struggle over land, culture, and identity. Rotem and Gordon (2017) maintain that state authorities used education among the Negev Bedouins as "an uprooting mechanism," through which they attempted to force Bedouins living in officially "non-recognized villages" to move into one of the state-established towns in order to gain access to schools and other services. At the same time, Bedouin activists have constantly invoked their right to education, using it as a tool for reinforcing their *Sumud* (steadfastness) and achieving official recognition of their villages (21).

The Arab Population's Standpoint toward Administrative Structure of Education

Since the early 1970s, the Arab population has adopted an integration strategy with respect to governmental offices in general. According to this strategy, the battle against separate departments for Arabs is part of the Arabs' struggle for equality and integration in Israeli society. The Arab leadership consistently declared that these Arab departments were being used as instruments of discrimination against Arabs designed to exclude them from an equal share in the opportunity structure (National Committee for the Heads of the Arab Local Authorities and Committee for Directors of Education Departments 1984, 76). In addition, they repeatedly argued that these departments existed mainly to support nepotism and paternalism. The fact that senior positions were blocked to Arabs also generated resentment among the Arab population. The directors of these departments came from an identifiable group, known in Hebrew slang as "Arabists"—Jews considered to be experts in Arab affairs (Mari 1978, 5).

The Arab population's struggle to decentralize the Department of Arab Education and to integrate the Arab schools into the Ministry of Education districts gained momentum during the Second Conference on Arab Education (May 23, 1984). This conference, run jointly by the National Committee and the Committee for Directors of Education Departments, called for accelerating the integration of Arab schools into the Ministry districts as a vehicle for equalizing services and bridging the gap between Arab and Jewish schools. The request was accompanied by a demand to form a special Pedagogical Secretariat for Arab Education in the Ministry of Education. Such a secretariat would be composed of Arab educators and chaired by an Arab and would handle all issues connected to content, curricula, and textbooks for the Arab schools (National Committee for the Heads of the Arab Local Authorities and Committee for Directors of Education Departments 1984, 76).

Meanwhile, the Ministry of Education continued to downgrade the status of the Department of Arab Education, among other things by reducing its staff. Hence, the Arab schools were trapped in a situation in which they were neither part of the districts nor under the auspices of the Department of Arab Education. The National Committee and the Follow-Up Committee on Arab Education issued a memorandum protesting this situation: "The process of abolishing the Department of Arab Education, without offering an alternative, has created chaos in Arab education. In many cases, there is no address to be approached by Arab teachers and local authorities in the case of a problem arising in the Arab schools. This situation of perplexity has caused a sense of helplessness in the Arab educational system and exacerbated the problem" (National Committee for the Heads of the Arab Local Authorities and the Follow-Up Committee on Arab Education 1986).

The administrative status of Arab education was a major issue in the negotiations between the Follow-Up Committee and the Ministry of Education. But these meetings had virtually no tangible results. The Follow-Up Committee severely criticized this situation, describing it as a "scattering instead of a dispersion of the Arab schools" (National Committee for the Heads of the Arab Local Authorities and Follow-Up Committee on Arab Education 1989).

At the Third Conference for Arab Education held in Shefa-'Amr in July 1989, the Follow-Up Committee on Arab Education took its claims for genuine Arab involvement one step further by demanding autonomous status in administering and directing their own educational system. This newly adopted decision was the first time the Arab leadership demanded the establishment of a separate Arab Pedagogical Secretariat affiliated with the Ministry of Education. In addition, the conference called for setting up a public committee that would closely monitor and share in making decisions about the different aspects of Arab education. This committee would be composed of representatives of the Arab local authorities and the Follow-Up Committee on Arab Education, together with representatives of the Ministry of Education.

A great deal of time went by before the Arab leadership adopted the next step toward changing the administrative structure of the Arab education system. As indicated in chapter 2, the 1990s were characterized by dramatic regional developments in the Israeli-Palestinian conflict, including the transition to conflict resolution (with the signing of the Oslo Accords in 1993) and then the collapse of this process after the assassination of Israeli prime minister Yitzhak Rabin and the outbreak of the Al-Aqsa intifada in 2000.

Meanwhile, the process of national localization among the Palestinian Arabs in Israel began intensifying. Their struggle was almost totally devoted to attaining their individual and collective citizenship rights as a national indigenous minority in Israel. Among other things, this struggle found expression in the Vision Documents (see chapter 2). The document issued by the National Committee in 2006 referred in detail to the educational and cultural rights of the Palestinian Arabs in Israel. This document portrayed the education system among the Palestinian Arabs in Israel as an integral part of their claims as an indigenous national minority. According to the document, the strategic vision in education stems from the "right of the Palestinian Arabs in Israel (as indigenous people in their homeland) to self-administration of the educational system and to self-determination of its policy" (National Committee for the Heads of the Arab Local Authorities 2006, 27–29).

The document specified three tracks for implementing the main principles of the Arabs' educational rights:

1. Legal track: Continuing to demand self-administration of the educational system in accordance with international laws and conventions by appealing to international organizations that deal with such issues and seeking justice in all matters of official discrimination.

2. Educational-Public track: Strengthening relations between the Follow-Up Committee on Arab Education and the community at large, and particularly with the Arab schools. The Committee should also engage in networking relations with all institutions active in the field of education and develop new alternative curricula.

3. Practical track: Conducting a detailed strategic study on building an Arab university, and creating a council of higher education for the Arabs. (National Committee for the Heads of the Arab Local Authorities 2006, 29)

In July 2010, the Follow-Up Committee on Arab Education announced the establishment of the Arab Pedagogical Council (APC). As in the case of the Vision Documents, the initiators of the APC emphasized that this council was to be an expression of the rights of the Arab minority as an indigenous minority to preserve its heritage and national identity and to determine its own education policy and content (Agbaria 2015; Jabareen and Agbaria 2017). Among the stated central goals of the APC are the following: "To combat widespread inequalities in resource allocation between Arab and Jewish education nationally; to gain recognition of the collective right of the Palestinian minority to include its national and cultural narrative within the curriculum (especially in key identity-building subjects, such as language, history, civics, geography, and social studies); and to improve engagement with Palestinian history and culture" (Jabareen and Agbaria 2017, 50–51).

Although the APC was established as an independent body, its initiators clearly hoped to be officially recognized by the Ministry of Education, to become grounded in Israeli law, and to work closely with state authorities, in particular the Ministry of Education (Jabareen and Agbaria 2017, 50). In fact, the educational rights declared by the Vision Documents and by the APC were formulated in the spirit of the United Nations Declaration on the Rights of Indigenous Peoples (UNDRIP), in which self-determination is a leading foundation for realizing the collective rights of indigenous groups, as follows: "Article 3: Indigenous peoples have the right to self-determination. By virtue of that right they freely determine their political status and freely pursue their economic, social and cultural development" (UNDRIP 2007, 8). Yet state authorities have been reluctant even to discuss any kind of autonomy with the Arab leadership, whether regarding the status of the indigenous Arab minority as a whole or regarding any kind of restricted educational and cultural autonomy.

What is the impact of the aforementioned state policy on the development of Arab education? What are the main quantitative trends in Arab education over time as far as educational expansion and attainment are concerned? What are the trends in terms of qualitative inequalities between Arabs and Jews? What are the main qualitative changes in Arab education in Israel in terms of school achievements and educational outcomes? Are quantitative changes concomitant with qualitative ones? Finally, what are the trends in qualitative inequalities between Arabs and Jews and within the Arab population? We answer these questions in the following sections.

Quantitative Changes:
Increasing Access and Educational Expansion

Until the early 1970s, the educational system in Israel was divided into three levels: kindergarten for children ages 5 to 6; a primary level from 1st through 8th grades; and a secondary level from 9th through 12th grades. As mentioned, the first two levels were compulsory and free by the virtue of the Compulsory Education Law, whereas the secondary level was neither compulsory nor free.

The main innovation where the Arab schools were concerned was the inclusion of kindergarten education in the category of compulsory education. During the Mandatory period, kindergarten had not been an integral part of government schools. The existing kindergartens were mainly private and, in most cases, exclusively served well-to-do families (Ben-Hanania 1947, 32). In the Arab system, kindergartens are attached to primary schools, mainly due to a lack of suitable facilities. In the Hebrew education system, in contrast, kindergartens are independent units. In 1969, compulsory education was extended to the end of 10th grade, and in 2007 it was once again extended to the end of 12th grade (Haddad Haj-Yehia and Rudentzky 2018). Another important development occurred in 2015, when the Compulsory Education Law was extended to include the 3-to-4-year-old age group. That is to say, since 2015 education in Israel is compulsory and free from age 3 through the end of secondary school.

Arab education in Israel started off with a handicap compared to education for the Jewish population. When the educational system in the Arab localities was launched in 1948/49, it included only 45 elementary schools and one secondary school, located in Nazareth. Within a single decade, the number of Arab primary schools tripled, a trend that continued throughout the 1970s and 1980s. In 1990/91 there were 338 Arab primary schools, 74 middle schools, and 90 secondary schools, covering the vast majority of Arab localities. Thirty years later, this number more than doubled, so in 2020/21 there were 667 Arab primary schools, 224 middle schools, and 250 secondary schools (SAI 2021, tables 4.5, 4.12).

This growing access to education among the Arab population is also reflected in the impressive growth in the number of Arab pupils at the various school levels (table 3.2). Today (2023) nearly one-third of the Palestinian Arabs in Israel are students at some stage of education. If the 2015 Compulsory Education Law, which grants free education to all from the age of 3 to the end of secondary schools, was fully implemented, nearly every second Arab citizen in Israel would be a student (see table 3.2).

Table 3.2. Number of Arab Pupils in the Education System, 1948/49–2020/21

	1948/49	1959/60	1969/70	1979/80	1999/2000	2009/10	2020/21
Kindergartens (1)	1,124	7,274	14,211	17,344	55,480	86,000	117,169
Primary schools (2)	9,991	36,729	85,449	121,985	181,640	247,000	250,091
Intermediate schools (3)	–	–	2,457	14,803	47,844	74,518	81,827
Secondary schools (4)	14	1,956	8,050	22,473	49,543	80,856	113,047
Total	11,129	45,959	110,167	176,605	334,507	488,374	562,134

Source: SAI, 2001, table 8.9, 8–25; SAI, 2021 tables, 4.5, 4.12, 4.3.

Notes: (1) Ages 5–6, for 2020/21 ages 3–6; (2) grades 1st–8th, starting from 1969 grades 1st–6th; (3) starting from 1969/70 grades 7th–9th; (4) grades 9th–12th until 1969, starting from 1969/70 grades 10th–12th.

Secondary Schools

Until the early 1970s, the development of Arab secondary schools lagged behind that of primary schools. During the first years of Israeli statehood, the Ministry of Education directed its main efforts toward increasing school attendance on the compulsory primary level. The official position was that developing secondary education could wait until the elementary level had been well established. This was despite the fact that with respect to secondary education, Arab responsiveness was described by officials as complete and even "over-enthusiastic" (*The Jerusalem Post*, August 5, 1954).

Indeed, documents obtained from the State Archives show that the Arab population was very enthusiastic about expanding the system of secondary education. In contrast, the Ministry of Education tried to cool down this enthusiasm and convince heads of Arab localities not to open secondary schools due to the high economic costs and shortage of qualified teachers (SA 1351/1616/GL). Nevertheless, the Arab population requested that more secondary schools be opened. By 1955 there were five full Arab secondary schools (up to 12th grade) with 700 pupils, as documented by Shmuel Salmon, director of the Division for Arab Education:

> It should be indicated that in those places with secondary schools, they (Arabs) spend large amounts on secondary education, which is totally maintained by parents and local authorities. Parents in small villages even spend additional amounts on their children who reside outside of their villages (during the course of their studies).
>
> If we take into consideration that 50 percent of eighth-grade graduates continued on to secondary education despite the minimal governmental support, we can see a very interesting phenomenon: At the time the Arab sector was willing to sacrifice a great deal for secondary education but was still far from understanding the value of elementary education. (SA 1351/1616/GL)

The Arab population's eagerness to obtain secondary education had to do with the returns on completing secondary school, which were relatively high in the 1950s. The small number of Arab university graduates at that time opened the way for secondary school graduates to obtain social and socioeconomic returns, although this situation was only temporary. As we shall see below, most secondary school graduates during the first years after

Israeli statehood found their way to teaching jobs in Arab schools. Moreover, taking into consideration the negligible number of Arab university graduates at that time, the Arab community saw graduates of secondary schools as the educated elite.

Hence, it can be argued that the quantitative changes implemented in secondary education among Arabs have been more rapid than at the primary level. The increase in the number of secondary schools continued throughout the 1980s, whereas for middle and primary schools during the same period the trend slowed down. By 1990/92 there were 90 Arab secondary schools. As indicated, in the 2020/21 school year, there were 250 secondary schools (SAI 2021, tables 4.5, 4.12). Almost all Arab localities with municipal status have their own secondary schools, in addition to Arab schools in mixed Jewish-Arab cities and regional schools shared by a number of Arab villages.

Coeducation

One of the main changes in Arab education in Israel is the radical rise in school attendance among girls. At first (1948/49) girls constituted only 18.6 percent of pupils attending Arab schools compared to 49 percent in the Hebrew schools. Within only one decade, Arab girls constituted 34.7 percent of all Arab pupils. This figure increased to nearly 44 percent in 1969/70, 46.4 percent in 1979/80, and 47.3 percent in 1990/91, a figure similar to that for Jews (Al-Haj 1995a, 88). The rate of Arab girls attending school has continued to increase, reaching 975 out of every 1,000 students by the 2020/21 school year, even higher than the rate for Arab boys (969 per 1,000) and for Jewish girls (959 per 1,000) (SAI 2022, No. 73, table 4.15).

From the outset, the Ministry of Education decided that the Arab schools were to be coed. This innovation was not based on educational considerations but rather was a purely technical consideration motivated by financial constraints and the overall lack of women teachers in most Arab communities (Ben-Or 1951, 3). Another important change entailed abolishing the regulation introduced by the Mandatory government, according to which women teachers had to quit teaching after marriage.

Despite initial difficulties, parents soon welcomed the new system enthusiastically. According to Ben-Or, a senior inspector of Arab schools at the Ministry of Education: "It proves once again the artificial pretenses made by the British educationalists who claimed that religious reasons prohibited co-education within the Muslim community. Mukhtars in Triangle villages revealed to Israel's officials that they had time and again requested the British Government to introduce co-education and were put off" (*The Jerusalem Post*, August 22, 1949). By the mid-1960s the vast majority of Arab schools in Israel were coed, though the issue continued to be disputed for some time after that. In 1967, a group of parents from Shefa-'Amr appealed to the High Court of Justice to force the Ministry of Education to allow their daughters to enroll at the local boys' school. They subsequently won their case and the school became coed (*Hapoel Hatzair*, May 10, 1967).

In the debate over this issue some teachers favored separate education, though their opposition to coeducation was not based on gender grounds. The only female Arab superintendent in the 1960s strongly opposed coeducation, claiming that girls achieve more at separate schools than at mixed schools. Some parents not only favored separate education but demanded that only female teachers be employed at girls' schools (*Hapoel Hatzair*, May 10, 1967).

Resistance to coeducation was especially prominent in the Druze community. The Druze spiritual leader Sheikh Amin Tarif strongly opposed coed schools and requested the establishment of separate schools for boys and girls in Druze communities. Nevertheless, Ministry of Education officials did not acquiesce to his request for the reasons already mentioned, that is, the shortage of female teachers and the extra expenses involved (SA 145/1733/G).

School attendance among girls was particularly low in the Negev Bedouin population. Caught between tradition and the lack of appropriate schools, for a long time Bedouin girls were deprived of the opportunity to obtain an education. Since the early 1970s several factors have contributed to changing this situation: the sedentarization of the Bedouin tribes, the establishment of stable and semi-stable settlements, the increasing number of schools within the confines of the tribes and the Bedouins' growing awareness of the importance of education. As a result, the percentage of girls in the Bedouin schools has been steadily increasing. By 1976, girls comprised 25 percent of the total number of Bedouin pupils in the Negev, a figure that rose to 33 percent in 1979 and 39.7 percent in 1986 (Meir and Barnia 1987, 163).

The dispute over coeducation was revived in the 1980s, with the rising influence of the Islamic Movement. Since 1989, some Arab localities in which the municipal council is headed by mayors affiliated with the Islamic

Movement have backed away from mixed education. The mayor of Um el-Fahm led the way when he decided in 1990–1991 to maintain separate classes for girls and boys in the local secondary school. This decision, however, has been criticized by large segments of the Arab population and by the appointee for Arab education at the Ministry of Education (*Al-Sinnarah*, September 7, 1990).

Over time, school attendance among both boys and girls in the Arab population has grown considerably. This increase is more dramatic among girls, in particular in the secondary schools. The gender gap in school attendance in Arab schools was very large up to 1970, when the rate for boys was almost double that for girls. Since then, this gap has steadily decreased. The most significant change occurred in the school year 2001/2, when for the first time the rate of girls surpassed that of boys. By 2019/20 the rates were 960 and 938 per 1,000, respectively.

At the same time, until the 1990s the discrepancy in school attendance between Arabs and Jews was extremely wide, mainly in secondary schools. The increasing rate of school attendance among Arabs has led to a considerable decrease in this gap, with the year 2000 marking the major turning point. Yet due to school dropouts there still a discrepancy in favor of Jews, mainly in secondary schools. In the 2020/21 school year, the total dropout rate for all students in grades 7–12 was 2.1 percent among Arab students (2.8 percent for boys and 1.4 percent for girls), compared to 1.6 percent among Jews (2.5 percent for boys and 0.8 percent for girls) (SAI 2021, table 4.26). Most dropouts occur toward the end of secondary school, in particular among the most disadvantaged groups, namely Arab Bedouins in the Negev, where the rate of secondary school dropout was 3.5 percent in 2020 (Ben-Gurion University and Negev Center for Sustainability 2020).

These statistics reflect overt/visible dropout. Yet, in addition to this visible dropout, there is also latent dropout in the form of students who come to school occasionally but do not really study or attend classes (characterized by absenteeism, low academic achievement, a sense of alienation from school, behavioral and social problems, and the like). The outbreak of the COVID-19 pandemic and the transition to distance learning intensified the phenomenon of latent dropout among students, especially from disadvantaged groups (see Dvir 2022).

It should be noted that although the discrepancy in school attendance between Arab and Jewish pupils has considerably narrowed at both the primary and the secondary levels, there is still a wide gap between the two groups at the pre-primary stage. Studies show that already in the mid-1980s, nearly 67 percent of 2-year-old Jewish children were enrolled in daycare centers, whereas in the Arab sector this figure was zero. Of Arab children aged 3, only 20 percent attended pre-compulsory kindergartens compared to 92 percent of Jewish children. Among 4-year-old children, preschool enrollment was 40 percent among Arabs compared to 99 percent among Jews. In other words, Arab pupils began their compulsory education at a disadvantage of 2 to 3 years behind Jewish children. This gap subsequently finds expression in disparities in school performance between Arab and Jewish pupils throughout their formal education (Habib-Allah 1984).

Although this situation has improved over time, the gap between Jewish and Arab children attending pre-primary education and daycare centers is still very wide, especially between the ages of 0 and 3 (see figure 3.1). Note that although the 3-to-4-year-old group has been included in the Compulsory Education Law since 2015, this law is still not fully implemented in many Arab localities due to a shortage of proper facilities and educational services. Figure 3.1 shows that during the 2018/19 school year about a quarter of Arab children aged 3 and 13 percent of those between the ages of 4 and 5 did not attend kindergartens or daycare centers.

Figure 3.1. Arab and Jewish Children by Age in Pre-Primary Education and Daycare Centers in the School Year 2018/19. *Source:* SAI; CBS.

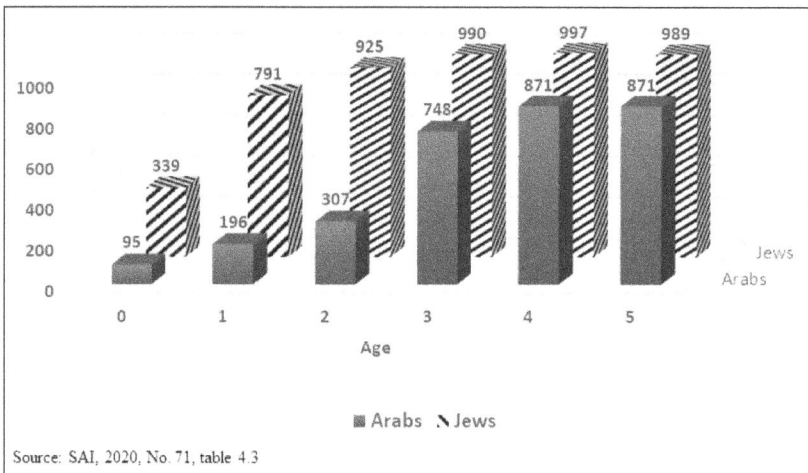

Source: SAI, 2020, No. 71, table 4.3

Qualitative Trends:
Cumulative Disparities and Persistent Gaps

THEORETICAL FRAMEWORK: NEOLIBERALISM, MARKETIZATION, AND STANDARDIZATION

Since the early 1980s, education systems in various countries, including Israel, have undergone an intensive process of privatization and marketization in the framework of neoliberal reforms. These reforms and other educational changes based on neoliberal ideology have engendered far-reaching changes in goals, educational content, teacher status, and educational administrative structure (for Western countries, see Doherty 2007; Baltodano 2012; Ball 2016; Zimmerman 2018. For Israel, see Yonah, Dahan, and Markovich 2008; Feniger, Israeli, and Yehuda 2016; Avigur-Eshel and Berkovitch 2017; Agbaria 2018; Bamberger and Kim 2022).

According to Michael Apple, neoliberal reforms have in effect been simultaneously combined with neoconservative values. Based on the neoliberal perspective the state must be minimized and should adhere to privatization of the school system. At the same time, the state should exert tight control over education so that the schools can teach "the correct knowledge, norms and values" (Apple 2006b). Although these positions seem contradictory, the neoliberal agenda has always found ways to reconcile them and present them as a coherent package. In this context, Apple concludes that the ultimate goal of such a combined neoliberal-neoconservative strategy is "the labelling of culturally and economically disenfranchised communities through media and political debate in ways that shift responsibility for their educational marginalization to both teachers and these communities themselves" (21).

Yonah, Dahan, and Markovich similarly discussed the ostensibly contradictory roles of the state as demonstrated through neoliberal policy in Israel: the "weak state" and the "strong state." The state appears to have withdrawn from educational affairs through decentralization, marketization, and privatization policies, whereas it has tightened its control over educational goals and content by enforcing a common core curriculum, setting comprehensive standards and criteria for assessment and evaluation of scholastic achievements, and imposing a national value system in an attempt to cultivate a society characterized by a common identity and shared goals (Yonah, Dahan, and Markovich 2008).

Concomitant with the marketization of the education system, one of the major goals of neoliberal education has been the development of human capital to enhance economic activity and to prepare the next generation for local and global market requirements. (For more on this topic, see the work of Milton Friedman [1955, 1997]—an economist and a driving force of neoliberal thought.) To measure and evaluate the quality of such human capital, national and global bodies have advanced a set of standardized tests. These tests are administered periodically, and their results are used for measuring, evaluating, and ultimately designing the education systems in various countries (Grek 2009; Feniger 2020; Bamberger and Kim 2022).

The Organization for Economic Cooperation and Development (OECD) is one of the foremost influential international apparatuses and policy setters for advancing global education policy in the context of national and global markets. The OECD's Programme for International Student Assessment (PISA) has become a major and influential component of the OECD, not only in Europe but also worldwide (Grek 2009). Another such influential apparatus is the International Association for the Evaluation of Educational Achievement (IEA), which administers another international test: Trends in International Mathematics and Science Study (TIMSS).

These organizations have generated a consensus regarding global education policy and have determined the educational agenda of governments in many countries across the globe. To a large extent, they have also imposed their definition for the criteria of "efficiency" and "quality" in education (Nóvoa and Yariv-Mashal 2003; Grek 2009; Feniger, Livneh, and Yogev 2012; Feniger 2020).

Nóvoa and Yariv-Mashal (2003) describe the power wielded by these organizations as follows: "Such researches produce a set of conclusions, definitions of 'good' or 'bad' educational systems, and required solutions. Moreover, the mass media are keen to diffuse the results of these studies, in such a manner that reinforces a need for urgent decisions, following lines of action that seem undisputed and uncontested, largely due to the fact that they have been internationally asserted" (425). Focusing on Israel and based on PISA data, Feniger, Livneh, and Yogev (2012) conclude that the debate over students' scores on the PISA exams has been magnified beyond all proportions. They claim that "the focus on the international grading of educational achievements deflects public attention from an understanding of the significance of inequalities within the country" (323). Similarly, Feniger (2020) indicates that in order to improve its worldwide ranking in the TIMSS, Israel revised the entire middle school curriculum in mathematics to align with the TIMSS test. Yet whereas students' TIMSS scores rose considerably, the mathematic scores of Israeli students on other international tests (PISA) did not exhibit a comparable improvement. Therefore, Feniger concludes that these international tests influence the way policymakers define "problems" and "solutions" rather than addressing issues of social inequality (363).

A similar trend is evident in standardized national tests designed in Israel. In this context, Feniger et al. examined the impact of the Meitzav tests, which target students in the 5th and 8th grades and were introduced in 2002 as part of the aforementioned neoliberal state reforms (see Feniger, Israeli, and Yehuda 2016; Yonah, Dahan, and Markovich 2008). The declared goal of these tests was to improve learning and instruction in major school subjects in the Jewish and Arab schools (Feniger, Israeli, and Yehuda 2016, 184). Nevertheless, as elsewhere (see, for example, Giroux 2010; Perryman et al. 2011) and in contrast to the Ministry of Education's declared goals, these tests have had negative consequences for principals, teachers, and students alike. Moreover, the public discourse, which was fueled by comparisons between schools and even neighborhoods based on these tests, has only exacerbated pressure on the school system and diverted public interest toward statistics rather than authentic educational issues. No less significant, these tests have changed the way in which major actors (in particular, parents and policymakers) speak about education (Feniger, Israeli, and Yehuda 2016, 184–85).

In the next sections, I analyze the standardization and the qualitative changes in Arab schools compared to Jewish schools. First, I focus on the national tests, specifically the Meitzav test and the matriculation exams. Then, I shift to the international tests, specifically PISA and TIMSS.

Standardization and Qualitative Trends in Arab Schools

THE MEITZAV TESTS

As mentioned, beginning in 2002 the Ministry of Education launched a series of achievement tests known as the Meitzav tests (Meitzav is an acronym for shortening efficiency and school growth indices). The Meitzav tests are administered in elementary and middle schools in Israel (5th and 8th grades) in the following subjects: science and technology, Hebrew mother tongue (in Hebrew schools), Arabic (in Arab schools), mathematics, science, and English. The Meitzav tests were first administered by the Ministry of

Education's Evaluation and Measurement Division, and since 2006 have been administered by the National Authority for Measurement and Evaluation (RAMA) under the auspices of the Ministry of Education. The following section discusses the results of the Meitzav exams over time in the 8th grades at Jewish and Arab schools. The analysis focuses on English, mathematics, and science because all students are tested in these subjects, thus allowing for a comparison of results between Jewish and Arab students. On the other hand, the tests in Hebrew and Arabic as mother tongues are different tests designed for and administered to separate population groups and therefore cannot be compared (see RAMA, Ministry of Education 2020a, 12). Here we provide the data from the exams for the 8th grade because the data collected for the 5th grade in some of the subjects do not meet the required quality and validity rules and therefore were not included in the RAMA report (RAMA, Ministry of Education 2018, 118).

Table 3.3 depicts a consistent gap between Arab and Jewish 8th-grade students in all subjects, including math, English, science, and technology, throughout the entire reported period of one decade, from 2008 to 2018. Yet despite the persistent gap, there are also internal differences in the extent of this gap, ranging from high to low as follows: English, math, and science and technology. Over the reporting period the gap in science and technology decreased significantly, from 66 points in 2008/9 to 21 points

Table 3.3. Mean Scores of 8th-Grade Arab Students on Meitzav Tests and the Gap in Favor of Jewish Students (2008–2018)

Year	Math	English	Science and Tech
2008/9	488	449	459
Gap	–32	–82	–66
2010/11	498	491	525
Gap	–34	–46	–22
2012/13	468	472	527
Gap	–46	–65	–46
2014/15	498	476	520
Gap	–50	–55	–47
2017/18	514	487	564
Gap	–40	–46	–21

Source: RAMA, Ministry of Education 2018, 20–27.

in 2017/18, while the gap in math increased from 32 to 40 points. At the same time, while the gap in English decreased over time, it is still very extensive (46 points).

As to the internal differences within each group, the report indicates a significant relationship between students' socioeconomic background and their achievements in all subjects among both Arab and Jewish students, such that those from low socioeconomic backgrounds are the lowest achievers. In this context, the negative impact of low socioeconomic background is much more significant among Arabs. This is because only a relatively small percentage (nearly 15 percent) of Jewish students are classified with low socioeconomic background, 40 percent with middle socioeconomic background, and 45 percent with high socioeconomic background, compared to 65 percent, 30 percent, and 5 percent, respectively, among Arabs. In other words, two-thirds of Arab students are from low socioeconomic backgrounds, whereas only a negligible portion (5 percent) are from high backgrounds (RAMA, Ministry of Education 2018, 39).

Note that the findings provided by RAMA did not mention how Meitzav scores were affected by funds invested in the school system. We can hypothesize that this financial investment has also had a significant impact in favor of Jewish students (for the strong impact of financial investment on students' scores in national tests, see Lavy 1998).

As far as the gender gap is concerned, the achievements of Jewish boys and girls in English and mathematics were similar over the different testing periods, whereas in science and technology boys' achievements were 6 points higher than those of girls (RAMA, Ministry of Education 2018, 45). In contrast, Arabs girls scored higher than boys in all subjects throughout the entire period examined. In mathematics, this gap increased from 20 points in 2008 to 28 points in 2018, whereas in English it decreased from 33 points to 17 points, and in science and technology it decreased from 54 to 26 points, a gap that is still significant in favor of girls (RAMA, Ministry of Education 2018, 48).

Entitlement to Matriculation (Bagrut) Certificate

Despite the progress exhibited by Arab secondary schools, these schools have always been at a disadvantage compared to Jewish secondary schools. Success on the matriculation exams (*Bagrut*) is considered one of the main criteria for evaluation of school achievement since it has a strong impact on the likelihood of obtaining a higher education. The matriculation certificate is considered a prerequisite for admission to academic institutions in Israel, together with the Psychometric Entrance Test (to be discussed in more detail in chapter 6).

During the first decade of the state, only a negligible percentage of Arab pupils passed their matriculation exams. In 1955 only four pupils out of 150 passed (3 percent) (Waschitz 1957, 272). The Ministry of Education then appointed a committee to examine the reasons for this high failure rate. This investigation found that the main reasons for failure were a lack of competent teachers, a poor standard of pupils entering secondary schools, and a lack of textbooks (Hussein 1957, 47).

Apart from the reasons stated above, two other factors may have been responsible. The first is that English is taught as a third language in the Arab schools, whereas it is taught as a second language in the Hebrew schools. In addition, the Hebrew schools also benefited from a "protective" grade granted by the school that was averaged with the Bagrut score, whereas the Arab schools did not offer this weighted grade (*Davar*, July 12, 1963).

The Knesset Committee for Education met in January 1962 to discuss these severe deficiencies in the Arab educational system and recommended the formation of a Pedagogic Council for curricula problems in the Arab schools (*Al-Hamishmar,* January 25, 1962). Consequently, by the mid-1970s academic performance in the Arab secondary schools had improved remarkably, in large part due to the fact that most Arab schools began granting a "protective" grade on the matriculation exams, similar to that granted by the Hebrew schools.

Since the mid-1990s, the matriculation exams have undergone a number of reforms, including reducing the number of required subjects and averaging the scores on external matriculation exams with those given by schools, with both components given equal weight. These reforms were aimed at increasing students' chances of succeeding on these exams, mainly among disadvantaged groups (for a full review of these reforms, see Shaik 2003). Indeed, these reforms have considerably increased the percentage of those entitled to matriculation certificates among Arab and Jewish students alike.

As figure 3.2 shows, the percentage of matriculation certificate entitlement among Arab students has gradually risen, from less than 50 percent in 1995 to nearly 70 percent in 2020. At the same time, among Jewish students this figure has increased from nearly 70 percent in 1995 to 83 percent in 2020. The relative rise in eligibility among Arabs was higher than that among Jews, thus narrowing the gap between the two groups from 20.4

percent to 13.1 percent. Yet despite the smaller discrepancy between Arab and Jewish students, average matriculation certificate entitlement among Arabs in 2020 resembles that among Jews in 1995. In other words, there is a 25 year separation between the two groups (figure 3.2).

As to gender differences, in 2018 the percentage of matriculation entitlement was 54.4 among Arab boys and 73.7 among girls, compared to 79.3 and 81.0, respectively, among Jewish boys and girls. In other words, whereas the percentage of entitlement for boys and girls was almost equal among Jews, nearly 20 percent more Arab girls were entitled to matriculation certificates than Arab boys (SAI 2019, table 4.20). In this regard, unlike boys, Arab girls have made tremendous progress toward closing the gap with their Jewish counterparts.

The gap between Arabs and Jews is also reflected in the percentage of students entitled to matriculation certificates at the level of 5 study units in English, math, and computer sciences (tables 3.4a and 3.4b). With the exception of physics, there is a wide gap between the two groups in all subjects, especially in English. This gap has a significant impact on admission to academic studies in general, and to prestigious programs of study in particular.

Figure 3.2. Entitlement to Matriculation Certificate among Arab and Jewish Students 1995–2020 (%). *Source:* SAI, CBS.

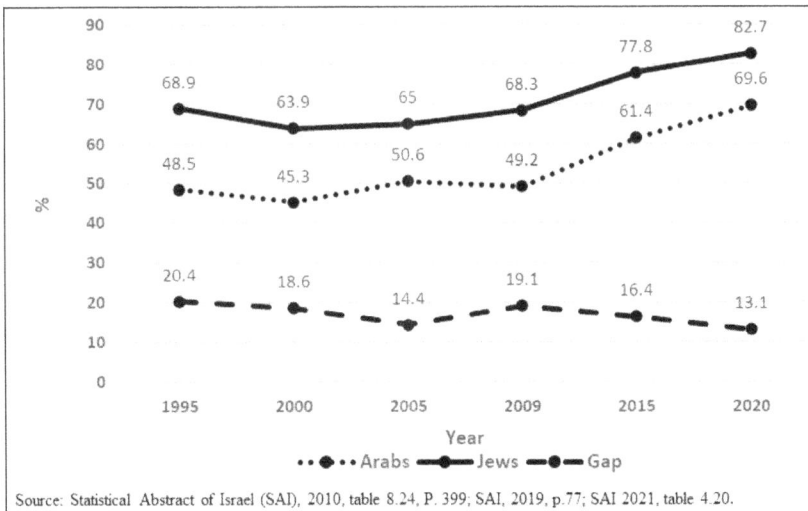

Source: Statistical Abstract of Israel (SAI), 2010, table 8.24, P. 399; SAI, 2019, p.77; SAI 2021, table 4.20.

Table 3.4a. Entitlement to Matriculation Certificate at 5 Study Unit Level in Selected Subjects among Jews by Gender (%) (2020/21)

Subjects	English	Mathematics	Physics	Computer Sciences
Total	62.3	23.3	15.1	12.0
Boys	63.9	26.4	21.3	17.7
Girls	60.9	20.5	9.6	7.0

Source: SAI 2021, table 4.22.

Table 3.4b. Entitlement to Matriculation Certificate at 5 Study Unit Level in Selected Subjects among Arabs by Gender (%) (2020/21)

Subjects	English	Mathematics	Physics	Computer Sciences
Total	34.3	13.8	15.4	8.0
Boys	30.6	12.1	17.2	9.2
Girls	36.8	15.0	14.1	7.1

Source: SAI 2021, table 4.22.

International Tests

In the following section, I analyze the achievements of Israeli students on two major international tests: PISA and TIMSS.

PROGRAMME FOR INTERNATIONAL STUDENTS ASSESSMENT (PISA)

As noted, PISA is an international study launched by the OECD in 1997. It was first administered in 2000 and encompassed both OECD member and nonmember countries. Every three years the PISA survey provides comparative data on the performance of 15-year-olds in reading literacy, mathematics literacy, and science literacy (see OECD, https://www.oecd.org/pisa/aboutpisa/pisa-based-test-for-schools-faq.htm). From 2000 through 2018, the PISA series included seven rounds. In 2018, 79 countries participated, including 37 OECD members and 42 nonmember countries (RAMA, Ministry of Education 2019, 7). Israel participated in all these rounds except for 2003.

As reported by RAMA, PISA tests in reading literacy, mathematical literacy, and science literacy examine students' ability to apply the knowledge and skills they have acquired during their lives, mainly through the formal education they received, to solve problems in real situations. These situations test whether students are able to analyze and understand a problem and express their ideas in an efficient and influential way, to what extent they use technological innovations, what degree of preparation they received for further study during their lives, whether they are equipped with appropriate learning strategies, and so on. These capabilities are summed up by the term *literacy*, a key term in the PISA approach. Level of literacy, and not just knowledge in and of itself, may be related to students' future financial success, their type of workplace, and the nature of the society and country in which they live (RAMA, Ministry of Education 2019, 10).

Due to space limitations and taking into consideration that all three parts of the PISA test (reading literacy, mathematical literacy, and science literacy) are similar in terms of scores, gaps between Arab and Jewish students, gender gaps, and inequalities according to students' socioeconomic status, I will focus only on reading literacy in the context of the PISA test. I subsequently provide a detailed analysis of mathematics and sciences as reflected in the TIMSS test.

Reading Literacy

The PISA 2018 study defines *reading literacy* as "individuals' ability to understand texts, to use them, appreciate them, criticize them and engage with them, in order to achieve their goals, to develop their knowledge and potential and be a part of society" (RAMA, Ministry of Education 2019, 15). The study examines the broader meaning of "reading skills," including enjoyment of and motivation for reading, critical understanding, evaluation, and use of written texts for different goals (23). Scores on the test are classified into six levels ranging from low to high, with level 1 being the lowest level. Level 2 is defined by PISA as a basic level, representing a score of 407–479 points. This level is required of graduates of the education system "in order to be able to enjoy learning opportunities and participate fully in all social, economic and citizenship aspects of society at large in a modern and global world" (65). Thus, students who score below level 2 are defined as having difficulties in reading literacy.

The findings show that despite improvement in the Israeli PISA average over time (2006–2018), the Israeli average score of 470 is still 17 points lower than the OECD average score of 487. This gap appears to be the result of the low scores of Arab students. Indeed, when the scores of Jewish and Arab students are analyzed separately, we see two completely different sets of results, such that the scores of Jews are compatible with those of developed-industrialized countries whereas those of Arabs are classified at the bottom of developing countries. In this context, the gap between the two groups has widened over time, from 84 points in 2006 to 144 points in 2018, a huge gap by all parameters (RAMA, Ministry of Education 2019, 82) (see figure 3.3).

Figure 3.3 clearly reflects the gap in PISA reading literacy between Jewish and Arab students over time. It shows that the scores of Jewish students have improved over time, bypassing the OECD average in 2018. During the same period, the scores of Arab students have even decreased, mainly between 2012 and 2018, thus widening the gap between Arab and Jewish students as well as the gap relative to the OECD average.

An examination of the percentage of students defined as having difficulties with reading literacy (i.e., scoring beneath the basic level 2) reveals a worrisome situation. In 2018, over two-thirds (or 69 percent) of Arab students were in this category, compared to 19 percent of Jewish students. Note that the percentage of Jewish students with reading difficulties was

Figure 3.3. Average Scores in PISA—Reading Literacy: Israel, Jews, Arabs, and OECD, 2006–2018. *Source:* RAMA and the Ministry of Education.

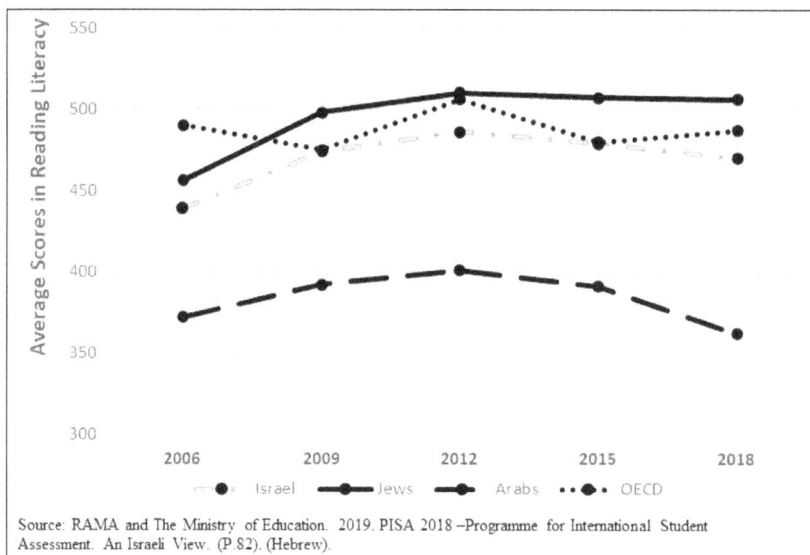

Source: RAMA and The Ministry of Education. 2019. PISA 2018 –Programme for International Student Assessment. An Israeli View. (P.82). (Hebrew).

even lower than that of the OECD (23 percent in 2018) (RAMA, Ministry of Education 2019, 82).

A study conducted by the OECD points to two central factors that play a decisive role in explaining PISA scores: students' socioeconomic background and the amount each country invests in its education system (mainly for ages 6–15). Indeed, state investment in education explains as much as 49 percent of the variance in student scores (RAMA, Ministry of Education 2019, 70).

As for socioeconomic background, the study shows that 74 percent of Arab students who have reading literacy difficulties are from low socio-economic backgrounds, compared to 67 percent among those from middle socioeconomic backgrounds and 45 percent among those from high socio-economic backgrounds. The wide gap between Arab and Jewish students is also reflected in the fact that the average score of Arab students from high socioeconomic backgrounds (418 points) is lower than the average score of Jewish students from low socioeconomic backgrounds (460) (RAMA, Ministry of Education 2019, 86–87).

Socioeconomic background clearly remains a central factor in deter-mining students' scores. It is especially crucial for Arabs, considering that 54 percent of Arab students who took these exams came from low socioeconomic backgrounds (compared to 22 percent of Jewish students), 30 percent came from middle backgrounds (compared to 44 percent of Jewish students), and only 16 percent of Arab students came from high backgrounds (compared to 34 percent of Jewish students) (RAMA, Ministry of Education 2019, 85).

In summary, state investment in education combined with socioeconomic background explain most of the variance in students' scores on the PISA exams. Indeed, there has always been a significant gap in school funding between Jews and Arabs. For example, a Knesset report shows that in 2015, the number of classroom hours allocated to students at Arab schools from weak socioeconomic backgrounds was 49.1, compared to 61.6 hours at state secular Hebrew schools and 78 hours at state religious Hebrew schools. Thus, Arab pupils from weak socioeconomic backgrounds received 80 percent of the number of classroom hours allocated at state secular Hebrew schools and only 63 percent of those allocated at state religious Hebrew schools. No less significant, Arab schools are more dependent on state funding due to the limited resources allocated by Arab local authorities (Weisblai and Veneger 2015, 22).

Note that the vast majority of Arab localities are classified at the bot-tom of the socioeconomic ladder. According to the 2017 CBS classification of localities by socioeconomic level, nearly 80 percent of Arab localities in

Israel were classified in the bottom 1 to 3 socioeconomic clusters. All the Bedouin localities in the Negev-Naqab were classified in the lowest cluster (1), and no Arab locality in Israel was classified in the top 8 to 10 clusters (CBS 2020a; classification ranges from 1-lowest to 10-highest).

Trends in International Mathematics and Science: TIMSS

Introduction

TIMSS is an international assessment of mathematics and science in the 4th and 8th grades administered by the IEA. The TIMSS series began in 1995 and continued every four years through 2019: 1999, 2003, 2007, 2011, 2015, and 2019. Many countries use TIMSS trend data for monitoring the effectiveness of their educational systems in a global context. Israel has participated in the entire series of this study since 1999. In 2019, 30 countries participated in the TIMSS study, including developing and developed countries. The following analysis focuses on the Israeli scores for 2019, which included 3,731 Israeli 8th-grade students, constituting a representative sample of the Israeli education system including Arab and Jewish schools. The test in Israel was monitored by RAMA, and our analysis is based on the RAMA report, which also relates to the main trends over the 20 years from 1999 to 2019. The analysis places the scores within a comparative context at two levels: the global level that compares Israel's achievements with those of other countries in the world and the local level that examines the achievements of Arab and Jewish students as well as gender and socioeconomic variables within each group.

A Global Perspective

In the 2019 TIMSS cycle, the average achievement of Israeli students was 519 points in mathematics and 513 points in science. These averages are higher than the overall average of all participating countries (489 points in mathematics and 490 points in science). Moreover, the rates of outstanding students in Israel (15 percent in mathematics and 12 percent in science) are higher than the international median rate (5 percent in mathematics and 7 percent in science). The rates of students with difficulty (13 percent in each field of knowledge) are similar to the international median rate (13 percent in mathematics and 15 percent in science) (RAMA, Ministry of Education 2020b, 2).

Gaps in the Achievements of Arab and Jewish Students

Examination of the achievements of Arab and Jewish students in the 2019 TIMSS cycle shows that Jewish students had higher achievements than Arab students in both fields of knowledge. The gap between the two groups is 60 points in mathematics and 42 points in science. Examining students from each group separately indicates that the average achievement of Jewish students is higher than the overall average for the participating countries (more noticeable in mathematics), whereas the average achievement of Arab students is similar to the average of participating countries (especially in science) (table 3.5). Note that the gap in the starting points for both groups (1999) was much wider: 75 points in mathematics and 90 points in science. This gap, though still very significant, has narrowed over time, mainly because of the dramatic improvement among Arab students compared to a slight improvement in the most recent two cycles among their Jewish counterparts. Tables 3.5a and 3.5b summarize the trends in the achievements of both groups.

Table 3.5a. Average Achievements of Arab and Jewish Students in Mathematics over Time (TIMSS 1999–2019)

	1999	2003	2007	2011	2015	2019
Arabs	397	465	408	465	460	476
Jews	482	505	484	536	533	536

Source: RAMA, Ministry of Education 2020b. The main findings of the TIMMS study "Achievements in Mathematics and Sciences of 8th Grades in Israel and Their Attitudes towards Fields of Knowledge." [A summary in Hebrew]. 2019, 6–7.

Table 3.5b. Average Achievements of Arab and Jewish Students in Science over Time (TIMSS 1999–2019)

	1999	2003	2007	2011	2015	2019
Arabs	394	463	422	481	458	483
Jews	484	496	485	530	528	525

Source: RAMA, Ministry of Education. 2020b. The main findings of the TIMMS study "Achievements in Mathematics and Sciences of 8th Grades in Israel and Their Attitudes towards Fields of Knowledge." [A summary in Hebrew]. 2019, 6–7.

Examination of the rates of those who excel and those who have difficulties among Arab and Jewish students shows that the rate of those who excel in mathematics among Jews is three times higher than the rate among Arabs (19 percent and 6 percent, respectively), whereas in science the rate of those who excel among Jews is double that of Arabs (14 percent and 7 percent, respectively). In contrast, in both areas of knowledge, the rates of difficulty among Arab students (about 20 percent) are twice as high as among Jewish students (about 10 percent) (RAMA, Ministry of Education, 2020b, 7).

A comparison of the achievements of Arab and Jewish students according to socioeconomic background reveals quite interesting findings. Among Jewish students, the average difference in achievement between students from high and low socioeconomic backgrounds is 110 points in mathematics and 95 points in science. Among Arab students, the average difference in achievement between students from middle and low socioeconomic backgrounds is about 65 points in each of the fields of knowledge. No findings were reported for Arab students from high socioeconomic backgrounds.

Nevertheless, when comparing the achievements in the TIMSS 2019 cycle for Arab and Jewish students from the same socioeconomic background, the gaps in average achievement between the two groups are considerably reduced or even disappear completely. Among students from low socioeconomic backgrounds there is an intergroup gap of about 15–10 points in favor of Jews. In contrast, students from middle backgrounds have similar achievements in mathematics and exhibit an intergroup gap of 20 points in science in favor of Arabs (figure 3.4). In other words, the gap in TIMSS achievements between Arabs and Jews is completely explained by differences in socioeconomic background for both groups (RAMA, Ministry of Education, 2020b, 9).

With respect to gender, in TIMSS as in PISA the situation among Arabs in Israel is completely different from that of Jews and of students from countries in the rest of the world. Among Jewish students, the average achievement of boys is higher than that of girls in both mathematics (15 points) and science (11 points). In contrast, among Arab students the average achievement of girls in science is higher by 22 points and in mathematics it is higher by 7 points, though this figure is not statistically significant (RAMA, Ministry of Education, 2020b, 11).

The PISA Tests in Israeli Media

To convey how these international tests are portrayed in the Israeli media, in the following section I briefly analyze two articles published on prominent

Figure 3.4. Average Achievements in the TIMSS 2019 Cycle of Arab and Jewish Students in Mathematics and Science by Socioeconomic Background. *Source:* RAMA and the Ministry of Education.

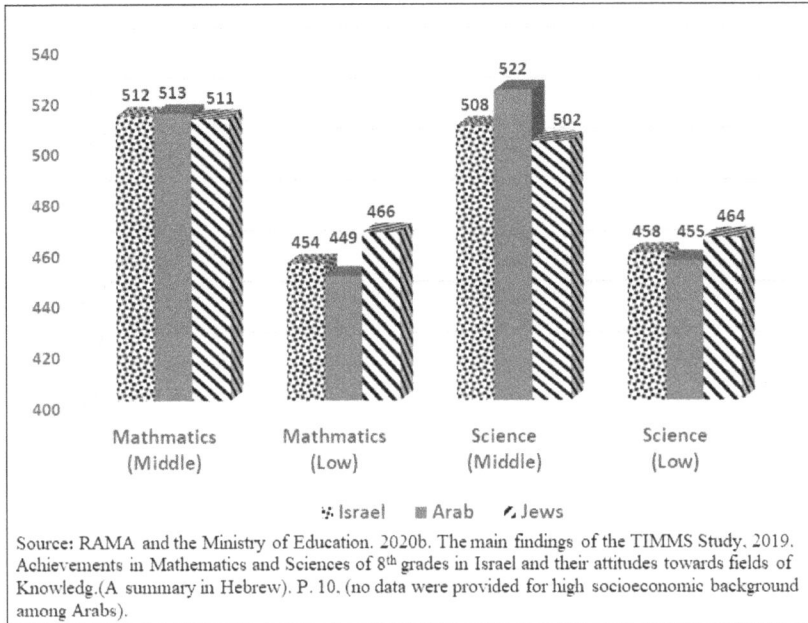

Source: RAMA and the Ministry of Education. 2020b. The main findings of the TIMMS Study. 2019. Achievements in Mathematics and Sciences of 8th grades in Israel and their attitudes towards fields of Knowledg.(A summary in Hebrew). P. 10. (no data were provided for high socioeconomic background among Arabs).

Israeli websites—*Ynet* and *Ma'ariv*—on the day the Ministry of Education announced the 2018 PISA results (December 3, 2019).

In an article titled "Drop in Grades, Huge Gaps between Jewish and Arab Students: PISA Exam Data," Adir Yanko provided a detailed report of the reading literacy, mathematics, and science scores of Jewish and Arab students. He indicated that

> Arab students show a particularly sharp decline, despite massive budgetary investments in Arab education, and even more so after government decision number 922 from 2015, which among other things aimed at strengthening the education system in Arab society. Against the background of the results among the Arab students, the Ministry of Education announced that it will establish a special team to examine the issue, which will focus on the curricula, the teaching methods and the use of the many hours of support that were allocated to reduce the gaps. (Yanko 2019a)

That same day, Ofer Livnat published an article in *Ma'ariv* titled "The Gaps Between Jewish and Arab Students: The Ministry of Education was Surprised at the Depth of the Crisis." The article's subtitle reads "in light of the growing disparities [between Jews and Arabs] as shown by the PISA test data, the Director General of the Ministry of Education announced the establishment of a working team that will examine the failures and draw lessons" (Livnat 2019). Livnat devoted a major part of the article to violence in Arab schools as the factor responsible for the gaps between Arab and Jewish students:

> According to educators, one of the factors that can explain the differences between Arab and Jewish students is the spread of violence among Arab youth and the lack of parental involvement. Off the record, teachers say that they have trouble teaching the curriculum due to students' violence toward each other and even toward the teacher. In addition, they cited their fear of verbal and physical violence on the part of parents, who often intervene in what is happening at school.

Nevertheless, the article does indicate that one of the reasons for this wide gap is the Ministry of Education's lack of understanding of the system in terms of developing and implementing programs adapted to Arab society, not necessarily a lack of investment, despite the budgetary gaps that favor Jewish schools over Arab schools.

Despite their slightly different explanations for the huge gap between the scores of Jewish and Arab students on the PISA tests, both articles incorporate basic implications that label Arab students as underachievers and that place responsibility on Arab schools and Arab society. At the same time, they highlight the concerns, positive intentions, and tremendous investment on the part of the state and the Ministry of Education, which immediately formed a special committee to examine the reasons for these gaps and draw conclusions.

We may conclude, then, that the way these test scores are reported in the media and the Ministry of Education's response have reinforced stereotypes concerning Arab schools and Arab society and assigned negative labels to Arab students, rather than dealing with social inequality and tackling its implications (in this regard, see Feniger 2020; Feniger, Livneh, and Yogev 2012). Also, as aptly concluded by Nóvoa and Yariv-Mashal (2003), the media reports determine how "good" and "bad" education systems and the required solutions should be defined. Indeed, according to the analyzed media reports, it is abundantly clear that the Hebrew education system is "good" and the Arab education system is "bad." The required solutions are also clear as far as officials in the Ministry of Education are concerned: to change Arab society, to prevent Arab schools from wasting public funds, and to make proper use of the government's generous investment in these schools.

New Challenges Brought on by COVID-19

The COVID-19 pandemic has had an unprecedented impact worldwide, not only on public health and the economy but also on education (see review in Greenhow et al. 2021). As schools began to close, the education systems in most countries across the globe had to make an immediate transition to remote learning. This transition and its concomitant challenges eventually expanded the gap between students from different socioeconomic backgrounds (Saito 2023). In this regard, the already existing digital divide between advantaged and disadvantaged groups came to the surface. This digital divide refers to lifelong digital skills that go beyond technical digital access (see Cohron 2015). Hence, "students with extensive technology experience, strong academic backgrounds and self-directed learning skills tend to do better in fully online learning situations, whereas students who are already vulnerable face greater challenges" (Greenhow et al. 2021, 9; see also Dynarski 2017). Disadvantaged students are doubly harmed, first because they often have less access to internet and digital services, and second, even if they have access to technology, they are less likely to have digital skills (Greenhow et al. 2021).

The situation described above applies to Arab schools in Israel. Although the far-reaching implications of the COVID-19 crisis on Arab education have yet to be studied in depth, initial studies and reports already show that this crisis has further widened the educational gaps between Arab and Jewish students in Israel. A Bank of Israel report indicates that Arab society had been especially harmed by the COVID-19 crisis due to its limited access to digital services. Another Bank of Israel report conducted prior to the COVID-19 crisis showed that only 30 percent of Arab households had adequate access to internet infrastructure that would allow remote learning, compared to 75 percent of Jewish households (Bank of Israel 2020, 85).

In a special survey of parents conducted by RAMA during the 2020 school year, 41 percent of Arab parents reported that their children had not regularly participated in remote learning, and 15 percent reported that their children had not participated at all (RAMA, Ministry of Education 2020c; see also Bank of Israel 2020, 85). Moreover, even after the return to regular schooling after the first closure (May–June 2020), 85 percent of Arab students did not return because the infrastructure and services in their schools did not meet Ministry of Health requirements (Follow-Up Committee on Arab Education 2020). In a follow-up parents' survey conducted by RAMA in 2021, 64 percent of Arab parents said there was a computer available for their children (to a large or very large extent), but only 52 percent said they had a strong and stable internet connection (compared to 48 percent and 54 percent, respectively, in 2020). That is to say, despite some improvements in computer availability, in 2021 nearly half of the parents still stated they had no stable and strong internet connection and one-third stated that no computer was regularly available for their children (RAMA, Ministry of Education 2021, 46–47).

Several factors are often mentioned as contributing to the devastating impact of COVID-19 on Arabs schools. One major factor is related to the difficult economic situation of the Arabs in Israel already existing prior to the crisis. A Bank of Israel report shows that in 2018, 45 percent of Arab households were below the poverty line. The report adds that the income of Jewish households was 32 percent greater than that of Arab households, and 40 percent of Arab households reported being in debt, compared to only 10 percent of Jewish households (Bank of Israel 2020, 79). In a survey conducted immediately after the breakout of the COVID-19 pandemic, 54 percent of Arabs reported that their economic situation had worsened, compared to 42 percent of Jews. At the same time, 17 percent of Arabs reported that their economic situation had severely worsened, three times more than among Jews (Bank of Israel 2020, 82).

A second factor is related to the weak standing of the Arab school system and the meager resources invested in the school system by local authorities. As mentioned earlier, Arab local authorities are largely disadvantaged compared to Jewish local authorities in terms of budgets, industrial zones, infrastructure, and local resources. This situation is reflected in the gap in resources invested in education by these municipalities. A 2020 report published by the Hashomrim organization on investment in students in local authorities in Israel revealed huge gaps between Jewish and Arab localities, both villages and cities. The ten municipalities that invested the most in students' education did not include a single Arab local authority, whereas of the 50 local councils that invested the least in each student, 46 were Arab. For example, the local council of the Jewish locality Rosh Pina invested NIS 15,000 per student, 35 times more than the Bedouin local council in the Negev, which invested only NIS 450 per student. This gap also exists in medium-sized municipalities. The city of Kiryat Bialik in the Haifa area invested NIS 11,000 per student per year, whereas the nearby Arab city of Shefa-'Amr invested only NIS 1,300 per student per year. In other words, the investment per student in Kiryat Bialik is eight times greater than in Shefa-'Amr (Shahar 2020).

It is no wonder then that the COVID-19 pandemic has further broadened the educational gaps between Jews and Arabs in Israel. Indeed, the response of localities to educational needs is closely connected to their socioeconomic standing. In this context, coping with the educational needs stemming from the pandemic requires unique organization of the education system, something more easily achieved in strong localities. Wealthy municipalities that function well know how to deal with changing situations, assimilate changes quickly, and allocate resources for the benefit of emerging needs (Shaked 2020).

Also, as morbidity from COVID-19 rose, a decision was made to shut down the education system in 40 Israeli localities, 37 of them in the bottom four socioeconomic clusters as determined by the CBS. This indicates that COVID-19 was primarily detrimental to the health of the weaker members of society, who consequently also suffered the greatest economic and educational harm. Precisely in localities situated in the socioeconomic periphery, the education system was closed for a long period, whereas in the strong localities studies continued as usual (Shaked 2020).

Summary

In this chapter I discussed the main developments in formal education among the Arabs in Israel since the establishment of the state, with a brief overview of the pre-state period. More specifically, I discussed the foundations of the state-designed policy of segregated control over the administrative structure of Arab education. I reviewed the destruction of the autonomous nucleus of private schools developed by the Palestinians in the Ottoman and Mandatory periods, thus demolishing Muslim private schools and subordinating Christian schools to the Israeli public education system. The major part of this chapter focused on the quantitative and qualitative developments in Arab education.

My analysis revealed a complex picture. On the one hand, there has been an impressive process of educational expansion over time at the various levels of formal education, from elementary school through middle school and senior high school education. Nevertheless, as far as early childhood education is concerned Jews still have an advantage over Arabs. On the other hand, a persistent qualitative gap remains between the two groups, as reflected in school achievements according to every national and international measure. In some respects, this gap has even widened over time, with the average scores of Arab students situated at the bottom of those of developing countries, whereas the scores of Jewish students resemble advanced Western and OECD standards. However, the analysis reveals that this gap mainly originated in structural-formal obstacles and discrimination that are related to differential state investment in education and socioeconomic background discrepancies between Jews and Arabs. Hence, the COVID-19 pandemic has just widened these qualitative gaps in favor of the advantaged Jewish students.

The differences in students' scores according to gender are especially interesting. In line with the international trend, the average scores of Jewish boys in mathematics are higher than those of Jewish girls, whereas girls score higher than boys in reading literacy and sciences. In contrast, the gender division among Arab students differs completely from that of Jews in Israel and of students from other countries in the world, with Arab girls scoring considerably higher than Arab boys in all subjects.

The next chapter focuses on another important aspect of formal policy that is reflected in the school curriculum in Arab and Jewish schools. More specifically, the chapter traces the main narratives that have been conveyed through the history curriculum to Jewish and Arab students over the past 70 years, from the establishment of Israel until the present period.

Chapter 4

Controlled "Multiculturalism"

A Comparative Analysis of the History Curriculum in Arab and Hebrew Schools, 1950–2020

Abstract

This chapter provides a comparative analysis of the history curriculum in the Arab and Hebrew schools in Israel. I begin by offering a brief theoretical framework. I then provide some background on Israeli society by discussing the discrepancy between the prevailing social structure that is marked by broad cultural diversity and the state's ideology that is devoid of multiculturalism. After that I discuss the development of a formal policy and goals for Arab education and trace the main narratives conveyed through the history curriculum to Jewish and Arab students from the establishment of Israel until the present period. The findings are examined through a critical multicultural perspective that sheds light both on the limitations of the education system and on the repercussions of the lack of a multicultural ideology on the possibility of enhancing peace education, diversity, and democratic citizenship.

The analysis is based on qualitative methods and on pertinent documents from the State Archives, in addition to specific reports on school curricula obtained from the Ministry of Education. The history curricula in the Arab and Hebrew schools over a period of nearly 70 years (1950–2020) underwent content analysis. Moreover, pertinent reports from Israeli newspapers, periodicals, and journalistic websites in Arabic, Hebrew, and English were extracted and analyzed.

Theoretical Framework:
History, Hegemony, and Multicultural Education

The teaching of history occupies a central place in Gramsci's discussion of the gap between school and society. According to Gramscian theory of cultural hegemony, dominant groups constantly attempt to maintain their hegemonic narrative while oppressing rival narratives. For this to happen, the state creates a myth in the form of a single narrative that ostensibly stands at the center of the national consensus. Hence, Gramscian theory of cultural hegemony revolves around the notion of "common sense," which he describes as a "collective noun" (Gramsci 1971, 325) that combines different worldviews into "a chaotic aggregate of disparate conceptions." This way of seeing the world is shaped by the dominant social class, yet its resilient capacity to absorb different and opposing conceptions also makes it "chaotic" and "unstable" (Bilton and Soltero 2020, 683). In this context, the worldview of the dominant social class is based on non-recognition and imposed homogenization of the aforementioned disparate conceptions with the aim of producing its own hegemonic conception (683).

In this regard, Apple (2013) maintains that the way educational systems structure knowledge and symbols is intimately related to the principles of social and cultural control in the society at large (20). Therefore, the claim of neutrality in the education system is patently false. Such a claim "ignores the fact that the knowledge that now gets into schools is already a choice from a much larger universe of possible social knowledge and principles. It is a form of cultural capital that comes from somewhere, that often reflects the perspectives and beliefs of powerful segments of our social collectivity" (25).

The above analysis, however, does not mean that no structural changes are made in the official knowledge introduced to subordinated schools over time. Drawing on Gramscian theory, Jones (2006) concludes that such changes are vital, mainly to maintain the hegemony of the dominant group. According to Jones, Antonio Gramsci recognized that social power is not a simple matter of domination on the one hand and subordination or resistance on the other. Rather than imposing their will, dominant groups within democratic societies generally govern with a good degree of consent from the people they rule, and maintaining that consent is dependent upon continuously repositioning the relationship between rulers and ruled. In order to maintain its authority, a ruling power must be sufficiently flexible to respond to new circumstances and to the changing wishes of those it rules (Jones 2006, 3–4). Therefore, the ruling group must introduce some changes to satisfy some of the expectations and values of the subordinated group. These controlled changes "treat the aspirations and view of subaltern people as an active element within the political and cultural programme of the hegemonizing bloc" (55). Such changes are introduced through school curricula as integral parts of the ideological and cultural hegemony, which are very effective in controlling the wider society, and particularly subordinate groups. Zimmerman contends that "through ideological hegemony, a dominant class is able to manufacture the rest of society's implicit consent to a particular way of seeing and making sense of the world" (based on Gramscian theory, Zimmerman 2018, 354).

Gramsci acknowledges that school is used by the dominant class as a mechanism of control and cultural hegemony. Nevertheless, he also asserts that education simultaneously contains the seeds of counterhegemony, as reflected in the community knowledge students bring with them and the possibilities of producing knowledge that serves as an alternative to the school curriculum (see chapter 1; also Tarlau 2017, 121). Yet under conditions of ongoing conflict, such a gap between school and community becomes unbridgeable. Indeed, under such conditions, nation states tend to use history to justify their ideological and territorial claims. Hence there is a dynamic relationship between wars and the development of national narratives. In nationalizing states, history constitutes a central subject in the school curriculum that is often used to shape collective identity and promote patriotism and national cohesion (Evans 2003; Ismailova 2004).

Not only do wars constitute a major source for producing national narratives, but such narratives can also serve as a tool for mass mobilization to war by providing a mythical and distorted interpretation of the past (Bar-Tal 1996). Hence, a model of cultural hegemony and homogenization yields only one "shared" narrative reflecting "one truth"—that of the dominant group. According to Bilton and Soltero (2020): "National cultural policies make sense of different interests, ideologies and values by providing a shared narrative, a foundational myth which underpins cultural policy outcomes. [These] mythic narratives are used to create harmony and consensus, especially 'historicising' narratives which retrospectively make sense of complex events into apparently uncontentious, simplified narrative truth" (681–82).

Students who belong to involuntary minorities find situations such as those described above to be especially problematic. (For a discussion of involuntary minorities, see Ogbu 1991; see also chapter 2.) Such situations produce a wide gap between the "formal knowledge" conveyed through the school curriculum and the community-informal knowledge these students acquire through unofficial sources (e.g., family, community, media, social networks).

The most problematic consequences of majority vs. minority narratives are usually associated with controversial dramatic events that erupted while the nation-state was being built and became an integral part of people's collective memories (e.g., wars and pogroms). Gross and Terra (2018) refer to such events as "difficult histories": "We call difficult history, periods that reverberate in the present and surface fundamental disagreements over who we are and what values we hold. Like the Civil War and its aftermath, these histories complicate the kind of positive patriotism that schools traditionally seek to develop" (52).

Liberal multicultural democracies today are investing more and more efforts in formulating an inclusive history curriculum that reinforces national cohesion while at the same time does not provoke conflicts between groups comprising the wider society. Indeed, the way the past is presented and constructed and/or reconstructed is crucially important to shaping future citizenship among majority and minority groups (see Jorgensen 2015; Banks 2004, 2017; Gross and Terra 2018). Yet in order for a curriculum to be inclusive it must recognize the "alternative narratives" of the majority and the minority alike (Ahonen 2001, 190). At the same time, alternative narratives can be introduced into the school system only in the context of critical multicultural education, which is a byproduct of a broader multi-cultural state policy.

Note that education systems often take a parochial approach to the history curriculum by considering it to be a "body of truth not to be questioned, criticized, or modified" (Banks 2006, 25). Hence, asking about the content of the curriculum is not sufficient. It is also important to ask what is missing. Raymond Williams (1976) referred to this practice as "selective tradition," in which the dominant group decides what kind of knowledge is to be defined as "official knowledge" worthy of being passed down to future generations: "From whole possible areas of past and present, certain meanings and practices are chosen for emphasis, certain other meanings and practices are reinterpreted, diluted, or put into forms which support or at least do not contradict other elements within the effective dominant culture" (205; see also Apple 1999, 11). Such a situation generates ongoing tension between the hegemonic discourses that form the official curriculum and the discourses of subordinate groups as "they might appear in 'forgotten' or erased histories" (Aronowitz and Giroux 1993, 128). Aronowitz and Giroux pointed out that the school curriculum should allow students to voice their opinions and to "check and criticize the history they are told against the one they have lived" (104). In addition, Banks (1996) proposed that students be given the opportunity to create alternative knowledge in a way that challenges the official knowledge offered by the formal curriculum (21). Other researchers suggested that in the global era, the school curriculum, including the history curriculum, should be internationalized by exposing students to international-global and cosmopolitan content rather focusing mainly on local-national issues (see Yemini and Bronshtein 2016). This is especially relevant for those living in conflict-ridden societies so as to enable them to acquire a "deep understanding of the 'other,' including knowing the history and the narratives of groups who are different from (and even competing with) our own" (Yemini and Fulop 2015, 42).

Israel: Multiple Cultures without Multiculturalism

In terms of its social structure and its population, Israel is a pluralistic society comprising many diverse cultures. The Jewish population is extremely heterogenous, originating from about 100 countries and differentiated by ethnicity—Ashkenazim (European/American origin) and Mizrachim or Sephardim (North African and Asian origin); religious orientation (religious and nonreligious); and length of time in Israel. Among the central immigrant groups are Russian Israelis, who immigrated from the former Soviet Union since 1989 and today form about 20 percent of the Jewish (or non-Arab) population (see Ben-Rafael et al. 2016; Ben-Rafael and Sternberg 2009; Al-Haj 2019; CBS 2017). These Russian immigrants clearly form a new distinct ethnic group in Israel (Al-Haj 2019). The Arab population is also heterogenous, comprising 85.5 percent Muslims, 7.5 percent Druze, and 7 percent Christians (SAI 2021, table 2.3, 4–5).

Yet despite Israel's many and distinct collective identities and its cultural pluralism, no multicultural policy has developed in the country (see Al-Haj 2002). Chapter 2 offers a detailed analysis of the obstacles to multiculturalism and multicultural democracy in Israel, especially in terms of Jewish-Arab relations. Among these are Israel's ethnonational character, securitization of state-minority relations, and blurred majority-minority boundaries. An examination of the entire spectrum of Israeli society may reveal additional barriers to multiculturalism, including the lack of separation between state and religion (see Kremnitzer and Fuchs 2016) and the "republican approach" that demands a single, homogenous, Hebrew-Zionist culture. As such, the dominant culture perceives the other cultures as inferior and rejects diversity and multiculturalism (see Smooha 2007). This fact has served to marginalize and alienate minority groups, including the Palestinian Arab citizens, the ultra-Orthodox population, and new immigrants whose mother tongue is not Hebrew (see Tannenbaum 2009).

The external Israeli-Palestinian conflict has deeply affected prospects for developing multiculturalism in Israel. This conflict is undoubtedly one of the most conspicuous national conflicts in modern history, with deep repercussions for the Middle East and the international community as a whole. The roots of this conflict go back to the late 19th century and it remains unresolved, so that it is considered to be an "intractable conflict" (see Bar-Tal 1996, 1999). The core of this conflict is the major dispute between the Zionist and Palestinian national movements over Palestine-Eretz Israel. Since the 1930s, the international community has devoted ongoing efforts to find a solution for this conflict that would be acceptable to both national movements. To date these efforts have been unfruitful, and the clashes between the two peoples have continued, peaking in the 1948 Israeli-Arab war, which marked a turning point in the history of the two peoples and of the Middle East as a whole. The war ended with the defeat of the Arabs, the establishment of the State of Israel, and the displacement of a large number of Palestinians, who became refugees in Arab countries (see Al-Haj and Yaniv 1983).

Beginning in the late 1970s, Israel signed a number of peace agreements with Arab countries. The first was the Camp David Accords in 1978, which laid the groundwork for peace with Egypt, the largest and leading Arab country. The Palestinian intifada, which erupted in the territories at the end of 1987, had a profound impact on both Palestinian and Israeli society, proving that the status quo option of occupation is not realistic (Al-Haj, Katz, and Shai 1993). In practice, the intifada paved the way for the Oslo Accords in 1993 and launched the Israeli-Palestinian peace process after a century of conflict between the Palestinian and Zionist national movements. Embarking on the road to resolving the Palestinian problem provided legitimacy for Jordan to sign a peace agreement with Israel and for a number of other Arab countries (Morocco, Tunisia, and Oman) to establish partial relations.

On September 15, 2020, the Abraham Accords were signed, normalizing relations between Israel and a number of Arab states, specifically the United Arab Emirates and Bahrain. Subsequently Sudan also joined the agreement. The Israel–Morocco normalization agreement, which is not officially included in the Abraham Accords but is substantially identical to them, was signed as well.

Nevertheless, the Palestinian issue remains the core problem of the Israeli-Arab conflict and continues to threaten political and regional stability in the Middle East. Since the Al-Aqsa intifada in 2000, the peace process between Israel and the Palestinians has continued to stagnate and even deteriorate. It seems that Israelis and Palestinians alike have shifted from conflict resolution to conflict management, such that all efforts toward promoting the Israeli-Palestinian peace have been frozen (see Al-Haj 2019).

This background raises a number of key questions about the educational system in general and the history curriculum in particular: What are the implications of the aforementioned contextual factors on the history curriculum in Arab and Jewish schools in Israel? How does the lack of multicultural ideology in Israel affect educational content? What official knowledge and narratives have been conveyed to Jewish and Palestinian Arab students through the history curriculum? What have been the main trends in the history curriculum over time? What has been the impact of the continuing Israeli-Palestinian conflict and the shift to conflict resolution (and the stagnating peace process) on how history is taught?

In the next section, I consider these questions. I begin with the stated policy and goals for Arab education. After that I trace the main developments over time in how history is taught to Jewish and Arab students in Israeli high schools.

Goals for Arab Education over Time

Three main periods emerge from an analysis of the goals for Arab education: 1950s–early 1970s, mid-1970s–1990s, and late 1990s–the present time.

The First Period: 1950s–early 1970s

According to conventional thinking, Arab education in Israel functioned for nearly three decades without any defined goals (Peres, Erlich, and Yuval-Davis 1968; Mari 1978; Nakhleh 1977). To support this claim, scholars have repeatedly quoted Emanuel Kupileivitch, former director of the Department of Education for Arabs, who criticized the lack of a specific goal for Arab education. In his article titled "Education in the Arab Sector," Kupileivitch had this to say:

> When the legislature defined the goals of Israeli education in general in the Law of State Education 1953, no thought was given to the goals of education for the Arab population. Indeed, most of the goals listed in section two of the law (achievement of knowledge, reverence for work . . .) also apply to the Arab students. Two additional goals (love of country and loyalty to the state) may also be considered as legitimate goals for Arab education. But the inclusion of two other goals (loyalty to the people of Israel, and the cultural values of Israel) raises suspicion. Actually, we cannot, nor do we want to sow in the hearts of Arab students a recognition of "mutual destiny and purpose with Jewish people." There is room at the top of the goals for Arab education towards the acquisition of Arab cultural values. Only after we establish this goal may we ask, to what extent they should be exposed to the cultural values of Israel. Put differently, the basic question is: Should we educate Israeli Arabs as Israelis, as Arabs, or as Israeli Arabs? (Kupileivitch 1973, 325)

Hence, most of those examining official policy toward Arab education came to the conclusion that this policy was ambiguous and lacked any particular direction. Some also claimed that policymakers were confused about decisions concerning the formal goals of Arab education and that the declared policy was more progressive and liberal than the actual one (*Haaretz*, February 19, 1971).

If the goals of education are analyzed merely at the declarative level, these conclusions may indeed be true. The main paragraph of the State Education Law 1953 stipulates the following: "To base elementary education in the state of Israel upon the values of Jewish culture and scientific achievements, upon love of the homeland and loyalty to the state and to the people of Israel, upon belief in agriculture and labor, upon pioneer training, and the aspiration towards a society built on freedom, equality, tolerance, mutual aid and, love of one's fellow man" (Tzartzur 1981, 114). The wording of this goal obviously does not take the needs of Arab education into consideration and clearly ignores the cultural and national uniqueness of the Arab minority in Israel. Educators and public figures have directed a great deal of criticism toward this omission, and many have asked about the social and political repercussions of avoiding any consideration of the national aspect of Arab education (Al-Haj 1995a).

Yet this does not mean that no goals were defined for Arab education. Our content analysis, which was based on a large number of documents from the State Archives that were formerly classified as secret or top secret, shows that formal policy regarding Arab education was an integral part of a wider policy toward the Arab minority in Israel. The prime minister's adviser for Arab affairs and other Arabists (Jewish "experts" on Arab affairs) in various government offices played an active role in formulating this policy, which was driven by the perception of Arabs as a security risk and a source of disturbances and instability. The means adopted to reduce this danger were control on the one hand and improving the conditions of the Arab population on the other (see chapter 3).

PUBLIC CRITICISM OF THE GOALS AND CURRICULA FOR THE ARAB SCHOOLS 1950S–EARLY 1970S

Criticism of the Arab school curriculum had already begun by the 1950s. Rashid Hussein, a renowned Arab poet, aptly described the social and political repercussions of stripping national content from Arab education:

> It is a known fact that he who has no self-respect will not respect others. He who has no national feeling cannot respect other nationalities. If the Arab student is hindered from learning about his people, his nationality and his homeland in school, he will compensate for the lack in his home and on the street. He will eagerly accept anything he hears from other people or reads in the newspaper, and this may lead him into a wrong and distorted view of nationalism. The school, which has deprived him of something in which everyone takes pride, will be regarded by him as an enemy. Instead of learning in school the meaning of a nationalism imbued with humanism, he will absorb only a distorted version. What will the school have achieved? What kind of generation of Arab youth will it have educated? Instead of educating its students to believe in fraternity and peace and to believe in the sincerity of its teachers, the school will bring forth a bewildered and confused generation, which looks at the facts in a distorted manner, and considers other nations to be their enemies; a generation filled with inferiority complexes, feelings of abasement, unable to take pride in its youth, in its homeland and its nationality. (Hussein 1957, 46)

A group of Israeli sociologists, including Yochanan Peres, Avishai Erlich, and Nira Yuval-Davis, later conducted a study comparing the goals and curricula in Arab and Hebrew schools (Peres, Erlich, and Yuval-Davis 1968). They indicated that policymakers sought to reach a compromise that would reconcile contradicting trends: achieving equality as opposed to preserving Jewish dominance, developing general values as opposed to national values, and granting autonomous status to Arab education as opposed to seeking total integration into the Jewish educational system. Hence, the curriculum in the Arab schools never achieved a balance between Arab national feelings and loyalty to the state, as policymakers had hoped (Al-Haj 1995a). Instead Arab national identity was blurred and Arab pupils were educated for inferiority and self-denial vis-à-vis the Jewish majority (*Hed Hakhinukh*, December 12, 1968; *Al-Hamishmar*, August 13, 1968).

The above analysis leads to the clear conclusion that Arab educational goals and curricula were aimed at creating submissive Arabs, ready to accept their inferiority vis-à-vis the superiority of the Jewish majority, while at the same time disparaging, weakening, and exterminating their Palestinian Arab identity (Peres, Erlich, and Yuval-Davis 1968; Mari 1978; Lustick 1980).

Restating Goals and Curricula for Arab Schools in the Mid-1970s

As indicated in chapter 2, since the early 1970s the Arabs in Israel have been undergoing a rapid process of social and political change that has boosted their national consciousness and accelerated their politicization. The Arab schools were not excluded from this new trend. Ministry of Education officials realized that continuing the former situation in the Arab schools in terms of goals and curricula might generate more alienation among the younger generations of Arabs. Indeed, they described this new trend among Arab pupils as disturbing and anti-Israeli (*Zu-Haderekh*, February 14, 1971). A study conducted by Peres lent support to these fears. This study revealed that purging any national content from the Arab school curricula may be responsible, at least in part, for the alienation of Arab youth from the State of Israel, which accelerated after the 1967 war (*Haaretz*, February 21, 1971).

In 1971, the Ministry of Education appointed a special committee headed by Aharon Yadlin, deputy minister of education, to draft new goals for Arab education (*Zu-Haderekh*, February 14, 1971). In February 1972, this committee submitted a document to Yigal Allon, minister of education, containing general recommendations for Arab education, including suggested principles for educational goals. According to this document, Arab education should be based on:

1. Education in the spirit of peace.

2. Education for loyalty to the state, emphasizing the commonality of all citizens while stressing the unique characteristics of Israeli Arabs.

3. Developing plans aimed to ease the social and cultural absorption of Arabs in Israel.

4. Development of Arab, Israeli and universal cultural values.

5. Educating female students toward autonomy and improvement of their status. (Ministry of Education and Culture 1975, 13)

The importance of the Yadlin document lies in the fact that for the first time it directed major public attention to the uniqueness of Arab education and the need to formulate particular goals for Arab pupils. Nevertheless, this document contained many internal contradictions and was far from reflecting the needs and aspirations of the Arabs in Israel. Arab educators harshly criticized the document's negligence in not dealing with the national identity of Arabs. They equally criticized the attempt to create a "unique Israeli Arab" identity divorced from the Arabs' genuine national and cultural roots, which are uncompromisingly linked to the Arab world and the Palestinians (see Al-Haj 1996, 2006).

Before the Yadlin document was implemented, the director general of the Ministry of Education formed a new committee headed by Dr. Matty Peled and composed of seven Arabs and eight Jews (hereafter the Peled Committee). The main purpose of the Peled Committee was to draw up Israel's goals for education for the 1980s. The Peled Committee examined several aspects related to Arab education, among them services, goals, and curricula. This committee published its conclusions in a report titled "Planning Education for the 1980s" (Ministry of Education and Culture 1975). The Peled Committee suggested the following goals for Arab education:

> The goal of state education in the Arab sector in Israel is to base education on the foundations of Arab culture; on the achievement of science, on the aspiration for peace between Israel and its neighbors, on love of the **shared country by all citizens, and loyalty to the state of Israel** through emphasizing their common interests and through encouraging the uniqueness of Israeli Arabs, on the knowledge of the Jewish culture, on respect of creative

work and on aspiration for a society built on freedom, equality, mutual help and love of mankind. (Ministry of Education and Culture 1975, cited by Mari 1978, 53–54)

For Hebrew education the committee proposed the following goals:

To help young people form a full personality as Jews who iden-tify themselves with the heritage and destiny of their nation; are keenly aware of their uniqueness as Jews; are keenly aware of the ties between the People of Israel and the Land of Israel, between the People of Israel and their State and the Jewish People in the Diaspora; and have a sense of common fate and responsibility for their nation.

    To inculcate the values of Jewish culture by the practical and academic acquisition of this heritage, as it was consolidated in all the ethnic groups of the People of Israel until recent gen-erations in their homeland and in the Diaspora. At the same time, they should be exposed to the best cultural heritages of other nations and become familiar with the culture of the Arab minority. (Ministry of Education and Culture 1975, cited by Smooha 1989, 117)

The Peled Report was submitted on September 29, 1976. Yet, the minister of education rephrased the suggested goals for Arab education by changing the pivotal sentence referring to the "**love of the shared coun-try by all its citizens.**" The word **"shared"** was deleted and the goal was changed to "**love the country**" (Ministry of Education and Culture 1977). According to this change, Arab pupils are not educated to love the country as their own country but rather as the homeland of the Jewish people, thus repudiating the spirit of the former goals. Unlike in the case of the goals for Arab education, the Ministry of Education made no change in the suggested goals for Hebrew education. Therefore, whereas Arab pupils were deprived of the opportunity to be educated as genuine partners in the State of Israel, Jewish pupils were educated to love Israel as their homeland and the home-land of the Jewish people everywhere. The recommendations of the Peled Committee were ultimately not implemented and the formal goals of Arab education remained unchanged until 2000. Nevertheless, the revised Peled Committee report served as a starting point for reformulating the curricula for the Arab schools (*Hinukh Mevugarim Beyisrael*, August 1977, 6).

Amendment of the State Education Law, 2000

The aforementioned recommendations were not included in the State Education Law until 2000, when the second clause of this law was amended (see Ministry of Education 2000). The 2000 amendment, which included 11 subclauses, reiterates the recommendations of the Peled Committee drafted in 1975. Nevertheless, the amendment highlights two main points based on the neoliberal approach adopted by the Ministry of Education since the mid-1970s:

First, the amendment emphasizes the character of Israel as a Jewish democratic state together with general principles of human rights, equality, and striving for peace and tolerance between peoples and nations (subclause 2 [2]). Second, for the first time the amendment mentions the principles of "equal opportunities, diversity and the right to be different": "Granting of equal opportunities to every child, to allow them to develop according to their way, and create an atmosphere that encourages and supports diversity" (subclause 2 [8]). Only one subclause (2–11) explicitly mentions the Arab population: "To get to know the language, culture, history and unique tradition of the Arab population in Israel and other groups in the State of Israel and to acknowledge the equal rights of all citizens in Israel."

An analysis of the 2000 amendment to the State Education Law reveals many internal contradictions among the various subclauses. The important principles of "equal opportunities, diversity and the right to be different" stated in subclause 2 (8) are contradictory to the underlying meaning of the entire amendment. While this subclause highlights well-known multicultural principles, the amendment as a whole emphasizes the character of Israel, first as a Jewish state and second as a democratic state in which equal rights for non-Jewish groups, including Arabs, are recognized at the individual rather than the collective-group level. In this sense, the Arab population in Israel is treated as a linguistic-cultural minority rather than as a national or indigenous minority. Unlike multicultural democracies that place special emphasis on group rights, and primarily the rights of indigenous groups (see Kymlicka 2007a; Banting and Kymlicka 2006), this amendment, like the original 1953 State Education Law, totally overlooks the group rights of the Palestinian citizens and in no way relates to them as an indigenous minority deserving of group differentiated rights.

Hence, the declared goal in subclause 2 (8) of "granting equal opportunities to every child, to allow them to develop according to their way, and create an atmosphere that encourages and supports diversity" does not apply when it comes to Palestinian children in Israel. For this reason, the 2000 amendment has been continuously criticized by Arab Palestinian intellectuals and political leaders, who sought modifications of Israeli legislation that would recognize the status of Palestinians in Israel as an indigenous national collective and guarantee educational autonomy for the Arab community to ensure equal educational and cultural rights between Jews and Arabs in Israel (Jabareen and Agbariya 2017, 55).

How have these general goals been reflected in the history curriculum in Arab schools? Taking into consideration that Jewish-Arab relations in Israel have developed in the context of an ongoing national conflict, how have the rival historical narratives been conveyed to Jewish and Arab students? Does the history taught in the Arab schools in Israel include any independent Palestinian narrative?

In the following sections, I attempt to answer these questions. First, I provide a brief review of the literature. Then, I conduct a systematic comparative analysis of the history curricula in Arab and Jewish schools in Israel over time.

History Curriculum in Arab and Jewish Schools in Israel: Literature Review

Studies on the history curriculum in Arab schools for the most part emphasized that, despite some changes over time, the Jewish-Zionist narrative has clearly dominated and no independent Palestinian narrative has been taught (see, for example, Barghouti 1991; Al-Haj 1995a, 2005b, 2021; Abu-Sa'ad 2008, 2019; Shemesh 2009; Hourani 2010). The main differences between these studies are related to terminology and the division into periods over time. Hana Shemesh differentiates between four main periods/generations, as reflected in the history textbooks produced by the Ministry of Education during each period. In the first period (1948–1970), which Shemesh refers to as the "Zionist generation," the textbooks in the Arab schools mirrored those used in the Jewish schools, with their dominant, Jewish-Zionist content. She calls the second period or generation (1970–1990) the "ambivalent generation." During this period, Arab (but not Palestinian) content was introduced into textbooks for Arab schools, along with universal democratic content emphasizing the shared values between Islam and Judaism, with the aim of enhancing citizenship orientation and boosting the integration of Arabs within Israeli society. Shemesh refers to the third generation of textbooks

(1990–2003) as the "challenging generation." For the first time during this period, a number of chapters on the Israeli-Arab conflict and the Palestinians were added to the history textbooks. Yet a large gap still remained between the declared goal of the official curriculum on the one hand ("to deepen the sense of belonging to the Palestinian people, the Arab nation and the State of Israel among Arab students") and the way these subjects were presented in the textbooks on the other. Thus, very few textbooks were written that corresponded to the curriculum (Shemesh 2009, 15). In the fourth period (2003–2008), known as the "generation of challenge," more Palestinian content was added and more Arab scholars were involved in preparing the history textbooks for Arab schools, yet no independent Palestinian narrative was introduced (Shemesh 2009, 18).

Hourani (2010), who analyzed the history syllabus through 1999, contends that the curriculum designed for Palestinian Arab schools in Israel passed through three main periods. The first period from the 1950s to the 1970s was characterized by "assimilation into the Jewish nationhood and de-nationalism from the Palestinian identity." The period from the 1970s to the 1980s "witnessed a trend of citizenship education," although this type of citizenship was oriented toward strengthening loyalty to the State of Israel, rather than "patriotic affiliation to the State of Israel." The third period was between 1982 and 1999, when national Arab values were introduced into the syllabus for Palestinian Arab schools, but the curriculum "remained detached from Palestinian-Arab national values" (Hourani 2010, 304–5).

Likewise, Abu-Sa'ad (2008) concludes that the history curriculum and textbooks in Arab schools have been oriented toward reeducating Arab students to "accept the loss of their history and identity" and to suppress their Palestinian Arab narrative (39).

As far as the curriculum in the Jewish schools is concerned, Bar-Tal (1999) concludes that despite changes that took place over time, the textbooks in the Jewish schools generally reflect the "intractable conflict," whereby the education system creates an ethos that supports the continuity of the conflict and produces psychological conditions that enable students to cope successfully with a state of conflict (480–81). In a detailed study of the curriculum in the Jewish schools, Bar-Tal examined 124 textbooks for teaching Hebrew language and literature, history, geography, and social studies, used at different grade levels from the 1950s through the mid-1990s. He found a variegated picture over time, showing more continuity than change with regard to Jewish-Arab relations. Societal beliefs emphasizing "security" and Jewish heroism, positive self-image, and victimization appeared frequently.

It should be noted that the history curriculum in the Jewish schools is not only a byproduct of formal decisions made by the Ministry of Education. Rather, to a large extent it mirrors the perceptions held by the Jewish public at large. This issue is well reflected in an article by journalist and columnist Kalman Liebskind published in the Hebrew newspaper *Ma'ariv*. In his attempt to explain why the Palestinian narrative regarding the 1948 war (which the Palestinians refer to as the *Nakba* [catastrophe]) should not be heard in the Hebrew education system, Liebskind had this to say:

> The "Nakba" issue is no longer an issue on the list of topics for class discussion. . . . To give the narrative of the "Nakba" a place in the Israeli classroom is to say that the view that holds that we have nothing to do here because our entire existence here is theft, robbery and injustice, is a view that needs to be heard. . . . To teach the Nakba narrative alongside our narrative is to say that there is no good and bad, no truth and lie, everything depends on the point of view, and all points of view are legitimate. There is our truth and the truth of those who tried to destroy us. . . . The Ministry of Education should not be ashamed to present a position, a clear position that says that if we had not won that war [the 1948 war], and if there had not been "the Nakba," we would not be here today to conduct this discussion. (Liebskind 2015)

Hence, the entire issue of contradictory Israeli and Palestinian narratives is considered by the Jewish majority, and mainly the political right-wing, to be a zero-sum game. In this context, any legitimacy given to the Palestinian narrative is tantamount to delegitimizing the very existence of the State of Israel and jeopardizing the Jewish-Zionist narrative, which is based on a single truth—that of the Jewish majority.

Some modifications were introduced into the education system in the 1980s, with the aim of enhancing democratic values and civil society in the Hebrew schools (Resnik 1999). By and large, though, the main content of school curricula has remained particularistic and very much loaded with nationalist religious content. This conclusion is based on Julia Resnik's comprehensive analysis of curricula in the public (nonreligious) Hebrew schools since the establishment of Israel. After a thorough analysis of the school curricula in Bible, history, literature, and civics, Resnik (1999) concludes: "The picture that emerges from this description is a gloomy one from the standpoint of democracy and the rule of law. The idea of civil society in the construction of the national subject is mere flotsam in a sea of Jewish religious particularism" (507). In a more recent study, Resnik (2006) concludes the following: "Formal education system in Israel is characterized by a centralistic structure, particularistic content and a clear domination of the collective Jewish identity vis-à-vis the Arab identity. This system has never adopted any multicultural orientation or agenda whether towards the Jewish-Arab divide, the labor migrants or even regarding ethnic and immigrant groups within the Jewish majority itself" (586). Hence, the school curriculum in Israeli-Jewish schools basically conveys a negative image of Arabs, thereby internalizing the stereotypes of the "backward" and "hostile" Arabs among Jewish students (see Abu-Sa'ad 2004, 2007).

The aforementioned situation is especially evident in the history curriculum, which is heavily based on local-national content (see Yemini and Fulop 2015). Arie Kizel (2008) reaches a similar conclusion. Based on his analysis of four versions of the history curriculum in the Hebrew schools over nearly 60 years (1948–2006), he concludes that both the history curriculum and the textbooks have been systematically used to convey the official narrative of the Israeli establishment with its three main components: Zionist, Jewish, and Western. In addition, since the establishment of Israel, the writers of history textbooks have tended to devote major attention to political and military history at the expense of social and cultural history (173). As a matter of fact, this trend is part of the "militaristic education" that is heavily conveyed in the Jewish state schools in Israel (see Ben-Amos and Bet-El 2003).

Comparative Analysis of History Curriculum in Arab and Jewish Schools

The aforementioned studies have made a major contribution to understanding the deficiencies of the history curriculum and the minor changes that have occurred over time. However, I contend that this curriculum must also be situated within a systematic comparative analysis that simultaneously delineates the main developments in the teaching of history in Arab and Jewish schools from a critical multicultural perspective.

To this end, I conducted a content analysis of the history curricula taught in Arab and Jewish high schools in Israel over nearly seven decades, from the establishment of Israel to the present time. My analysis shows that the aforementioned trends regarding the formulation of the general policy and goals of education have also affected school content, including the history curriculum. Therefore, I divided the major developments in the history curriculum into three main periods, in parallel to my above analysis of the policy and goals of education: the 1950s to the early 1970s, the mid-1970s to the 1990s, and the late 1990s to the present. In what follows, I briefly outline the main characteristics of each period.

THE FIRST PERIOD: 1950s–EARLY 1970s

As early as January 1949 a special subcommittee was formed through the Ministry of Minorities to handle the problem of goals and textbooks for Arab schools. This committee was authorized to disqualify textbooks defined as politically or pedagogically defective or for other reasons. The committee was also asked to find ways to produce new and suitable syllabuses (Ministry of Minorities 1949, 23).

For at least two years after the establishment of Israel, Arab pupils used the textbooks that had been used during the Mandatory period. Some of these books included national and sometimes even anti-Zionist content (*The Jerusalem Post*, August 11, 1954). Yet they were soon replaced by manuals written by Arab teachers or Arabic-speaking Jewish teachers under the supervision of the Ministry of Education. Arab teachers received very strict instructions to omit parts of history and geography books defined as "nationally oriented" (Ben-Or 1951, 5).

This dismantling of the former curriculum and textbooks was aimed at tightening state control over the content of Arab education. Taking into consideration that no books were allowed to be imported from neighboring Arab countries, Arabs in Israel had no alternative but to accept books and curricula produced by the Israel Ministry of Education (Copty 1990, 316).

Until the end of the 1950s, there was no special history curriculum in the Arab schools. As in the case of other subjects, instruction depended on the teachers, each of whom prepared a course book that contained all the material to be taught. These books were naturally subject to supervision and monitoring by the inspector, who could control the material. Only in 1961 did the Ministry of Education begin to prepare an Arabic version of history textbooks. In practice, books were translated from Hebrew into Arabic almost word for word. The only difference was the addition of a chapter on the history of the Arabs, which was nowhere to be found in the Hebrew textbooks (Barghouti 1991, 115).

A comparison of the objectives of teaching history in the Jewish and Arab schools during this period reveals consistency in everything associated with the goals mentioned above. Whereas in the Jewish schools the emphasis was on the Jewish national theme, the curriculum for Arab students ignored the Arab national theme. Arab students were taught "that human culture is the fruit of the combined endeavors of all peoples of the world," whereas Jewish students learned that the "Jewish people played a central role in shaping human culture." Curricular goals were aimed at indoctrinating Arab students to believe in Jewish superiority through repeated emphasis on the passive role of Arabs in creating human culture, while magnifying the role of the Jewish people, and the shared destiny of the two peoples. Values of coexistence were not conveyed to Jewish students, for whom the Arabs as a people were included under the term "other nations." What is more, Arab students were expected to understand the importance of the State of Israel to the Jewish people rather than to Jews and Arabs alike.

That is to say, the history curriculum precisely reflected the asymmetric Jewish-Arab relations in Israel. Furthermore, the identity of Arab students was totally overlooked, and there was no mention whatsoever of strengthening national consciousness, which constituted a core value in the history curriculum of the Hebrew schools. Moreover, the Arab narrative was totally ignored, with Arabs referred to as "others" who are submerged within "other nations" and have no specific narrative or history to be recognized, either by Jewish students or by Arab students themselves.

This asymmetry between the Arab schools and the Jewish schools was also reflected in the allocation of teaching hours between world history, Arab history, and Jewish history. World history occupied about 60 percent of the curriculum in both the Arab and the Jewish schools. Other historical topics were divided quite asymmetrically. Whereas the Jewish schools devoted about 40 percent of their history classes to Jewish history, the Arab schools dedicated only about half as much time to Arab history. What is more, whereas about 20 percent of the history classes for Arab students was devoted to Jewish and Zionist history, Jewish students spent less than 2 percent of their history studies on parallel Arab topics (based on Al-Haj 1996a, 104–6).

THE SECOND PERIOD: MID-1970S–1990S

Since the early 1970s, criticism of the school curriculum among the Arab population in Israel has been growing. For its part, the Ministry of Education formed a number of committees to deal with changes in the Israeli education system in general and in Arab education in particular. As mentioned earlier, two major committees were appointed by the Ministry of Education: the Yadlin Committee (1971) and the Peled Committee (1975). While the report of the first committee had no substantial impact on Arab education, the revised report of the Peled Committee paved the way for some changes in the school curriculum. These changes were reflected in the second version of the history curriculum, which went into effect in the early 1980s.

In its statement of objectives this new curriculum made a distinction between information and values. In addition to the study of "historical facts," information also included the development of an analytical approach and the ability to analyze social phenomenon in the present and past (Ministry of Education and Culture 1982, 2–3).

With regard to values, the following objectives were defined:

1. To develop skills for judging historical events on the basis of general human values.

2. To instill a spirit of tolerance and understanding of the feelings, traditions, and ways of life of other people and other nations.

3. To develop a feeling of identification with the Arab nation and its culture and with the State of Israel and all its inhabitants.

The main change in the new history curriculum was its reference to *identification with the Arab nation* as a central objective. But this new version was also vague, cautiously stated, and far from being parallel to the objectives set for the teaching of history in the Hebrew schools. Furthermore, the notion of identification with the Arab nation was accompanied by "identification with the state of Israel and all its inhabitants," without any indication of the status of Arabs in the state or even a general declaration indicating that Israel is a "state shared by all its inhabitants." No less significant, identification with the Arab nation was not necessarily associated with an intensification of national consciousness. What is more, the Arab nation was mentioned in general terms, with no reference to the Palestinian people.

It also should be noted that the revised high school curriculum for Arab schools emphasized Jewish-Arab coexistence, including an understanding and appreciation of the Jewish people's contribution to human culture and advancement. The curriculum for Jewish schools did not incorporate parallel objectives (Al-Haj 2021).

Arab intellectuals criticized the lack of balance and symmetry in the official objectives proposed for Arabs and Jews. The core of this criticism was that the proposed objectives included no recognition, either overt or indirect, of the fact that the Arabs in Israel constitute a national minority and are an inseparable part of the Palestinian people. What is more, only in the Arab schools did the goals emphasize the aspiration for peaceful Jewish-Arab coexistence. The goals drafted for Jewish schools made no mention of aspirations for peace or coexistence (Tzartzur 1981).

The Third Period: A New History Curriculum, Late 1990s–Present

General Guidelines

The new history curriculum for Jewish junior high schools was published in 1998, and an experimental history curriculum for Arab senior high schools was published in 1999. Even though the two stages are not parallel, it is possible to remain faithful to the comparative perspective because the analysis focuses on the overarching declared goals that guide the curricula, which do not differ significantly between junior and senior high school. This fact is conspicuous in the general guidelines, which explicitly state that the two curricula are complementary: the curriculum for junior high school focuses on chronology, while the curriculum for senior high school delves more deeply into the subject matter (Ministry of Education 1998, 6).

The section of the curriculum that covers the general objectives of teaching history includes the following statement: "The abundance of past events and the sources that deal with them make it impossible to become familiar with all of history. Historical study is selective by its very nature, in accordance with various criteria" (Ministry of Education 1998, 9). This is an important statement and reflects the familiar situation of "selective tradition" that is followed in most educational systems. It is true that the authors of the curriculum did not append any clarifications to their statement, thereby leaving a number of key points without defined answers: What is the basis for selection in the curriculum under discussion? What standards are used to determine what information should and should not be conveyed to pupils? And what precisely are the "various criteria" referred to, which in the final analysis are responsible for setting the goals and content of the study of history in Arab and Jewish schools?

The second significant section is section 4, which outlines the specific central objective of the study of history: "In the teaching of history we must provide the pupils with a knowledge and understanding of Jewish history and human history, with an emphasis on the distinctive course of the Jewish people" (Ministry of Education 1998, 9). This section in fact demonstrates continuity rather than change in the history curriculum. Similar to the situation in the 1950s, the enhancement of Jewish national awareness is the central axis of the history curriculum. There is also no mention of exposing Jewish pupils to the rival narrative of the Palestinian national movement or that of pan-Arab nationalism. This goal is subsumed under the general objective of familiarity with human history.

The other three sections in the curriculum for Jewish schools are general and relate to pedagogical principles relevant to the study of history, such as the need to emphasize social and cultural variety and to learn about earlier generations, the need for perspective on trends in human development, and the importance of seeing the present as the outcome of the past (Ministry of Education 1998, 9–10).

The goals associated with information were conventional and, as noted, were also included in the previous version of the history curriculum published in the early 1980s. The heading of values, however, included something new, although not far-reaching. The first two sections referred to very important educational values, such as fostering judgment of historical events on the basis of humane and ethical values and fostering understanding for and tolerance of the feelings, traditions, and ways of life of other peoples and nations. Yet after having stated these liberal generalities, the curriculum in practice failed to engage with the cardinal point of placing the Palestinian narrative alongside the Zionist narrative throughout the teaching of history in Jewish and Arab schools.

In addition, because the history curriculum was drafted after the beginning of the peace process in the region, and specifically after the signing of the Oslo Accords with the Palestinians (1993), the peace treaty with Jordan (1994), and the first steps toward a comprehensive peace in the Middle East, one might have expected the Ministry of Education to confront the central question: What is the role of the history curriculum in the transition from conflict to peace? What new themes, both informational and value-driven, reflect the historical change taking place in the region?

These questions were overlooked in the enumeration of the general goals, which related to information, skill acquisition, types of historical concepts, analysis of social phenomena, development of historical thinking, fostering judgment of historical events, fostering understanding and tolerance, and fostering identification with the people and the state.

In fact, the only innovation with regard to values can be found in the goals set for the Arab schools: "Fostering a sense of affiliation with the Palestinian Arab people and the Arab people on one hand, and with the State of Israel and its citizens on the other" (Ministry of Education 1999a, 8–9). This statement about fostering a sense of affiliation, though not identification, with the Palestinian Arab people appeared for the first time as a central objective of the history curriculum in Arab schools. In the previous curriculum (1982), the stated goals related to developing "a feeling of identification with the Arab nation and its culture," with no specific reference to the Palestinian people.

It should be mentioned that in the Arab curriculum (1999a), the goal of "fostering a sense of affiliation with the Palestinian Arab people" was followed by the additional goal of fostering a sense of affiliation "with the State of Israel and its citizens," without any reference to the nature of the State of Israel. What is more, one of the key goals in the curriculum for Jewish schools was "recognition of the role of the state in the life of society and fostering a desire for active participation in shaping its destiny." This section, which was missing from the curriculum for Arab schools, aimed at perpetuating the status quo in order to internalize the perception that Israel is a Jewish state rather than a civil state shared by Jews and Arabs. Unlike Jewish students, Arab students were not called upon to participate actively in shaping the destiny of the state or to feel they were full members of the society. From this perspective, then, whether consciously or unconsciously, the new curriculum of the 1990s urged Arab students to enhance their sense of belonging to the State of Israel as a *Jewish state* and not as a binational or a multicultural democratic state (see Al-Haj 2021).

Noteworthy was the section on values: in both the Arab and Jewish schools the general clauses were phrased in a balanced fashion, referring to the need "to foster humane ethical values to permit judgment of historical events, fostering critical thinking and avoiding dogmatism, fostering recognition of the reciprocal influences among peoples, and evaluation of individuals according to their actions and not their group affiliation." With regard to knowledge and understanding of different historical narratives, the curricula for Jews and Arabs alike emphasized the following goals: "To foster the ability to understand the position of the other from the other's point of view and to foster the recognition that there are other points of view (and not just one) that can be accepted with regard to national problems as well" (Ministry of Education 1998, 12 [Hebrew curriculum]; Ministry of Education 1999a, 8 [Arabic curriculum]).

Yet when considering how these general principles were translated into the specific national context, an asymmetric picture emerges, with different standards for Jews and Arabs. In the Arab schools, the general principles were applied meticulously and with a broad "multicultural" perspective. The curriculum presented the two narratives, Jewish-Zionist and Arab-Palestinian-Muslim, in the same breath. Students were required to grasp the place of Palestine in the Palestinian Arab and Islamic consciousness vis-à-vis the place of the land of Israel in the history and consciousness of the Jewish people (Ministry of Education 1998, 12 [curriculum for Jewish schools]; Ministry of Education 1999a, 8–9 [curriculum for Arab schools]).

A comparison of the goals prescribed for Arab schools and for Jewish schools reveals that the principle of fostering the ability to understand the other's position and to become familiar with other points of view of the same events and national problems was applied in Arab schools. In Jewish schools, however, a one-sided picture was given, weighted in favor of Jewish nationalism and providing a historical perspective based on learning about the distinctiveness of the Jewish people "with regard to its essence and destiny." The state's Arab Palestinian citizenry and their connection to the land were simply not mentioned.

What is more, in the Jewish schools the specific goals of fostering a sense of identification with the Jewish people were conveyed in an active, sentimental manner and were based on knowledge, understanding, and appreciation of the most important historical figures in Jewish history. Conversely, the general goals of enhancing Arab students' sense of affiliation with the Palestinian people and the Arab nation were conveyed in a dry and factual manner, emphasizing knowledge rather than cultivating sentiment and attitudes as part of the educational process (see also Al-Haj 2021).

Textbooks Based on the New Curriculum: A Comparative Analysis of Arab and Jewish Schools

In general terms, both the curriculum and the textbooks in Jewish schools in the third period (the late 1990s–present) devote the lion's share to Jewish history, the Israeli-Arab conflict, and the State of Israel, although as separate units, with the largest single unit among the required hours devoted to world history. The textbook devotes slightly more to world history than suggested by the Ministry of Education, at the expense of Jewish history. Another conspicuous discrepancy between the textbook and the curriculum involves the section on the Israeli-Arab conflict, which receives more attention in the textbook at the expense of issues associated with current Israeli society. This is the greatest discrepancy between plan and implementation, with the textbook focusing more on the external political conflict and much less on domestic conflicts and social and cultural issues within Israel (see also Kizel 2008).

All in all, despite the changes in the new curriculum in the Jewish schools compared to its predecessor, more is similar than different. Like the previous curriculum, the new one ignores Arab, Islamic, and general Palestinian history. Jewish students learn about these subjects only in the context of conflict and not in a broad context of general human history. As a result of recent developments in the Middle East, however, the new curriculum does offer a specialization in the transition from conflict to peace and the chances for a continuation of the process.

Unlike the aforementioned situation in Jewish schools, in Arab schools there is no essential divergence between the formal curriculum and its implementation in textbooks. The main divergence is between the general guideline, which for the first time mentions "enhancing the sense of belonging of Arab students with the Palestinian Arab people and the Arab nation and its culture," and its lack of implementation in the textbooks, as I will discuss subsequently. Also, the curriculum for Arab schools provides incomplete treatment of the Israeli-Palestinian conflict because the analysis ends with the 1948 war and the establishment of Israel. By contrast, domestic and external developments from 1948 through 1990 occupy a central place in the curriculum for Jewish schools.

The following section outlines the main differences in the content of Hebrew and Arabic textbooks. I focus mainly on two parallel textbooks: for Arab schools I focus on *The Modern History of the Middle East*, part 2 (Barghouti 1998; and the revised version by Salameh 2009); for Hebrew schools I examine *Modern Times*, part 1, 1870–1920, and part 2, 1920–2000 (Bar-Navi and Naveh 1999).

The analysis reveals profound differences between the textbook intended for Arab schools and the one for Jewish schools, mainly reflected in the way the two narratives—Palestinian and Zionist—are presented to students in both groups. Whereas Arab students are exposed to the Zionist narrative, Jewish students are given no opportunity for direct exposure to the Palestinian narrative. What is more, Arab students learn about the Zionist movement as one that came into being upon its own initiative, with defined goals that integrate pragmatism and ideology. Jewish students are exposed to the Arab national movement in general, or its Palestinian part, only in the shadow of the Zionist movement and not as a movement in its own right (see Barghouti 1998, 276–318).

It should be emphasized that the textbook used in the Arab schools treats many issues connected with the Israeli-Palestinian conflict with extreme caution or even ignores them. These include issues that are considered "sensitive" or "difficult history," such as the massacres that took place during the 1948 war and the debate behind the creation of the Palestinian refugee problem, as shown in table 4.1.

Table 4.1. The 1948 Israeli-Arab War in Arabic and Hebrew Textbooks in Israeli Schools (1990s)

	Arabic textbook	Hebrew textbook
Terms used for the 1948 war	Uses the neutral expression "the 48 Arab-Israeli War"	Uses the Zionist ideological term "War of Independence"
Massacres and difficult events during the war	Ignores the massacres that took place during the war and ethnic cleansing actions directed against the Palestinians	Refers to the Deir Yassin massacre but in a fashion that diminishes the impact
Chronology of the war	Describes the chronology of the war in a factual manner	Description of the war highlights "Jewish heroism"
Comparison between Arab and Jewish forces	No reference to this topic	The war of the few (Jews) against the many (Arabs) and victory of quality over quantity
Palestinian refugees (number)	"Israel annexed 80% of the territory of mandatory Palestine, and most of the Arab inhabitants of this area were forced to leave their homes and villages for camps set up for them in Arab countries" (316).	For the most part the Palestinians fled—"Ran away for their lives"—except for "about 10,000 villagers who were expelled after the end of the fighting in order to clear border areas of hostile elements" (238).
Palestinian refugees (how the refugees' problem was created and the developments after 1948)	No discussion of the debate behind the creation of the Palestinian refugee problem	Discussion of the emergence of the Palestinians from refugees into a national group, including the Palestinian intifada

Source: For Arab schools, Barghouti 1998, 276–319; for Jewish schools, Bar-Navi and Naveh 1999, 226–39, 316–23.

The selective tradition in the history curriculum as discussed in the theoretical framework is clearly reflected in both the Hebrew and Arabic textbooks, not only with respect to the history of the Israeli-Palestinian conflict but also concerning the current status and conditions of the Palestinian Israeli citizens and of Jewish-Arab relations in Israel in a state of flux between conflict and peace. It is precisely these points that interest Arab students as they examine their environment in search of answers to questions that arise in their daily lives regarding political, economic, and social developments that affect the community in which they live, the state in which they are citizens, and the Palestinian people of which they are members. The Hebrew textbook, in contrast, devotes several chapters to the wars between Israel and the Arab countries, the Palestinian national movement after 1948, the issue of the occupied Palestinian territories, the implications of the intifada, and the transition from a century-old conflict to the beginnings of resolution and mutual recognition between Israel and the Palestinians, all this from a totally Jewish-Zionist perspective.

One might expect that a textbook intended for Arab students would devote significant space to addressing how the Palestinians shifted from a majority into a minority group and became marginalized citizens of Israeli society. Indeed, treatment of these issues could offer a framework for discussing the links between past, present, and future. Yet the Arabic textbook ignores these topics, referring to the Arab citizens of Israel in only a single sentence: "In the territory of the State of Israel there remained about 150,000 [Arabs] who received citizenship [in Israel], with about 25 percent of this number considered refugees because they had been forced out of their villages and resettled in neighboring villages and towns" (Barghouti 1998, 316).

Moreover, as noted, even though the Hebrew textbook includes a detailed discussion of developments in the Israeli-Palestinian conflict after the establishment of the state, its discussion of Jewish-Arab relations within Israel and the complex citizenship issues of the Palestinian Arab minority in Israel remains quite marginal. Two chapters in the Hebrew textbook are devoted to the social structure of Israel. The first chapter deals with "the emergence of the Israeli nation" but completely disregards the existence of the indigenous Palestinian population that was formerly the majority (Bar-Navi and Naveh 1999, 260–65). This chapter surveys Israel's struggle for economic independence, the creation of the Israeli nation, and the influences of mass immigration, economic challenges, wars, and the principle of ingathering of exiles, a principle that generated social tensions and divided Israeli society into ethnic groups. This chapter does not include a single word about the Palestinian Arab minority in Israel. Jewish students, therefore, learn about *Israeli society as a purely Jewish society.* The textbook makes no reference to the fact that one of the central challenges that faced the nascent state, aside from the creation of the Jewish nation, was its treatment of the indigenous Palestinian population—a population that until 1947 was the majority and that after the state was established involuntarily became a small minority of second-class citizens, constituting about 13 percent of the population (see chapter 2).

A revised version of the history textbook for Arab schools was published in 2009. Like its predecessor, this version included only one chapter on the Palestinian issue. A careful comparison between the two versions leads to the conclusion that they are practically identical. Both versions conclude with the establishment of Israel. The only minor difference is that while the first version used a neutral term for the 1948 Israeli-Arab war (see Barghouti 1998, 307), the second version uses the two names given to this war, one by Jews and the other by Arabs. Nevertheless, this difference is reported only through a single question directed to the students, without any in-depth discussion: "The Jews refer to the 1948 War as the War of Independence, while the Arabs call it *Nakbat Falastine* (the Catastrophe of Palestine); what do you think of these names?" (Salameh 2009, 185).

Moreover, all the new history textbooks in both the Jewish and Arab schools relegate students to a passive role. The curriculum as reflected in the textbooks does not enable students to think critically, confront existing myths and narratives, or take part in the development of alternative narratives. Even the issue of peace in the Middle East is conveyed in a "banking" fashion (the "banking" method in education was phrased by Freire 1972) that involves depositing information rather than in a way that turns students into partners in thinking and potential partners in action, eventually advancing education for peace. Hence, students are provided no chance to produce their own thoughts or generate any alternative narrative that might challenge official knowledge and narratives.

Recent Developments

Recent changes in the school curriculum in both the Arab and Jewish schools have been affected by two major factors. The first is associated with the neoliberal state policy regarding education and the second is related to sociopolitical radicalization occurring among the Jewish population.

As mentioned, since the early 1980s Israel has adopted a neoliberal policy toward education. This trend has intensified over time and has found expression in various educational reforms (see chapter 3). The privatization and marketization of the public education system, which are an integral part of the neoliberal reforms, have paved the way for nongovernmental stakeholders, including private actors and NGOs, to penetrate the education system and exert a massive influence on Israeli education policy and content (Amiel and Yemini 2023, 586).

In effect, most of these actors are affiliated with extreme Zionist right-wing parties and missionary education systems (Pinson 2022; Caspit 2023). This is the outcome of wider political processes that have taken place in Israeli society since the beginning of the 21st century. Ethno-religious right-wing neo-Zionism has gained the upper hand, thus marginalizing democratic, civil society voices to become the exclusive hegemonic political force (Pinson 2022, 124; see also Ben-Eliezer 2019; Ben-Porat 2013).

This trend has weakened the general public school system, both in terms of financial resources and in the massive infiltration of religious Zionist missionary content in formal education. Ben Caspit, one of Israel's leading journalists, highlights Israel's concerning decline of general state education in contrast to the rise of the state Zionist stream and the missionary and Orthodox Jewish streams: "And that's how we got to where we are: On the one hand, ideological, funded, purposeful, political and missionary education systems. On the other hand, a depleted, neutral system [general state-system]. . . . This is how religious Zionism became a new and cohesive political elite, while its institutions became the ideological-spiritual infrastructure of its principles" (Caspit 2023).

The aforementioned changes have further marginalized the Palestinian schools and led to tightened control over their curriculum and content. According to Agbaria (2018), these neoliberal reforms reflect the ongoing interface between ethnonationalism and neoliberalism in the Israeli education system and have led to the adoption of two completely different sets of goals for Palestinian and Jewish education. Whereas Palestinian education has been subject to standardization and de-contextualization in a way that excludes ideology and politics, rightist ideology has been deeply enhanced in the Jewish education system (18).

Indeed, since 2009 the Ministry of Education has been controlled by minsters with clear rightist leanings, reflecting a growing trend toward Zionist ideology and narrative in Jewish and Arab schools alike (see Al-Haj 2021). According to Pinson (2022), these ministers of education have been "actively pushing a neo-Zionist agenda by reshaping the curriculum, amending the State Education Act, and attempting to intervene in the content of teaching in academia" (128).

On November 1, 2012, the director general of the Ministry of Education issued a circular to all Arab schools in Israel informing them that the history of the Zionist movement and the Holocaust should be taught as a compulsory unit (Ministry of Education 2012). What this means is that Arab students will not be able to get a matriculation certificate without passing the exam on this specific unit. Note that although the Zionist history unit was included in the matriculation exams for Arab schools since 2007, it was an optional unit and most Arab students found a way to get around it and replace it with another subject (see *Elfger*, November 9, 2012).

The Nationality Law (*Hok La'leum* in Hebrew) that was approved by the Knesset in July 2018 has intensified this trend toward enhancing the Jewish-Zionist narrative (Knesset 2018; see chapter 2). Soon after the Nationality Law was passed, it found expression in the education system, as reflected, among other things, in a number of changes in the new version of the civics textbook for Arab high schools. This textbook, which is an Arabic translation of the text taught in Jewish schools, employs several expressions aimed at emphasizing the Jewish character not only of the State of Israel but also of the entire territory of Mandatory Palestine. Thus, instead of *Al-Quds* (the Arabic name of Jerusalem) the new book uses the name *Or-Shalim-Al-Quds* (the name used by formal Israeli authorities), and instead of Palestine (*Filastin* in Arabic) the translators use the term *Palestina* (commonly employed in Zionist writings) (Yanko 2019b).

In addition, the new textbook teaches the Jewish-Zionist narrative exclusively and completely disregards the Palestinian narrative. It should be noted that the Ministry of Education committee responsible for translating this book did not include a single Arab member. These changes have already drawn wide protests from Arab public figures and politicians (see interview "MK Jabareen," *Bokra*, January 31, 2019).

The aforementioned trend gained further support in June 2019 with the nomination of Rafi Perez as the new minister of education. Perez, chair of the right-wing Habayit Hayehudi party and one of the leaders of the extreme right in Israel, declared his intention to include teaching the Nationality Law as an integral part of the civics curricula in both Jewish and Arab high schools beginning in the 2019/20 school year (Ben-Porat 2019). This step incited strong opposition among the Arab population. The Follow-Up Committee on Arab Education and some public figures expressed their intention to oppose these plans. Moreover, the parents' association in Nazareth urged Arab teachers to reject the Ministry of Education's decision in this regard (see Jabareen 2019).

Meanwhile, the most recent elections (held on November 1, 2022) led to the formation of the most extremist government in Israel's history. This government includes radical nationalist and fanatically religious quasi-fascist right-wing parties (see Bauer 2023, 1). One of the immediate steps this government initiated is a so-called judicial reform aimed at subordinating the judiciary to the political system, a step that is believed to have far-reaching anti-democratic implications (see Bauer 2023, 2). While we are still in the midst of the process, these developments will undoubtedly be reflected in the education system, thus posing more challenges to the general public state education system, and particularly to Arab schools.

Summary

In this chapter, I have analyzed the history curriculum in the Hebrew and Arab schools over a period of nearly 70 years, from 1950 through 2020. I examined the findings through a critical multicultural perspective that sheds light on the limitations of the education system and the repercussions of the lack of a multicultural ideology regarding the possibility of enhancing diversity and mutual acceptance of rival narratives in a deeply divided society.

A comparison of successive versions of the curricula in the Jewish and Arab schools reveals a number of changes both in the general goals related to the values imparted through teaching history and in the specific content of the curricula. This is especially true in the Arab schools, where there has been a shift from a curriculum quite devoid of Arab national content in the 1950s to one that referred to fostering identification with the Arab nation in the 1970s and ultimately to identification with the Arab nation and the Palestinian people in the late 1990s. Whereas these goals encourage the fostering of Arab students' affiliation with the State of Israel, they do not examine how the declared nature of the state hampers such affiliation.

These changes have failed to make any considerable progress toward education for multiculturalism in Israel. Moreover, no alternative narrative has been introduced to Jewish students or to Arab students. The narrative taught to Jewish students has remained predominantly Jewish-Zionist, ethnonational, and particularistic, while Arab students have been denied any independent Palestinian narrative (see also Shemesh 2009; Kizel 2008; Abu-Sa'ad 2007; Hourani 2010; Al-Haj 2021). Furthermore, school segregation between Arabs and Jews in Israel has been used by the state to develop a form of one-sided, controlled multiculturalism that is inculcated exclusively in the Arab schools, while the curriculum of the Jewish schools is completely devoted to developing exclusive patriotism, collective memory, and national ethos among the majority members. In addition, starting in 2009, the power of the extreme political and religious Jewish right in Israel has been on the rise. Since then, the Ministry of Education has enhanced Zionist ideology and narrative in Jewish and Arab schools alike, while further marginalizing the Palestinian narrative and Palestinian identity in Arab schools.

The next chapter examines the policy of controlling Arab education by means of exerting control over teachers and nurturing a culture of silence among them. More specifically, it discusses the status and conditions of Arab teachers, the factors behind their high burnout rates, the impact of the COVID-19 pandemic, and the impediments blocking them from assuming a role as educational leaders.

Chapter 5

Status of Arab Teachers

Attitudes, Burnout, and the Culture of Silence

Abstract

This chapter examines the status of Arab teachers in Israel and the dilemmas they face. First, I offer a brief theoretical framework for this discussion. After that, I provide some background to explain the policy of control applied to Arab teachers immediately after the State of Israel was established. Then, I discuss the findings of a nationwide survey of Arab teachers that examined the characteristics of Arab teachers, their interrelationships within the school, and their attitudes toward cardinal issues in the school system, the local community, and the Ministry of Education. I conclude by examining recent developments and factors that have affected the status of Arab teachers and have contributed to their sense of burnout, including local and global changes and new challenges brought about by the COVID-19 pandemic.

The data are based on a synthesis of qualitative and quantitative methods, including analysis of documents from state archives that provide a unique opportunity to understand how formal policies of control and cultural hegemony were designed during the first decade of the state. A major part of this chapter is based on the findings of the first representative nationwide survey of Arab teachers in Israel conducted in November 1993. In addition, I conducted two focus groups of Arab teachers, one comprising 10 elementary school teachers and the second comprising 12 teachers from secondary and middle schools. Both focus groups were conducted in January 2020. During January–February 2020 I also carried out systematic observations at a number of elementary, middle, and secondary schools in the Galilee (north) and the Little Triangle (center). These school observations provided an opportunity to conduct a number of unstructured interviews with teachers, principals, and superintendents.

Theoretical Framework: Challenges Faced by Minority Teachers

Research shows that teachers who belong to minority and disadvantaged groups face more difficulties and barriers than those usually reported among teachers from dominant groups (Hall, Lundin, and Sibbmark 2020; Chiang, Clark, and McConnell 2017; Atkins, Fertig, and Wilkins 2014; Sass et al. 2012). In addition to the usual challenges faced by teachers in all school settings (Hall, Lundin, and Sibbmark 2020), minority teachers must cope with a wide range of issues stemming from their students' impoverished and disadvantaged social backgrounds and from problems in cooperation between school and parents. Moreover, both students and the community at large have high expectations of teachers belonging to their minority group. Indeed, minority teachers who work with students from the same group serve as role models for their students and can affect their self-esteem and prospects for the future (Atkins, Fertig, and Wilkins 2014, 508).

Critical theoreticians highlight the difficulties minority teachers face, stemming from the large discrepancy between school and society and from the contradictory expectations of the establishment and their own community. According to Giroux, schools are not merely a site for transmitting knowledge but also a cultural site that legitimizes the culture and the historical narratives of the dominant group and disregards or delegitimizes the narratives of other groups (Giroux 1987). Thus, the mainstream pedagogy reflects the dominant culture of the broader society, which teachers convey without raising any doubts or criticisms. This mainstream pedagogy drives teachers and students alike to adopt a culture of silence, further marginalizing their role. According to Sleeter and McLaren (1995):

> The dominant culture of schooling mirrors that of the larger culture in so far as teachers and students willingly and unwittingly situate themselves within a highly politicized field of power relations that partake of unjust race, class and gender affiliations. . . . Such a "culture of silence" teaches students to harmonize a world of incongruity and faction antipathy and to

domesticate the unruly and unpleasant and messy features of everyday life in which costs are imposed for being different and rewards given for 'fitting in' compliantly. (6–7)

Moreover, Gramscian theory of cultural hegemony acknowledges that the culture of the school often contradicts the culture of the community in that the school culture is used as a mechanism of cultural hegemony. In one of his letters, Gramsci (1971) notes: "The individual consciousness of the overwhelming majority of children reflects the social and cultural relations which are different from and antagonistic to those which are represented in school curricula. . . . There is no unity between school and life, and so there is no automatic unity between instruction and education" (35–36). Gramsci explains that the strong hegemonic powers of the dominant group in the wider society make it difficult to change the education system. These powers also weaken the status of teachers, who are trapped between school and community: "It was right to struggle against the old school, but reforming it was not so simple as it seemed. The problem was not one of model curricula but of men, and not just of the men who are actually teachers themselves but of the entire social complex which they express" (25).

The above theoretical introduction raises a number of questions regarding Palestinian Arab teachers in Israel (hereafter, Arab teachers): What are the main contextual factors that have affected the status, self-image, conduct, attitudes, and teaching practices of Arab teachers within the school system and in the wider community? How do Arab teachers cope with the contradictory expectations of their students and their community on the one hand and of the official school system on the other?

Background: The Military Government and the Foundations of a Culture of Silence

In the wake of the *Nakba* (the 1948 war), very few Arab teachers remained in Israel. A report by Ben-Or (then in charge of education among Arabs) states the following: "In Jaffa only one woman teacher was left out of a total of 125 in former government schools; in Ramle and Lydda only three were left and one of them was soon arrested and deported. In Haifa, out of 46, only one was left. . . . The same held true of a number of other localities" (Ben-Or 1950, 226). Thus, in many cases Arab teachers appointed during the first years of the state did not have the same qualifications as those who had taught in Arab schools under the Mandate. In 1950/51 there were 601 teachers in the Arab schools, of whom 154 were women (25 percent). Most of these teachers were unqualified, and some of them had not even completed elementary school (Ben-Or 1951, 4). To deal with this teacher shortage in the Arab schools, the Ministry of Education employed some Jewish teachers, who constituted 13.5 percent of all teachers in Arab schools in 1950/51. The vast majority of these Jewish teachers were bilingual, either because they were originally from Arab countries (mainly Iraq) or because they had studied Arabic during their secondary education (2). As will be shown later in this chapter, some of these teachers came from the security services or other government offices and were slated to return to their permanent jobs after completing a one- or two-year stint as teachers.

The shortage of qualified Arab teachers continued until the late 1970s. In 1953, out of 780 Arab teachers only 73 were actually qualified, whereas more than 300 had no more than 10 years of general education. This picture becomes even more striking in contrast to the situation in Jewish education, where only 73 of 13,000 teachers had 10 years or less of education (*The Jerusalem Post*, August 11, 1954). As of the 1960/61 school year, 879 (or 65 percent) of the 1,340 teachers employed in the Arab educational system were unqualified. As of the 1969/70 school year, more than half of Arab teachers were still unqualified (Al-Haj 1995a).

Yet the shortage of qualified teachers was only part of the problem faced by Arab schools immediately after the establishment of the state, and more specifically through the late 1960s. As indicated earlier (chapter 2), during that period the Arab citizens in Israel were under the strict control of the military government. In the following section, I briefly describe the principal methods used by the formal authorities during this period to establish a system of control over Arab schools and to construct a *culture of silence* among Arab principals, teachers, and students—a system that continued after the military government was abolished.

According to several studies, during the crucial period of Israel's first decade the state formulated its strategic orientation and policy toward Arab citizens in various fields (see Al-Haj and Yaniv 1983; Al-Haj and Rosenfeld 1989; Lustick 1980; Ozacky-Lazar 1996, 2002; Forman 2006; Erez and Degani 2021). This was particularly the case in the field of education. State authorities considered education to be an important mechanism for controlling Arab society at large. Indeed, education was used to introduce the Arabs to a type of citizenship in which they express their loyalty to the state, rationalize their inferior status, and internalize the majority perception of Israel's Jewish character (see report by Shmuel Salmon about Arab education, SA 1351/1616/GL).

From the outset, the ruling establishment and the Arab community had contradictory expectations of Arab teachers. On the one hand, these teachers were under the strict control of the military government apparatus and were forced to refrain from any political involvement, for otherwise they would have been fired (Jiryis 1976; Cohen 1951, 132). On the other hand, because teachers were all that remained of the Arab educated elite, their community expected them to serve as role models and assume leadership positions (Mari 1978).

These pressures made it almost impossible for Arab teachers to function as educators and leaders. One teacher working during that period had this to say about the situation:

> The Arab teacher does not have psychological security, which might allow him to fulfill his mission as a teacher and educator. It is no secret that in Arab villages, teachers are appointed by favoritism, according to the recommendation of military governors or people affiliated with them, often not by merit. The fear of being dismissed is always on the shoulders of the Arab teachers who do not dare to express any political opinion in light of their conscience, because of the fear their career may be harmed. (*Al-Hamishmar*, May 31, 1960)

Indeed, Yehoshua Palmon, the prime minister's adviser for Arab affairs, sent a letter (then classified as secret) to the prime minister, the minister of education, and the foreign minister requesting special legislation that would make it possible to fire tenured Arab teachers suspected of being involved in anti-Israel agitation. Palmon estimated that about 10 percent of the Arab teachers in 1952 belonged to this category of teachers with Communist-nationalist inclinations (SA 25/2402/Foreign Ministry).

In response to Palmon's suggestion, the minister of justice wrote that no special legislation was needed to fire Arab teachers involved in political activity, since according to the existing regulations teachers could be dismissed for such reasons, as stated in article 8(3) of the Education Law: "The Director General of the Ministry of Education is allowed to demand that a teacher in a public, supported or non-supported school be fired if the teacher was convicted of a criminal action which involves a disgraceful act, or if the Minister of Education was convinced, after a judicial investigation by a judge who was especially nominated for this purpose, that the teacher provided a provocative, disloyal or immoral education or education oriented to harm in any other manner" (SA 25/2402/Foreign Ministry). The Ministry of Education used this firing policy to intimidate Arab teachers. Toward the end of every school year a number of Arab teachers, mainly those who were political activists, received letters from the Ministry of Education informing them that their employment in the following year could not be guaranteed. In 1953 about half of the Arab teachers received such letters. At the same time, officials spread rumors that teachers involved in "provocative actions" against the government's policy would be fired (*Al-Ittihad*, June 26, 1953).

Exerting such control over Arab teachers was extremely important to the state authorities. By controlling teachers' behavior, the authorities could ensure that planned official goals would be implemented and the stability of the education system would be maintained. The Ministry of Education's policy of firing Arab teachers was very effective in light of the economic distress of the Arab population. The Arab localities had no economic base, and educated Arabs were completely dependent on state authorities. Hence, the sanctions against Arab teachers were multipurpose: they served as a deterrent, discouraged nonconformist elements, and forced those who sought to remain neutral to actively demonstrate their identification with the official policy. These points were well reflected in a letter that a dismissed principal sent to the minister of education (August 25, 1952) demanding to be reinstated:

> My livelihood is completely dependent on teaching: I have no other source of income, no lands and no private property; my only asset is my job. Is it logical, then, that a man like myself would attempt to commit any action in violation of the existing laws? In particular, I was a principal in . . . for three years and I certainly know what is permitted and what is prohibited! I got married only a short time ago and I am responsible for supporting my family. Is it possible that I would abuse my position that enables me to survive?
>
> I swear to God that I am innocent of all accusations attributed to me, which are as far from me as the distance between sky and earth. I request therefore that you reconsider my case and will be grateful if I am given mercy [*sic*]. (SA 3822/1631/GL)

The military government (1949–1966) played a major role in this policy of control over Arab teachers. Through this apparatus, Arab teachers were closely monitored both within and outside the schools. For example, in August 1950 the Ministry of Education organized a training course in Nazareth, attended by about 300 teachers. During the course Arab teachers were given detailed instructions regarding what places they should not visit, what restaurants they are allowed to patronize, and how they should spend their leisure time. They were also prevented from visiting the office of the Communist party (*Al-Ittihad*, August 20, 1950). During the military government period, Arabs who did not comply with the formal policy or did not cooperate with the military government authorities were blacklisted. Arab intellectuals who sought to obtain a teaching job or get a promotion made every effort to avoid being blacklisted (Lustick 1980, 193).

One major component in the policy of controlling the Arab population via the school system was to reinforce a type of inferior citizenship in which Arabs continuously had to prove their love for and loyalty to the state and to internalize the superiority of the Hebrew language and culture. In this sense, celebrations of Israel's Independence Day served as central form of political control and a means of forcing a downgraded form of citizenship upon Arab teachers and students. Erez and Degani (2021) analyze music education in Palestinian Arab schools under the military government. They discuss the patterns of loyalty and self-denial imposed on Arab students and educators through songbooks produced in the 1960s, in particular Independence Day songs that pay homage to the state and praise the joy and accomplishments of its Arab citizens. The authors point out that Israel imposed a policy of "subordinate integration" on Arab citizens that was based on granting individual rights while extinguishing claims for collective rights based on indigeneity (1010; see also Degani 2018). At the same time, the political goals of the Arab public school system were directed toward monitoring and suppressing any dissent among the Arab minority, whether real or perceived (Erez and Degani 2021, 1013).

Arab educators felt humiliated by Independence Day ceremonies, not only because they were forced to participate but also because these ceremonies meant nothing to them and did not reflect their actual feelings. Indeed, these ceremonies were even insulting to their Palestinian identity. One of the interviewees put it this way:

> I felt very sad while I was preparing my pupils for the Israeli Independence Day ceremony. On exactly the same day Israel had

declared its independence, my people became refugees and lost their liberty. In these ceremonies we spoke about the freedom of the Jewish people but not ours. We knew that most Arab lands had been confiscated but we spoke about the progress and achievements of our people. We spoke about the dignity inspired by independence, but for us it was just humiliation. (Al-Haj 1995a, 180; interview in November 1991)

In the early 1970s some Jewish officials began voicing opposition to the Independence Day ceremonies in the Arab schools. They realized that the way these ceremonies were organized only increased alienation and disappointment among students and teachers alike. Ran Lerner, former chairman of the Division for Arab Teachers in the Teachers Federation, had this to say:

The way the Arab schools celebrated Independence Day until the 1970s was disconcerting. To me these celebrations were very strange and even inhuman. I received many letters from teachers who complained that the superintendent forced them to work overtime in order to prepare the Independence Day celebration. Sometimes superintendents even threatened teachers, stating that failure to implement the formal instructions would be considered an action against the State of Israel.

I told Kupeleivetch (then Director of the Division for Arab Education) that we should request only the minimum from Arab schools as far as Independence Day celebrations are concerned, and I am happy that today the situation is different. (Al-Haj 1995a, 181; interview by author, October 1991)

The Independence Day ceremonies in the Arab schools were subsequently canceled. Today Arab schools have adopted a low-profile approach to Independence Day. The day is recognized as a holiday and Israeli flags are raised over school buildings, but no ceremonies or special events are organized.

Security system interference in the affairs of Arab teachers diminished considerably, but it did not vanish, even after the military government was abolished in 1966. Security clearance still serves as an effective instrument for controlling Arab teachers, and through them for controlling the Arab educational system. For this purpose, in addition to completing the regular forms needed to attain a teaching job, Arab teachers who wish to obtain a teaching post are required to complete a personal background questionnaire that has nothing to do with professional requirements. Based on this questionnaire and other clandestine checks, Ministry of Education officials decide whether the individual is "qualified" to be appointed to a teaching position (Wergift 1989). According to these officials, any civil servant who did not serve in the Israeli Defense Forces (IDF) must undergo a security check. Yet officials fail to explain why Orthodox Jewish teachers who also did not serve in the IDF are exempt from security checks (Wergift 1989).

Unlike in the elementary and middle schools, teacher appointments in the secondary schools are not completely controlled by the Ministry of Education. The local authority plays a major role in hiring and firing teachers. A joint professional committee comprising municipality and Ministry of Education representatives interviews the candidates and chooses those that are suitable. Sometimes a representative of the parents is included on the committee. Nevertheless, the committee's professional decision is not sufficient. The list of selected candidates must be submitted to the Ministry of Education for final approval (see Al-Haj 1995a).

Continuity and Change:
Findings from a Comprehensive Survey and Focus Groups

From the 1970s onward, a growing number of studies have focused on teachers, their self-image, and their interaction with the school environment. Nevertheless, Arab teachers have been the focus of very few field studies, particularly those based on representative nationwide samples. In the following sections I provide a detailed analysis of the first, and to the best of my knowledge the only, nationwide survey of Arab teachers in Israel to date. I conducted this survey in 1993 under the auspices of the Center for Educational Research at the University of Haifa and in collaboration with the Israel Teachers Union. Part of the findings of this survey were published only as a research report in Hebrew (see Al-Haj 1995b).

The survey examined a series of topics associated with teachers' work, social image, cultural life, and attitudes about various aspects of the school system. A special section was devoted to the issue of burnout among Arab teachers. As in every comprehensive survey, here too the desire to examine a wide range of topics limited the possibility of studying each one in depth. Therefore, in the discussion, the main conclusions of this survey are juxtaposed with and enriched by the findings of two focus groups of Arab teachers, one comprising 10 elementary school teachers and the second including 12 teachers from middle schools and high schools. Both groups were conducted in January 2020. I have integrated relevant direct quotations from these discussions into my analysis of the teacher survey.

METHODOLOGY

The survey was based on a representative sample of 852 teachers selected in three stages. First, 26 localities were randomly chosen to represent the different categories of Arab communities: geographical area (the Galilee, the Triangle, and the Negev); religion (Muslim, Christian, Druze, mixed); size; and municipal status. Second, a sample of schools was selected from each locality according to a predetermined quota based on population data regarding school level, type, and affiliation. Third, I selected a random sample of teachers from the chosen schools in accordance with the predetermined quota based on school size (number of teachers in each school).

The research tool was a multiple-choice questionnaire distributed to participants, who completed it individually and anonymously. The teachers were asked to complete the questionnaire without the presence of any colleagues or the principal in order to ensure maximum candor and truthful answers. While the participants filled out the questionnaires, a member of the survey staff was available to answer questions and provide clarifications.

After the teachers completed the questionnaires, the forms were placed in a large box and thoroughly mixed to ensure complete confidentiality. This step was much appreciated by the teachers, for it reinforced their confidence in the survey staff's preliminary declaration that the data would be analyzed statistically with no attempt to discover any identifying details. The teachers' response rate was high, with a negligible rate of refusal.

The final questionnaire was formulated after a pilot study using a small random sample of 50 teachers from various categories. The pilot study enabled us to check the clarity of the questions, examine the likelihood of reservations or refusal to answer questions in certain categories, and assess other important information related to the questionnaire and the interviewers.

The field work was conducted in November 1993 and lasted one month. The survey staff consisted of Arab students who were specially trained for this job. Based on our experience in previous surveys in Arab localities, we made certain that the survey personnel were not sent to their home communities. Cumulative experience has shown that such a step is extremely important in increasing respondents' trust and cooperation.

The data obtained from the study indicated that the sample did indeed faithfully represent the population of Arab teachers in Israel (for comparison, see Al-Haj 1995a). The overwhelming majority of participating Arab teachers (82 percent) taught in state/public schools; 12 percent taught in private/Christian schools (which constitute 8 percent of all schools but were overrepresented in the sample to obtain a reasonable number of cases for the statistical analysis); the third group taught at Amal vocational schools. The "other" category refers to other private schools that are not affiliated with any of the previous categories.

Women in the Education System

As in the Jewish schools and worldwide, the Arab education system is undergoing a process of feminization, though at a much slower rate and mostly in the primary schools. The findings of our survey (1993) indicate that about 58 percent of teachers in Arab schools were men and 42 percent were women. This proportion accurately reflected the nationwide picture. According to statistics published in the Statistical Abstract of Israel (SAI), in the 1992/93 school year there were 12,516 Arab teachers, of whom 5,285 (42 percent) were women, thus providing another indication that our sample faithfully represented the situation of Arab teachers nationwide. One notable conclusion from these data is that the higher the level of the school, the lower the number of female teachers. Women teachers were concentrated mainly at the lower end of the school system, in primary schools and special education. According to our data, women constituted 54 percent of the teaching staff in primary schools (52 percent according to SAI 1996, table 22.23) and 26 percent in middle and high schools (25.6 percent according to SAI 1996, table 22.23). These differences were largely due to differences in level of education between men and women in the mid-1990s. The survey reveals that 57 percent of male teachers were university graduates holding at least a bachelor's degree, compared to 25 percent of female teachers with university degrees.

This picture has changed considerably over time. Since the mid-1990s higher education among the Arab population in Israel has expanded significantly. Moreover, the percentage of Arab women who have acquired academic education has risen much faster than that of men for all academic degrees. (For information on the development of higher education among Arab men and women over time, see chapter 6; see also SAI 1984, 54; CBS 1995, 71; SAI 1997, 64; SAI 2020, 5).

The aforementioned expansion of higher education is reflected in the rising educational level and dramatic increase in feminization among Arab teachers. As table 5.1 shows, the division between qualified and unqualified Arab teachers is no longer relevant because almost all Arab teachers today hold academic degrees. In the 2018/19 school year, 95 percent of all Arab teachers held academic degrees compared to 91.6 percent of Jewish teachers. That is to say, for the first time since the establishment of the state, the percentage of teachers with academic education is slightly higher among Arabs compared to Jews.

Moreover, the Arab education system has experienced the same feminization trend as in the Jewish population and worldwide (e.g., Drudy 2008; OECD 2005). As shown in table 5.1, in 2019 the majority (71.9 percent) of Arab teachers were women. This was also the case among Jewish teachers (81.2 percent). Although women teachers are in the majority in the secondary schools, in Arab schools they constitute a lower percentage (57.7 percent compared to 73.7 percent for Jewish teachers). Taking into consideration the broad expansion of higher education among Arab women (see chapter 6), it is safe to claim that within a few years, women will become the prevailing majority at all school levels, including secondary schools. Yet while women constitute the majority of the teaching staff, they are still in the minority as far as senior administrative positions are concerned. Indeed, most Arab school principals are men, particularly in the high schools. The same picture emerges regarding senior positions as superintendents and officials in the Arab education system.

As table 5.1 shows, Arab teachers are clearly younger than Jewish teachers. The percentage of Jewish teachers over the age of 50 is almost twice as high as among Arab teachers (30.5 percent compared to 17.7, respectively). One possible reason is that Arab teachers continue on to higher education and training right after secondary school. Moreover, if Arab teachers become tenured, they most likely remain in the system until retirement, rarely shifting to other jobs. Indeed, the limited employment opportunities for Arab academics drive Arab teachers to seek socioeconomic mobility within the school system. Unlike their Arab counterparts, an increasing number of Jewish teachers are second career teachers or career switchers, in line with international trends (Sarid et al. 2022).

Table 5.1. Arab and Jewish Teaching Staff in Schools by Level of Education and Other Characteristics* 2018/19 (%)

	Average			Academic Degree	Experience
	Number	Women	Age 50+		
Arabs					
Total number of staff	38,912	71.9	17.7	95.0	14.5
Primary schools	20,982	78.4	16.7	93.9	14.8
Lower secondary schools	8,786	71.4	17.7	98.6	15.1
Higher secondary schools	10,803	57.7	20.1	93.6	13.5
Jews					
Total number of staff	122,402	81.2	30.5	91.6	16.3
Primary schools	65,017	85.7	25.6	89.4	15.2
Lower secondary schools	29,839	79.6	33.6	97.4	16.7
Higher secondary schools	42,276	73.7	37.2	92.6	18.1

*Primary (1st–6th grades); Lower secondary (7th–9th grades); Higher secondary (10th–12th grades)

Source: Based on SAI 2020, table 4.33.

RELATIONSHIPS WITHIN ARAB SCHOOLS

A great deal of research on relationship dynamics within the Arab educational system has emphasized its rigid hierarchical structure: the inspectors are at the top of the hierarchy, followed by principals, and then teachers, with pupils in the least important position (Mari 1978; Bashi, Kahan, and Davis 1981; Al-Haj 1995a, 2006). Hence, the Arab school system is characterized by authority, coercion, and a lack of democracy in terms of internal relationships. This situation raises the following questions: Who has the strongest authority in the schools? What are the factors affecting internal relationships within the schools?

The findings of my survey are somewhat surprising and suggest that the answers to these questions are complex. I examined the four central relationships in the school system: teacher-inspector, teacher-principal, teacher-teacher, and teacher-pupil. The data show that inspectors maintain only a weak relationship with the school system and that their authority is less central. Only about one-third of our respondents indicated that an inspector had sat in on one of their classes during the past three years, and 10 percent answered that the inspector had not sat in on a class but had discussed their work with them. The majority (55 percent) reported that the inspector had neither visited their classroom nor discussed their work with them. Most teachers (53 percent) said they had no faith in administrative inspectors.

In contrast to the waning authority of the inspectors, the principal wields enormous authority and enjoys a great deal of power and influence in Arab schools. In general, teachers refrained from criticizing the principal, even in this anonymous questionnaire. The principal's authoritarian position is quite evident in respondents' reports on faculty meetings: 39 percent of the teachers stated that they do not express their opinions at faculty meetings, and 27 percent stated that the principal either does not listen to their opinions or else listens but does not take their opinions into consideration. In other words, two-thirds of the teachers do not express their opinions at faculty meetings or else the principal disregards their opinions. Yet, some 86 percent of the teachers reported being satisfied with their relationship with the principal, 70 percent reported that the principal exhibits positive involvement with their work, and 75 percent stated that they have faith in their principal.

The increasing power of principals is a result of the gradual decentralization of the school system and the introduction of school autonomy. Hence, teachers are dependent upon the principal for almost everything connected to their work, including class scheduling, promotion to various administrative positions at the school, selection for in-service training, and other benefits.

Most of the teachers defined their relationships with the other teachers as satisfactory. Some 80 percent stated they were "satisfied" or "very satisfied" with the relationships among the teaching staff, and 60 percent said they trusted their colleagues. One explanation of this high level of satisfaction with the school's social atmosphere is the "power of conformity" that prevails in the Arab educational system. When teachers begin working at a new school, they find themselves in an inflexible environment. In most cases, they choose to fit into the school climate rather than confront the system or try to change it. The existing culture of silence in the Arab educational system encourages teachers to toe the line with the school climate and become part of the prevailing social order.

Teacher satisfaction with the school atmosphere can also be attributed to the social networks within the system, in particular those based on *hamula* (family/clan kinship group) or other primary ties. The data point to a positive (though not statistically significant) correlation between the number of people from the same hamula working at a school and the level of satisfaction with the social atmosphere. The average number of teachers from the same hamula in a particular school is 3.2. As noted in chapter 2, the kinship structure among the Arab population has survived conspicuous modernization processes. One central factor in the survival of this structure is related to what was defined earlier as "social localization," that is the high demographic concentration of these hamulas in the same Arab localities. Unlike other developing societies where proletarianization has, among other things, resulted in extensive internal immigration from rural to urban centers, Arab society in Israel has been marked by urbanization without immigration (see chapter 2). This, in turn, increases the concentration of hamula-based staff at the same school. Naturally, principals exert a significant influence in hiring teachers from their own hamula to work in their schools (Mari 1974).

The aforementioned picture reflects the central role played by the hamula in the education system (see Arar and Abu-Asbah 2013). Because local politics in Arab communities are to a large extent hamula-based (Al-Haj and Rosenfeld 1990; Al-Haj 1995c), the interests of the hamula infiltrate the educational system as well. Hence, in many cases the hamula-based leadership of local authorities constitutes a source of control that retards the development of Arab education (Arar and Abu-Asbah 2013). In other words, Arab education is subject to a dual system of control: that of the state and that of the local authority.

Freire (1998b) described such a situation as a "dual system of oppression": "The culturally alienated society as a whole is dependent on the society that oppresses it and whose economic and cultural interests it serves. At the same time, within the alienated society itself, a regime of oppression is imposed upon the masses by the power elites that in certain cases are the same as the external elites and in others are the external elites transformed by a kind of metastasis into domestic power groups" (478). Note that the highest concentrations of people from the same hamula in the schools are found in homogenous Druze localities and small villages, and particularly in Bedouin localities in the Negev, where kinship groups are most dominant numerically. The number of teachers from the same hamula in the same school has only increased over time. In an interview conducted on February 15, 2020, a principal from a secondary school in Wadi Ara (Little Triangle) said the following:

> The *hamula*-based concentration of teachers in a particular school is the natural and immediate outcome of the demographic concentration of people from the same *hamula* in the same locality. In Wadi Ara, large *hamulas* numbering two thousand people or more live in the same town or are spread over a number of towns and villages. It is natural, then, to find a large number of teachers and students from the same *hamula* at a single school. For example, in almost every class at my school there is a large concentration of children from the Mahajneh and Jabareen *hamulas*. This is a reality we have to face, despite all the problems involved.

Going back to power relationships within the school system, the aforementioned authoritarian structure within the Arab schools extends to the teacher-pupil relationship, with the pupil in a marginal position. Our findings reveal that teachers had difficulty answering direct questions about the teacher-pupil relationship. Most teachers preferred to give noncommittal answers to the questions we posed on this subject rather than unequivocal ones. Nevertheless, the responses reflect the hierarchy in the decision-making process. For example, we asked teachers the following question: "In the event of a disagreement between yourself and your pupils on a particular matter, whose opinion matters in the end?" Of the teachers who answered this question, 66 percent responded "sometimes that of the teacher and sometimes that of the pupils," 32 percent responded "the teacher's opinion," and only 2 percent responded that the pupils' opinion took precedence.

TEACHING OF ACTUAL ISSUES

One factor that impaired the pupils' image of the teacher as an educator and leader was the fact that the schools do not permit any discussion of current affairs, and particularly of issues related to the students' national identity and the Arab citizens' collective national rights. Despite the extremely high politicization of Arab society in Israel, for many years teachers refrained from discussing current political issues (Mari 1978; Al-Haj 1995a).

A number of historic and dramatic political events over the years served to increase the confusion and sense of powerlessness among Arab teachers. These included Land Day (March 30, 1976), Egyptian president Anwar Sadat's historic visit to Jerusalem in 1977 (see *Al-Hamishmar*, January 25, 1978), Israel's invasion of Lebanon in 1982, and especially the massacre of the Palestinians at the Sabra and Shatila refugee camps in Lebanon (*Al-Hamishmar*, January 28, 1983) and the first Palestinian intifada in the occupied territories (1987).

The outbreak of the first intifada in the occupied Palestinian territories caused further confusion in the education system in Israel as a whole and in the Arab schools in particular. Faced with the dynamic events of the intifada, Arab teachers found themselves in a tricky situation. They were puzzled about whether and how to deal with these events and to what extent they should express their own opinions (Mari 1988).

The Ministry of Education distributed a special circular calling upon the schools to "soothe their pupils' tempers" and "inculcate optimism and hope for overcoming all the barriers." Based on this circular, a formal working paper was disseminated in the Arab schools discussing the national and citizenship components of the identity of the Arabs in Israel. This working paper raised a number of questions regarding these components, yet most remained unanswered. The crux of this working paper was to convince Arab pupils, through their teachers, that all contradictions stemming from the complicated status of the Arabs in Israel can be reconciled. In addition, the paper tried to simplify crucial issues, for example by assuming that Israel's status as a Jewish state as stated in the Declaration of Independence does not necessarily contradict its status as a democratic state (Ministry of Education and Culture 1988, 3).

Since the early 1990s, and especially after the Israeli-Palestinian Oslo Accords in 1993, the reins of control in Arab schools have been somewhat loosened. Nevertheless, most teachers have not been able to shake off all traces of their old fears. In our survey, which as noted was conducted in November 1993, right after the Oslo Accords were signed, only 26 percent of the teachers stated that they discussed current affairs with their students on a regular basis.

Notwithstanding some degree of openness, the formal education system in Israel still suppresses any content that has the potential to foster a collective national identity among Arab students. This suppression is aimed at sustaining the dominance of Israeli citizenship content as part of the official definition of citizenship (e.g., Crossley and Tikly 2004; Al-Haj 2005b; Agbaria, Mustafa, and Jabareen 2015; Sabbagh and Resh 2018). Indeed, the Ministry of Education's ban on any discussion of current affairs seeks not only to maintain the hegemonic culture within Arab schools but also to suppress any counterhegemonic discourse and to inculcate a culture of silence among both students and teachers.

Nevertheless, studies show that by means of extracurricular activities Arab teachers have begun to launch more initiatives to counterbalance the fact that current issues are not taught in Arab schools. Arar and Ibrahim (2016) note that some teachers have developed a coping strategy in which they use the overt curriculum to inculcate covert learning that provides students the chance to address issues connected to their national identity and cultural values (681). Some of these activities are organized through parents' committees and the local municipality in an attempt to block any possible objections from Ministry of Education officials. In this way, teachers and principals attempt to reconcile the expectations of their students and the local community without interfering with their official commitment to the Ministry of Education (691). Similarly, Agbaria and Pinson (2019) analyze the strategies developed by Arab high school teachers under the auspices of citizenship education. They show how these teachers attempt to initiate a discussion that would allow students to deal with citizenship rights without breaking the rules of the game dictated by the formal system.

In a comparative study examining how Jewish and Arab teachers discuss controversial issues of Jewish-Arab relations (referred to as "controversial public issues" [CPI]), Gindi and Erlich-Ron (2019) reach a conclusion similar to that of the aforementioned studies: Arab teachers were "less knowledgeable of Ministry of Education guidelines regarding teachers' freedom of speech, conducted fewer discussions of CPI and rated the importance of their role in promoting active citizenship lower than their Jewish counterparts" (44). Thus, although Arab teachers hold more pluralistic views than their Jewish counterparts, they make every effort not to endanger their status and professional interests. As a result, Arab teachers have chosen a strategy of compromise through which they direct their students to engage in a pragmatic-localized discussion of current issues rather than a value-oriented discussion with a global-political orientation (52).

The matter of discussing actual issues with students was repeatedly mentioned by the participating teachers in our focus groups at all school levels, especially middle school and senior high school (January 2020). This repetition suggests how important it is for these teachers to satisfy the community's expectations and be recognized as "authentic" educators in the eyes of broader Arab society. Secondary school teachers appear to be more daring in expressing their attitudes about current political issues than elementary school and middle school teachers. This may be because secondary school teachers are university graduates and are usually more politicized. As discussed in chapter 6, for Arab students, university studies constitute a significant period of political socialization (see also Mari 1978; Al-Haj 2003, 2006). In contrast, elementary and middle school teachers usually are trained at teachers colleges. These colleges are directly controlled by the Ministry of Education and thus prohibit any political activity among trainees. In addition, secondary schools are managed by Arab local authorities and thus are less dependent on the Ministry of Education. Hence, secondary schools usually have more leverage in administering their activities, though they are far from autonomous. Moreover, by the time students reach secondary school, they exert more pressure on their teachers to discuss current issues. Equally important, teenagers are naturally much more politically involved in issues related to their collective national identity.

In what follows I present two typical citations from these discussions. Omar, a participant in the secondary school teachers focus group, made the following comment on this issue:

> I have been teaching history at this school for nearly 25 years now. I can say that over time, discussion of current issues has become much more apparent. As a matter of fact, this trend has been very much affected by the atmosphere our mayor introduced at the school, as reflected in his speeches at the annual graduation ceremonies. Last year [2019] he even participated in a symposium about the Nationality Law held at our school. He severely criticized this law, which completely overlooks our existence and rights as an Arab minority. This atmosphere has very much encouraged me to engage my students in discussion of this law during regular classes and to speak more openly about our citizenship rights. Yet, in line with instructions from our principal, I am still very cautious when dealing with collective issues such as the Nakba.

Mahmoud, a middle school teacher, added:

Let's speak frankly, we [teachers] are always lagging behind our students. We try to respond to their queries, but we rarely lead a discussion on our own initiative. I do think that in many cases, students bring up such questions on actual issues just to provoke teachers, because students have all the answers from the media and through their social networks and they simply do not need us for this purpose. Yet as a veteran teacher, I can see that unlike my students 20 years ago who were very preoccupied with national-political issues, today's students are more concerned about individual-pragmatic issues connected to their own future and needs. (Secondary-middle school teachers' focus group, January 2020)

Burnout among Teachers

Since the early 1980s, numerous studies worldwide have examined teacher burnout in both developing and developed societies (see, for example, Farber and Miller 1981; Jackson, Schwab, and Schuler 1986; Kyriacou 1987; Friedman 1992a, 2000; Näring, Briët, and Brouwers 2006; Sadeghi and Khezrlou 2014; Maslach, Jackson, and Leiter 2018; Squillaci 2020). Whereas many studies have examined teacher burnout among Jewish teachers in Israel (Friedman and Lotan 1987, 1993; Friedman 1991, 1992a, 1992b; Friedman and Farber 1992), to the best of my knowledge, not one study on burnout has been conducted among Arab teachers, despite the importance of this issue to teachers' status and performance.

In the following sections, I briefly review the literature on the central issues and factors associated with teacher burnout. After defining burnout and outlining the major factors that affect its extent, I discuss the findings of our nationwide survey on Arab teachers in Israel in the context of burnout.

Most researchers define the complex concept of burnout along three main dimensions: mental exhaustion, depersonalization, and low sense of self-fulfillment (Jackson, Schwab, and Schuler 1986, 630). These dimensions are included in the Maslach Burnout Inventory (MBI), which has become the central tool for measuring burnout (Jackson, Schwab, and Schuler 1986; Maslach, Jackson, and Leiter 2018). Burnout encompasses the negative impact of workplace stress as manifested by fatigue, increased mental distance from one's job, and diminished professional efficacy (Squillaci 2020, 1). Accordingly, Maslach and Leiter (2016) define burnout as "a psychological syndrome emerging as a prolonged response to chronic interpersonal stressors on the job. The three key dimensions of this response are overwhelming exhaustion, feelings of cynicism and detachment from the job, and a sense of ineffectiveness and lack of accomplishment. The significance of this three-dimensional model is that it clearly places the individual stress experience within a social context and involves the person's conception of both self and others" (103). In the past few decades, burnout has been recognized as an occupational hazard in people-oriented professions, including education, health services, and human services. These professions involve intense personal and emotional contact together with complex and frequently exhausting relationships with clients (Maslach and Leiter 2016). According to Friedman (1992a, 257), of the three variables of burnout, sense of exhaustion—in particular mental exhaustion—represents the highest level.

Various researchers have noted that the symptoms of burnout encompass a wide range of responses: rigidity, inflexibility, a feeling that life lacks meaning, diminished enthusiasm for work, boredom, frustration, emptiness, cynicism, a drop in sensitivity threshold, and a feeling of being overworked (see Friedman and Lotan 1993; Freudenberger 1974; Kyriacou 1987; Squillaci 2020). In the case of teachers, the signs of burnout also include a drop in teaching quality, protracted absences from work, and a lack of commitment to pupils. Teachers experiencing burnout are liable to become impatient when faced with frustrating classroom situations and to be overly strict with pupils (Farber and Miller 1981). Burnout generally culminates with the teacher leaving the profession (Friedman 1992a, 285).

A review of the literature indicates that the level of burnout among public service workers in general, and among teachers in particular, varies from place to place but does not exceed 25 percent. In a series of studies of school teachers in England, Kyriacou (1981) found that one in four teachers claimed that "being a teacher puts a lot of pressure on you." A similar study conducted by the Szold Institute in 1990 found that 25 percent of teachers reported having recently considered leaving the profession due to burnout and about 20 percent reported being "sick and tired" of the work (Friedman 1992b, 5). Recent literature shows that the potential for burnout in the teaching profession is high. Squillaci (2020, 6) reported that more than 80 percent of teachers are in the danger zone, 13 percent in the at-risk zone, and only 1 percent are in the desired zone (see also Näring, Briët, and Brouwers 2006; Baran et al. 2010).

Burnout levels vary not only from one country to another, but also within the same education system, due to different attributes of the teachers themselves. Whether men and women experience different levels of burnout is open to debate. Some studies show a higher level of burnout among women due to the additional burden of having to maintain the home (Enteman and Shirom 1987; Dumitru and Talpos 2012). Other studies demonstrate the opposite—male teachers complain of burnout more than their female counterparts (Friedman 1992a; Schaufeli and Buunk 2003; Buunk et al. 2007). Still other researchers found no significant differences between men and women (Maslach, Schaufeli, and Leiter 2001; Sadeghi and Khezrlou 2014).

Similar to the controversy regarding gender differences in burnout, findings also vary regarding the extent to which burnout is a function of years on the job. Enteman and Shirom found a higher rate of burnout during the early years of teaching. This finding can be explained by reality shock: teachers embark upon their careers with high expectations but are quickly disappointed by the disparity between their expectations and reality (Enteman and Shirom 1987; Friedman 2000). Indeed, according to research conducted in England, teacher absenteeism is highest during the first years of teaching (Avraham 1986, 140).

In contrast, Friedman (1992b, 5) found that burnout increases steadily during the first 20 years of employment (up to age 45 or so), after which it decreases from year to year. Similar findings were reported in the United States (Schwab and Iwanicki 1982). This can be explained by the pressure, tension, and frustration that build up over the years. Teachers over the age of 45 tend to demonstrate resilience and survive the system. In addition, at this age family pressures decrease because teachers' children tend to be older (Friedman 1992b, 6). It is reasonable to assume that teachers with many years of experience have come to terms with the system and adapted their expectations to reality (Enteman and Shirom 1987, 351, 356). Nevertheless, some studies report no significant differences based on teaching experience (Sadeghi and Khezrlou 2014).

Studies also found a positive connection between level of education and burnout. The more highly educated the teacher, the more likely he or she is to complain of burnout. According to Friedman (1992b, 6), the main difference can be seen between graduates of teachers colleges and university graduates. Teachers with university degrees have higher expectations, both of themselves and of the system, and their disappointment is correspondingly greater. Moreover, teachers who teach higher grade levels report greater burnout.

To examine burnout using our data, I selected a number of questions based on Friedman's 1991 study[1] that would enable me to make comparisons with Jewish teachers. Other questions were specially formulated for Arab teachers. Four questions reflected negative aspects (e.g., fatigue, frustration, burnout) and four questions reflected positive aspects (e.g., satisfaction, desire to continue in the profession). One question reflected the collective positive aspect (no. 8 in table 5.2). Three questions specially written for Arab teachers were added after a pilot study based on open discussions with the teachers. These discussions led me to conclude that Arab teachers saw the following as major factors in burnout: achieving upward mobility as a result of nonprofessional considerations, entering the profession due to a lack of alternatives, and seeing teaching as a national mission.

A comparison of my figures with those of Friedman (1991) shows that the burnout rate is similar for Arab and Jewish teachers (39 percent and 36 percent, respectively). Nevertheless, Jewish teachers have a greater sense of self-fulfillment than Arab teachers (93 percent vs. 63 percent). The proportion of teachers who feel that teaching prevents them from getting anywhere in life is similar, though slightly greater in the Arab sector (40 percent for Jews, 44.4 percent for Arabs).

Viewing teaching as a national mission yielded the highest rate of positive responses among Arab teachers. Indeed, the political-ideological context plays a significant role among Arab teachers, who are highly sensitive to the Arab community's expectations regarding the national significance of education. As my data show, the vast majority of Arab teachers (92 percent—the highest of all results) think teaching is a national mission. The assumption is that this attitude is influenced by strong public acceptance. As noted in chapter 6, among Arabs education has replaced land as an economic resource and a symbol of national pride. Most public discussions define education as a national mission and criticize teachers for failing to carry out this mission adequately (Al-Haj 2006).

One interesting finding is that although a large number of Arab teachers joined the profession due to a lack of alternatives, only 8.4 percent claimed to be in the teaching profession for reasons beyond their control. It is reasonable to assume that teachers have rationalized their work as teachers and have developed internal mechanisms to deal with their frustration. The proportion of those who claimed they became teachers for lack of an alternative was twice as high among high school teachers (12 percent) as among primary

---

1. The burnout scale used by Friedman was actually based on the Maslach Burnout Inventory (MBI) (see Maslach and Jackson 1981).

Table 5.2. Variables Comprising the Burnout Index*
(Means and Standard Deviations)

	Mean	SD	N
1. I feel that teaching and working with pupils causes me to burn out.	2.49	0.88	842
2. Teaching does not enable me to use my talents.	2.50	0.87	844
3. I am a teacher for reasons beyond my control.	1.49	0.71	849
4. Promotion is based on connections with one's superiors and not on professional ability.	2.49	1.05	844
5. As a teacher, I will not get anywhere in life	2.36	0.97	844
6. I am very interested in my work	1.64	0.48	846
7. Teaching gives me satisfaction	1.72	0.45	846
8. Teaching is a national mission.	1.44	0.49	843
9. If I had to make the choice again, I would choose to be a teacher.	1.72	0.45	829

*The burnout index has a high internal reliability: Cronbach's alpha = 0.74; mean = 1.96; standard deviation = 0.38.

school teachers (6 percent). Indeed, the mismatch between education level and job is most noticeable in the case of teachers with university degrees, who became teachers only because of the limited employment possibilities for Arab university graduates (Lewin-Epstein, Al-Haj, and Semyonov 1994). My findings show that if given another chance to choose a profession, nearly 40 percent of Arab teachers would not go into teaching.

BURNOUT INDEX

The items I included in the burnout index cover four main areas: mental exhaustion (one item: no. 1 in table 5.2); professional self-fulfillment (three items: nos. 2, 3, 4); personal self-fulfillment (four items: nos. 5, 6, 7, 9); and national fulfillment (one item: no. 8 in table 5.2). Respondents were asked to reply on a 4-point scale (totally disagree, disagree, agree, totally agree). Note that while analyzing the data from the pilot questionnaire I reached the conclusion that intermediate categories like "agree somewhat" or "disagree somewhat" should be avoided, since most of the respondents tended to take refuge in these categories rather than give unequivocal answers. The experimental questionnaire also enabled me to identify the items that made a larger contribution to the content of the burnout index (in accordance with a factor analysis applied to the experimental questionnaire).

In table 5.3, I examined the burnout index using a large number of independent variables, classified into four main groups:

- Background variables: gender, education, marital status, years of experience.

- Organizational variables: school affiliation, school level.

- School climate: degree of innovation at the school.

- Self-fulfillment: level of achievement of Arab education, teachers' status in society's eyes, perceived criteria by which society determines status.

Table 5.3 reveals an interesting set of correlations between the burnout index and the independent variables. Gender and education exhibited a significant relationship with burnout, such that men experience more burnout than women and teachers with university degrees experience more burnout than those without higher education. When level of education is statistically controlled, the difference between men and women still remains but becomes insignificant, such that the main distinction is simply between those who have university degrees and those who do not.

Marital status is not an important factor in burnout, although the burnout rate is higher among married teachers than among those who are not married. The correlation between years of experience and burnout is also not significant. Note that the main difference emerges between teachers in their first years (one to four) of teaching and all the rest, such that novice teachers experience less burnout than other teachers.

My findings tally with those of Friedman (1992a, 1992b) and Friedman and Lotan (1987), especially with regard to gender and education. The major difference is related to years of experience. Friedman's findings indicate that burnout level rises during the first 20 years of work, whereas my data showed that number of years of experience did not make much difference after the fourth year (Friedman 1992b, 5–6). This confirms the above claims regarding the power of conformity in the Arab educational system. New

Table 5.3. Teachers' Scores on Burnout Scale according to Various Independent Variables (Means and Standard Deviations)*
Significance at P < 0.05 level

Background Variables

Table 5.3a.

Gender	N	SD	Mean
Male	489	0.34	2.06*
Female	354	0.38	1.82

Table 5.3b.

Education	N	SD	Mean
Non-university	486	0.37	1.91*
University	352	0.38	2.03

Table 5.3c.

Marital status	N	SD	Mean
Married	671	0.38	1.97
Not married	180	0.36	1.94

Table 5.3d.

Years of teaching experience	N	SD	Mean
1–4	179	0.37	1.93
5–14	295	0.37	1.97
15–24	266	0.38	1.96
25+	112	0.41	1.97

Organizational Variables

Table 5.3e.

Affiliation	N	SD	Mean
State school	689	0.38	1.98*
Private-Christian	100	0.35	1.86
Amal network	29	0.35	1.95

*Significant at P <.05

Table 5.3f.

Level of school	N	SD	Mean
Primary	385	0.38	1.94*
Special education	14	0.35	2.14
Junior high	81	0.34	2.01
High school	199	0.38	1.99
Comprehensive (junior high and senior high)	82	0.35	2.07
Comprehensive (primary and secondary)	65	0.36	1.92

School Climate

Table 5.3g.

Amount of innovation			
Low	501	0.37	2.03*
High	340	0.37	1.86

Self-Perception

Table 5.3h.

Level of educational achievement in the Arab sector	N	SD	Mean
Low	454	0.38	2.04*
Average	336	0.36	1.89
High	61	0.33	1.79

Table 5.3i.

Society's view of teachers' status	N	SD	Mean
Low	411	0.36	2.06*
Average	413	0.37	1.88
High	27	0.33	1.74

*Significant at P <.05

continued on next page

Table 5.3. Continued.

Table 5.3j.

Perceived criteria by which society determines status			
Financial situation	404	0.37	2.05*
Education	360	0.36	1.86
Family ties or connections to the authorities	32	0.33	1.95

Table 5.3k.

Total sample	852	0.38	1.96

*Significant at P <.05

teachers quickly adapt to the system, such that differences between them and teachers with more experience gradually disappear.

The data reveal a significant correlation between each of the school organizational variables and burnout. Teachers at private schools experienced less burnout than those at state schools and Amal vocational schools, likely because the private schools are more exclusive and selective with regard to both pupils and teachers. Moreover, these schools maintain stronger ties to the community than do state schools and enjoy much greater social support from the community and from church organizations.

Special education teachers exhibit the highest rates of burnout compared to teachers in regular education. This finding is in line with the findings of many field studies. In their literature review, Pavlidou, Alevriadou, and Antoniou (2022, 192) note that burnout rates are more elevated among special education teachers than among teachers in regular classes. This is due to lower work satisfaction, low self-esteem, increased work-related stress, and turnover among special education teachers (also Antoniou, Polychroni, and Kotroni 2009; Emery and Vandenberg 2010).

In line with the findings in the literature, burnout rate increases at higher grade levels. Teachers at comprehensive schools (combined middle and senior high schools) exhibit the highest rates of burnout. At middle schools that are not combined with high schools, the extent of teacher burnout is lower than at comprehensive schools that encompass both middle and senior high school classes. Studies show that this may result partly from the nature of teacher-student relationships at the different school levels. Indeed, primary school students are usually closer to their teachers and often seek out this proximity (Furrer and Skinner 2003, cited by Pavlidou, Alevriadou, and Antoniou 2022, 199). In contrast, teenagers enrolled at secondary schools "are less willing to develop interpersonal relationships with their teachers, and sometimes they may even show aggression towards them" (199; also McGrath and van Bergen 2015).

A significant correlation emerged between school democracy and burnout rate, such that the more democratic the school atmosphere, the lower the burnout rate. Concurrently, the more the principal listens to the teachers and takes their views into consideration, the lower the burnout rates. This conclusion reiterates other studies highlighting the importance of respect and support provided by principals in building trust and confidence in the school community (Arar 2019). Hence, principals with more autocratic and authoritarian leadership styles tend to diminish teacher autonomy, negatively affecting the school climate (Arar and Massry-Herzallah 2016). Note that my data also reveal a strong relationship between school innovation and burnout, such that burnout is lower at schools with educational innovation projects than at schools with only a few or no such projects.

My findings are also in line with studies that highlight the impact of school climate on teacher burnout (Kyriacou 1981, 1987; Dunham 1984; Gavish and Friedman 2010; Luleci and Coruk 2018). These studies show that an improved school climate is crucial to increasing teachers' job satisfaction, boosting their morale, and ultimately improving their conduct at school (Luleci and Coruk 2018). Furthermore, clarity in what is expected of teachers has been mentioned as a central factor affecting burnout. Thus, the information provided to teachers regarding their rights, obligations, and responsibilities must be sufficiently clear and consistent (Lavian 2012).

The findings show that as teachers' perceptions concerning the standard of Arab education and concerning their own status in society's eyes improve, the burnout rate decreases. In the questions on self-image, I asked teachers to rank teaching relative to other professions. The teachers placed themselves at the middle of the social status scale and at the lower end of the financial status scale. This result explains why teachers who think that a person's status in society is determined by financial status experience the most burnout, whereas teachers who believe that education is the most important criterion for determining status have the lowest level of burnout. Furthermore, teachers who believe that promotion in the education system is determined by hamula-clan connections or ties with authorities experience higher rates of burnout. Note that teachers are highly responsive to the expectations and attitudes of the society in which they live. Those who think that the standard of Arab education is high and believe that society considers teaching to be a high-status profession are least likely to experience burnout.

These findings go hand in hand with the conclusions derived from the relevant literature regarding the relationship between self-fulfillment and burnout. Indeed, the literature points to the gap between expectations and perceived reality as a major factor in burnout levels and consequently in deciding to leave the teaching profession (Friedman 2000; Gavish and Friedman 2010). At the same time, as self-fulfillment rises, burnout rates and teacher dropout rates drop (Tomic and Tomic 2008). Based on the social exchange theory, Van Horn, Schaufeli, and Enzmann (1999) similarly conclude that teacher burnout results from the discrepancy between investment and outcome and in this sense social exchange processes affect all relationships within the school system, including teacher-student, teacher-teacher, and teacher-school relationships.

Recent Trends: Local and Global Challenges

What characterizes burnout trends among Arab teachers over time? What are the local and global factors contributing to these trends? To answer these questions, I analyzed the discussions in my teacher focus groups, the unstructured interviews, and the conclusions of my systematic observations at a number of Arab schools. My analysis shows that the factors enhancing teacher burnout have become stronger over time as a result of several developments in the local and global arenas. I discuss the major factors in the following sections.

The first factor is the widening gap between the expectations of Arab teachers and the returns from their teaching jobs. As indicated earlier, the level of education and training among Arab teachers has undergone quantitative and qualitative changes. Indeed, Arab teachers have become much more qualified. The vast majority of Arab teachers today (96 percent) hold academic degrees, and one-third hold master's degrees (SAI 2020, table 4.33). Yet employment opportunities for these teachers have remained very limited. As of 2020, nearly 39,000 Arab teachers are employed at the different levels of education (SAI 2020, table 4.33), and estimates show that nearly 15,000 unemployed teachers (over one-third) are on waiting lists for teaching jobs. Note that there are very few vacant teaching positions at Arab schools each year.

The main vacancies are to replace teachers who retire. As mentioned earlier, a considerable portion of Jewish teachers either change jobs or quit teaching. In contrast, Arab teachers tend to remain in the school system throughout their entire career, primarily because they have no other alternative. Like other Arab academics, they have very limited options on the labor market and are therefore completely dependent on their current job. As a result, the number of unemployed Arab teachers is expected to increase in the future. In an interview, one of the superintendents had this to say:

> According to current estimates, nearly 15,000 Arab teachers are unemployed. There is, indeed, employment distress among graduates of academic teachers colleges. The number of graduates is much higher than the number of available teaching posts. Therefore, in many cases most of these graduates remain unemployed for a couple of years because we have to give priority to those already on the waiting list. The waiting period can range from three to seven years until they are offered a job, and in most cases just a part-time job. On the other hand, there is a shortage of teachers in Jewish schools. Some Arab graduates have changed their career path in order to work in Hebrew schools. But these are only a small number and this cannot solve the acute problem of teachers' unemployment. (Interview by author, January 23, 2020)

These hardships in acquiring teaching jobs have far-reaching implications for self-perceptions and sense of burnout among Arab teachers. Samira, an elementary school teacher who participated in the focus group, aptly expressed this reality:

> I graduated from teachers college eight years ago, but I am still a first-year teacher! It took seven whole years until I was offered a teaching job, which I first thought would be available immediately after graduation. For three years after graduation, I was unemployed. I searched for a job in other fields but did not find one. Eventually, I worked as a teacher in a private kindergarten. Needless to say, the salary and conditions were

much lower than those granted by the Ministry. I applied to the Ministry of Education again and again, and every year I was told I am still way down on a long list of candidates who are ahead of me. As a matter of fact, nobody knows what the criteria are for hiring Arab teachers or how to advance on this waiting list. Finally, a friend who was offered an appointment told me frankly that without support from a well-known public figure, I would never be offered a teaching position. My husband spoke with the mayor, who promised to handle this shortly. Indeed, in the next school year, I was offered the appointment I had been dreaming of for the past seven years! Yet already during my first year of work I feel completely exhausted. I always ask myself whether it was worth investing so many years in my academic studies and training just to go through such a humiliating process!

Samira corroborates my aforementioned analysis that the gap between expectations and perceived reality is a major factor in teacher burnout. Indeed, among other things teacher burnout results from the dissonance between the investment teachers make and the outcomes they gain. In addition, teachers believe that promotion is based on social networking and connections rather than on objective professional ability. This perception constitutes a major factor that exacerbates burnout. Samira's experience reflects that of thousands of Arab teachers, who experience burnout from the outset due to the wide gap between expectations and reality.

Indeed, the above factors contributing to teacher burnout have become stronger over time, and unemployment or underemployment among Arab teachers has increased. Equally important, the failure of government ministries to hire Arab academics and graduates of teachers colleges has made the local government a major employer for a considerable number of educated Arabs, who are forced to compete for available jobs in their residential localities, mainly in the secondary schools (Al-Haj 2003). Yet the interests of the local government are not necessarily in line with those of the schools. Therefore, interference in Arab schools is not restricted to the central government but is also exercised by local authorities, mainly in the secondary schools, as manifested in the hiring and promotion of teachers and principals (see Arar and Abu-Asbah 2013). As a result, most teachers are convinced that hiring, firing, and promotion policies are influenced by nonobjective criteria that have not changed over time but rather have become more acute and painful.

The second factor contributing to rising burnout rates is linked to the widening gap between Arab schools and society. My above analysis reveals that teachers are highly responsive to the expectations and attitudes of the society in which they live. Those who believe that the standard of Arab education is high and that society considers teaching to be a high-status profession are the least likely to experience burnout. An examination of developments in Arab schools shows that even though physical conditions have improved considerably over time, Jewish schools still surpass Arab schools in terms of qualitative criteria, as reflected by scores on national and international tests and by matriculation exam results (see chapter 3).

As indicated, my findings show that burnout rates are negatively associated with the use of advanced methods based on creativity and innovation. Based on my systematic observations at a number of Arab schools, it is safe to argue that, despite some important changes, most Arab schools still use the frontal method of teaching, in which the teacher is the main actor and the pupils play minor roles. Only a few schools have made considerable efforts to introduce high-order skills such as innovation, critical thinking, and creativity or life skills that students can use outside the classroom. As Alayan (2012) concludes, "Palestinian society today needs teachers who will provide young people with the ability to ask relevant questions and to identify problems, cultivating their intellects in accordance with the spirit of the time, creating bold and independent thinkers" (226).

My analysis in chapter 3 shows that the performance gap between Arab and Jewish schools has broadened over time, as reflected in the differential performance of Arab and Jewish students on international tests (PISA and TIMSS). The analysis shows that the scores of Jewish and Arab schools on international exams reflect two completely different entities: the figures for the Jewish schools resemble those of Western industrial countries, whereas the figures for the Arab schools are classified at the bottom of third world countries (chapter 3).

These facts have clearly had a negative impact on the self-efficacy perceptions of Arab teachers, in turn raising burnout rates. Moreover, as a result of high rates of failure in these tests, parents and the Arab community at large put major pressure on teachers, who are blamed for this failure. Most of the participants in the teacher discussion groups raised this point. Suha, a middle school teacher, bitterly stated:

> It is very annoying that, regardless of our efforts as teachers, once the results of the PISA exams are published, criticism is directed at us. It's as if we are the only ones at blame for this. When I speak with people in my community, I always feel as if I am guilty. . . . It seems that people forget that we [Arab

teachers] do our best under difficult conditions. Our schools also suffer from difficult conditions and budget shortages. But parents in my community seem to think we are representatives of the authorities [Ministry of Education], and it's easier to direct all their criticism at us. This demoralizes me a lot, because I do think there are many achievements to be proud of at my school, thanks to the efforts we make together with our principal. But it seems that people do not recognize these achievements, because all the headlines in the media speak only about the failure of Arab schools on the PISA exams.

The third major factor in the rise of teacher burnout is linked to changes in teacher-student relationships. As previously noted, students are extremely marginalized in the educational process because teacher-student relations are deeply rooted in notions of teacher authoritarianism and students' blind obedience (Al-Haj 1995a). Hence, Arab schools have always had a problem of internal democratization. Indeed, studies have repeatedly shown that Arab teachers are sensitive to democracy and civil rights when it comes to Jewish-Arab relations, but much more narrow-minded and intolerant when it comes to internal democracy in the Arab schools (Al-Haj 2006).

In the meantime, some far-reaching changes have occurred in the dynamics of student-teacher relationships, at least on the part of the students. Even though the teachers' traditional authoritarian approach to students has practically not changed, the approach of the formerly obedient students has changed radically. This transformation is a byproduct of social processes taking place in society at large. As noted in the background chapter (chapter 2), a conspicuous social change has occurred within the Arab family. In the past, women and children exerted limited and even marginal influence in the family's decision-making, but over time women and children have become more central in the life of the family. Indeed, most families have adjusted their consumer patterns and lifestyles to the needs and requirements of their children (Al-Haj 1987; Al-Krenawi and Graham 1998; Haj-Yahia and Lavee 2018; Meoded Karabanov et al. 2021). Moreover, parent-children relationships have also been affected by technological changes. As in other contemporary societies, one of the major developments in family lifestyles among the Arabs in Israel is that more families have introduced digital technology and internet-based media into their homes, primarily oriented to children's needs (Meoded Karabanov et al. 2021; Tzischinsky and Haimov 2017).

Consequently, the traditional relationship between the authoritarian teacher and the obedient student has been undermined and is constantly being challenged by students and their parents. Backed by their parents, most students today are not prepared to accept the authoritarian formula once dictated by teachers. Furthermore, the atmosphere inspired by social media has led to increased aggression directed against teachers. The wide discrepancy between school and society on the one hand and the changing nature of teacher-student and teacher-parent relationships on the other have made teachers' jobs more difficult, thus increasing their despair and their burnout. Nasser, a middle school teacher, expressed this feeling during the teachers' focus group discussion:

> Being a teacher has become extremely difficult. I feel marginalized not only regarding my status and economic conditions, but also in my relationships with my students. It is very difficult to maintain any sort of discipline in the classroom because most students are not even willing to listen! Today, it is common for students to arrive late, make noise in the class, not do their homework, and often play with their smartphones during class time. As a teacher I can do nothing to combat such unruly behavior. Unlike in the past when parents used to cooperate with teachers and make their children obey the teacher's rules, today the immediate response of parents is to back up their children against the teacher.

As mentioned earlier, teacher burnout resulting from relationships with students is especially evident in the middle and senior high schools. The discussions with teachers and principals show that this situation has even worsened over time. This was well expressed by Laila, a secondary school teacher who participated in our discussion group:

> I have been a teacher for over two decades now and can certainly say that the relationships with students are becoming more and more difficult. We [teachers] often are the victims of student violence and we can do nothing to prevent that. In fact, I feel very threatened, because unlike in the past when I could count on the help of parents to prevent students' deviant behavior, today's parents do not cooperate, whether because they side with

their children or because they are afraid of them. Let's face it, we live in a violent society, and this violence has trickled down from social networks and society at large into the school system. What is probably the most threatening is that you can never know when students use their phones to document every move you make and share it with thousands of people via the social media. . . . It is really frightening.

The above statements reflect a sense of helplessness among Arab teachers, especially because they are attempting to face a deeply changing reality through stagnant traditional teaching methods and authoritarian means of control. Indeed, during the systematic observations at a number of Arab schools (January–February 2020), I had the chance to speak with teachers and observe some classes in different subject areas. I must admit that a substantial number of schools have made the transition to new methods that are based on discussion, creativity, and active learning. Yet I was surprised to find that the majority of schools still use traditional methods that are based on listening and knowledge transfer and that relegate students to a passive role of extracting information from readymade materials. Teaching is often conducted in the form of a monologue, with the teacher as the main actor. A method that is a bit more advanced is the dialogue method, in which materials are conveyed in a way that allows limited interaction between the teacher and one student, while the rest of the students listen. Only a minuscule number of teachers use dynamic methods that involve brainstorming and give all students the opportunity to ask questions, take part in the discussion, and act as knowledge producers. In these dynamic methods, students are also offered the possibility of autonomous work and dynamic interaction among themselves and with the teacher.

Teachers who used dynamic methods expressed the highest levels of satisfaction and consequently exhibited the lowest rates of burnout. In contrast, teachers who used traditional methods exhibited higher levels of frustration, burnout, and powerlessness. This is because traditional methods produce mistrust and alienation and generate a wide gap between teachers and students. As a result, students often respond with disobedience. As Nasser stated in the discussion groups, with such methods it is "very difficult to maintain any sort of discipline in the classroom, because most students are not even willing to listen."

Indeed, treating students as passive listeners goes against the very nature of children, who are curious and active. Children seek to be involved in the educational process, which is supposed to be designed to meet their needs and match their development. Hence, the educational process should provide room for students' experiences, insights, and identity reflections. As Dewey (1915) noted long ago, treating children passively contradicts their natural tendencies. Dewey identified four main interests among schoolchildren: conversation or communication; inquiry or finding things out; making things or construction; and artistic expression (33, 45). Similarly, Freire (1973, 1985) highlighted that education is not merely the transference of knowledge but rather communication and dialogue and the practice of freedom. In the education system, students do not merely receive knowledge passively but rather seek it actively. Gramsci concurs with Freire's transformative pedagogy in that both see education not only as a system for knowledge transference but also as a place of knowledge production and development (see Tarlau 2017, 119–20).

In addition to the aforementioned local factors that have contributed to the growing burnout among Arab teachers, global factors related to neoliberal ideology and reforms have also had an impact. These factors have been in effect since the 1980s but have particularly intensified during the past two decades (see chapter 3). As a result, teachers today face many more challenges than in the past. These challenges are related to imposed curriculum, increasing bureaucracy, expanded responsibilities resulting from school reforms, rising expectations, declining teacher autonomy, and a growing climate of distrust. Moreover, the job of teaching has become more complex and intense, often as a result of societal and technological changes and the confusion of teachers within a system dominated by standardized tests and the "politics of numbers and scores" (see review by Flores 2020, 219–21).

Research shows that neoliberal reforms have in fact been detrimental to teachers' status and conduct (see, for example, Giroux 2010; Ball 2016; Zimmerman 2018; Acuña 2023). Giroux maintains that as a result of neoliberal reforms, teachers have been under unprecedented attack by those forces that view schools less as a public good and more as a private right. He further states that the standardization of school curricula and the subjugation of the educational process to the results of fixed evaluations for students and teachers alike have undermined the very essence of teachers' mission as educational leaders: "Questions regarding how teachers motivate students, make knowledge meaningful in order to make it critical and transformative, work with parents and the larger community, or exercise the authority needed to become a constructive pedagogical force in the classroom and community are now sacrificed to the dictates of an instrumental rationality largely defined through the optic of measurable utility" (Giroux 2010, 709).

Based on my systematic observations in the schools and my discussions with teachers, I feel confident stating that most of these global factors apply to Arab teachers as well. Such factors have exerted a negative impact on motivation and job satisfaction and have increased feelings of helplessness and fatigue among these teachers. (For a discussion of the major reforms in the Israeli education system during the past decade and their impact on schools, see Tamir and Shaked 2016; Tamir and Arar 2019; Arar, Tamir, and Abu-Hussain 2019. For the impact of global and national school tests, see Feniger, Israeli, and Yehuda 2016; Feniger 2020.) A number of teachers and principals mentioned the matter of teachers' expanded responsibilities as a result of school reforms. Hassan, an elementary school principal, had this to say: "There have been countless reforms during the past two decades. Almost every minister of education institutes a new reform, regardless of the many already in effect. Thus, before we have time to comprehend the previous reform, we are faced with another one. These reforms make our lives as principals more complicated because they are associated with expanded responsibilities, bureaucracy, reporting requirements, tracing the implementation of each reform, assessments, and other responsibilities vis-à-vis teachers, superintendents and the Ministry of Education." Hassan concluded: "It's really exhausting, in particular because we do not see any considerable improvement from these reforms. . . . These reforms make it even more difficult for teachers because they have no choice but to accept them without questioning" (interview by author, February 15, 2020).

A number of teachers also raised this point in the teachers' focus group discussions. Riham, an elementary school teacher, commented:

> I have been a schoolteacher for nearly 30 years now. I never have had such a heavy work load as in recent years. It is because of these reforms that we have to stay many hours after the regular school day in order to earn some extra salary, which in fact does not make a big difference. To the contrary. As a mother of four children I feel very exhausted by not being able to coordinate between my work as a teacher and my duties as a wife and mother. This does not even take into consideration the dramatic increase in the amount of training we have to take as part of these reforms. Yet nobody asks us what kind of training we need and how we feel about the relevance of this training in our day-

to-day work. . . . In fact, most of this training is irrelevant and does not help me cope with the difficulties I face as a teacher.

After a few minutes, Riham added the following: "I want to mention another point that has made our work even more difficult in recent years. This is connected with parents' expectations, which have become really exaggerated. . . . You cannot imagine the amount of stress we feel as teachers. Because this comes from all directions: the superintendent, the principal and parents" (teachers' focus group, January 2020). Participants in the teachers' focus group also complained that as a result of these reforms they have been reduced to "small technocrats" who have been "left behind" in that they must spend their time filling in forms and writing reports about tests and students' scores instead of doing the job they like: being teachers. Ihab, a middle school teacher, stated:

> These reforms are driving us crazy. . . . We don't have time to teach because we are busy all the time filling in forms and writing reports about tests and evaluations. We (teachers) have simply become small technocrats, we are irrelevant as teachers. Unfortunately, nobody wants to listen to us, we have been left behind. Our job has been reduced to satisfy the expectations of the superintendent who, in turn, wants to please the Ministry (of Education). All they want us to do is to give tests and use every measure to prove that our students' scores on the next test are better. I even began thinking about taking early retirement because I feel completely detached from my job. I am exhausted and full of despair. (Teachers' focus group, January 2020)

The Implications of the COVID-19 Crisis

The COVID-19 crisis has undoubtedly increased teachers' confusion, enhanced their sense of helplessness, and consequently raised their burnout rate. The health, economic, and social consequences of this pandemic have served to exacerbate the stress teachers feel both at school and at home under conditions of an uncertain and complicated reality.

In chapter 3 I showed that the shift to remote learning during the pandemic closure periods was especially difficult and demanding in Arab schools. As indicated, my systematic observations in Arab schools show that despite changes in teaching methods over time, a large proportion of Arab teachers still use traditional methods based on listening and transmitting knowledge. They are less likely to use methods based on creative and critical thinking, active learning, and independent work, even though these dynamic methods are crucial for regular as well as remote learning. Moreover, Arab students are disadvantaged in terms of digital access and they lack digital skills. While this digital disadvantage characterizes socio-economically disadvantaged groups worldwide (see Cohron 2015; review by Greenhow, Lewin, and Willet 2021; Saito 2023), the situation is especially prominent in Arab society: nearly 50 percent of Arab families live under the poverty line and 80 percent of Arab localities in Israel are categorized in the bottom clusters of the Central Bureau of Statistics socioeconomic ladder in Israel (see chapter 3).

A survey on teacher stress conducted among Jews and Arabs in Israel during the COVID-19 crisis shows that Arab teachers exhibited significantly more stress than Jewish teachers on both personal and work-related stress factors, and consequently on the general stress index as well (Boneh et al. 2021, 12). The survey found that Arab teachers were especially concerned about factors related to the collective, such as the reactions of school principals, the Ministry of Education, and parents. In contrast, Jewish teachers were concerned about personal factors associated with their personal well-being and the well-being of their family (Boneh et al. 2021, 1).

Summary

In this chapter I examined the circumstances of Arab teachers in Israel, including their status, their attitudes and orientation, and the difficulties and dilemmas they face as educators. The conflicting expectations of the school system and the Arab community at large from teachers were also discussed. I provided background by explaining the origins of the formal government policy of control and suppression of Arab education as a whole and of Arab teachers in particular—a policy that in essence prevails until this day. Based on a pioneering and representative survey of Arab teachers, I discussed various issues connected with how their professional identity, self-esteem, and job satisfaction have evolved. Finally, I devoted a special discussion to recent trends and factors that have led to rising burnout among Arab teachers.

According to my analysis, the factors affecting the status, conditions, and burnout of Arab teachers can be classified into four main levels: (1) the state-political level, which is tied to formal policy; (2) the school level, which is in fact related to the first level though is also affected by internal relationships in the Arab schools and Arab society; (3) the community level, which is related to the influence of parents and other power relationships in the local community; and (4) the global level, which describes general factors such as expanded responsibilities in the wake of neoliberal-neoconservative reforms and technological changes affecting teachers worldwide, including Arab teachers. Equally important are the challenges brought on by the recent COVID-19 pandemic, which have negatively affected Arab schools and increased teachers' sense of powerlessness and burnout rates.

The next chapter focuses on higher education among the Palestinian Arabs in Israel. This chapter underscores the main developments in attaining higher education among the Arabs, the cumulative difficulties faced by Arab students before and during their academic studies, and the socioeconomic returns from higher education as reflected in employment inequalities between Jewish and Arab graduates of the higher education system and their chances of translating higher education into upward mobility in the labor market.

Chapter 6

Higher Education

Quantitative Expansion, Obstacles, and Qualitative Inequalities

Abstract

This chapter provides a comprehensive picture of higher education among the Palestinian Arabs in Israel, from the establishment of the state through the present period. After a short theoretical overview, I trace the main trends in the expansion of tertiary education among Arabs compared to the Jewish majority. I underscore the factors that have retarded educational attainment among the Palestinian Arabs. More specifically, I discuss the role of the Psychometric Entrance Test (PET) as a gatekeeper that has had a negative impact not only on Arabs' access to higher education but also on their chances of being admitted to prestigious areas of study. Next, I outline the main problems of adaptation among Arab students during their academic studies, with special emphasis on cultural adaptation and its implications for their identity and sense of belonging. I conclude this chapter with a detailed discussion of employment opportunities for Arab graduates and the relationship between educational expansion and socioeconomic mobility.

The data are based on a synthesis of quantitative and qualitative methods, including a detailed analysis of statistics and reports available from the Israel Council for Higher Education (CHE), the Central Bureau of Statistics (CBS), and other pertinent sources. Moreover, I analyze the findings of a 2001 survey examining adjustment patterns among Palestinian Arab students in comparison to Jewish students. The qualitative analysis is based on a focus group conducted in November 2019 that included 14 undergraduate and graduate Arab students enrolled in various faculties at the University of Haifa.

Theoretical Framework: Higher Education and Inequalities

One of the main debates in the sociology of education centers on determining the impact of higher education on inequalities and socioeconomic gaps between dominant and disadvantaged groups. The theoretical perspectives developed to address these issues can be classified under two main headings: the positivist approach and the critical approach. In line with the positivist approach, the human capital theory of education and society postulates that education is a form of investment in that the "individual acquires skills and knowledge that can be converted into income when used to get a job" (Schultz 1977, 322). Accordingly, as people develop their human capital through education, they attain more opportunities for mobility, thus improving the economy and society as a whole.

In a frequently cited study espousing the aforementioned approach, Michael Hout concludes that higher education is a key engine for upward mobility, independent of social background. In this sense, intergenerational mobility is higher among college graduates than among people with lower levels of education. According to Hout (1988): "Origin status affects destination status among workers who do not have bachelor's degrees, but college graduation cancels the effect of background status. Therefore, the more college graduates in the work force, the weaker the association between origin status and destination status for the population as a whole" (1358).

In a recent study, Hout (2012) concludes that in addition to the individual socioeconomic returns of higher education, communities, states, and nations also benefit from a higher level of education among their populations. Some estimates even suggest that these social returns exceed the private returns. Hout adds that "college graduates find better jobs, earn more money, and suffer less unemployment than high school graduates do. They also live more stable family lives, enjoy better health, and live longer. They commit fewer crimes and participate more in civic life" (380; for reviews of US patterns, see Fischer and Hout 2006, 18–22). In this context, education is often referred to as the *great equalizer*. Thus, Torche (2011) concludes that a "college degree may fulfill an important meritocratic function: erasing the advantages of social origin in the competition for economic success" (797).

Unlike the positivist approach, the critical approach sees formal education as a mechanism of reproduction that reflects the power relations prevailing in the broader society, where education is used exclusively by the dominant group as a mechanism for economic exploitation and sociocultural control (Apple 1982, 1999, 2006a; Nieto and Bode 2008). Accordingly, advocates of the critical approach see the education system as an obstacle to development among disadvantaged groups and as a tool for preserving the status quo and for generating inequalities through its powerful mechanism, thus exerting a major impact on students' lives and future opportunities (Nieto 2000; Sleeter and Grant 2001; Apple 2004, 2006a, 2013).

The critical approach contends that institutions of higher education serve as vehicles for social reproduction, since the major portion of parental influence on children's socioeconomic standing is transmitted through education (for a review of this approach, see Zhou 2019). In this context, Lucas (2001, 2009) proposed the theory of effectively maintained inequality, which posits that "socioeconomically advantaged actors secure for themselves and their children some degree of advantage wherever advantages are commonly possible" (2001, 1652). Therefore, as quantitative advantages narrow as a result of the expansion of higher education, dominant groups will attempt to maximize their qualitative advantages at the high school level by selecting lucrative fields of study in higher education that ultimately yield higher returns (1680; see also Lucas 2009).

The critical approach was developed to explain class-based gaps in higher education. Nevertheless, its logic has been also used to interpret inequalities based on ethnicity and race (see Feniger, Mcdossi, and Ayalon 2014; Zhou 2019). Using this approach, Feniger, Mcdossi, and Ayalon (2014) examined how the expansion and diversification of higher education in Israel since the 1990s affected the gaps between the various ethnic and religious groups. They conclude that despite the dramatic expansion of higher education in Israel over the past two decades, Muslims, Christians, and Druze remain the most disadvantaged groups, both in terms of vertical (access) and horizontal (field of study) inequalities (7).

Whereas the positivist approach sees the expansion of education as a catalyst for intergenerational mobility and the emancipation of human potential, the critical approach underscores the uneven returns and asymmetrical utility of public schooling for the masses. Those who espouse the critical approach claim that the dominant groups are the main beneficiaries of educational expansion since they use the education system to consolidate their economic and political domination (Johnston 1985, 333).

In line with the critical approach, Zhou (2019) concludes that the expansion of higher education per se cannot guarantee intergenerational mobility and that social origin—as measured by family income—remains the key engine of upward mobility. Thus, "origin-based disparities in skills, in turn, translate into origin-based disparities in education, employment, and income, sustaining the 'inherited meritocracy'" (480). Zhou also showed that parental influence is not limited to financial resources. A great deal of parental influence on educational and labor market outcomes tends to be indirect "through the development of cognitive and non-cognitive skills well before college attendance" (480).

In addition to socioeconomic dominance, scholars have pointed to cultural hegemony as a central factor in perpetuating inequality in higher education. Through his concept of "cultural capital" Bourdieu highlighted cultural transmission as a carrier of social inequality, such that the structural conditions of higher education embody class interests and ideologies, reproduce the unequal distribution of cultural capital, and reproduce unequal levels of academic attainments and achievements (cited by Swartz 1997, 547; see also Bourdieu and Passeron 1990).

Research also shows that dominant groups maintain their cultural hegemony in higher education institutions through overt and covert policies. Explicit cultural hegemony is conveyed by faculty members, administrative staff, and curriculum, all of which are typically controlled by the dominant group (e.g., Margolis and Romero 1998; Adam 2019, 368). At the same time, implicit cultural hegemony is practiced through what is framed as a "hidden curriculum" (see Apple 1982, 2004) that is reflected in the nature of teaching and learning strategies and in programs that ignore the original culture of minority students (Sonn, Bishop, and Humphries 2000, 128). Such cultural exclusion generates alienation among minority students, who eventually tend to operate within an "enclave system" in which their informal relations take place mainly within their own ethnic or racial group (133).

Decolonial Theory

Decolonial theory was first invoked by Latin American scholars, who asserted that despite the disappearance of political *colonialism*, the relationships between European/Western culture and other cultures continue to reflect various forms of *coloniality* (Quijano 2007; see also Mignolo 2007, 163–64). Maldonado-Torres (2007) further differentiates between colonialism and coloniality: "Colonialism denotes a political and economic relation in which the sovereignty of a nation or a people rests on the power of another nation, which makes such nation an empire. Coloniality, instead, refers to long-standing patterns of power that emerged as a result of colonialism, but that define culture, labor, intersubjective relations, and knowledge production well beyond the strict limits of colonial administrations. Thus, coloniality survives colonialism" (243). Advocates of decolonial theory have described the use of higher education as a tool for cultural hegemony in terms of cultural coloniality that seeks to serve the interest of colonial powers, whether directly or indirectly (see Adam 2019; Regmi 2023). According to Adam (2019), this type of cultural coloniality "aims to convince the colonised to think of the coloniser—his epistemologies, his philosophies, his policies, his languages, his cultures—as superior. This colonisation of the mind is still deeply embedded in previously colonized countries, decades after formal political independence" (368).

Indeed, scholars contend that higher education is among the main arenas strongly affected by the hegemony of coloniality (Mbembe 2016; Jansen 2019; Adam 2019). While the methods used to implement coloniality in higher education may differ from one country to another, the colonial components conveyed through the education of minorities, indigenous peoples, and other marginalized people tend to be similar (e.g., Adam 2019; Mullen 2020). Furthermore, scholars have delineated a number of restructuring and decolonizing measures that should be introduced by institutions of higher education (Hayes, Luckett, and Misiaszek 2021, 887). Quijano (2007), for example, notes that first and foremost decoloniality is "epistemological decolonization, as decoloniality is needed to clear the way for new intercultural communication, for an interchange of experiences and meanings, as the basis of another rationality" (177).

Accordingly, educational activities toward decolonization that have been adopted in various countries have underscored the need to replace European/Western knowledge with local indigenous knowledge (see, for example, Mullen's 2020 analysis of the Canadian education system). Similarly, Mbembe (2016) highlights the need to strengthen students' sense of belonging, especially among students from disadvantaged groups. These students should be encouraged to pursue and produce alternative knowledge that reflects their culture and identity (30).

The above theoretical overview raises a number of questions regarding higher education among the indigenous Palestinian Arabs in Israel: What are the main trends in the expansion of higher education among the Arabs in

Israel? What are the odds of educational attainment among Arabs compared to Jews? Do institutions of higher education perpetuate the power system and cultural dominance of the wider society, or do they act as a catalyst for social change? What are the main difficulties faced by Arab students at Israeli institutions of higher education? Is there any formal strategy for dealing with these difficulties which takes into consideration needs and culture of Palestinian Arabs as an indigenous minority?

Higher Education among the Arabs in Israel: Background and Developments

Several factors in the background of the Palestinian Arab population in Israel have made education in general, and higher education in particular, top priorities. Both the low starting point of the Palestinian Arabs and the crisis experienced by Arab political and intellectual elites as a result of the 1948 war contributed greatly to the status accorded to university graduates as the mainstays of the political and social rehabilitation of the Arab population. As in other developing societies, educated Arabs are considered to be agents of social change who are carrying out an important mission by providing direction and leading the struggle to improve the political and social status of their people (Al-Haj 2003). The economic changes marking Arab society (chapter 2) have assigned even greater value to education. The drastic transition from agricultural work in one's own village to hired labor outside the village has fundamentally changed the criteria determining status and prestige. As mentioned, there was massive confiscation of Arab lands by Israeli authorities, mainly during the first decade after the establishment of the state (see chapter 2; see also Abu-Kishk 1981, 31). In an agrarian society, land ownership was more than an economic resource—it was a status symbol. After the Arabs lost their land, education became the "new land," serving as an economic asset, a status symbol, and a source of pride. Thus, acquiring an education became the main objective of the Arab population, and investment in land was replaced by investment in human capital through educational attainment (Al-Haj 1995a, 2006).

Moreover, for Arab women the significance of higher education extends far beyond its socioeconomic returns. Education is related to women's personal identity, social status, and standing and is fundamental to establishing their relationships within the family and community (e.g., Arar 2011; Abu-Sa'ad 2016; Cinamon, Habayib, and Ziv 2016). According to Cinamon, Habayib, and Ziv (2016) women's consciousness of the social implications of pursuing higher education and the expected impact of education in boosting their status within their own family and community are major factors in their motivation and career development (136).

Focusing on Palestinian women from Israel studying at Jordanian universities, Arar (2011) concludes that despite the difficulties and complex implications involved, the experience strongly influenced the women's gender identity and their empowerment orientation. He adds that "the Palestinian women's new identity, formed during their studies, assists them in their efforts to reintegrate and establish their status when they return from their academic studies abroad to their society of origin" (625).

The experiences of Arab students studying at Israeli universities are unique in that the universities are almost the only place in the Israeli education system where Arabs and Jews meet. Separate education systems keep Arabs and Jews apart during their primary and secondary school studies, such that they meet only at institutions of higher education. This encounter is a very important factor in the consolidation of Arab students' civic and national identity and their relations with the Jewish majority. In addition, their encounter with students from all over the country gives them an opportunity to become politically and socially active, such that university is the most intensive stage of political socialization for educated Arabs (Mari 1978).

The social experience of Arab students during their academic studies is no less important. The universities and colleges in Israel are quite far away from Arab localities, such that many students must move out of their parents' homes and find a place to live closer to these institutions. This offers Arab students an exceptional opportunity for a freer lifestyle without being scrutinized by the community. Such experience is particularly important for women, who still struggle with restrictions in their own communities that keep a watchful eye on their social life (Al-Haj 2003).

Main Trends in Higher Education

The starting point of the Palestinian Arabs in Israel in terms of higher education was extremely low. Until the late 1960s, representation of Arabs in Israeli universities was negligible. In fact, only a few Arab high school students went on to higher education (see table 5.1). In analyzing the differential attainment trends between Arabs and Jews, I chose universities for several obvious reasons. First, the use of university statistics allows us to maintain consistency in analyzing developments in higher education among Arabs since the establishment of Israel. As indicated below, the academic colleges and the academization of teachers colleges (later referred to as colleges of education) only began in the early 1990s. Furthermore, the CBS did not begin systematically reporting on students at universities, academic colleges, and colleges of education by population groups until the 2004/5 academic year (see SAI 2010, 429; SAI 2018, table 8.59; SAI 2019, table 4.66). The representation of Arab students at academic colleges and colleges of education is analyzed in a different section below.

In the early 1970s, the number of Arab students at Israeli universities rose significantly. Several factors can explain this trend. Abolition of the military government in 1966 put an end to restrictions on Arab movement. Improvements in the secondary school system and an increase in the number of those obtaining matriculation certificates also contributed to the rising number of applications to academic institutions. At the same time, Arabs increasingly aspired to integrate into Israeli society as part of a strategy of acculturation. With this aim in mind, they perceived higher education as a means of advancing their individual and collective status. The establishment of the University of Haifa in the early 1970s also contributed to this. The proximity of this university to the Galilee made it attractive to Arabs, most of whom live in the north of the country. The fact that the University of Haifa was close to Arab localities was particularly advantageous to women in that it helped traditional families come to terms with the idea that their daughters were studying at university because they were still able to return to their village every day.

As shown in table 6.1, the increase in the number of Arab students began to wane in the late 1980s, despite the growth of the Arab population and the rising number of Arab high school graduates. From the mid-1990s, the number of Arab university students began to rise again, increasing from 3,966 in 1989/90 (5.4 percent) to 9,606 in 2001/2 (8.2 percent). The past two decades have seen a steady increase in the number of Arab students at Israeli universities. In 2018, there were 18,244 Arab students at all Israeli universities, representing 14.5 percent of all university students (not including the Open University).

This analysis leads to the conclusion that there has been an impressive expansion of higher education among the Arab population in Israel. Yet despite this expansion, a wide gap in higher education attainment still remains between Jews and Arabs in Israel. Figure 6.1 illustrates this gap by showing the ratio between Jewish and Arab students in Israel per 1,000 population.

As can be seen in figure 6.1, until 1996 the number of Jewish students per 1,000 population at Israeli universities was three times higher than the number of Arab students. The number of Arab students considerably

Table 6.1. Arab and Jewish Students at Israeli Universities (1956–2019)*

Year	Jews (%)	Arabs (%)	Total N	Total (%)
1956/57	99.4	0.6	7,228	100.0
1964/65	98.7	1.3	18,368	100.0
1970/71	98.3	1.7	36,136	100.0
1974/75	97.1	2.9	49,148	100.0
1979/80	97.0	3.0	54,480	100.0
1984/85	93.5	6.5	61,155	100.0
1989/90	94.6	5.4	67,770	100.0
2001/2	91.8	8.2	117,146	100.0
2008/9	89.9	10.2	120,134	100.0
2018/19	85.5	14.5	125,487	100.0

Source: SAI 1972, no. 23, 599; 1977, no. 28, 625; 1981, no. 32, 637; 1982, no. 33, 649; 1990, no. 41, 644; 1995, no. 46, 512; CBS 1997, pub. no. 1068, 58; Council for Higher Education, based on CBS 2000. Data for 2008–2009 are based on SAI 2010, no. 61, table 8.50, 429; data for 2018–2019 are based on SAI 2020, no. 71, table 4.66.

*These figures do not include the Open University, which has its own system with no admission requirements.

Figure 6.1. Jewish and Arab University Students in Israel per 1,000 Population, 1957–2018. *Source:* CBS, SAI.

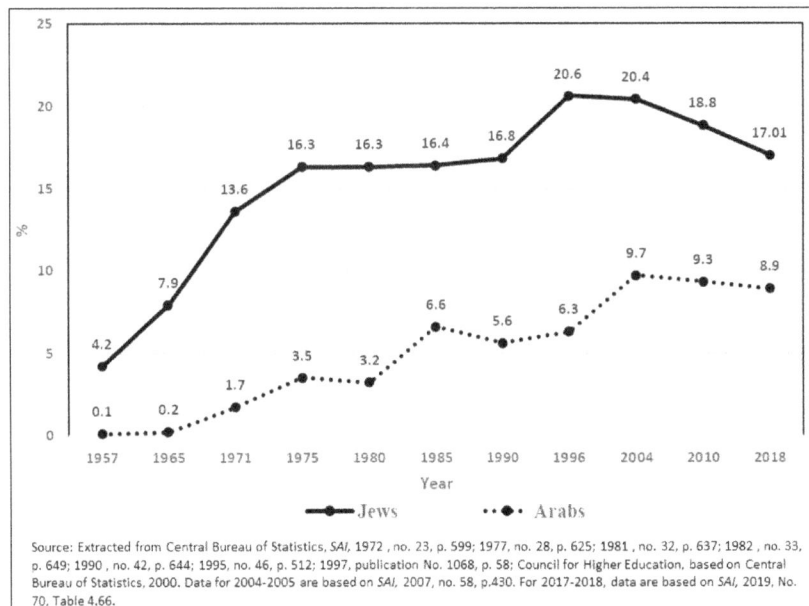

Source: Extracted from Central Bureau of Statistics, *SAI*, 1972 , no. 23, p. 599; 1977, no. 28, p. 625; 1981 , no. 32, p. 637; 1982 , no. 33, p. 649; 1990 , no. 42, p. 644; 1995, no. 46, p. 512; 1997, publication No. 1068, p. 58; Council for Higher Education, based on Central Bureau of Statistics, 2000. Data for 2004-2005 are based on *SAI*, 2007, no. 58, p.430. For 2017-2018, data are based on *SAI*, 2019, No. 70, Table 4.66.

increased during the late 1990s, thus narrowing the gap between Arab and Jewish students. From 2004 through 2018, the gap in favor of Jews remained almost unchanged, such that the proportion of Jews in academic institutions was 2.0 and 1.9 times higher than that of Arabs in 2010 and 2018, respectively.

The gap between Jews and Arabs extends beyond their differential representation in academic institutions and is reflected in differential attainment of advanced academic degrees (see table 6.2).

Table 6.2 demonstrates a wide gap between the percentage of Arab students pursuing undergraduate degrees (first degree) and those studying for advanced degrees. This gap has narrowed since 2004/5, mainly with respect to second degrees. This change is related to the inclusion of students from academic colleges, which have begun granting second degrees. In 2017/18, nearly 51 percent of students pursing second degrees were enrolled at academic colleges and education colleges (SAI 2019, table 4.66). Yet most of these second degrees do not entail writing a thesis, hindering the possibility of continuing on to doctoral studies at the universities, which still have the exclusive right to grant PhDs.

ACADEMIC COLLEGES AND COLLEGES OF EDUCATION

When we include the academic colleges and colleges of education, the picture of Arab students enrolled in undergraduate studies at institutions of higher

Table 6.2. Arab Students by Degree 1984–2018 (%)*†

Year	1984/85	1995/96	2004/5	2009/10	2017/18
First degree (BA)	7.9	7.0	10.1	11.9	16.5
Second degree (MA)	3.2	3.0	5.2	6.9	13.6
Third degree (PhD)	2.7	3.5	3.4	4.0	6.6

*Figures for 1984 and 1995 are only for universities; from 2004/05 onwards, these figures include universities, academic colleges and academic colleges of education.

†Excluding the Open University.

education changes drastically. The proportional representation of Arab students is considerably higher at the colleges than at the universities. During the academic year 2018/19, the total number of Arab students enrolled at Israeli institutions of higher education was 45,845, or 17.1 percent of all enrolled students. Of the Arab students, 61.5 percent studied at academic colleges or colleges of education and only 38.5 percent at universities (SAI 2020, table 4.66). The differential representation of Arabs at colleges compared to universities can be attributed to differential admission requirements and selectivity criteria, which are much higher at universities than at colleges (see Caplan et al. 2009, 5).

The establishment of the academic colleges and the academization of the teachers colleges (or colleges of education) in the early 1990s contributed immensely to the expansion of higher education in Israel as a whole. This expansion was influenced by the increasing demand for higher education as a result of rapid demographic growth in the wake of the mass immigration from the former Soviet Union to Israel, as well as the significant increase in the number of high school graduates and the labor market's growing demand for academic credentials (Guri-Rosenblit 1999, 94).

Within three decades (1990–2020), the total number of students enrolled in higher education in Israel increased by a factor of 3.5, from 75,487 to 268,555 students. During the same period, the population grew by a factor of 1.9, from nearly 4.8 million to 9 million people (SAI 2020, table 2.1). This expansion in higher education was mainly due to the dramatic increase in the number of academic colleges. The total number of students at these colleges increased from 3,668 in 1989 to 107,456 students in 2018/19, almost a thirtyfold increase! During the same period, the number of university students increased by a factor of only 1.9 (from 67,202 to 125,286). In other words, whereas in 1989/90 students at academic colleges and teachers colleges constituted only 11 percent of the total student population, by 2018/19 their proportion in higher education in Israel had increased dramatically to 53.3 percent

This change in the structure of tertiary education reflects the new policy adopted by the Israel CHE and its planning and budgeting committee (PBC) in the early 1990s. According to this policy, academic colleges would be established in Israel's peripheral regions, mainly in the north and the south, in order to make higher education more accessible to disadvantaged groups. The original plan was to serve population groups living in these areas, mainly Arabs, Sephardic Jews, and Ethiopians. Indeed, the CHE's report for 2018 highlights the fact that opening academic colleges drastically increased the number of students in northern and southern Israel (CHE and PBC 2018, 10). The report adds that about a quarter of all undergraduate students in 2018 studied at colleges in these peripheral regions. During the past two decades, the percentage of students enrolled at colleges in the northern region (where most of the Arabs in Israel live, constituting a majority in this region) quadrupled three times (CHE PBC 2018). Furthermore, the number and geographic distribution of these colleges expanded. Driven by commercial and political considerations, new private colleges have been established in major cities in Israel, in addition to the public colleges. Moreover, the capabilities of these colleges have rapidly expanded, from focusing solely on teaching and granting first degrees to granting second degrees and engaging in research.

The impact of this dramatic expansion of tertiary education through academic colleges (both public and private) and colleges of education on inequalities in Israel is the subject of widespread controversy (see Swirski and Swirski 1997; Ayalon and Yogev 2006; Shwed and Shavit 2006; Caplan et al. 2009). Doubts regarding the efficacy of public colleges in advancing disadvantaged racial and ethnic groups are backed by extensive literature discussing the experience in the United States in this regard (e.g., Moore 2006; Carnevale et al. 2018; and review by Grubbs 2020). Carnevale et al. (2018) conclude that instead of advancing equality, the public college system in the US has developed such that Whites are disproportionally represented at selective, well-funded, top-tier colleges, while Blacks and Latinos are primarily funneled into bottom-tier colleges (1).

In the Israeli context, Swirski and Swirski (1997) contend that the academic colleges serve as an obstacle to development among disadvantaged groups and as a tool for reproducing social inequalities because they push their graduates into an inferior position on the labor market relative to university graduates. Shwed and Shavit (2006) paint a more complex picture. They contend that university graduates attain more desirable occupations than graduates of other tertiary education institutions. Nevertheless, graduates of private colleges earn incomes similar to those earned by university graduates. At the same time, graduates of public colleges are more disadvantaged than all other graduates of postsecondary education in terms of desirable occupations and income (439). Similarly, Ayalon and Yogev (2006), who identified these colleges as a second tier of less selective institutions, differentiate between public and private colleges in terms of fields of study. They claim that the "private colleges offer mainly prestigious and lucrative fields of study, thus producing a mobility channel for economically established members of otherwise disadvantaged social groups" (201).

In a study titled "The Quality of Israeli Academic Institutions: What the Wages of Graduates Tell About It?" Caplan et al. (2009) examined the returns on education in terms of salaries earned by college graduates compared to university graduates, controlling for cognitive abilities and socioeconomic characteristics. They conclude that in many fields of study (excluding business management), college graduates in their first jobs were paid on average 20 percent to 30 percent less than university graduates (87). The study emphasizes that even though public academic colleges have helped make higher education accessible to disadvantaged groups in Israel, the outcomes for graduates of these colleges in terms of labor market returns are lower than those of university graduates (29).

My analysis thus far shows that higher education among the Palestinian Arabs in Israel has expanded significantly. Two main waves of expansion are noteworthy. The first took place in the early 1970s, in the wake of the abolishment of the military government imposed on Arabs between 1949 and 1966, which restricted their movement and their integration into the wider society, education, and economy in Israel. The second wave of expansion in higher education started in the late 1990s, influenced by the establishment of academic colleges and the formal policy of the Israel CHE that sought to promote access to higher education among Arabs and other peripheral groups.

Along with the quantitative expansion of higher education among the Arab population, some qualitative changes have occurred as well. Arabs are enrolled in a wide range of faculties and departments at all institutions of higher education in Israel. Furthermore, the percentage of Arab women enrolled in higher education has risen steadily. In 1984, women accounted for about one-quarter of Arab students. For the first time in 1999, over half (or 50.9 percent) of Arab students at Israeli universities and institutions of higher education were women. This trend has continued over the past two decades at both the universities and the colleges, for both undergraduate and graduate degrees. In 2019/20, the percentage of women among Arab students was as high as 67.1 percent for BA studies, 72.9 percent for MA studies, and 63.4 percent for doctoral programs (see SAI 1984, 35; CBS 1995, 71; SAI 1997, 64; SAI 2020, 5).

The major fields of study pursued by Arab students have changed significantly over time as well. For example, between 1988/89 and 1998/99, the proportion of Arabs among first-year engineering students rose from 4.8 percent to 7.5 percent (SAI 2000, 22–52). Today (2023) medical and paramedical subjects have become the main fields of study for Arab students. In 2005/6, 19.7 percent of Arab students studied medicine, while 21.3 percent majored in paramedical fields (mainly nursing and pharmacy). That same year, 8.7 percent majored in science and mathematics, while only 5.6 percent of Arab students majored in engineering and architecture (SAI 2007, table 8.53).

In an article in the leading newspaper *The Marker*, Arlozorov explains the relatively high representation of Arab students in medical and paramedical fields in terms of a tendency to focus on a limited number of fields. She states that "the success of Israeli Arabs in medical studies is sectoral and spotty. Arabs tend to focus on a limited number of academic departments: they constitute 42 percent of pharmacy students and 36 percent of nursing students. In contrast, they refrain from trying to be admitted into other necessary and important fields, such as economics and management (5 percent Arabs), engineering (6 percent) or agriculture (3 percent)" (Arlozorov 2013).

In a previous study, I showed that the tendency among highly skilled Arab students to apply for medical and paramedical studies is affected by the availability of employment opportunities in this field. There is a severe shortage of doctors in Israel. Moreover, highly skilled Jewish students tend to seek jobs in high-tech and other profitable fields, in which Arab students still face many barriers for so-called security reasons (see Al-Haj 2003; Yaish and Gabay-Egozi 2021). A special report issued by the Israel Medical Association reiterates my conclusions. This report cautioned that special measures should be taken to encourage students to continue their studies in medicine and emphasized the following points:

> The growing shortage of physicians is endangering the field of medicine in Israel, as shown by studies conducted in recent years. It is important to emphasize that this is not a pessimistic future prophecy, but an emerging reality before our eyes. Another worrying parameter is the finding that the demand for medical studies is declining compared to the demand for other professional studies. The report indicated that the reasons for the shortage of doctors are many. For example, in recent years, many alternatives have been opened up to doctors, such as working abroad in developed countries where there is also a shortage of doctors. Another alternative is to leave the profession in favor of

other prestigious professions with high income, such as high-tech, biotechnology, etc. (Israel Medical Association 2016)

Yet despite the aforementioned qualitative changes, expansion of higher education among the Arabs in Israel has been mainly restricted to the quantitative level and consequently has failed to bridge the gaps between the Arabs and the Jewish majority. These gaps are reflected in the likelihood of attaining a higher education, and particularly in the large differential representation of both groups at the universities, where the ratio of students per 1,000 population among Jews is nearly double that of Arabs. Moreover, there is still a major discrepancy between Jewish and Arab students in terms of prestigious and profitable fields (such as high-tech subjects) and advanced academic degrees, as previously noted. In fact, a large part of the expansion in higher education among Arabs is due to the aforementioned dramatic increase in chances of obtaining tertiary education through public academic colleges and colleges of education. Consequently, many Arab students who failed to be admitted to desired profitable fields of study at Israeli universities searched for new opportunities at foreign universities, particularly in Jordan, the Palestinian Authority, and Eastern European countries, as briefly discussed below.

Arab Students at Foreign Universities

Even though this monograph focuses on Arab students at Israeli institutions of higher education as compared to Jews, in this section I briefly discuss the case of Arab students studying at universities abroad. A special report published by the Israeli Knesset (Parliament) titled "Academic Institutions for Minority Groups: A Comparative Overview" points to an increasing trend among Arab students to pursue their academic studies abroad. In 2012, nearly 9,000 Arab students, representing 27 percent of the total number of Arab students, studied abroad. About two-thirds of these students studied at Jordanian and Palestinian universities in the West Bank (Avger 2015, 3). Most of the remaining students studied in Moldavia, Romania, Italy, and Germany (OECD 2013; UNESCO 2012, cited by Haj-Yehia and Arar 2016, 507).

A number of studies have examined Israeli Palestinian students in Jordan and the Palestinian Authority (see Arar and Haj-Yehia 2010, 2013, 2016; Arar 2011; Arar, Masry-Harzalla, and Haj-Yehia 2013; Vurgan 2012; Haj-Yehia 2013; Haj-Yehia and Arar 2016, 2022). The main reason behind this trend is related to difficulties in being admitted to Israeli universities, primarily in the fields of medicine, dentistry, pharmacy, nursing, and other paramedical fields that are considered prestigious and offer high employment potential after graduation. The principal barriers to admission in these fields are the PET and age requirements (Haj-Yehia and Arar 2016, 513) in that most universities in Israel set age 21 as a threshold condition for admission to paramedical fields of study. In contrast to these admission barriers at Israeli universities, at Jordanian and Palestinian universities Arab students enjoy smooth admission and acceptance criteria (Haj-Yehia and Arar 2016; see also Arar and Haj-Yehia 2013, 2016).

Haj-Yehia and Arar contend that cultural alienation among Palestinian students at Israeli universities, in conjunction with other practical problems, serves as a catalyst for deciding to study at Arab universities outside Israel. These researchers note that one of the main factors affecting Palestinian Arab students' decision to pursue their academic studies in Jordan and the Palestinian Authority is related to the fact that these locations offer them a cultural and ideological milieu similar to their own and a sense of belonging and feeling at home (Haj-Yehia and Arar 2016, 505).

The Psychometric Entrance Test (PET) as a Gatekeeper

As shown in the previous chapters of this book, Arabs in Israel experience cumulative disadvantages, beginning in early childhood and continuing through elementary and secondary school. These disadvantages are eventually reflected in ongoing disparities between Jews and Arabs in the attainment of higher education. The PET has been widely mentioned as one of the central obstacles facing Arabs in accessing higher education and as a fundamental barrier that reduces Arab students' chances of being admitted to prestigious and highly competitive areas of study. Almost every study examining the obstacles to educational attainment among Arabs in Israel mentioned this conclusion (e.g., Mari 1978; Al-Haj 2003; Mustafa 2009; Arar 2011; Arar and Mustafa 2011; Arar and Haj-Yehia 2016; Haj-Yehia and Arar 2016; Hager and Jabareen 2016; Abu-Sa'ad 2016; Arar and Abu El-Hija 2018).

Nevertheless, very few studies provide in-depth analyses of the PET scores of Arab applicants according to the test's various components, and almost no study has traced trends in the PET scores over time. Equally important, initiatives launched to enhance fairness in access to education among Arabs have not been systematically investigated, nor has the impact of such initiatives on university admission policies. My study seeks to fill this lacuna by providing a comprehensive picture of the content of this test, the gaps in PET scores between Arabs and Jews over time, and the efforts made to enhance fairness of access. It also assesses the policy of admission to higher education in Israel compared to global trends.

In the following sections I provide a brief theoretical background outlining the development and basis of standardized entrance tests and their implications with respect to discrepancies between established and disadvantaged social groups. Then, I focus on the Israeli case in the context of the Arabs in Israel and the PET score gap between Arab and Jewish applicants over the past 30 years (1991–2020). I devote a special section to the initiatives launched to enhance fairness in admission to higher education institutions in Israel and to the response of stakeholders in the higher education system.

STANDARDIZED ADMISSION TEST (SAT): MERITOCRACY AND UNFAIRNESS

The SAT for college admission was introduced in the United States in the late 1950s. Since then, standardized tests such as the SAT have become the central tool for admission to higher education worldwide due to their presumed scientific validity in predicting success and academic potential and their reliance on the principle of meritocracy (Sulphey et al. 2018, 651).

In this context, the term meritocracy refers to the assumption that "people with the same level of merit—IQ plus effort—should have the same chance of success" (Swift 2003; 24, cited by Lim 2016, 161). This term highlights the principle of equality of opportunity, which is based on merit, as the guiding principle for division of scare resources. In other words, meritocracy is equivalent to rewarding individual merit with social rank, socioeconomic returns, general recognition and prestige, and greater educational resources (Lim and Tan 2020, 281).

Meritocracy is seemingly based on the principle of equal opportunity. Nevertheless, meritocracy has been repeatedly criticized for embodying the very opposite principle—that is, inequality that is often based on ethnicity, class, race, and other affiliations (see, for example, Erichsen and Waldow 2020; McNamee and Miller 2018; Tan 2008). Some scholars argue that stakeholders in the higher education system deliberately manipulate this principle to justify the privileges that "advantage the advantaged" (see Erichsen and Waldow 2020, 103; McNamee and Miller 2018). In this regard, Lim (2016) concludes that "the dynamics of meritocracy needs to be appreciated as an ideology that is negotiated by dominant social groups as these seek to legitimize particular distributions of social resources. Such dominant ideologies, however, are not only produced in the education system; they are also reproduced through it, often in far more complex ways" (160).

Meanwhile, criticism of standardized admission tests is on the rise, with focus on three major areas: their credibility and their ability to predict success in academic studies, the social implications related to the perpetuation of inequalities and socioeconomic gaps, and violations of the principle of diversity. Even studies asserting that standardized admission tests do have high predictive validity still contend that the scores need to be interpreted with caution, as they explain less than half of the variance in students' academic success (McKenzie and Schweitzer 2001, 29). Other studies emphasize that in addition to predicting academic performance, admission procedures should also predict which students have the greatest potential to complete their studies on time and are least likely to drop out (Makransky et al. 2017).

Critics of standardized admission tests contend that they perpetuate social gaps and reproduce socioeconomic inequalities because they are positively correlated with students' socioeconomic backgrounds (e.g., Mardones and Campos-Requena 2021; Zwick 2019; Zwick et al. 2021). Many studies show that students from low socioeconomic backgrounds score lower on college admissions tests even though their high school grades are high (Zwick et al. 2021, 21; see also Giancola and Kahlenberg 2016). Furthermore, typical test score requirements for higher education serve as a barrier to campus diversity. As a result of the large performance gap on these tests between different ethnic and socioeconomic groups, the education system is largely populated by dominant groups and well-to-do families, with minor representation of students from disadvantaged backgrounds, particularly in highly selective fields of study and at prestigious institutions (Zwick 2019).

According to students of decolonial theory, standardized admission tests—which still determine access to higher education in many countries—are reflections of Western thought and practice that perpetuate inequalities through the hegemonic ideology of meritocracy (e.g., Mbembe 2016; Regmi 2023). In this regard, meritocracy was invented as a hegemonic ideology for convincing the general masses that racial, social, and economic inequalities are the result of variations in intelligence (Regmi 2023, 2; see also Piketty 2020, cited by Regmi 2023).

Hence, studies examining higher education have begun focusing on the need to adopt serious measures to decolonize universities. Specifically, these studies underscore the importance of dismantling mechanisms that perpetuate racial and colonial formations in the systems governing access to and management of universities (e.g., Hayes, Luckett, and Misiaszek 2021; Mbembe 2016; Jansen 2019; Zembylas 2023; Regmi 2023). Mbembe proposes detailed practical steps necessary to build the "university of tomorrow." One such step is to enhance the democratization of university access. For this to happen, "the doors of higher learning should be widely opened . . . we need to decolonize the systems of access and management insofar as they have turned higher education into a marketable product, rated, bought and sold by standard units" (Mbembe 2016, 30).

Over time, various strategies have been developed to address admission inequalities and underrepresentation of disadvantaged groups at higher education institutions. In a detailed review of globalization and equity norms in higher education, Goastellec (2008) offers a chronology of the development of benchmarks in different countries regarding "fairness in access" to higher education, highlighting three major periods. At the outset, higher education institutions were designed for a small urban elite and gave preference to a limited number of prestigious professions (73). Beginning in the early 1990s, higher education began encouraging open access for previously excluded groups, such that alongside the ideal of meritocracy the principle of equal rights became fundamental in higher education (74). Yet the simultaneous existence of the equality norm and the meritocracy ideal generated many contradictions. Because academic performance is largely considered a byproduct of "natural intelligence," it overlooks the influence of socioeconomic determinants on scholastic achievement. At the same time, efforts to recognize and implement the principle of "equality of rights" (or formal equality) focused on geographic decentralization and diversification of higher education (74). These efforts led to the creation of a second tier of largely nonselective academic institutions (such as community colleges in the United States and academic colleges in Israel) with the purpose of increasing access to higher education among formerly excluded and peripheral groups. Goastellec defines this period as "formally equal, but apart" (75).

The typical strategy of minimizing unfairness and increasing equality in access to higher education in this second period was based on affirmative action and designating entrance quotas for specific disadvantaged groups. Yet such a strategy is highly controversial and many scholars are skeptical about its effectiveness. (For a discussion of contradictory attitudes toward affirmative action, see the review by Mangum and Block Jr. 2021.) Consequently, during the 1990s affirmative action was abandoned and replaced by a policy of "holistic admission," also referred to as "contextualization." Through this method, universities request and use data and information that can help them understand applicants' social and educational context. This method allows for individualized, holistic, case-by-case consideration to improve chances of admission among disadvantaged applicants (Mountford-Zimdars and Moore 2020, 754). Ivy League institutions in the US practice this form of contextualization, as do other colleges that use the holistic admissions method (Stevens 2007).

According to Goastellec's chronology, in many countries the late 1990s marked the third and perhaps most significant period in terms of enhancement of fair access to higher education. During this period, issues of fairness and equality in access to higher education became international norms and were subsequently formalized by such international bodies as the World Bank and UNESCO. Goastellec (2008) points to the report of the Paris 1998 World Conference on Higher Education as perhaps the most important document in recognizing universal normalization of equal access to higher education and the right to higher education as integral human rights (77). One of the central decisions of the World Conference on Higher Education reads as follows: "Access to higher education for members of some special target groups, such as indigenous peoples, cultural and linguistic minorities, disadvantaged groups, peoples living under occupation and those who suffer from disabilities, must be actively facilitated" (UNESCO 1998).

The above summary raises a number of questions in the Israeli context: What has been the impact of standardized admission tests on access to higher education among the Arab population in Israel? Where is Israel situated along Goastellec's chronology of "fairness in access" to higher education? What kind of initiatives have been proposed in Israel to enhance "access fairness" in higher education? Do Israeli academic institutions conform to the international trends marking the third period, and specifically globalization of equity and equality in higher education? Have stakeholders made any efforts to decolonize higher education in Israel in terms of democratization of access and cultural contents? As an indigenous minority with obvious linguistic and cultural uniqueness, do the Palestinian Arabs in Israel enjoy any special status in terms of admission requirements and culturally responsive curriculum in institutions of higher education?

THE PET AND ADMISSION INEQUALITIES

In reviewing the history of the PET in Israel, Beller (2001) notes that until the late 1960s, the *Bagrut* (matriculation certificate) served as the main criterion for admission to higher education. The Bagrut certificate is based on scores on a set of exams students take toward the end of their secondary school studies. For various reasons, including the growing demand for higher education, Israeli universities decided to seek an additional selection tool to be weighted with the Bagrut grades. According to Beller (2001), "The universities explicitly stated that admissions requirements should be based on meritocratic criteria" that favor those who have higher potential to succeed in academic studies (320).

Ultimately, all Israeli universities decided to use the PET, which takes the form of a standardized non-curricular test. To this end, in 1981 the universities established the Inter-University National Institute for Testing and Evaluation (NITE) as an independent body governed by the heads of the seven research universities. The new admission criterion for all universities is now based on a combination of the weighted average of students' Bagrut grades and their scores on the PET (composite score). Note that the original language of the PET was Hebrew, but it was later translated into a number of languages (including Arabic) to allow non-Hebrew-speaking applicants (along with Hebrew speakers) to complete the test in their native language (Beller 2001, 320–21).

As mentioned earlier with respect to the SAT in the United States, and in Israel as well, the PET's predictive validity for success in academic studies is highly controversial. One group of researchers asserted that this standardized admission test has relatively high validity in predicting academic success (see Beller 2001, 320; see also Kenneth Cohen 2001; Beller 1994; Ben-Shakhar, Kiderman, and Beller 1996). Yet as shown by international studies (McKenzie andSchweitzer 2001, 29), even researchers claiming the high predictive validity of the PET admit that the test explains less than half of the variance in students' academic success (see major study by Kenneth Cohen, Bronner, and Oren 1999, 63).

In contrast, Rosenthal and Ben-Shakhar (1990) found that the predictive validity of matriculation grades (0.36) was higher than that of the PET (0.29) (Rosenthal and Ben-Shakhar 1990, 480, cited by Kenneth Cohen, Bronner, and Oren 1999; see also Haimovich and Ben-Shakhar 2004, 446). Gamliel and Kahan (2004) accordingly highlight the unfairness of higher education admission criteria for disadvantaged groups in Israel. This unfairness is reflected in the extremely large gaps between "strong" and "weak" social groups in admission scores (matriculation grades and PET score), which are larger than the gaps in academic success between these groups (433).

The predictive validity and hence the fairness of the PET for different social groups are controversial. Yet as noted earlier, and as most researchers claim, Arabs are the group that is most disadvantaged by this admission criterion. Indeed, the PET serves as a gatekeeper that significantly reduces Arab students' access to higher education at particular universities and to prestigious areas of study (see, for example, Gamliel and Kahan 2004; Mustafa 2009; Arar 2011; Arar and Mustafa 2011; Arar and Haj-Yehia 2016; Haj-Yehia and Arar 2016; Hager and Jabareen 2016; Abu-Sa'ad 2016).

Despite the lower odds of educational attainment among Arabs, an analysis by Feniger, Mcdossi, and Ayalon (2014, 12) does not corroborate the claim that the PET is a barrier to Arabs' enrollment in higher education, though their study does suggest that the PET may play a role in certain selective fields such as medicine. In what follows, I examine these contradictory arguments by analyzing the gaps in admission scores between Arab and Jewish applicants to institutions of higher education over time.

Statistics derived from the NITE, which is responsible for preparing and implementing the PET, reflect a wide performance gap between Arab and Jewish students over time, as shown in figure 6.2.

Figure 6.2 shows that Jews score significantly higher on average on the PET than Arabs. Over the three decades from 1991 to 2020, the discrepancy

Figure 6.2. Scores of Jewish and Arab Students on the Psychometric Entrance Test (1991–2020). *Source:* National Institute for Testing and Evaluation.

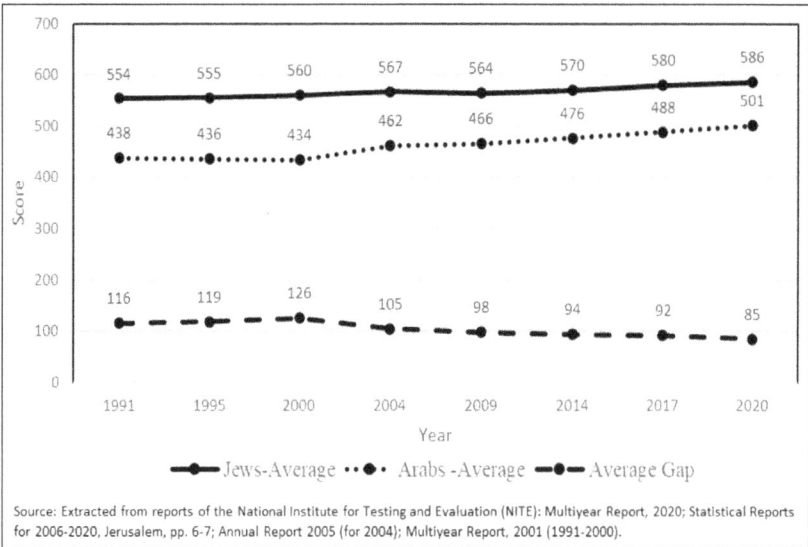

Source: Extracted from reports of the National Institute for Testing and Evaluation (NITE): Multiyear Report, 2020; Statistical Reports for 2006-2020, Jerusalem, pp. 6-7; Annual Report 2005 (for 2004); Multiyear Report, 2001 (1991-2000).

between the two groups ranged from 85 to 126 points, exhibiting an increase in the period between 1991 and 2000. Since then, the rising trend has been halted, replaced by a diminishing trend through 2020. Indeed, the discrepancy decreased by 31 points (from 126 to 85 points), an important development in light of the fact that every point counts in admission to different fields of study, mainly those that are highly competitive. Nevertheless, the wide gap in favor of Jewish applicants has persisted over time.

English constitutes an additional barrier that reduces the chances for Arabs to pursue higher education. Advanced English on the matriculation certificate is an admission requirement for Israeli universities and most colleges. According to Feniger and Ayalon (2016), this requirement constitutes a "gatekeeper" that hinders access to higher education for many Arabs. They contend that this requirement places Arabs in a disadvantaged position compared to their Jewish counterparts. For Jewish students, English is the only compulsory foreign language they must study. Note that Arabic is not a compulsory subject for Jewish students. In contrast, Arab students are obliged to study two foreign languages, English and Hebrew, in order to meet matriculation certificate requirements (104). In other words, whereas English is a *second language* for Jewish students, for Arab students it is a *fourth language*. Their mother tongue is spoken Arabic (*Ammiya*), which they use in their day-to-day communication. At school they must study classical literary Arabic (*Fusha*), which differs substantially from spoken Arabic dialects. Hence, Arab students must study three languages (Arabic *Fusha*, Hebrew, and English) in addition to their mother tongue—spoken Arabic!

In addition to being penalized by the advanced English requirement for the matriculation certificate, Arab students are "doubly penalized" in that English is one of the three major components of the psychometric exam, in addition to the verbal and quantitative components. This double penalty can be seen in figure 6.3, which illustrates the gaps between Jewish and Arab applicants on the main PET components during the period 1995–2020: verbal thinking, quantitative thinking, and English.

As figure 6.3 shows, the greatest discrepancy between Arab and Jewish applicants is in the scores on the English section. This discrepancy ranges between 20 and 29 points. The second most difficult component is verbal thinking, where the gap in favor of Jewish students ranges from 17 to 24 points. The least difficult component is quantitative thinking, though it still exhibits a steady gap in favor of Jewish students ranging from 12 to 24 points.

Figure 6.3. Trends in the Gap between Jewish and Arab Students (in Points in Favor of Jews) on the Psychometric Entrance Test According to Exam Components (1995–2020). *Source:* National Institute for Testing and Evaluation.

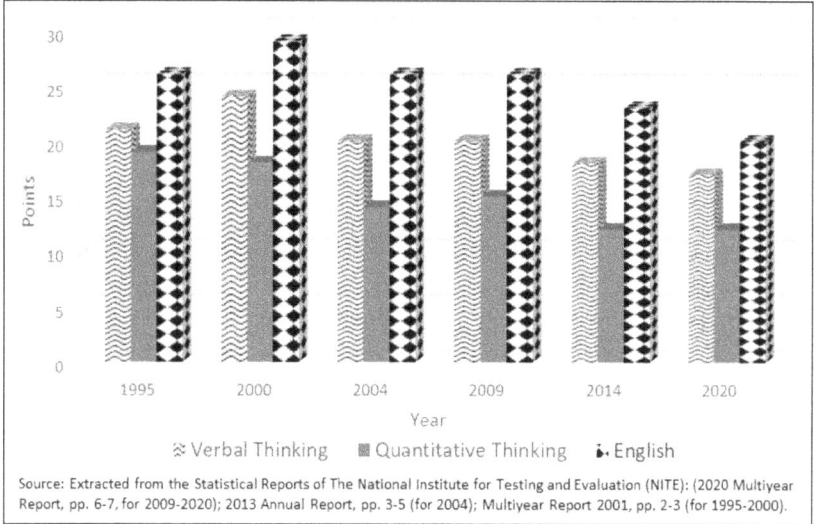

Source: Extracted from the Statistical Reports of The National Institute for Testing and Evaluation (NITE): (2020 Multiyear Report, pp. 6-7, for 2009-2020); 2013 Annual Report, pp. 3-5 (for 2004); Multiyear Report 2001, pp. 2-3 (for 1995-2000).

My findings show that while the PET as a whole is problematic for Arab students, the most challenging sections are those with cultural connotations—namely the sections on verbal thinking and English. Indeed, several studies have indicated that the PET is culturally biased in that its contents have a clearly European/Western orientation (Hager and Jabareen 2016, 461; OECD 2011, 49; see also Mustafa 2009; Arar and Mustafa 2011). While other groups, mainly Mizrahi Jewish students who are the descendants of Jewish communities from the Middle East and North Africa, are also negatively affected by this cultural bias (see Al-Haj 2003; Bitton 2012), Arab students are at a particular disadvantage due to the aforementioned cumulative barriers and difficulties throughout their years of schooling.

As mentioned, university admission is determined by a composite score consisting of the PET score and the matriculation grade average. This composite score was supposed to compensate Arab students to some extent. Whereas Jews have always scored higher on the PET than Arabs, Arab students' matriculation grade average has always been a bit higher than that of Jewish students. Indeed, over the past decade Arab students have consistently demonstrated higher matriculation averages than Jews: in

2010, 89.1 vs. 86.0; in 2014, 89.5 vs. 87.1; in 2017, 90.0 vs. 86.6; and in 2020, 89.9 vs. 87.1, for Arabs and Jews, respectively (NITE 2013, 4; NITE 2020, 15–16). Nevertheless, most universities have found a way to reduce the impact of the matriculation grade by assigning greater weight to the PET score. That is, instead of an equal 1:1 ratio between the two scores, the PET score is usually assigned twice as much weight as the matriculation grade. In highly competitive fields that are in high demand, this ratio is 1:3 in favor of the PET score.

The aforementioned gaps in PET scores between Jews and Arabs and the extra weight universities assign to these scores provide Jewish students, especially those from privileged social backgrounds, a steady advantage over Arab students and other peripheral groups in all academic fields of study. This situation has to a large extent been responsible for limiting Arab students' access to universities, particularly in prestigious areas of study. In 1998/99, Arabs accounted for 13.5 percent of university applicants, but only 9.0 percent of those who were admitted that year (SAI 2000, 22–54), reflecting the fact that only 41.2 percent of Arab applicants are admitted, as opposed to 65.1 percent of Jewish applicants. In addition, in 1999, 30.6 percent of all applicants rejected by the universities were Arabs (SAI 2000, 22–54). Reports for 2017/18 showed a minor improvement: 21.3 percent of applicants were Arabs, but only 13.4 percent were admitted. Among applicants who were rejected, the percentage of Arabs was nearly twice that of Jews. That is, 38.6 percent of Arab applicants were rejected compared to 20 percent of Jewish applicants (SAI 2019, table 4.61).

Initiatives to Enhance Fair Access to Higher Education

In the wake of the aforementioned Paris 1998 World Conference on Higher Education, this author, then a member of the Israel CHE, submitted a position paper titled "Higher Education among the Arabs in Israel: Condition, Needs, and Recommendations" (Al-Haj 1999). The topic was brought up for discussion in the council's PBC, as well as in the full council plenum. On July 27, 1999, in the context of deliberations on the matter of higher education among the Arab population, the CHE decided to comply with the PBC's decision to appoint a special committee chaired by Professor Al-Haj (hereafter, Al-Haj's Committee). The members of this committee included prominent Arab and Jewish academics from the different Israeli universities. In addition, for the first time a representative of the National Union of

Arab Students in Israel was appointed a member of this committee (for the full list of members, see CHE and PBC 2001, 3).

Al-Haj's Committee dealt with various aspects of higher education among the Arabs in Israel, including fair access, programs to prepare high school students for academic studies, adaptation problems of Arab students at higher education institutions, diversity and multiculturalism in higher education, employment of Arab graduates, and other related issues. The committee devoted a central part of its report and recommendations to the PET.

The opening section of the committee's report reads as follows:

> The discussions of the committee emphasized that one of the central barriers limiting acceptance of Arab students to institutions of higher education, especially to universities, is the PET. The discussions also noted that this test discriminates against three main groups in Israel: women, Jews of Sephardic origin, and Arabs. . . . On the other hand, the committee is aware that the PET photographs, as it were, a situation in which there are gaps in the starting point between Jewish and Arab students. Therefore, the use of the PET as a major part of the admission requirements to institutions for higher education perpetuates the existing disadvantages and gaps. (CHE and PBC 2001, 7–8)

The committee's report delineated the main factors in the PET that discriminate against Arab students. Among other things, the report noted that the PET was intended and designed mainly for students with Western cultural backgrounds. Consequently, it is not suitable for Arab students or even for Jewish students from Mizrahi-Sephardic backgrounds. To redress the imbalance, the committee called for revising the PET, and particularly the section on verbal thinking. This section should be based on material from Arab students' cultural and cognitive world and not on material translated from Hebrew into Arabic. Moreover, Arab students have a problem with diglossia stemming from the immense difference between spoken vernacular Arabic and literary Arabic. Even when Arab students are tested in Arabic, they are actually dealing with a second language. The problem is not, then, with their level of Arabic but with the nature of the literary texts chosen. The texts chosen for the verbal section should be written in more practical literary Arabic and not in the classical language, which is very far removed from the students' cognitive world. That is to say, in addition to the cultural bias of the PET, this test also reflects the gap in starting points between Arabs and Jews. Indeed, the use of the PET as a central criterion for admission to institutions of higher education in Israel serves to perpetuate and even to increase the gaps between the groups as far as access to higher education is concerned (see CHE and PBC 2001, 9).

Clearly, then, the PET constitutes a main gatekeeper that hampers access to higher education among Arabs and other students from disadvantaged backgrounds. Hence, Al-Haj's Committee strongly recommended shifting to a system in which students are allowed to choose one of the two components used as admission requirements—either their matriculation grade average or their PET score. According to this new system, the PET would become optional rather than compulsory, as it is now. The Committee's recommendations read as follows:

1. The Committee favorably views any change in admissions requirements that may advance access of peripheral groups to higher education.

2. The use of the matriculation examinations as a classification tool for admission to institutions of higher education is a positive step. Nevertheless, the Committee recommends that prior to deciding on any formula for matriculation scores, the implications of this decision regarding admission to academic studies in general, and prestigious subjects in particular, should be examined with respect to the admission chances of groups with low starting points, especially the Arab population.

3. In discussing changes, the cultural uniqueness of the different groups must be taken into consideration, and the group's mother tongue should be included in any agreed-upon version.

4. In the event that the Committee's aforementioned recommendations in regard to the PET are implemented, the Committee views in a positive light leaving the PET as an option to be selected by students should they so desire. (CHE and PBC 2001, 8–9)

These recommendation by Al-Haj's Committee provided important backing to growing public pressure protesting the use of the PET as the central criterion for admission to higher education institutions in Israel. Meanwhile, two initiatives were launched in the Knesset that sought to discontinue the use of the PET as a major admission criterion for higher education.

In 2001, former education minister Yossi Sarid and MK Ilan Gilon submitted a draft law to the Knesset calling for abolishing the PET. Sarid argued that the PET is culturally biased and not suitable for students from weaker classes. The law passed its preliminary reading but was subsequently canceled due to opposition from then education minister Limor Livnat (Bar-Gefen 2001). MK Silvan Shalom formulated a similar proposal calling for open admissions to the first year of study at institutions of higher education, followed by selection based on first-year achievements (see Beller 2001, 329). This proposal was also not passed into law.

It should be noted that because the PET symbolizes the elitism of Israeli universities, a number of leading politicians made an effort to bring about its abolition. In fact, some of the public criticism leveled at the PET called for abolishing it for the good of the students from the periphery. For example, then finance minister Silvan Shalom claimed that abolishing the PET as a prerequisite for university admission would bring students from the outlying development towns (Mizrahi Jewish students) to the law and economics departments. Today these students hesitate to apply to these departments because of the barrier imposed by the PET (Sa'ar 2001).

In response to public pressure, VERA (the Hebrew acronym for the Association of University Heads, a voluntary body comprising the heads of Israel's research universities) decided that starting from the 2002/3 academic year, students would no longer be required to pass the PET as a compulsory requirement for university admission. Instead, applicants would have to decide between their PET score and their grades on the matriculation exams in three subjects: math, English and language, and expression in their mother tongue (Hebrew for Jewish students or Arabic for Arab students) (Sa'ar 2001). This method was in line with the recommendation of Al-Haj's Committee to shift to a system in which students are allowed to choose one of the two components used as admission requirements—matriculation grade average or PET score. Also, it recognized Al-Haj's Committee recommendation that "the group's mother tongue should be included in any agreed-upon version" (see CHE and PBC 2001, 8–9).

This new admissions procedure was implemented for one academic year only (2002/3). During that year, the number of Arab students admitted to universities increased dramatically, and their representation in prestigious faculties almost doubled (cited by Abu-Sa'ad 2016, 100). When the administrations of Israel's universities recognized this change, they immediately decided to stop using the new admission procedure and to return to the way things were before, thus giving primacy to the PET. According to Sa'ar:

> As soon as Israel's top university administrators noticed that the big winners from admissions policy changes were not Jewish youngsters from low income towns, but rather Arabs, they reverted back to the old admissions system. . . . The universities did little . . . to conceal the fact that the admissions policies are being altered to benefit Jewish applicants. The Association of University Heads declared: "Admissions policies based on [high school] grades do not make studies more accessible to [Jewish] students from the periphery. The opposite is true." In this statement, the association was careful not to use the words "Jews" or "Arabs," but the intention was clear. (Cited by Abu-Sa'ad 2016, 100)

On January 28, 2004, the Association of Civil Rights in Israel petitioned the High Court of Justice on behalf of a coalition of organizations that opposed abolishing the new method of admission to universities. Among other things, this petition stated: "The totality of the circumstances indicates that the decision stems solely from a discriminatory consideration of the preference of Jews over Arabs in admission to academic studies" (Association of Civil Rights in Israel 2004).

The High Court of Justice severely criticized the university leaders' decision to abolish the new method of admission and return to the former one. Among other things, the judges wrote that "the decision has a serious impact on the chances for weak populations to be admitted to universities." Yet despite their harsh criticism, the judges ruled that the petition could not be heard because the High Court is not allowed to order universities to reverse a decision. On the advice of the judges, the Association of Civil Rights withdrew its petition (Zlikovich 2006).

Subsequently, some Israeli universities began employing a form of affirmative action regarding Arab students. After years of being excluded from university programs geared to Jewish students from disadvantaged social backgrounds, Arabs began to be considered a "population group deserving of advancement." Thus, they became eligible for a program that had formerly been restricted to Jewish students from disadvantaged groups, including new immigrants, residents of development towns, residents of distressed neighborhoods, and students with learning disabilities (see CHE and PBC 2001, 10). Beller (2001) mentions that the Hebrew University implemented this policy with the aim of increasing access of disadvantaged students (including Arabs) to some prestigious departments. Yet Beller notes that "the University has not abandoned its policy of gradual raising of the admission threshold. Rather it has opened an additional avenue of admission to the existing, competitive one, and additional places (5 percent), over and above the departmental quotas, were allocated to this new avenue" (328–29). In fact, as shown in our earlier analysis, this measure has failed to bring about any significant change in the gaps between Arabs and Jews in terms of access to Israeli universities.

Adaptation Difficulties of Arab Students during Academic Studies

The cumulative disadvantages of Arab students are also reflected in difficulties in adaptation once they begin their academic studies. Among these difficulties are economic, housing, learning, and other personal difficulties, coupled with problems of cultural adaptation (see also Al-Haj 2003; Arar and Haj-Yehia 2016; Abu-Kaf and Khalaf 2020). While all these difficulties are significant and very much affect the academic attainment and performance of Arab students, most research has focused on cultural adaptation, which is considered the most complex and perhaps most difficult of these problems (e.g., Abu-Sa'ad 2016; Halabi 2016; Haj-Yahia and Roer-Strier 1999). This is because adaptation is tightly connected with issues of identity and culture that are especially prominent in the Israeli reality. Researchers have noted that Israeli universities, which are considered the most prestigious component of the Israeli higher education system, are closely tied to Israel's ethnonational project. In addition to academic excellence, the essence of these universities is based on their leading role in nation-state building and in formulating the national ethos (see also Erdreich, Lerner, and Rapoport 2005; Halabi 2016). While my study considers cultural adaptation to be central, it places this issue within a holistic approach that encompasses the various difficulties faced by Arab students during the course of their academic studies.

In May 2001, I conducted a comprehensive survey among a representative sample of Arab and Jewish students at the University of Haifa. This university was chosen for my survey since, as noted earlier, it has the largest concentration of Arab students of all Israeli universities. Moreover, the Arab students at the University of Haifa constitute a cross-section of Arab students in Israel in terms of religious affiliation, residential localities, gender, and other pertinent characteristics. The sample of Jewish students enabled me to place the findings within a comparative perspective.

This survey used three-step sampling. First, I selected the main faculties in which Arab students are enrolled: humanities, social sciences, healthcare and welfare, natural sciences, education, and law. Second, I randomly selected one department from each faculty. Third, I selected one mandatory course from each year of undergraduate studies and one course from the first year of graduate studies. In total, 410 Jewish and 193 Arab students were interviewed. Arab students were overrepresented in the sample (32 percent in the sample compared to 18 percent of the student body) in order to represent the different subgroups among the Arab students and have enough cases for statistical analysis.

The survey asked a series of questions that sought to identify the main problems students encounter, primarily during their first year of studies. These problems included economic distress, learning difficulties, cultural adjustment, social relationships with Jewish students, and housing. Arab students ranked their difficulties from highest to lowest as follows: English, getting used to new teaching methods at the university, adjusting to a new social and cultural environment, relationships with Jewish students, housing, economic distress, and Hebrew. Jewish students also ranked problems associated with learning difficulties in first place, though to a lesser degree than Arab students. Jewish students, and particularly Ethiopian and Russian-speaking immigrants, ranked cultural adaptation in second place. This category does not include relationships with Arab students, which Jewish students saw as a minor problem. The final and least serious problems identified by Jewish students were connected to economic distress and housing (table 6.3).

Table 6.3. Adjustment Difficulties of Arab and Jewish Students (Large or Very Large Extent [%]).

Difficulty	Arabs	Jews
English language	48.4	18.2
Getting used to new academic teaching methods	42.5	27.2
Adjusting to a new cultural atmosphere	37.0	14.5
Relationships with Jewish/Arab students	26.7	6.7
Housing	27.5	9.8
Financial distress	25.1	10.0
Hebrew language	18.7	5.6

Source: Students' Survey, conducted at the University of Haifa, May 2001.

Based on the focus group with Arab students (November 2019), I grouped the adaptation difficulties of Arab students into three categories: The first category—learning difficulties—incorporates the topics of English, getting used to new teaching methods at the university, and Hebrew. The second category—cultural and sociopolitical difficulties—combines two closely related topics: adjustment to a new social and cultural environment and relationships with Jewish students. The third category—material difficulties—includes housing and economic distress.

In the following sections, I provide an up-to-date and detailed picture of the central difficulties faced by Arab students and the significance of these difficulties over time, as assessed by the students who participated in the November 2019 focus group.

LEARNING DIFFICULTIES

Learning difficulties connected with the English language and teaching methods indeed constitute a major barrier for Arab students and have a substantial impact on their adjustment and academic performance. These difficulties are related to the relatively disadvantaged background of Arab students in the formal education system as well as to the Western and Hebrew orientation of the curriculum at Israeli universities. As discussed in chapter 5, despite changes in the Arab education system over time, teaching in many Arab schools at both the elementary and high school levels is still based on the frontal methods of "banking" or "depositing knowledge" and less on educating pupils to use creative and critical thinking (the term *banking method* is derived from Freire 1972, 1985). Thus, Arab students find it difficult to adapt to the methods used in higher education, mainly at the universities and academic colleges, which place more emphasis on independent work, analytical discussion, and independent use of different sources. In addition, there is no effective occupational counseling system at Arab high schools. Therefore, a large number of Arab students run into difficulties due to their ignorance regarding areas of study, admissions criteria, the right way to choose a major, and so on. Indeed, many Arab students begin their higher education without knowing exactly how to choose an area of study that takes into consideration their preferences and capabilities and the conditions on the labor market (see Al-Haj 2003). Several students in our 2019 focus group brought up this difficulty. A second-year student studying occupational therapy stated:

When I decided to apply to the university, I had no idea how to choose my major. I asked the counselor at my school, but the answers she gave me were general and even confusing. I ultimately decided to apply to the Faculty of Law, because since I was a child the two professions frequently mentioned in my family were doctor and lawyer. My psychometric score was good, but not good enough to be admitted to medicine, so I decided to study law and was accepted. It took a whole year for me to realize that I had made a mistake and decided to quit. Completely by coincidence, I met an Arab student who was studying art and she convinced me to apply to the arts department. But once again, after one year I felt lost, with no motivation to continue my studies. . . . I ended up studying occupational therapy, where I really enjoy every moment and I have excellent grades that make me eligible to continue to graduate studies. Yet, I always think of the two years of my life that I wasted and I know of other Arab students who quit university studies after the frustration of frequently changing majors.

FINANCIAL AND HOUSING DIFFICULTIES

Financial difficulties also make it harder for Arab students to adapt. As indicated in chapter 2, the Arab population is underprivileged and most Arab families live below the poverty line (see Israel, National Insurance Institute 2018, 5–6). Housing also constitutes a problem for a considerable number of Arab students (27.5 percent of Arab students compared to 9.8 percent of Jewish students). This problem stems from the high percentage of Arab students who must find off-campus housing in nearby cities since they are not granted rooms in dormitories on campus. Therefore, the problem is twofold: an economic problem caused by relatively high rent and the problem of Jewish landlords who often refuse to rent to Arab students. In my 2001 survey, 10 percent of Arab students reported housing problems based on racist discrimination. In view of the current tense political circumstances, such problems are on the rise.

A fourth-year student in the focus group spoke about her experience:

During the first three years of my studies, I lived in the university's dormitories, which were reasonably priced. Prior to my fourth year, I was denied a dorm room on campus. I believe this was because the dormitory administration wanted to give priority to Jewish students who had served in the army. Therefore, I had to rent a room off campus. I eventually found a small apartment in Romema, a Haifa neighborhood close to the campus. The rent was reasonable. I called the landlady, told her my name and asked about the one-room apartment. She sounded very nice and we agreed in principle on the rent and conditions. Then I told her that my dad, who was sitting beside me, wanted to speak with her to set up a time to see the apartment and finalize issues connected with rent payments. Once my dad came on the phone, the landlady sounded very surprised, apparently because my dad speaks Hebrew with an accent and has an Arabic name. I, in contrast, have a universal name and speak Hebrew without an accent. The landlady asked my dad when he had immigrated to Israel. My dad asked her why she was asking such a question. She replied: "Because you speak Hebrew with an accent." My dad answered: "I am not an immigrant, I am a native-born Sabra." She seemed a bit confused, and continued: "How long has your family been living here?" My dad answered: "For a long time, for many years." She became very impatient, as if she wanted to know something, and asked loudly: "Be frank. Are you from the Migzar?" [Migzar, literally "sector," is a word Jews use to refer to Arabs in Israel.] My dad answered: "Yes." Once the landlady heard that, she completely changed her attitude. She said: "I am sorry, I have to ask my son, it seems he has already rented the apartment. In case something changes, I'll call you back." As we expected, she never called back.

A number of students in the discussion group reported similar cases of Jewish landlords refusing to rent them apartments for racist reasons.

Cultural Adjustment and Identity

Cultural adaptation is one of the main problems faced by Arab students, particularly women. Upon arriving at university, Arab students must negotiate two different cultures: that of the Arab community and that of the campus. This need to adjust challenges components of their personal and cultural identity in that they must move from an Arab community that, despite modernization trends, still retains many traditional elements, to a new sociocultural environment in which Hebrew/Western culture is dominant.

Studies conducted on Arab students' problems in adjusting to campus life at Israeli universities show that these students experience a deep sense of alienation and estrangement. Arab students are marginalized by the dominant culture and the formal system (e.g., Arar, Masry-Harzalla, and Haj-Yehia 2013; Arar and Abu El-Hija 2018). Moreover, Jewish students and stakeholders alike consider Arab students to be outsiders and even somewhat threatening (e.g., Haj-Yehia and Arar 2016; Halabi 2016; Haj-Yahia and Roer-Strier 1999; Cnaan 1988). Halabi (2016) examined the adjustment difficulties of Palestinian Arab students at the Hebrew University of Jerusalem. He concludes that these students experience ongoing and systematic discrimination and a sense of rejection both in their courses of study and in campus life: "Arab students feel as if they are outsiders on campus, and worse, they feel unwanted. They feel alienated from the teachers, the Jewish students and from the curriculum. The only goal that these students have during their years at the university is to complete their studies and receive the much-desired degree" (562–63).

The focus group discussion revealed problems of culture shock, lack of adaptation, and alienation among Palestinian Arab students. The fact that during the course of their academic studies Arab students are hardly exposed to any content related to Arab culture merely exacerbates these cultural difficulties. This is reflected in the language used on the campus, where instructions and names of departments, faculties, buildings, and the like are in Hebrew and sometimes in English, but rarely in Arabic. The administrative staff members of the different departments and sections responsible for providing services to students include almost no Arab employees or even Jews who speak Arabic. Such an atmosphere serves to increase feelings of estrangement and lack of belonging among Arab students.

Participants in the focus group spoke openly, though painfully, about problems of cultural adaptation. One third-year student had this to say: "I can never forget how I felt like a stranger when I first arrived at the university. I looked around, everything was written in Hebrew and sometimes Hebrew with English translation. But none of names of the buildings or the signs giving directions at the university was in Arabic." She hesitated for a moment: "Yeah, I recall that there was only one sign with Arabic translation: 'Smoking is prohibited. Offenders will be punished!'" Another second-year student who was studying Arabic and Hebrew literature added: "I had a similar feeling during my first year. Every time I met with the secretary of the department of Hebrew literature I wondered when she would be able to pronounce my name correctly, something that had given me a bad feeling of not belonging to this place. What surprised me more was that in the department of Arabic literature as well, the secretary was not an Arabic speaker, but at least she could pronounce my name correctly."

This culture shock is clearly compounded by the nature of the curriculum, which is based on Hebrew/Western content and lacks any cultural sensitivity or cultural content derived from the Arab students' own culture and experience, even in fields that provide culturally dependent training, such as social work and educational counseling. Studies examining Palestinian students enrolled in specific university faculties report adjustment difficulties stemming from the formal curriculum and the teachers' attitudes. A study conducted by Roer-Strier and Haj-Yahia on Arab social work students found that these students experience both "adjustment and acculturation related stresses." Moreover, some teachers expect Arab students to adopt Western-oriented ideologies that do not take the students' own experiences and culture seriously (Roer-Strier and Haj-Yahia 1998, 465; see also Haj-Yahia and Roer-Strier 1999). This situation has not changed over time. According to Mahajne and Bar-on (2022, 1112), social work training and practice at Israeli institutions of higher education are essentially Western-oriented, without a single course on Arab society.

As mentioned in the literature review, cultural incompatibilities in higher education are especially problematic among students who belong to indigenous-involuntary minorities because these students may develop an oppositional identity to that of the dominant group, who they perceive as responsible for their oppression and ultimately for their exclusion (see Ogbu 1991). This assumption applies to the case of Palestinian Arab students at Israeli universities. Researchers have noted that the marginalization of these students and even their exclusion from the dominant student body serve a catalyst for Palestinian students to engage in political activities and establish their own organizations to help reconstruct their identity (e.g., Erdreich 2006, cited by Halabi 2016, 564; Erdreich, Lerner, and Rapoport 2005). Indeed, already in the 1970s Mari (1978) noted that university studies constitute a central period of political socialization among Palestinian students in Israel. During this period, many students become involved in political activities, whether through existing parties or through other authentic organizations they form. Such involvement ultimately serves as a trigger for wider nationwide political involvement among Arab graduates.

I examined the impact of cultural alienation among Palestinian students at the University of Haifa through the focus group discussion. Students spoke enthusiastically about their own experiences. One student, who eventually became a leading figure in the Arab student organization at the university, had this to say:

> There is no doubt that my studies at the university helped me sharpen my Palestinian identity. It is true that I have always been proud of my Palestinian Arab identity, but at the university I discovered different aspects of this identity through my countless debates with Jewish students and also with other Arab students. After so many years at secondary school when we couldn't say anything about our Palestinian identity, here at the university, for the first time, I feel free to speak openly about my national dreams and identity. But, unfortunately, these debates take place outside the lecture halls, during our free time, and rarely as part of our classes.

Another third-year communication student intervened:

> Let us speak frankly, the major thing that drives Arab students to embrace their Palestinian identity is their rejection by Jewish students and the university. I remember that during my first year, and even my second year, I always felt so strange sitting in class, like somebody from another planet. In the class discussions, the lecturers used examples and materials that are far from my culture—the names, the stories and all the contents were far from my own world. Eventually, I decided to voice my opinion in a discussion about the establishment of Israel, in which the lecturer didn't even mention the existence of the Palestinians. Once I started to speak, I told a different story, the story of the Palestinian people who are the natives in this country and until 1948 were the majority, with their own culture, press and intellectuals! The lecturer abruptly stopped me in a way that was extremely offensive. I felt very humiliated, and from that moment on I decided not to speak in class anymore. Yet, after every class I felt something burning inside me, which I couldn't express in front of the lecturer. Therefore, I was eager for class to

end, when I would rush to meet other Arab students sitting on the famous sofas in the hall of floor 600, which was known as the Arab gathering place. There, I felt free to express my Palestinian identity and share my thoughts with other Arab students.

A second-year political science student added the following comment: "I can certainly understand your feelings because of this lecturer, but I have to say I had a different experience, apparently with a different type of lecturer. My lecturer was always open to listen to different opinions and every time I wanted to speak, he made every effort to get the other students to listen to me, though in some cases the debate became heated once we started to speak about identity issues."

The above discussion describes the complexity of student-teacher relations at the university. While some lecturers conform to the formal system and suppress any tendency among Arab students to challenge this system, other lecturers do respect diversity and encourage students to express their own attitudes. Yet the system as a whole at the universities is less than open and far from being based on diversity and multicultural orientation. As noted, this system shows no sensitivity toward the identity and orientation of Arab students, who are perceived not only as different but even as threatening. As in other cases of cultural incompatibility among indigenous students (see Sonn, Bishop, and Humphries 2000), this situation has a negative impact on their adaptation and generates a feeling of alienation and lack of belonging. The immediate response of indigenous-minority students is usually to create their own enclave where they can safely and openly practice their identity, attitudes, and culture.

Employment and Socioeconomic Returns of Education

The cumulative nature of the disadvantages experienced by Arabs in higher education also extends to the labor market and the socioeconomic returns of education. Various studies demonstrate wide inequalities between Arabs and Jews in their ability to translate their academic degrees into profitable outcomes on the labor market. These studies also point to the disadvantaged position of Arab college and university graduates with respect to attaining lucrative jobs and the barriers they encounter in society at large, and specifically in the Jewish-controlled labor market (Lewin-Epstein and Semyonov 1986, 1993; Lewin-Epstein 1990; Lewin-Epstein, Al-Haj, and Semyonov

1994; Al-Haj 1988, 1995a, 2003; Al-Krenawi and Graham 1998; Semyonov and Yuchtman-Yaar 1988; Semyonov and Lewin-Epstein 2011; Abu-Sa'ad 2016; Yonay and Kraus 2018; Yaish and Gabay-Egozi 2021).

In the following sections I outline the main trends in the employment distress of Arab college and university graduates over time, the key factors that retard their integration in the labor market, the implications of this situation on Arabs' motivation to pursue higher education, and the repercussions regarding Arab-Jewish relations in Israel.

Employment Distress of Arab College and University Graduates over Time

Even during the 1950s when there were only a few Arab university students and graduates, employment distress among the Arab intelligentsia was widespread. Since then, officials have repeatedly proclaimed that this problem should be dealt with and that Arab university graduates need to be integrated into government offices. As far back as April 7, 1959, the Knesset held a special debate on the problem of the Arab intelligentsia (*Lamerhav*, April 8, 1959). In his remarks, Prime Minister Ben-Gurion stated that he was aware of the problem and had already appealed to different ministries to hire Arab academics. He added: "The state of Israel should take care of the Arab intelligentsia and facilitate their employment in the labor market and in public and private offices, not because of the naive belief that this might bring peace, but because they are Israeli citizens who deserve equal rights like all other citizens" (*Lamerhav*, April 8, 1959). Despite discussions of this issue and the prime minister's statement, the government adopted no measures to fulfill its promise to hire Arab university graduates, who were relatively few at the time. Meanwhile, in 1959 Arab students at the Hebrew University of Jerusalem established a committee. Among this committee's main goals was to fight for "the promotion of higher education among Arabs, including the integration of Arab graduates in appropriate jobs" (*Haaretz*, January 1, 1966).

In the early 1970s, similar committees were established at other Israeli academic institutions, particularly at the universities in Haifa and Tel Aviv and at the Technion. In 1972 these committees were united into one umbrella organization called the National Union of Arab Students (*Zu-Haderekh*, January 1, 1972). Naturally, one of the declared aims of this unified organization was to fight for equal opportunities for Arab university graduates on the labor market (*Post Mortem*, June 6, 1972).

The government for its part was aware of the Arab intelligentsia's growing resentment about the scarcity of jobs and opportunities for mobility. In 1972, Shmuel Toledano, the prime minister's adviser on Arab affairs, initiated a special survey on the situation (Rekhess 1973). This survey revealed that the Jewish sectors, both private and public, were virtually closed to Arab university graduates and that this discrimination consequently engendered deep feelings of estrangement and frustration.

In the wake of this survey, a committee comprising the general directors of several ministries was formed to devise a plan for "the integration of Arab graduates." The committee recommended that 44 new government jobs be offered by public tender to university-educated Arabs. These positions would be located mainly in the Ministries of Interior, Justice, Education and Culture, and in the minorities' section of the prime minister's office (*The Jerusalem Post*, May 22, 1974). The recommendations of this committee were also never implemented. Eli Rekhess, who had conducted the 1972 survey for the government, stated that since his survey almost nothing had been done to alleviate the distress of Arab university graduates (Rekhess 1988, 49–50).

As a result of limited access to the wider labor market, Arab university graduates compete with one another for positions available in their own localities. Bearing in mind the economic dependence of Arabs on jobs outside their own communities and the absence of an economic base in Arab localities, one can understand why the increase in the number of university graduates has not brought with it a significant number of new jobs. The relatively rapid increase in educational level has been accompanied by only limited economic expansion. Consequently, educated and highly skilled people have very limited opportunities for finding suitable employment (Lewin-Epstein 1990, 31).

The situation described above was reflected in the findings of the 1983 Population and Housing Census published by the CBS (see Al-Haj 1995a, table 8.8, 205). These findings show that in 1983 some 38.7 percent of Arab university graduates were employed in education, as opposed to 15.3 percent of Jewish graduates. The concentration of Arab graduates in the field of education derives mainly from the lack of alternatives. Given the lack of opportunities for finding suitable work in the Jewish sector, engineers, architects, and graduates in the exact sciences turn to the educational system—in many instances against their will (see chapter 5). Therefore, whereas 14.5 percent of Jewish graduates worked as engineers and architects, this percentage was only 4.9 percent among Arab university graduates. Also, whereas 16.1 percent of Jewish university graduates worked in the life sciences, natural sciences, and social sciences, the percentage was only 6.6 among Arabs. No less significant, because of the deep employment distress, 11 percent of Arab university graduates worked in blue collar jobs (as drivers, waiters, and unskilled construction workers in garages and other places) compared to 2.8 percent of Jewish university graduates. Because of the dismal employment situation, Arab university graduates are willing to work in any available job in hopes of eventually finding a position commensurate with their education (Al-Haj 1995a, 205).

An examination of data from a 1990 survey of the labor force shows that in management and technical positions, the proportion of Arabs was significantly lower than that of Jews. Almost no Arab women hold managerial positions and fewer than 1 percent of Arab women are employed in technical professions. The situation is not very different for men: slightly more than 1 percent (1.3 percent) of Arab employees hold managerial positions outside the public sector, whereas the figure for Jews is five times greater—7 percent of all employed Jewish males (Lewin-Epstein, Al-Haj, and Semyonov 1994, 34–35). The number of Arabs employed at academic institutions is also very small. Only about 1 percent of all university lecturers in Israel are Arab. In 1998/99, of some 5,076 teaching posts at the universities only 57 were held by Arabs. There are almost no Arabs among university administrative staff and no Arabic speakers among those providing services to students.

Note that in recent years there has been an important—albeit limited—change in the hiring of educated Arabs at senior levels. In this context, more than half of the Arab university lecturers today were appointed thanks to stipends provided by the Ma'of Fund, which was established in 1995 through the PBC of the CHE and the Kahanoff Foundation. Ma'of stipends are given to outstanding Arab scholars who the university is interested in hiring. The program provides four to six three-year stipends each year, and the universities pledge to finance these positions from their regular budget at the end of the three-year stipend period (see CHE and PBC1997, 97). After the CHE adopted the recommendations of Al-Haj's Committee (2001), the number of Ma'of stipends increased to up to 10 grants annually. Moreover, the category of institutions eligible for these grants has been expanded to include academic colleges (see CHE and PBC 2001, 12–13).

Furthermore, there has been no significant change over time in the representation of Arab university graduates in lucrative public sector jobs. These graduates are still largely underrepresented in government offices and civil service units. The Report on Diversity and Representation in the Civil Service for 2020 reveals that while Arabs constitute about one-fifth of

Israeli citizens, 14 percent of civil service units have no Arab employees, 28 percent of these units have less than 5 percent Arab representation, and 32 percent have only 5 to 10 percent Arab representation (Israel Government, Civil Service Commission 2021, 26).

Expansion of Higher Education among Arabs and Persistent Inequalities

Meanwhile, higher education among the Palestinian Arabs in Israel has expanded dramatically. As my analysis shows, despite the remaining gap between Jews and Arabs in the attainment of higher education, the number of Arab undergraduate and graduate students at the various levels has increased. In addition, there has been a significant rise in the number of Arab women in higher education, so that by 2017/18 women became the majority of Arab students at both the graduate and undergraduate levels. This raises the following question: What has been the impact of this educational expansion on socioeconomic inequalities between Jews and Arabs on the one hand and between men and women in the Arab population on the other?

The employment distress and mismatch between area of study and employment among Arab graduates came up in our discussion group (November 2019). Students from different faculties sounded very pessimistic regarding their possibilities of finding a suitable job after graduation. While these attitudes characterized both men and women, male students were even more despairing than female students, perhaps due to different types of expectations. Whereas male students emphasized economic and professional motives, female students tended to speak about another goal that appeared equal in importance to economic returns: social fulfillment within their family and community (see also Arar 2011; Abu-Sa'ad 2016; Cinamon, Habayib, and Ziv 2016).

Following are a number of student responses in the discussion group (November 2019) to the following question: How do you evaluate your employment opportunities after graduation?

A third-year male student in statistics and mathematics had this to say:

> Based on the experience of my brother, who graduated five years ago from the Technion (Israel Institute of Technology) with distinction in civil engineering, it is hard to be optimistic. After graduation, my brother tried every possible way to find

a job. He applied to many places in the Jewish sector that had vacancies in his field. But he was turned down for various and sometimes even strange reasons, all of which were apparently connected to security issues. Some employers stated this clearly in the interview, while others did not state this openly but it was obviously the case. Some tenders even require military service as a precondition, leaving him no reason even to apply. My brother began working in temporary jobs, even in construction, with the hope of eventually finding a job. . . . When I think of my brother's experience, I frequently ask myself why I decided to continue my academic studies? Because if I end up working in construction, I do not need an academic degree for that!

Another fourth-year female student in education noted:

The unemployment problem among Arab academics is very discouraging. I know many women in my village who graduated from the seminar (teachers college) and after many years are still unemployed. In the Ministry of Education and the local councils we always hear that there is a surplus of graduates, so they must apply objective criteria for appointments in the education system based on credentials and graduation year. But this is not true, because in most cases those who belong to a large hamula (kinship group) and have other connections are the first to get jobs, while the others are left behind. . . . As the previous student said, I constantly ask myself why we need to go to university under such circumstances. But these thoughts are balanced by thinking about what alternative I have as an unmarried woman. I derive a lot of self-fulfillment when I think about positive changes in my personality and the respect I now enjoy in my family and my village. I am certain that even if I do not find a job, I will continue on to graduate studies.

A second-year male student in the master's degree program at the Faculty of Law had this to say:

I graduated with distinction from the Faculty of Law nearly 10 years ago. For two years after graduation, I searched for a job in the private sector, but in vain. Then I submitted my candidacy to a tender for a government job. I was informed that I need to pass an entrance exam, which is held at the main office in Tel Aviv. When I arrived the other day to do this exam, I was shocked! Because there were about 300 applicants waiting, all of them for the same job. I realized that my chances were very small, so I decided to give up and return home. I ended up working as a civics teacher at our local secondary school. This is not exactly what I wanted but it's better than being unemployed. But I do realize that we (Arabs) have no other alternative but to stick with education. Therefore, I decided to continue for an advanced degree in the hope of finding a job that fits my credentials.

Spatial segregation between Jews and Arabs exacerbates employment distress among Arab university graduates. Arabs are heavily concentrated in peripheral regions in Israel, which are underdeveloped, provide a lower level of services, and offer relatively scant employment opportunities (Goldscheider 2015; Haj-Yahia and Lavee 2018). Unlike the Jewish majority, which is concentrated in major cities and urban communities in central regions that form the nation's economic hubs, most Arabs in Israel reside in small villages and towns in the northern and southern (Negev) regions (Semyonov and Tyree 1981; Goldscheider 2015; Shdema, Abu-Rayya, and Schnell 2019). In fact, Arab cities are not much different from large Arab villages in terms of their economic structure. They are heavily dependent on a commuting labor force in that they are part of peripheral regions, lack the basic characteristics of urban centers (mainly industrial zones), and can only offer a few employment opportunities (see Haj-Yahia and Lavee 2018, 29).

ARABS IN THE HIGH-TECH INDUSTRY

The impact of the aforementioned spatial segregation and the concentration of Arabs in peripheral regions find expression in their underrepresentation in the prestigious high-tech industry. A recent Bank of Israel report provides important data about the underrepresentation of Arabs in high-tech (Bank of Israel 2021).

In the following section, I briefly summarize the main points of this important report. The report indicates that the high-tech sector has been a key component in the growth of the Israeli economy in recent decades. In 2019, high-tech constituted nearly 13 percent of Israel's GDP, and about 9 percent of all employees in Israel worked in the high-tech industry (Bank of Israel 2021, 1). Thus, employment in high-tech jobs is considered both prestigious and highly rewarding in terms of income.

Yet the representation of Arabs in Israel's high-tech industry is remarkably negligible. In 2019, only 1.2 percent of Arab employees worked in high-tech, compared to 10.7 percent of Jewish employees. These differences between Jews and Arabs in the high-tech sector are also reflected in wage gaps. The wage gap between Jews and Arabs employed in the high-tech sector is 31 percent (in favor of Jews), even slightly higher than the wage gap between Arabs and Jews in other branches of the economy. A large part of this gap is due to the difference in occupation types between the two groups. This is mainly manifested in low-ranking jobs, in particular those providing high-tech services (44 percent), while the gap among core high-tech employees is only 13 percent. These wage gaps reflect various differences between Jews and Arabs in aspects such as human capital, types of jobs, types of companies, working hours, bargaining differences, and more (Bank of Israel 2021, 13–14).

The report aptly points to a number of factors that explain the extreme underrepresentation of Arabs in high-tech. While we have already referred to some of these problems in this chapter, it is useful to reiterate these issues as phrased by the report. First, the low representation of the Arab population in high-tech industries is due primarily to cumulative gaps in human capital in the various educational settings, from childhood to university. The differences in achievement are reflected in differences in international test scores, as discussed in chapter 3. Nevertheless, the report overlooks the aforementioned significance of the PET as a gatekeeper that considerably reduces Arab students' chances of being admitted to lucrative areas of study, including high-tech fields.

The aforementioned gap in skills and the barrier of the PET find expression in the low percentage of Arab students studying high-tech fields at Israeli universities and colleges and the even lower percentage who earn degrees in these majors. In 2018, Arabs constituted only 4 percent of degree recipients in high-tech fields (Cohen-Kovach and Kasir 2020), significantly lower than the percentage of Arab students studying these subjects (12 percent). This is largely due to the high number of Arabs who drop out of high-tech studies. Mazuz-Harpaz and Krill (2016) found that among those born between 1975 and 1985, only 51 percent of the Arab students who began studying high-tech professions were eligible for a degree in the field, compared to 68 percent of the Jewish students (Bank of Israel 2021, 6).

Despite some improvements over time, even the very few Arabs with degrees in high-tech face many problems when they search for employment in the high-tech industry. A recent study reported that in 2012, only 30 percent of Arabs with high-tech degrees were employed in their field. By 2017 this rate had doubled to 60 percent but it is still low when considering the shortage of employees in Israel's high-tech industry (see Cohen-Kovach and Kasir 2020).

The Bank of Israel report underscores two major problems regarding the labor market. The first is related to the mismatch between the location of high-tech employment centers and the places where most Arabs live—as noted, in the peripheral regions in Israel. The majority of high-tech companies in Israel are located in the central region, mainly in the Dan metropolitan region (Tel Aviv area). Thus, while in 2019, 62 percent of high-tech employees in Israel worked in the Tel Aviv and central area, only 12 percent of the Arab population lives in the central region, compared to 50 percent of the Jewish population (Bank of Israel 2021, 6).

The second factor that may explain the integration difficulties of Arab high-tech graduates is that Arabs lack relevant social networks similar to those of Jews, for example through military service in technological units (Tsofen 2020). Many Arabs have no prior acquaintance with the high-tech world. According to a 2020 survey conducted by Presentense, 78 percent of Arab respondents reported not knowing anyone who works in the high-tech field, compared to only 32 percent of Jewish respondents. This difficulty is exacerbated because many high-tech companies recruit workers by informal means of "a friend brings a friend" (Bank of Israel 2021, 7).

Indeed, various studies worldwide have shown that networks of social contacts are crucial for transmission of job information and exchange of knowledge regarding specific jobs as well as for creating connections with potential employers. Therefore, a lack of social network connections may decrease the likelihood of finding employment and serve as a source of inequality between racial and ethnic groups (Calvo-Armengol and Jackson 2004; Dustmann, Schönberg, Brücker 2016; Loury 2006).

While I agree with the above analysis of the factors explaining the low representation of Arabs in the high-tech industry, I contend that other factors stemming from discrimination and exclusion of Arabs in the wider Israeli labor market should be also addressed. Arabs face overt and covert discrimination that limits their access to the labor market (see Yaish and Gabay-Egozi 2021; Yonay and Kraus 2018; Margalioth 2004). Yet since direct discrimination in the labor market is prohibited, most forms of discrimination are motivated, justified, and implemented through indirect means.

In this context, prejudices, hostile attitudes, and perceptions of Arabs as a security risk may affect employers' behavior, thus reinforcing the informal apparatus of discrimination against Arab employees (see Smooha 2004; Goldscheider 2002, 2015; Yaish and Gabay-Egozi 2021). Security considerations and army service requirements constitute a serious barrier to Arabs in Israel for obtaining jobs connected to military or defense industries, in particular in the high-tech sector (Yaish and Gabay-Egozi 2021, 4). Margalioth (2004) offers a detailed discussion of the methods that employers in the private sector may use to bypass the need for individual security screening and to prove that "nationality is the best alternative for ascertaining who is qualified" and who is not: "An employer may prove that individual screening is impossible and that reference to nationality is the best alternative to ascertain who is unqualified. It is obvious that some Arabs can pass a security clearance check. However, employers, especially those in the private sector, may claim that they cannot conduct the comprehensive security clearance checks required" (865).

Summary

This chapter has discussed developments, conditions, and policies concerning higher education among the Palestinian Arabs in Israel. I surveyed the main trends in Arab student representation at Israeli institutions of higher education, the major barriers that impede Arab access to these institutions, the problems faced by Arab students during the course of their studies, and the returns on education for Arabs, as reflected in their position in the labor market and on the socioeconomic ladder. I analyzed these trends relative to the Jewish population, which constitutes the reference group for Arabs when evaluating their socioeconomic situation.

My analysis shows that Arab students are trapped within a set of cumulative disadvantages that start from early childhood education, continue through elementary and secondary school, and remain with them before, during, and after their higher education. As far as higher education is concerned, despite the wide expansion of tertiary education, Arabs are still the most disadvantaged group in terms of vertical (access) and horizontal (field of study) factors (see also Feniger, Mcdossi, and Ayalon 2014). My analysis clearly shows that the PET serves as a gatekeeper that considerably reduces Arab students' access to higher education institutions in Israel, and particularly to universities and prestigious areas of study. Although there has been some improvement over time, a significant gap remains in the scores of Jewish and Arab students, thus positioning Arabs as the most disadvantaged group in Israel in terms of higher education attainment.

My findings reveal that employment distress has increased over time and that the expansion of higher education among Arabs has not been accompanied by a parallel broadening of employment opportunities, especially in the wider Israeli labor market. This situation has further deepened labor market segregation, marginalized Arab academics, exacerbated their alienation, and limited the potential impact of higher education as an engine for socioeconomic mobility at the individual and group levels.

Thus far, I have dealt with education among the Palestinian Arabs in Israel at the various stages, from early childhood through elementary, junior, and senior high school and up to higher education. I have delineated the main developments and inequalities in terms of quantitative educational access compared to qualitative developments and educational outcomes and returns. The next chapter shifts significantly from a discussion of formal policy and minority-state relationships to a consideration of the role of civil society organizations among the Palestinian Arabs in Israel in terms of self-empowerment and contesting the status quo. More specifically, this chapter traces the unique experience of INSANN, the first nationwide Arab civil society organization, over the course of 30 years of educational and cultural activity and community empowerment.

Chapter 7

Self-Empowerment and Civil Society Organizations among Indigenous Palestinians

The Case of the INSANN Association

Abstract

This chapter focuses on self-empowerment among indigenous Palestinian Arabs in Israel through civil society organizations. I begin with a brief introduction about the nexus between research and the academic activism of researchers. Next, I provide a theoretical overview in which I consider the approaches to empowerment and define civil society and its role as a counter-hegemonic force. I then examine nongovernmental organizations (NGOs) as a catalyst for community empowerment among indigenous peoples in general and briefly discuss the obstacles to the development of such organizations among the Palestinian Arabs in Israel. The rest of the chapter is divided into two parts. The first part discusses the profile, organizational structure, and strategic model of the INSANN Association, which was established in 1991 as the first national Palestinian NGO in Israel in the field of education and culture. The second part provides a detailed analysis of the empowerment philosophy and practice developed by INSANN, as reflected in its various community projects and initiatives. The chapter concludes with a discussion of the lessons to be learned in the context of using civil society organizations to enhance social change and community empowerment among the Palestinian Arabs in Israel.

It should be noted that this chapter describes a venture in which I have been personally involved as a social activist. I strongly believe in the connection between theoretical and applied sociology and in the leading role organic intellectuals should play in promoting community well-being and combating oppression and inequalities. Hence, I begin the theoretical introduction by describing a unique type of sociology known as public sociology, which combines theoretical and practical aspects. After that I discuss the advantages and dilemmas posed by academic activism when it comes to the question of objectivity.

Introduction: Public Sociology and Academic Activism

The nexus between research and community activism is by no means a new issue, nor is the connection between sociological theory and practice. Durkheim already mentioned both in his classic work *The Division of Labor in Society* (1984): "Because what we propose to study is above all reality, it does not follow that we should give up the idea of improving it. We would esteem our research not worth the labour of a single hour if its interest were merely speculative. If we distinguish carefully between theoretical and practical problems it is not in order to neglect the latter category. On the contrary, it is in order to put ourselves in a position where we can better resolve them" (xxvi). (See also Bradly 2004, 1630).

In 2004, Michael Burawoy, former president of the American Sociological Association, coined the term *public sociology* to express the outcome of this connection between theory and practice. The term seeks to transform sociology into a more public social science that extends beyond its theoretical significance by reaching a broader public audience and improving the public well-being. According to Burawoy (2004): "Public sociology engages publics beyond the academy in dialogue about matters of political and moral concern. It has to be relevant to such publics without being faddish, that is subservient to publics" (1607).

Indeed, Burawoy (2004) contends that "sociology's specific contribution lies in its relation to civil society, and, thus, in its defense of human interests against the intrusion of states and markets" (1603). In other words, in order for sociology to have a real impact, it should aspire to acquire public knowledge at the grassroots level, become more interventionist, and contribute to improving the public's well-being through close connections to civil society organizations to counterbalance inequalities caused by hegemonic forces (1607–8). Burawoy believes that public sociology does not contradict other disciplines within sociology but rather complements them: "Public and policy sociologies could not exist without professional sociology, which provides legitimacy, expertise, distinctive problem definitions, relevant bodies of knowledge, and techniques for analyzing data. An effective public or policy sociology is not hostile to, but depends upon the professional sociology that lies at the core of our disciplinary field" (1609).

In addition to considering the role of sociology, scholars and intellectuals have often mentioned activism and social responsibility as an important mechanism for protecting human rights, bridging gaps, and combating inequalities between disadvantaged and dominant groups (see Chomsky 1987; Ladegaard and Phipps 2020; Clennon 2020). In his strong argument supporting the role of organic intellectuals in developing real forms of life, Gramsci (1971) emphasizes: "The mode of being of the new intellectual can no longer consist in eloquence, which is an exterior and momentary mover of feelings and passions, but in active participation in practical life, as constructor, organizer, 'permanent persuader' and not just a simple orator; from technique-as-work one proceeds to technique-as-science and to the humanistic conception of history, without which one remains 'specialized' and does not become 'directive' " (10). In this context, Gramsci differentiates between two types of intellectuals: "traditional professional intellectuals" and "organic intellectuals." According to Gramsci, "These organic intellectuals are distinguished less by their profession, which may be any job characteristics of their class, than by their function in directing the ideas and aspirations of the class to which they organically belong" (3).

Indeed, organic intellectuals can support and even lead processes of social change by combining scholarly work with activism and by turning their research and academic expertise into an instrument for the political, economic, and social transformation and empowerment of disadvantaged communities and minority groups (Webster 2008; Clennon 2020, 46–49). In addition to activity in the field, multiple forms of applied research can contribute to advocacy and connect to the activities of social movements in various social arenas (Gutierrez and Lipman 2016). Yet this is possible only by crossing the boundary separating academic theory and research from actions seeking to transform the lives of ordinary people (Webster 2008, 175).

This discussion raises the traditional question of how to maintain objectivity in the social sciences while becoming personally involved in the researched subject. How is it possible to separate between subject and object—the researcher's own life—when analysis of the venture initiated by a particular researcher must inevitably be at least in part autobiographical? To answer this question, I build on Jaume Aurell's discussion of how the issue of objectivity is treated in autobiographical work. In examining the experiences of several historian autobiographers, Aurell distinguishes between two main approaches: constructionist and experimental. Constructionist autobiographers tend to establish a critical distance from their own lives in order to present it objectively. They often use empirical-analytical language that makes their narratives seem like monographs. Experimental autobiographers, in contrast, are less concerned with their identity as academics/ historians. They place their narratives within an epistemologically skeptical frame, which paradoxically is more worthwhile from the perspective of the theoretical debate (Aurell 2006, 435).

Based on the above classification, my analysis in this chapter adheres to the constructionist approach. I use the same analytical methods throughout this monograph in order to establish as much critical distance as possible between the researched subject and the object—my own life. Nevertheless, I do realize that maintaining total separation between subject and object is to some extent impossible. Hence, any attempt to speak about such separation in order to present a plausible and objective analysis would be artificial. Speaking about his own experience, well-known cultural anthropologist Clifford Geertz contends that it is extremely hard "to separate what comes into science from the side of the investigator from what comes into it from the side of the investigated." Geertz (1995) goes on to say:

> Representing what one has been doing as the result of just about everything in the world except one's beliefs and intentions—"it just happened"—is hardly plausible, a way of removing oneself from the picture in the guise of putting oneself into it. Since the decline, in most quarters, of belief in a single and sovereign scientific method and the associated notion that truth is to be had by radically objectivizing the procedures of inquiry, it has become harder and harder to separate what comes into science from the side of the investigator from what comes into it from the side of the investigated. In anthropology, in any case, and in my case anyway, assuming either has anything to do with science, the indivisible experience of trying to find my feet in all sorts of places and of the places themselves pressing themselves upon me seems to have produced whatever has appeared under my professional signature. Indeed, it has produced that signature itself. (134–35)

Beyond the dilemma of objectivity, I contend that combining theory and practice has a clear advantage, in particular in the context of education as a complex and multifaceted arena. Various studies have shown that connecting theory, practice, and research is of major importance for effective educational planning and development, in particular when it comes to culturally relevant education (see Aronson and Laughter 2020; Valeeva and Gafurov 2017). Rebecca Tarlau raises this issue in her interesting analysis of the Gramscian theory of cultural hegemony. She bases her analysis on close observation of a network of schools known as Itinerant (Mobile) Schools. This network constitutes one of the most important parts of the political struggle of the Brazilian Landless Workers Movement (Tarlau 2017). Based on observations, she identifies a major shortcoming in the work of important theoreticians in that they themselves never put their own ideas into practice: "While Gramsci offers a framework for analyzing public schools as terrains of dispute and even offers a few recommendations for reforming schools, he was never able to experiment with putting these ideas into practice. Similarly, while Freirean theory spurred hundreds of popular education and literacy experiments around the world, there are fewer examples of how these practices have been implemented in a systematic form within the public-school system" (Tarlau 2017, 122).

Indeed, theoretical concepts, important as they may be, would become richer if transformed into a form of field application. Systematic work on the part of researchers that combines both theory and practice has the potential to enrich their own understanding and provide insights that otherwise would be difficult to obtain. In this context, although education is among the most dominant topics in research on Arabs in Israel, most studies on Arab education have focused on state-minority relationships, thus emphasizing official policy dictated from above. In my analysis I also show the other side of the coin: initiatives launched by indigenous Palestinian Arabs on behalf of their own education, culture, and identity.

Theoretical Framework:
Empowerment, Civil Society, and Indigenous Peoples

Empowerment is one of the theoretical frameworks most frequently used by both researchers and professionals (Joseph 2020, 138). The theory of empowerment is based on conceptions of power and power relations. In social theory, power is usually defined as the capacity of an individual or a group to influence the actions, beliefs, or conduct of others, regardless of their own wishes or interests (Weber 1946). Among other things, power derives from economic, political, and military sources as well as from control over hedonic interests. It also encompasses the control exerted by belief and value systems, such as religion, education, specialized knowledge, ideology, and propaganda (Swartz 1997). Pierre Bourdieu's contention that culture is a main source of power makes a major contribution to the sociological theory of human conflicts. Bourdieu identifies two major and competing principles in the social hierarchy of modern industrial societies: (1) the distribution of economic capital (wealth, income, and property), which Bourdieu calls the "dominant principle of hierarchy," and (2) the distribution of cultural capital (knowledge, cultural competence, and education credentials), which Bourdieu calls the "second principle of hierarchy" (Swartz 1997, 136–37).

In the context of education and culture, Paulo Freire adds an important aspect to the theoretical analysis of power by emphasizing the dialectical nature of power relations. He differentiates between two types of power: negative and positive. Negative power is exercised by the oppressor and serves to maintain its interests. In contrast, positive power accumulates in the hands of the oppressed and serves as means of liberation and creation of a better world. Power operates on and through people in that "it is not exhausted in those public and private spheres where governments, ruling classes, and other dominant groups operate. It is more ubiquitous and is expressed in a range of oppositional public spaces and spheres that traditionally have been characterized by the absence of power and thus any form of resistance" (review by Giroux 1985, xix).

As a byproduct of power, the concept of empowerment also has different definitions and interpretations (see Zimmerman 2000; Rappaport 1984). Yet most definitions of empowerment are understood and interpreted in relation to the definition of power as "the ability to take the initiative to make something happen that otherwise would not happen" (Abu Samah and Aref 2009, 63–64). Abu Samah and Aref (2009) suggest the following definition: "Empowerment is the process whereby power is developed, promoted, gained, shared, facilitated, or adjusted by the individual or group members in their social interaction through which they are able to exercise their capabilities to make, affect and bring about changes in the community, as the product of being empowered" (63–64). That is to say, the concept of empowerment simultaneously incorporates the two dimensions of process and product and the complex relationship between them (Zimmerman 2000). In the same vein, the Connecticut People Empowering People Program has adopted the following definition: "Empowerment is a multi-dimensional social process that helps people gain control over their own lives. It is a process that fosters power in people for use in their own lives, their communities and in their society, by acting on issues they define as important" (Page and Czuba 1999, 1).

Analyses of empowerment usually emphasize three levels: organization, community, and individual. The organization level of analysis encompasses organizational processes that improve participation and organizational effectiveness to achieve goals. The community level focuses on collective action aimed at improving quality of life in the community and on the connections between various community organizations and agencies (Zimmerman 2000). At the community level, creating a sense of collective well-being, providing mutual support to effect change, and strengthening networks to improve the quality of community life are of major importance (Jennings et al. 2006). Rissel (1994) adds that "community empowerment includes a raised level of psychological empowerment among its members, a political action component in which members have actively participated, and the achievement of some redistribution of resources or decision making favorable to the community or group in question" (Rissel 1994, 41).

Empowerment at the individual level is addressed as psychological empowerment, which encompasses "beliefs about one's competence, efforts to exert control and understanding of the sociopolitical environment" (Zimmerman 2000, 46; see also Jennings et al. 2006). Zimmerman (1995) contends that an empowered person exhibits different dimensions of empowerment that can be identified as intrapersonal, interactional, and behavioral components. Thus, "an empowered person might be expected to exhibit a sense of personal control, a critical awareness of one's environment, and the behaviors necessary to extent control" (Zimmerman 2000, 47).

Empowerment is closely connected with the restoration of individual and collective identities among disadvantaged groups. Chen (2012) points out two approaches to empowerment in the context of the relationship between identity and empowerment: empowerment for self-efficacy and empowerment for group identity and collective action. The first approach focuses on changes at the individual level, whereas the second concentrates on the collective group level. Reconstruction of individual and group identities among minorities and disadvantaged groups is an effective way to cope with stigmas and stereotypes attached to members of these groups in society at large. Hence, the empowered identity of minority groups emerges through collective dialogue and raised consciousness among the members of these groups when they come together and share discriminatory experiences, develop group bonds, and exchange ideas and strategies to cope with their experiences (Chen 2012, 164). In many cases the individual and group levels of identity reconstruction and empowerment intermingle in that empowered individuals exert collective group efforts to bring about broader and more effective social changes.

By definition, empowerment is intended to enable disadvantaged groups and individuals to shift from a condition of powerlessness to a state of power that may be applied in different psychological, political, social, economic, and cultural fields and levels (see Zimmerman 2000; Rappaport 1981, 1984). Zimmerman (2000) claims that the definition of empowerment to a large extent determines its outcome. Hence, empowerment should not be perceived from a paternalistic or benevolent perspective. That is to say, organizations and agencies that launch empowerment initiatives should not see their role in terms of empowering disadvantaged groups and individuals but rather in terms of providing them the skills, knowledge, and required tools that will enable them to take an active role in setting their priorities and goals and in changing their lives as they see fit. No less important, the targets of empowerment should be involved in making decisions and tracking their own performance. They should have a sense of ownership and pride in their work and their organization, and feedback should come from within the group rather than imposed from above (see also Shor 1992, 3–4).

Moreover, empowerment should be perceived and treated as a process that is internalized over time rather than as a one-time event. Throughout this process, emphasis should be placed on *strengths* rather than on *weaknesses* to restore self-confidence among disadvantaged individuals and groups (Page and Czuba 1999). In their literature review, Gutierretz and Cox (1998, 4–5) identify a number of important components in the empowerment process, among them attitudes, values, and beliefs related to self-efficacy, self-belief and sense of control, validation through collective experience, knowledge and skills for critical thinking, and involvement in action for change. Although these components are interconnected, there is no linear relationship between them.

DEFINITION AND ROLE OF CIVIL SOCIETY

Various definitions of civil society have been proposed, depending on the historical period and the prevailing theoretical approach (see, for example, Nielson 1995; Kaldor 2003; Jones 2006; Kleibl and Munck 2017). Discussion of these theoretical approaches throughout the different periods is beyond the scope of my study. For the purpose of my analysis, I adopt the World Bank's broadly cited definition of civil society, as follows: "The wide array of non-governmental and not-for-profit organisations that have a presence in public life, expressing the interests and values of their members or others, based on ethical, cultural, political, scientific, religious or philanthropic considerations" (Kleibl and Munck 2017, 203). The World Economic Forum adds that "when mobilized, civil society—sometimes called the *third sector* (after government and commerce)—has the power to influence the actions of elected policy-makers and businesses" (World Economic Forum 2018).

One point of special importance to our analysis is associated with the critical definition of the role of civil society organizations. In this context, Gramsci emphasizes that the significance of civil society lies in its role as a counter-hegemonic force that contests the hegemony of the state and the ruling class. This also applies to education, as Gramsci differentiates between two contradictory powers affecting the school system and the contents of education. The state or the political society applies a hegemonic strategy to education with the aim of controlling curriculum and conveying a perception that fits the interest of the dominant classes. In contrast, the counter-hegemonic forces mobilized through civil society contain the seeds of social change and play a significant role in bridging the gap between school and society (Gramsci 1971, 35–36).

CIVIL SOCIETY AND INDIGENOUS PEOPLES

Research places special emphasis on the role played by NGOs in enhancing the status and rights of indigenous people worldwide. As noted in chapter 2, since the early 1960s international NGOs have played a key role in bringing the concerns of indigenous peoples to the attention of the United Nations and its agencies (Zinsser 2004, 79). In addition, various indigenous and international NGOs have joined efforts toward making the international community more aware of the human rights of indigenous and minority groups. These efforts culminated in the 2007 United Nations Declaration on the Rights of Indigenous Peoples (UNDRIP) (see Hatzikidi, Lennox, and Xanthaki 2021).

Note that most studies that examine the rights of indigenous groups do so from a human rights perspective (see Fierro 2020; Sieder and Vivero 2017; Lightfoot 2010; Macklem 2008). For example, most research examining self-determination among indigenous people has focused on issues associated with human rights from a universal perspective. Nevertheless, very little research has examined how the concept of self-determination can be utilized to develop strategies of empowerment among indigenous groups at the individual and community levels (e.g., Gordon and Datta 2021; Murphy 2014). Murphy (2014) contends that this lack of research is partly explained by the fact that the right to collective self-determination among indigenous people is largely still unrealized, even in its most restricted forms. Hence, self-determination among indigenous people must be examined not only as a human rights issue but also in terms of the human need for well-being (329). To this end, the collective capability of indigenous groups must be seen as a component in their struggle against disempowerment and oppression and as their means of achieving individual and collective development and empowerment (330).

Over the past two decades, a growing body of research has examined the involvement of indigenous organizations in the development and well-being of indigenous peoples in various fields. Issues of education, culture, language, and identity reconstruction occupy a central place in the activities of civil society organizations among indigenous groups (Nash 2006; Odello 2012; Nesterova 2019; Hatzikidi, Lennox, and Xanthaki 2021; Gordon and Datta 2021). One of the basic issues emerging from this research is connected to the right of indigenous groups to redefine education to reflect their cultural, social, spiritual, and linguistic values (Aikman and King 2012). The struggle of indigenous groups to realize this right has been accompanied by self-empowerment strategies reflected in the establishment and development of authentic organizations. Studies show that community-driven organizations and projects among indigenous groups are vital venues for promoting narratives to counteract the existing narratives in formal education, which is controlled by majority groups (Gellman and Bellino 2019, 19).

Indigenous civil society organizations play an important role in counterbalancing the absence of authentic multicultural education that recognizes the identity and historical narratives of indigenous peoples. In a review of indigenous knowledge and education, Aikman and King (2012) note that indigenous organizations at the community, national, regional, and global levels have lobbied and worked for intercultural and multicultural education to shatter centuries of discrimination and domination. These organizations have a wealth of experience and understanding regarding how to attribute value to indigenous knowledge. Similarly, Gellman and Bellino (2019) explain how the fact that the formal curriculum has overlooked the historical narratives of indigenous groups has magnified the role played by civil society organizations in counterbalancing this reality: "Until the formal sector engages in both teaching the violent past and promoting multiculturalism as worthy and interrelated goals, community-driven cultural promotion projects remain vital venues to promote counter-narratives" (19). Nevertheless, Gellman and Bellino suggest adopting a "realistic" approach regarding the ability of civil society organizations to bring about a comprehensive change in society as a whole. Hence, the role of such organizations is basically to serve as a source of inspiration and a catalyst for creating a discourse that challenges the past of marginalized groups and provides them with a space of their own. According to Gellman and Bellino (2019): "These community-based organizations should not have to shoulder the whole burden of addressing intersectionalities of marginalization, but could rather serve to inspire deeper engagement in formal education settings, creating new discursive spaces that acknowledge indigenous people and the violent pasts that have marginalized them" (19).

CIVIL SOCIETY AMONG INDIGENOUS PALESTINIAN ARABS IN ISRAEL

The seeds of Palestinian civil society already existed during the British Mandatory period. These encompassed a wide range of civil associations, including religious groups, sports and youth clubs, labor unions, women's societies, charitable organizations, and village guest houses. These associations acted outside the framework of the colonial British authority (Muslih 1993, 260). Except for the village guest houses, however, most of these associations were restricted to Palestinian urban centers. Also, since that period was characterized by national struggle in the Palestinian community, many of these associations were drawn into the orbit of the political apparatus of the Palestinian national movement (Muslih 1993; see also Abu Ghazaleh 1972).

Various factors retarded the establishment of civil society organizations among the Palestinian Arabs in Israel. As indicated in the background chapter (chapter 2), the Palestinian community had been totally shattered in the wake of the *Nakba* (the 1948 Israeli-Arab war). From being part of a large majority, the Palestinian Arabs who remained within the boundaries of the new state of Israel constituted only a small minority. Moreover, until 1966 this population was governed by a military government apparatus imposed by the state as a conspicuous system of control that restricted movement and development among the Arab minority.

One of the basic problems of the remaining Palestinian Arabs is related to their low starting point. Most of the Palestinians who remained in Israel after 1948 lived in rural peripheral regions and localities that were economically disadvantaged. It is no wonder, then, that establishing Arab civil society organizations has not been an easy mission. In addition, the hamula-based social structure of the Arab population constituted a serious barrier. As noted in chapter 2, despite the profound social changes that have taken place among the Arab population, hamula kinship groups still play a major role in local politics. Indeed, hamula-based politics are a source of ongoing internal conflicts and tensions in Arab localities. This structure exacerbates the difficulty in constructing modern community organizations that bring together activists and professionals from different hamulas.

As a result of the aforementioned situation, civil society organizations in the field of education were launched in the Jewish sector almost two decades before they began to appear among the Arab population. Already in the mid-1970s, a large number of Jewish NGOs began operating at both the local-community and national levels (Berkovich and Foldes 2012). This trend was part of the neoliberal policies that have been adopted in Israel, including the growing privatization and decentralization of the public education system (see chapter 3). Today Israel is considered to have one of the world's highest rates of NGOs per population. According to Gidron and Katz (2004), the relative size of the Israeli third sector is fourth in the world.

Another important factor that has retarded the establishment of Arab civil society organizations in the field of education is related to the centralization and state control of Arab education. As shown in the various chapters of this book, formal education among the Palestinians in Israel has been subjected to a systematic policy of control and disempowerment (see also Mari 1978; Mazawi 1994; Al-Haj 1995a, 2006; Abu-Sa'ad 2004; Arar and Abu-Asbah 2013; Arar 2022).

It should be noted that political and religious civil society organizations began to emerge in Arab society long before general educational civil society organizations. Furthermore, the rise in political consciousness among the Palestinian Arabs in Israel since the mid-1970s (see chapter 2) resulted in the formation of a number of nationwide organizations aimed at advancing the Arabs' struggle for equal rights in various fields. Among these are the National Committee for the Heads of the Arab Local Authorities (1974), the National Committee of Arab Students (1975), and the Committee for Defense of Arab Lands (1975).

In the 1980s Arab national public committees focusing on specific civil issues began to appear on the scene: the Follow-Up Committee on Arab Education (1984), the Committee for Health Affairs (1986), and the Committee for Welfare Affairs (1987). In 1987, the Arabs in Israel established their most important extra-parliamentary organization: the Supreme Fol-low-Up Committee of the Arab Population. This committee includes all the elected Arab leaders in Israel from across the political spectrum, together with representatives of Arab religious and national organizations (see Al-Haj and Rosenfeld 1990; Al-Haj 2005a).

Along with these political organizations, a large number of Arab NGOs linked to religious groups operate as a network that serves charities, medical clinics, education facilities, and daycare centers, as well as commercial and revenue-generating enterprises (Haklai 2009, 868). While systematic nation-wide research on these religious NGOs is lacking, it is safe to assume that a large number of them are connected to the Islamic Movement in Israel.

The strategy of the Islamic Movement in Israel in enhancing independent community-based organizations stems from the communitarian society legacy of Islamic movements worldwide. This legacy, known as *Al-Muj'tama' Al-A'hli'*, calls for the establishment of authentic Islamic organizations as "opposed to civil society which seeks to affect state and policy, especially regarding the community" (see Agbaria and Mustafa 2014, 46; also see Tamimi 2001). Using this strategy, the northern part of the Islamic movement led by Sheikh Ra'ed Salah established a large number of Islamic community organizations in various fields, including private educational institutions and the *Eqraa* Association for the Promotion of Education in the Arab Sector, established in 1996 (Agbaria and Mustafa 2014, 49).

Yet only since the late 1990s has a conspicuous trend toward NGOs among the Palestinians Arabs in Israel become evident (e.g., Gidron, Bar, and Katz 2004; Haklai 2009; Khalaily and Ghanem 2023). During that period a number of nationwide Palestinian NGOs emerged, most of them advocacy-oriented organizations. These include Adalah ("Justice" in Arabic): The Legal Center for Arab Minority Rights in Israel (1996); Mossawa ("Equality" in Arabic): The Advocacy Center for Arab Citizens in Israel (1999); and the Arab Center for Alternative Planning (ACAP) (2000), which is involved both in lobbying and in development.

According to Khalaily and Ghanem (2023), the proliferation of civil society organizations among the Palestinian Arabs in Israel is the outcome of internal processes among the Palestinian community. These include the growth of human capital as reflected in the rise of higher education and the expansion of the middle class. This has led to a strengthening of the "politics of faith" in that increasing numbers of Arab academics are willing to engage in collective action through civil society organizations in order to change the status quo at both the community and state levels. This trend has been accelerated in light of the failure of Arab political parties and institutions to bring about a genuine change in the status and conditions of the Palestinians in Israel (1–2, 14).

The INSANN Association

The INSANN Association (hereafter, INSANN) was established in 1991. Since then, INSANN has become the first nationwide independent (nonreligious and nonpartisan) Arab NGO in the field of education and culture. In the following sections I trace the development of INSANN; outline its main activities, major challenges, and achievements; and point out what can be learned from this unique practical experience.

The establishment of INSANN was motivated by a dramatic 30 percent drop in the number of Arab applicants to institutions of higher education in 1991 (see INSANN 1992, 6). That same year, performance on nationwide arithmetic exams in Arab primary schools was also at a low point: more than 70 percent of 4th graders in the Arab schools and two-thirds of 5th graders failed to master basic arithmetic skills. Indeed, the failure rate among Arab students was 2.5 times higher than among Jewish students (Lavy 1998, 177).

For the sake of full disclosure, this author initiated the establishment of INSANN and has been deeply involved in formulating its vision and its various projects. Within a short period of time, a number of distinguished Arab academics and educators joined this challenging and demanding venture. The name we chose for this NGO was INSANN, which means "human being" in Arabic. All the founders agreed to this suggested name out of the belief that human beings are at the center of every society and constitute the most important pillar for development and social change.

Subsequently, I conveyed this message together with the crucial importance of education, identity, and cultural capital for the Palestinian Arab community through countless meetings with students, parents, and educators who participated in INSANN's projects. The following paragraphs reflect the very essence of my message:

> Education for the Palestinian Arabs in Israel is a crucial part of their survival strategy and their very existence and future. After the Nakba (the 1948 Catastrophe), most of the Palestinian lands

were confiscated by the state, and the economic base of Arab society was devastated. But we remained with the human base, and the investment in human capital through education has replaced the investment in land. **Education has become the New Land**. . . .

Yet, development of human capital should be accompanied by the preservation of cultural capital. The conclusion is: in order to build our Palestinian Arab society, **we have to combine the power of knowledge with the power of culture and identity**. The latter should be derived from pride in our national and cultural identity and, at the same time, openness toward diversity and the embracing of other identities and cultures. (Different forms of this statement have been published in various Arabic newspapers, e.g., *Fasl el-Makal*, January 31, 1997; *Kul el-Arab*, January 26, 2001; *Kul el-Arab*, March 2, 2001; *Al-Ittihad*, February 1, 2002; *Al-Akhbar*, November 21, 2003.)

INSANN's Vision and Goals

INSANN's first and most critical mission was to formulate its vision and goals, which are based on the following central principles:

- INSANN is an independent nongovernmental Palestinian Arab organization, and all of its activities and contents derive from the needs, culture, narrative, identity, and aspirations of indigenous Palestinian Arabs in Israel. The organization seeks to provide alternative and authentic educational models that are based on values of equality, equity, excellence, and pride in the Palestinian Arab national identity and culture, along with multicultural and equal citizenship in the state of Israel among Arab students, teachers, and the community at large.

- INSANN does not aim to help or empower Palestinian Arab society, but rather to work with Arab communities and stakeholders to mobilize community initiatives. Together with all parties involved, INSANN seeks to set up priorities and plans through which it can make a difference and pave the way for social change and a better reality and future.

- Despite the conspicuous changes among the Arab population, women are still subject to double discrimination in that they are marginalized and excluded both as Arabs in Israel and as women in Arab society. Therefore, one of INSANN's priorities is to tackle this inequality and enhance internal equality within the Arab population, alongside its efforts to promote collective rights, equality, and equity for the Arab citizens in Israel.

After INSANN determined its vision, the second step was to form a wide support group that identifies with its goals. This group included Arab and Jewish academics, community leaders, cultural icons (e.g., writers and poets), and other public figures. After that, the organization devised a fundraising strategy; decided upon its organizational structure that included administration, managerial staff, and a cadre of professionals; and devised an operational strategy and a practical plan, including priorities and specific projects.

Major INSANN Projects and Initiatives

Based on the aforementioned principles and available financial resources, INSANN formulated an action plan that included three major projects:

1. A mobile community cultural center targeting non-recognized Arab villages, remote Arab communities, and Arab Bedouin tribes.

2. A national project on alternative education for creativity and innovation.

3. A national project targeting Arab high schools to bridge the gap in higher education by enhancing qualitative change and fairness of access to institutions of higher education for the Arab population.

In addition to these major projects, we initiated a number of small experimental projects, such as a leadership community project in which students from the University of Haifa, the Technion, and Ben-Gurion University were trained to promote community initiatives in 40 Arab villages and towns, including Bedouin villages and tribes in the Negev. We also designed a comprehensive plan for public activity in Arab schools and communities, including lectures, seminars, study days, and conferences in various Arab villages and towns. These activities targeted teachers, school principals, students, parents, and community leaders.

Because of space limitations, in the following discussion I focus only on the first two projects mentioned above. In the following sections, I briefly describe the content, applications, and public responses to these projects, together with their main challenges, limitations, and difficulties. I begin with the Mobile Community Cultural Center, the first project implemented by INSANN.

The Mobile Community Cultural Center

The Mobile Community Cultural Center (hereafter, the Center or the Mobile Community Center) was the first of its kind, not only in Palestinian Arab society but in Israel as a whole. The goal of the Center was to serve Arab villages located in the northern region (the Galilee) and the center (Little Triangle) that lacked official recognition. Later, a special unit was also activated in al-Naqab (the Negev) that offered services to remote Bedouin tribes and villages, most of which were not officially recognized.

When INSANN's activities were launched in 1990, 51 Arab villages in Israel lacked formal recognition by the state (Al-Haj and Rosenfeld 1990). Most of these villages were populated by Bedouins who had settled there during the Ottoman period, the Mandatory period, or as part of the government's settlement program for Bedouins during the 1950s and 1960s. Since the establishment of Israel, the government has made ongoing attempts to eliminate a large number of these villages and transfer their inhabitants to nearby large settlements under the auspices of a Bedouin sedentarization program (Falah 1989; Reiter 2022). The inhabitants of these "non-recognized" Arab villages have resisted these attempts. In response, the state has applied constant pressure on the inhabitants of these village by denying them many basic human services, such as running water and electricity, education, and other vital infrastructure components. The residents of these villages were denied the right to build houses. Therefore, most lived in tents or buildings that are officially defined as illegal in that they were built without formal permission from regional planning and building committees (see Reiter 2022).

The struggle of the residents of these villages to attain educational services and other organized cultural activities not only sought to improve the educational level of the population. It has also served as a survival strategy, since establishing schools and cultural services is tantamount to official recognition of people's right to exist on their land. Hence, INSANN's efforts were aimed at supporting these villages' demand for formal state recognition and for basic human rights in housing, education, and culture. INSANN also sought to connect these villages to broader society through educational activities, cultural festivals, public events, and meetings, with participation of Arab leadership from the whole country. The main philosophy of this venture was based on **community empowerment and social change** by enhancing educational and cultural activities and strengthening women and young leaders.

We selected the following villages for the first phase of the project:

- Officially unrecognized villages in the north: Kammaneh al-Sharqiya, Kammaneh al-Gharbiya, Arab Elna'im, Demida, and Galaseh.

- Remote villages in the Triangle region: Barta'a, Mu'awiya, and Mosmos.

- Remote villages in Marj Ibin Amer (Emeq Yizrael): Na'ura, Kufr Masser, and Sandala.

The project was eventually expanded to Arab Bedouin villages and encampments, including non-recognized Bedouin villages and tribes in al-Naqab (Negev) in southern Israel. The Mobile Community Center offered the following services:

1. A mobile library on wheels containing nearly 6,000 books in Arabic, Hebrew, and English, in addition to cassettes and audio-visual aids. This library was administered and operated by professional librarians and a trained staff. It visited every village participating in the project once a month for an entire day. A variety of activities were organized throughout the day, including lending books to children and adults in addition to activities aimed at enhancing reading literacy.

2. A mobile creativity center containing a mobile theater and a mobile exhibition of children's paintings that used a large van or truck adapted for this project. We organized all the other cultural and community activities through the mobile

creativity center, including creativity workshops; lectures for students, teachers, and parents; an early childhood learning center; and classes for painting, theater, art, and various cultural activities. In the officially unrecognized villages and small villages without local schools, the center's activities took place in a room donated by local residents or in a tent dedicated to such activities. Some of the villages with local schools provided facilities for these activities.

The services provided by the Mobile Community Center were directed by highly professional instructors and well-known Arab artists and writers, who were carefully selected to reflect the prestigious nature of this venture, make it more attractive, and turn it into a source of community pride. We also organized an annual Creativity Week in one of the participating communities. Students, parents, and teachers from all the surrounding communities took an active part in this festival, which has become the project's trademark.

Within a short period after its establishment, INSANN became a success story that spread by word of mouth to the entire Arab population and to Israeli society in general. Because it was the first project of its kind in the Palestinian community, and particularly in villages that offered no educational or cultural activities whatsoever, it also attracted wide media interest.

The enthusiasm about this extraordinary project is reflected in a detailed article written by well-known journalist David Rudge and published in *The Jerusalem Post* on March 31, 1993, under the headline "Bridging the Gaps in Arab Education." The article's subtitle speaks for itself: "Arabs in Israel, for the first time, are taking an active part in trying to improve Arab education and promote the level of education and training."

Rudge focused on INSANN's major projects, which very quickly became a role model and gained tremendous interest and cooperation among the Palestinian population. He began by referring to the Mobile Community Center, which aims at promoting educational and cultural activities in places no one had ever imagined this was possible. In Rudge's words:

INSANN's mobile library is the nucleus of the first mobile community center in the country. Around INSANN's library a number of rich cultural activities had been initiated, such as creative writing, drama, painting, art and parent education. In many villages, such as the formally unrecognized village of Arab

Elna'im, there were no schools or buildings to use as classrooms, so INSANN together with the local leadership set up a special tent where cultural and art classes were held, which children of all ages came to with unparalleled enthusiasm, and in many cases accompanied by parents, who do not rush home but participate with the children. These activities were directed by famous Arab artists and writers.

The Mobile Community Center was later adopted by formal authorities through the Israel Association of Community Centers, thus becoming the first Mobile Community Center in the country. This cooperation, however, did not last long. It was terminated after a few years because of a dispute between INSANN and the Association of Community Centers regarding the project's contents and the type of communities it should serve.

Ayman Agbaria, who later earned his doctorate in education and worked as a researcher and is currently an associate professor in the Faculty of Education at the University of Haifa, was appointed as first national director of the Mobile Community Center. Agbaria, who is also a writer, published several articles about the Mobile Community Center, one of which appeared in the magazine of the Israel Association of Community Centers (*Bamantnassim*) in October 1995. At the beginning of the article, Agbaria provided background on INSANN:

INSANN initiated a number of innovative projects tailored to the uniqueness and needs of the Arab population. Among the pioneering projects are community entrepreneurship projects in forty Arab villages, which were carried out by activist students from the University of Haifa, the Technion, and Ben-Gurion University of the Negev. Another project was in the field of academic counseling and professional guidance for high school students across the country. And above all, the Mobile Community Center was one of the most disciplined initiatives of the INSANN and had become an incubator for programs in the field of creativity.

Agbaria added: "INSANN has initiated modeling intervention in a number of unrecognized villages adopted by the association, which has operated a mobile library and enrichment classes on its behalf; the goal is to be a catalyst for social change within the villages and to institutionalize these activities through permanent bodies, in order to turn them into regular and continuous activities."

The article went on to describe the activities of the Mobile Community Center in detail and outlined how this center was run under the harsh conditions in these villages:

> The Community Center runs under harsh conditions, within the only school located in each village. It offers five classes: painting, dance, creative writing, theater and music, run according to a community empowerment vision. This vision was reflected in the establishment of parent committees for each class and in the organization of community events, such as community theatre, meetings with writers and music days. Parents took an active part in these classes, along with their children in an impressive manner.

Ayman Agbaria concluded the article by mentioning the staff of the Mobile Community Center, which was chosen based on a philosophy of community empowerment and social change: "Every community center in each village was operated by a community coordinator, who also served as an operations coordinator and liaison with the schools. In addition to the coordinators, there were a number of well-trained instructors. These instructors were selected from the best professionals in the Arab sector, in order to give the project a prestigious image and attract wide participation of students, teachers and parents, children and adults, and community leaders in the various classes and activities" (Agbaria 1995, 18–19).

In the following sections, I describe the case of the village of Kammaneh, at the time one of the officially non-recognized villages where INSAAN ran a wide range of activities, including the Mobile Community Center and a number of other educational and public activities. After providing some background about this village, I present an in-depth interview I conducted with E'id Sawaed, a leading figure in Kammaneh. In the interview we discuss INSANN's activities and their impact on the educational and cultural life of the village and on promoting official recognition for the village.

The Case of Kammaneh

Kammaneh is a Bedouin village located on Mount Kammaneh (or *Kamun* in Hebrew), the highest mountain in the Lower Galilee. The top of Mount

Kammaneh offers a panoramic view of the Sea of Galilee and the Golan Heights to the east and of the Mediterranean Sea and Haifa Bay to the west. Three small Arab Bedouin villages were built side by side on this mountain. They are actually three neighborhoods of a larger village, all inhabited by the Arab Bedouin tribe of Sawae'd: Kammaneh al-Sharqiya (eastern Kammaneh), Kammaneh al-Gharbiya (western Kammaneh separated from the eastern village by a wadi), and Galaseh, located to the north of these villages.

The village of Kammaneh has been in existence for over 200 years, dating back to 1810 during the Ottoman period. The stone houses in the village were built in 1925/30. Immediately after the establishment of the state, a modest school built of tin huts was established in the village, providing the children an educational setting until the end of elementary school and also offering the village semi-official recognition. In 1962/63 the state closed this school as part of an effort to pressure the inhabitants of Kammaneh to move to permanent population concentrations the state had established for Arab Bedouins in several places in the Galilee. In addition, the state passed an official law in 1965, according to which the village lands were declared as agricultural lands, which meant that buildings in the village would be considered illegal. Yet the residents of Kammaneh refused to move and embarked on a long and persistent struggle for official recognition.

The Jewish settlement of Kamun was established in 1981 right next to the Bedouin village of Kammaneh as part of the government's Mitzpim project of the 1980s, whose main purpose was to Judaize the Galilee (see chapter 2). Unlike the Arab village of Kammaneh, the Jewish settlement of Kamun, which numbered only a few dozen families, enjoyed all types of services, including electricity, running water, paved roads, and educational and cultural services.

INSANN's Activities in Kammaneh

INSANN launched its activities in the villages of Kammaneh in 1992 as part of the above-mentioned nationwide project in the non-recognized Arab villages. The educational activities took place in a large room in the home of the parents of community leader E'id Sawaed, which he donated for this purpose. He also donated the yard where the mobile library parked. Children, adolescents, and women from all parts of the village came to borrow and exchange books. A large number of elementary school children participated in the various activities. Very often their mothers also joined in, together with their other children. According to E'id Sawaed, the entire venture turned into a major happening in the life of the village.

In addition to the Mobile Community Center, INSANN offered extensive public community activities. We held art and culture festivals that attracted a large audience, including children and young people. After each festival, a public event and symposium were held. A large audience from the village and other Arab surrounding communities participated in these symposia, as did public figures, politicians, and academics from across the country. Every year, INSANN organized a large public event during the Muslim fasting month of Ramadan. The event is called *Iftar* (the fast-breaking meal of Ramadan) and thus has special social significance. The participation of public figures, heads of councils, and politicians from all over the country lent this event added importance.

Interview with E'id Sawaed

To learn about the long-term impact of INSANN's activities in Kammaneh, on March 13, 2022, I conducted an in-depth interview with E'id Sawaed, an elementary school teacher who now also works as an instructor in the Ministry of Education on the subject of heritage. The residents elected him as the village's representative on the Misgav Regional Council, which is responsible for the municipal affairs of the 35 communities within its jurisdictions: 29 Jewish and 6 Bedouin communities.

E'id represents the new generation of Kammaneh residents. He and his two cousins, Hashem (a lawyer and today a judge) and Mahmoud (a teacher), led the 1990 struggle of the three villages (Kammaneh al-Sharqiya, Kammaneh al-Gharbiya, and Galaseh) for official state recognition. Today E'id is the only one who has remained politically active. In the following section I quote directly from this in-depth interview, in which E'id spoke in great detail about INSANN's activities, the participants, the main events, and their short- and long-term impact on the village, the children and their parents, and the significance of these activities in gaining formal recognition for Kammaneh.

Question: What do you think was the significance of INSANN's activities in Kammaneh?

Answer: The activities you (INSANN) organized for the children were very important to them and to the whole community. For the first time our children felt that someone cared about them at a time when the rest of the world was depriving them of their natural human rights. A large number of children participated, especially those in primary school. Moreover, other young people made sure to take part in the creativity workshops and cultural activities, which were also suitable for adults. These activities were also very significant to parents. When we saw that someone had been instilled with a new spirit of hope and action, this raised our morale and fortified our resilience in our struggle for formal recognition.

Question: Tell us briefly what was entailed in gaining recognition.

Answer: Recognition of Kammaneh al-Sharqiya, Kammaneh al-Gharbiya, and also Galaseh took place in several stages. In 1992 we began talking seriously with government representatives regarding official recognition. On December 24, 1995, the government recognized both Kammaneh al-Sharqiya and Kammaneh al-Gharbiya, and in 1999 the High Court of Justice ruled that more neighborhoods should be recognized, including Galaseh.

Question: In your opinion, what was the impact of INSANN's activities on the formal recognition, if any?

Answer [*without hesitation*]: INSANN certainly had an impact! Every INSANN activity in the community was important in boosting our morale and reinforcing our belief in our struggle to get the authorities to recognize our human rights. INSANN's activities contributed a great deal in terms of exposing the general Israeli public, politicians, and government representatives to our rights. For example, the Iftar event that INSANN organized during Ramadan was attended by dozens of public figures and politicians, including MK Abd Elwahab Darawshe and MK Talab Alsania', leaders of the Supreme Follow-Up Committee of the Arab Population and its chairman Ibrahim Nimer Hussein, as well as the mayor of the Ba'ana Council, the mayor of Sakhnin, and others. This Iftar celebration and the other festivals, as well as the activities organized by INSANN, made us feel that we were not alone and that there are others who stand with us and support our just struggle. In the wake of these activities, official government representatives also began to treat us differently. The Knesset members who participated in your [INSANN's] activities also felt a commitment and brought up our demands in the Knesset and at meetings with various ministry representatives. In short, with INSANN's support we were able to position our struggle such that policymakers could no longer ignore us or our just demands. INSANN's presence along with all the public support you brought and the activities you initiated, and especially the mass festivals, put us on the map and gave our just struggle a very important boost.

Question: How about the educational activities?

Answer: INSANN's activities made us aware of our rights to education and culture. Until then, these issues were not exactly at the top of our priorities because all our attention was focused on physical survival and being able to continue living on our lands. INSANN's legacy has served as a catalyst for placing education at the center of our concerns. Today [2022] I am proud to say that the elementary school in Kammaneh is one of the best schools in the region. These are the seeds that INSANN planted and today we are reaping the fruits of these seeds.

Media Coverage of INSANN Activities in Kammaneh

As mentioned by E'id Sawaed, the activities and public festivals and lectures that INSANN organized in Kammaneh attracted major public attention. Indeed, the media gave extensive coverage to the Mobile Community Center model in Kammaneh and in other non-recognized villages. In the following section, I briefly discuss two articles published in prominent Arabic newspapers.

In 1997 journalist Wadi' Awawdeh wrote a review of one of these festivals held in Galaseh-Kammaneh. The article, titled "INSANN Works in Unrecognized Villages to Compensate Their Children for What the State Has Deprived Them Of," was published in the newspaper *Kul el-Arab* on November 21, 1997. Awawdeh provided an overview of the festival and its activities. He pointed out that the festival featured two types of activities. The first type was intended for children and entailed cultural classes and competitions in which children and parents participated throughout the day. At the end of the day, the adults met with Arab leaders and activists from across the country.

Another interesting example is an article published in the weekly magazine *Al-Sinnara* under the heading "The Mobile Community Center Provides Its Services to Villages Rich in Their Children's Skills." The article was written by a journalist named Ilham who also worked as an educator:

> Dear readers, no doubt you are used to seeing people in your communities gathering around a van or truck selling vegetables or clothes, but the spectacle of groups of children and adults, women and men thirsty for reading and for education, gathering around a truck loaded with books from all over the world, books in different languages and cultures, such a scene is certainly not customary either for me or for you. . . . Yes, it is the achievement

of the INSANN, which initiated the unique Mobile Community Center enterprise that has become the only source that feeds the remote and secluded (Arab) villages, with books in different fields from all over the world, that places special emphasis on children's books, in order to deepen their reading culture and open their horizons to the wider world.

INSANN initiated the idea of the mobile library in 1992. It should be noted that the idea of a mobile library had been known in various countries around the world for decades and had been used by various institutions and foundations but without success. In contrast, the mobile library of INSANN has become a success story within a short period, and this is thanks to the holistic plan that INSANN formulated after conducting a comprehensive field study in the unrecognized (Arab) villages. This study examined the attitudes of the residents, the social structure, the residents' needs, aspirations, priorities and expectations, and the existing economic and social obstacles—and that is really the secret of success.

Note that the journalist made reference to one of the important factors behind the success of the Mobile Community Center project, as well as other INSANN's projects: the comprehensive study of the local population's needs and attitudes conducted before planning each project. Based on this study, we built a strategy that took into account the social structure of each locality, the needs and expectations of the residents, and other important variables. That is to say, INSANN saw the local residents as the leaders of each project and involved them in the various stages of planning, content decision-making, and practical implementation. This model was based on my knowledge and examination of the reasons behind the success, and mainly the failure, of many other projects in the Palestinian Arab community, despite their large budgets. In most cases, these projects were based on a perception that was detached from reality and far from the culture and expectations of the local population. Moreover, these "top-to-bottom" projects overlooked the indigeneity of the Palestinian Arabs and the local residents' aspirations to restore their identity and narrative through authentic contents reflecting their needs, history, and culture.

This point was mentioned in an opinion piece by Ilham, which appeared adjacent to the article about the Mobile Community Center of INSANN under the headline "Libraries without Audiences, and Audiences without Libraries":

Many Arab localities have libraries rich in budgets and material resources, but only a few readers come to these libraries and use them, while other villages were deprived of the basic right of being given opportunity to gain knowledge. . . . And so, the inhabitants of these villages are thirsty for this knowledge and thirsty for books and begging for someone to come and connect them with the outside world. And that's exactly what INSANN did, and that's exactly the role of the Mobile Community Center that revived these villages and put them on the map, after having been forgotten. The Mobile Community Center with its modest budget brought joy and happiness to the residents of these villages of all ages and has become their bridge to the wider world. (Ilham Hanna, *Al-Sinnara*, November 21, 1997)

THE CREATIVITY PROJECT: AN ALTERNATIVE MODEL FOR EMPOWERING MULTICULTURAL EDUCATION

Rationale and Main Principles

Innovation and creativity are two major skills that have always been affiliated with human progress and sustainable development. Both professionals and policymakers firmly believe that the future of nations in the 21st century depends to a large extent on creativity and innovation. This is especially true in today's globalized world, which is based on rapid changes, fast growth of knowledge and technology, increasing competition over scarce resources, and rising challenges facing the human race (see Schleicher 2018; Eduah 2019).

Creative writing methods that include prose writing, poetry writing, storytelling, and other creative endeavors are considered to be groundbreaking and innovative pedagogical strategies. Even a cursory literature survey reveals a wide range of studies that highlight the importance of creative methods for student self-empowerment and for providing students real-life skills they can apply outside the classroom and in their life. According to these studies, creative and critical thinking broadens students' horizons to include important values and social competencies, such as cultural competence, diversity, multiculturalism, and intercultural dialogue (see, for example, Bremner 2021; Lorenz 2020; Howe and Van Wig 2017; Ryan 2014; Thomas and León 2012; Mazza 2012; Sommer et al. 2012; Blumenfeld 2010; Clegg 2008; Lave and Wenger 1991).

In a detailed review of 21st-century educational strategies, Howe and Van Wig (2017) provide an interesting analysis of creative writing pedagogy as a major student-centered learning strategy and a vital method for developing deeper cognitive learning skills, critical thinking, and collaborative problem-solving, all of which serve as the basis for globalized, technologized, and innovative education. They show how multiple theories of creative learning, including transformative, reflective, and experiential learning theories, position the creative writing workshop model at the "intersection of pedagogies supporting metacognition, transformative education, identity development, creativity, and critical thinking, across multiple demographics of writing students" (139).

The aforementioned principles were integrated into the second area of INSANN's activity, which aimed at creating an alternative model for *empowering multicultural education* among the Palestinians in Israel based on critical-transformative methods of creativity and innovation (hereafter, the creativity project). In what follows, I briefly describe the contents of the creativity project. Then, I discuss the project's impact on Arab schools and its reception by Arab community. After that, I briefly discuss the shortcomings and main difficulties of the project. I conclude this section by summarizing the project's pedagogical philosophy.

Content of the Creativity Project

TEACHER TRAINING

From the outset, our project aspired to create an alternative critical model of educational empowerment for both students and teachers. Hence, there was a crucial need to offer teachers appropriate methods not usually provided by their conventional training, especially in an era of neoliberal policies (see chapter 5). To this end, every year, we organized a special training course for creativity project teachers and coordinators through the Center for Multiculturalism and Educational Research at the University of Haifa. The course covered a variety of topics directed at strategies for developing educational initiatives and introducing alternative educational methods based on creativity and critical thinking.

The theoretical part of the course was complemented by practical workshops held at the participating schools. These workshops focused on creative methods, including creative writing, music, painting, and basic skills in mathematics literacy, computer literacy, and science. In addition, a series of study days and conferences were organized in those parts of the country with a high percentage of Arab residents: the Galilee, the Little

Triangle, the Negev, and the mixed cities. These meetings included lectures, discussions, and workshops that were open to teachers, principals, parents, and municipality representatives. Thus, all interested parties were exposed to the project's main philosophy and teachers had the opportunity to present their projects and obtain feedback from professionals and other colleagues.

MOBILE CREATIVITY CENTER

The Mobile Creativity Center employed in INSANN's first project in the non-recognized Arab villages was also used in the creativity project. This center included a special creativity library that contained books, cassettes, and audio-visual aids. The Mobile Creativity Center also included a mobile exhibition of children's paintings, produced solely by students from the participating schools. This exhibition was cumulative in that we continuously added new items to the gallery and replaced some of them to give students from across the country a chance to display their work. The exhibition was organized and directed by well-known Arab artists, thus enriching its activities and lending it a prestigious image.

PUPIL WORKSHOPS

Workshops were organized for students at each of the participating schools and run by the teachers who had taken part in the intensive training described above. Some of the participating schools organized these workshops as an integral part of their school curriculum, and most schools ran them after school hours. In these workshops, teachers applied the new creativity and innovation methods they learned in the training courses, under close professional guidance from the course instructors. This guidance was of major importance in making a direct connection between theory and practice with respect to various creative writing methods.

THE ANNUAL BOOK OF CREATIVITY

One of the main parts of the project was the publication of an annual book produced entirely by the participating children. The book included creative writing, paintings, and other forms of artwork. The well-known writer Dr. Mahmoud Al-Abbasi assessed some samples of the students' work. His analysis appears later in this chapter.

CREATIVITY FESTIVALS

In addition to the aforementioned events, each year a number of creativity festivals were organized in various Arab towns, villages, and Arab Bedouin encampments. Each such festival lasted an entire day and included a large number of workshops and creative activities: creative writing, creative drama, creative folklore, and music. The festivals each culminated with an exhibition of students' works and a special show organized and moderated by students.

Evaluation of the Creativity Project

For the sake of scientific assessment of the project, each year we evaluated a representative sample of participating schools. Each evaluation study included a field survey, analysis of students' work, and interviews with teachers, principals, and parents. These evaluation studies were intended mainly for internal purposes. They enabled us to determine which parts of the project were successful and should be strengthened and which were less successful and should be improved or replaced. As part of this evaluation, I also conducted a longitudinal content analysis of students' works published in the *Annual Book of Creativity* during the period 1993–1998 (see Al-Haj 2004).

School Steering Committees

A steering committee was set up in every school. This committee was composed of the superintendent, the school principal, and representatives of the teachers, students, parents, and the local authority. These committees closely monitored the project and were involved in planning, implementation, and decision-making for all the activities.

Impact on Students: A Brief Analysis of the Annual Book of Creativity

The *Annual Book of Creativity* contains selections of the children's creative writing and art products. Selecting the products for publication in the annual book was very competitive and took place in two stages. First, each school submitted a sample of its students' products. After that, a special committee of judges was appointed, composed of teachers, school principals, and famous poets and writers. Among the members of the committee were the poet and writer Salman Natour, the poet Sua'd Karaman, the writer Dr. Mahmoud Al-Abbasi, and two educators, Dr. Ibtisam Al-Haj and Dr.

Rihab Abd el-Halim. Every year the committee or its representatives selected what it considered the most outstanding of the children's paintings, poems, thoughts, and more. In selecting the best products, the committee made every effort to choose at least one product from each school.

In addition to the general *Annual Book of Creativity*, each school produced its own creativity volume or published its students' work in class magazines and in the annual school gazette. In this way, every participating child had the chance to see their product recognized and published in one or more channels. Needless to say, this was extremely important for children, parents, and schools in boosting morale and pride.

Dr. Mahmoud Al-Abbasi helped enrich the creativity project. In particular, he served as a judge in selecting works to be included in the *Kalat Lia Elriahin* (*The Roses Told Me*) book series. He also participated in the festivals at which the children presented their works. On December 9, 1997, Dr. Al-Abbasi published an article about the book in the culture section of the *Al-Sinnarah* newspaper under the following headline: "Motifs, Themes and Foci in the Fourth Book of the *Kalat Lia Elriahin* Series" (Al-Abbasi 1997). In the article Al-Abbasi states: "This book is an embodiment of the process of creativity, and the works in it resemble a 'selection of rainbow colors' produced by true creators in every sense of the word."

Al-Abbasi also compares this book to previous volumes: "Over the years one has seen a welcome change in students' thinking, in the depth of their works and in the diversity of topics. What stands out in the fourth book (1996/97) are the diverse motifs that students have expressed in their works, through poetry (42 works), prose (40 works), stories (12), and short essays on personal and general topics (25)." According to Al-Abbasi, the most dominant focus was the personal focus, which encompassed issues related to relationships with self-identity, childhood and personal dreams and hopes, parents, siblings, and immediate family members. The second focus was on school and relationships with teachers and other students. The third focus was more general and referred to community, land, environment, village, heritage, and national identity. The fourth focus was on human culture, war and peace, students' identification, and their longing for peace between peoples, especially between Palestinians and Israelis. The fifth focus was global, with references to nature, the sun, the stars, treatment of animals and relations with them, and other topics related to nature and the environment. Al-Abbasi adds: "This is an impressive rainbow of colors, indeed, arranged in spherical circles, from the personal circle to the universal human circle, where in every circle children expressed themselves in the most beautiful way, when the standard of literature and poetry would not embarrass the best writers and poets—it even sounds more authentic and more natural" (Al-Abbasi 1997).

My content analysis of the *Kalat Lia Elriahin* volumes, published in the period 1993–1998, reiterates Al-Abbasi's conclusions (see Al-Haj 2004). My analysis reveals a considerable increase in individual subjects over time, from 17 percent of the total works in the 1993/94 volume to 52 percent in the 1997/98 volume. Among these individual themes are self-identity, national identity as viewed from the individual perspective, and social identity among girls, who protested their marginalization within the family and community (Al-Haj 2004, 10–14).

In addition, a large part of the children's writings focus on their personal feelings and experiences: my dreams, my school, my teacher, my parents, my hand, myself, my candle, my pencil, my friends, my birthday, my flower, my fears, my hopes, and other items connected to their personal lives. Indeed, the participating students gradually moved from the margins of their collective identity to the center of identity formation. In this sense, the children's individual identity became centralized over time. Yet this does not mean that collective national and cultural identities diminished. These forms of collective identities remained central but were absorbed within the children's self-identity and creatively expressed in the children's own words rather than as slogans, such as my national flag, my village, my memorial day, my grandfather told me, and others. At the same time, human topics increased from 4 percent in the 1993/94 volume to 19 percent in the 1997/98 volume. These topics include peace and war, identification with the poor, the environment, and essays about life, wisdom, and other topics with general human orientations (Al-Haj 2004, 18).

Already in 1915, Dewey noted the importance of giving the students the chance to express their own individual experience. He wrote that this is what differentiates between modern methods and traditional methods that consider children as aggregate units: "The moment children act, they individualize themselves; they cease to be a mass and become the intensely distinctive beings that we are acquainted with out of school, in the home, the family, on the playground, and in the neighborhood" (Dewey 1915, 33).

My findings also point to a gradual increase in "human" topics in the children's products. This finding indicates that their increasing self-confidence and self-esteem is accompanied by a growing sense of being human and rising interest in global-multicultural subjects. Due to space limitations, we unfortunately cannot provide examples of these works.

Response of Arab Schools and Community

Already in the first year (1993) about 50 schools registered for the project, many more than we expected. In the second year this number increased to 70 schools, and after nearly three years close to 100 Arab schools across the country participated in the creativity project. These schools constituted a representative sample of the entire education system, ranging from government schools (mostly Muslim) to Christian private schools to schools representing various sectors of the Arab population, including Druze and Bedouin schools.

Note that when INSANN launched its activities, a question was raised as to whether the Druze sector should also be included in its projects. As mentioned in chapter 3, Druze schools are treated as "non-Arab" schools and are administered as a separate unit that is not part of the Arab education system. Yet INSANN made an unequivocal decision to consider the Druze sector as an integral part of the Arab public, despite policymakers' attempts to divide and rule. Therefore, from the outset we contacted the people in charge of Druze education, including mayors, superintendents, and principals, who exhibited great enthusiasm and wonderful cooperation. Already in the first year, Druze schools from the villages of Beit Jan, Maghar, Daliet Al-Carmel, Peki'in, and Yarka participated in the project.

This great enthusiasm about the creativity project was reflected in various Arab newspapers throughout the country. In the following section I offer a brief sample of these articles and reports. In an article titled "The Winds of Change Are Blowing in Arab Schools," journalist and columnist Wadi' Awawdeh conducted a number of interviews with the educators who formed the project's pedagogical field leadership. Dina Zu'abi, who served as director of the creativity project at the 'el-Amal school in the remote Arab village Kufr Maser, noted that after 17 years as a teacher she thought it was crucial to attend training workshops organized by INSANN in order to learn creative educational methods. Zu'abi had this to say about her experience with students who participated in creativity workshops at the 'el-Amal school: "Through these workshops I sense a day-by-day improvement in students' conduct and the way they express themselves freely through creative writing methods, painting and drama. I also notice considerable progress in students' writing and expression skills. . . . This has even improved the mutual trust between teachers and students, as many students started to call me at home in order to speak with me about their work and new ideas." One of the workshop participants was Faisal Assadi, principal of an elementary school in Deir el-Assad. He came to this workshop together with a number of teachers from his school. Assadi spoke enthusiastically about the basic notion behind the creativity project, which seeks to "give students a voice by respecting their right to speak openly and frankly about their dreams, thoughts and ideas" (Awawdeh1995).

Iskander A'mal, a well-known writer and journalist (and himself a teacher who attended INSANN's seminars and led the creativity project at the Carmelite School of the Italian Sisters), wrote a detailed article about the creativity project that was published in *Al-Itihad* (the oldest Arabic language daily newspaper in Israel). The article was titled "INSANN Continues the Journey of Creativity" and subtitled "The establishment oppresses creativity and creators out of fear of their intellectual creativity." A'mal had this to say:

> INSANN . . . continues the creative journey, which began three years ago in Arab schools. INSANN has always accustomed us to presenting innovative and leading ideas, and day after day it proves that it is a pioneering association in enhancing innovative and creative methods in our Arab schools. We already feel the change, a change that is not something transient or seasonal, but a change based on long-term vision. INSANN proved that creativity is not an empty slogan, but an ongoing process and revolution, a real one built on in-depth vision and content that meets the needs of the Arab education system.

In this article, Iskander A'mal provided a comprehensive picture of all the activities in the INSANN creativity project, including seminars for teachers and principals, courses and training for project instructors in Arab schools, student workshops, and publication of the *Kalat Lia Alriahin Annual Book of Creativity* (A'mal 1996). In analyzing the 1995/96 volume, A'mal wrote:

> Literature that is aimed at children is of major importance to the development of their imagination and language. We still have a long way ahead of us, because most children's books are translated from other languages into Arabic. But INSANN has gone a step further by encouraging children to create and unleash their imaginations. **This is indeed the first Arabic language book of its kind in the country where the writers are the children themselves**, and the students' poetry, short stories and paintings are all presented in such an impressive way. This

is definitely the closest creativity to the child's world, and this world is more real because it expresses in depth the children's dreams and their worries and what they feel most directly and without the mediation of adult writers . . . because this literature is often translated literature, it is the literature of adults who write for children, and here we see a different kind of literature written by the children themselves, and drawn from the world of the children, and it is directed to both children and adults. For many years we have complained that no one cares about creativity and cultivating creative thinking in Arab education, and this was largely true, but today thanks to the efforts of INSANN, a real revolution is taking place, and this is not to glorify the head of INSANN and its leadership, but to point out a true fact which created a different reality in the Arab schools. (A'mal 1996)

It is worth noting that over time the school principals internalized the core tenets of the creativity project. This is reflected in statements they made upon many occasions, both in personal conversations and in media interviews. For example, in an article published in the *Fasl el-Makal* newspaper (May 30, 2003), Omar Darawshe, principal of the Omar Ben Al-Khattab School in Nazareth, noted:

We were lucky at school to have been chosen to participate in the creativity project developed by INSANN. The importance of the project stems from the fact that it is the only way that allows our students to express their potential and express their true talents. Through the project we discover that our students have many skills. We came to the conclusion that every student Can and every student Has a Point of Light and a Point of Strength that in traditional methods are difficult to discover, but they are reflected in the creativity project.

The well-known journalist Sai'd Hassanin published an article in the *Kul el-Arab* newspaper (May 30, 2003) about the Festival of Creativity organized by INSANN at the Al-Nahda Elementary School in the village of Yarka. He enthusiastically described the various parts of this festival, including workshops for creative writing, puppet theater, painting, mud art, music, drama, and more, which were attended by over 400 students from the school. Hassanin interviewed Anwar Ghbish, the school principal, who highlighted the importance of this creativity festival and its culminating creativity exhibition, "which provides an extraordinary opportunity to express the talents of the students, their points of strength, and their abilities in the various fields" (Hassanin 2003).

Shortcomings of the Creativity Project

Alongside the various successful aspects of the creativity project, there were also problematic parts that must be addressed. I became aware of these aspects during my observations of the creative writing workshops held at the schools, both those that were part of the curriculum and the extracurricular activities. I was particularly impressed by the depth of understanding of Salma, who was among the first instructors in the creativity project. Since then she has retired and completed a master's degree in creative writing. Below I offer several direct quotations from an in-depth interview I conducted with Salma that point to two central problems or difficulties that arose during implementation of the project's activities.

To begin, one of the problematic aspects of the creativity project resulted from the wide gap between the innovative methods used throughout the project and the traditional methods used in the regular school curriculum. This gap was especially difficult for students defined as "underachievers" or "weak" in the traditional subjects. According to Salma:

> Students who are weak in the traditional subjects and often feel neglected by teachers in the regular classes were suddenly exposed to a different world that they love, where they can express themselves without fear, speak and write about their feelings and their own experiences, hopes and fears, and are also appreciated by the instructor and by their classmates. Indeed, everything was fine and dandy until these students returned to their regular class, where everything was turned upside down. They again felt neglected and sometimes even humiliated by the teachers, and again felt they were worthless. But now this became more problematic, because after having experienced a different situation they were no longer prepared to accept the former bad treatment, and for many students this caused a crisis.

A second problem was cited by a small number of parents, especially those who worked as teachers. This problem was related to their expectations that teachers should comply with the traditional mission of teaching as defined by the system, not as defined by the creativity project. That is, they believed that teaching should be clearly assessed and evaluated using traditional testing methods, such as the Meitzav exams (see chapter 3). Salma stated in this regard:

> I will never forget a father, himself a teacher at another school, who complained to the school principal that "I was just wasting the students' time on activities that will not help them in the future." This father also came to me, and of course I talked to him, but it was not easy to convince him because he was locked in his conservative views. He also raised the following criticism of me: "Why don't you mark the students' mistakes with a red pen, as we usually do, so we can keep track of them?"

Salma further stated: "I felt that there should be more activities targeting the parents. Because the parents who participated in the creativity workshop together with their children had become very supportive of the project, and this had a very positive impact on both parents and their children, and was even encouraging to us as teachers. But this was limited because the parents who participated in the workshops were usually those whose children were good in regular classes" (interview, March 15, 2022).

Salma's critique is indeed very important and reflects what we observed in the field. The limited resources of INSAAN made it difficult to expand the project's activities further. Nevertheless, despite this limitation we tried to set up a model to handle the discrepancy between the innovative methods used in the creativity project and traditional teaching methods. To this end, we organized study days and workshops attended by all the teachers (not only instructors in the creativity project) in each participating school to expose them to the new method of creativity and creative writing. While these activities proved useful, they were limited to schools that could fund them through parents and the Association of Teachers.

The second problem referred to the standardization of education. This problem was much more difficult to handle because it is associated with the tremendous pressure imposed on the school system in the wake of the standardization of education through the neoliberal-neoconservative reforms mentioned in chapter 3. This pressure and the extensive formal discourse accompanying it have generated the common belief among many teachers that every activity introduced in the education system should be subject to statistical assessment and evaluation and that without such assessment it is considered ineffective (see chapters 3 and 5; for general discussion of the impact of neoliberal reforms on teachers, see Giroux 2010).

Nevertheless, the INSANN project has clearly offered different ways of thinking and practice that challenge the status quo, including the afore-mentioned neoliberal standardization ideology and the traditional methods still used in Arab schools. In the following sections I discuss these changes as reflected in the pedagogical philosophy of the creativity project.

Pedagogical Philosophy of the Project

I have discussed the pedagogical philosophy of the creativity project in var-ious articles and interviews published in the Arabic media, as well as at the many lectures I have given to Arab educators during study days and teacher training. My goal was to obtain responses and input from these educators and to raise their awareness of the need for a transition from traditional methods to the transformative and empowering method of creativity. This message was well-received by the Arab schools, as reflected in the interview with principal Omar Darawshe described above (*Fasl el-Makal*, May 30, 2003).

This educational philosophy, which was designed according to the needs of Arab schools, incorporated unique components that were culturally and socially sensitive alongside universal pedagogical features. Hence, the project was predesigned to achieve twin goals: developing students' creative and inno-vative skills while enhancing *holistic cultural competence* that simultaneously makes room for nourishing students' own identity and narrative and offers a universal orientation based on diversity and intercultural dialogue. (For a discussion of critical multicultural education, see Grossman 1995; Banks 2001b; Sleeter and Bernal 2004; see also theoretical framework, chapter 1.)

Because the project was designed to counterbalance the traditional school curriculum that does not recognize the identity and narratives of Arab students, it naturally needs to secure *authentic content* derived from Arab culture and values. Hence, unlike many projects imported from Hebrew schools, that are introduced into the Arab schools with the same content and even with same Hebrew name, an Arabic title was chosen for this project: Estibdal al-Ida'a bil-Ibdaa' (Replacing the Knowledge Depositing Method with Creativity). Moreover, from the outset we designed the educational model underlying the creativity project to place emphasis on providing students with alternative methods that would enable them to reflect upon how they viewed their individual and national identity, their experiences, and their authentic-indigenous culture. In this context, for the first time, students have been given a voice in that they were able to *produce knowledge* that touches the various circles, from the personal circle up to the national and the universal human circles.

Equally important, our *empowering education model* is designed to change the existing traditional conception, according to which empowering education merely represents a transition from teacher-guided to student-centered education (for a discussion of student-centered vs. teacher-guided education, see Salinas and Garr 2009; Frambach et al. 2014; Kim, Turner, and Mason 2015; Goldschmidt, Scharfenberg, and Bogner 2016; Brown 2021; Bremner 2021). Although I believe that teacher-guided education marginalizes students and needs to be changed, it should not be replaced by another extremist method such as the student-centered method, which ultimately marginalizes teachers. Indeed, no empowerment strategy can stand a chance without *encompassing transformative pedagogy* that sees the two central pillars in the educational process—students and teachers—as complementary partners rather than contradictory opponents. Therefore, empowering education should be based on a strategy in which students and educators are simultaneously empowered, that is, student-teacher centered strategy (see chapter 1). According to this new strategy, empowerment is a dynamic and reciprocal process in the sense that the party presumed to be empowered (the students) can be also a source of empowerment for the assumed empowering party (the teacher).

Hence, INSANN's project was oriented to *empowering—not replacing—* the local staff in the participating schools, ultimately securing the principle of continuity. As noted earlier in this chapter, empowerment should be treated as a process rather than as a one-time action. Thus, time is needed for empowerment to be internalized and it should not be imposed from above (see also Maeroff 1988; Abu Samah and Aref 2009). Unlike many projects based on instructors recruited outside the school system, this project was based solely on local school staff who received training, backing, and ongoing professional support from experts. After receiving the proper training, teachers and principals led the project on a daily basis and served as a source of support for students and parents alike. Based on my many conversations with school principals and teachers, I came to the conclusion that "importing" outside mentors and excluding local school teachers and principals would generate a great deal of alienation and animosity between these mentors and the local staff, thus minimizing the chances for collaboration and even creating conflicts between the outside mentors and the local staff. These outsiders would be perceived as a threat to the local staff, thus producing an anti-change atmosphere. Equally important, the local staff and administration are naturally the ones who remain at the school, and only they can guarantee continuity and ongoing change.

A central component of the project's educational philosophy entails *focusing on the strong side of students.* I contend that one of the central deficiencies of traditional "enrichment programs" is that they focus on students' weaknesses. Thus students who are weak in mathematics are given more classroom hours in mathematics with the aim of dealing with their difficulties. As our teacher focus group discussions show (see chapter 5), such methods often exacerbate these difficulties and strengthen the sense of helplessness and frustration among both students and their teachers.

We adopt a completely different strategy in the creative workshops, one that unleashes the imagination of students by letting them express themselves through any method they choose, be it writing, drawing, drama, or some other method. Once students discover their *points of strength*, or the *inside point of light*, they gain self-confidence and reinforce their belief that they can do it and are capable of overcoming their points of weakness. At the same time, they are given the chance to have fun and enjoy learning and interacting with their teacher and classmates.

No less important, the method behind the creativity project is based on *power sharing.* Shor (1992, 3–4) outlines a number of principles for empowering education as follows: people are involved in making decisions, they track their own performance, they have a sense of ownership of their work, and they are proud of their work and their organization. We carefully integrated these principles in our project. As mentioned earlier, all relevant decisions for every school were made through a local steering committee composed of school system stakeholders, including the principal and representatives of the students, teachers, parents, and the local council. Moreover, students played a major role in managing and making decisions about contents and activities. Thus, one of the basic components of the creativity project's educational philosophy has been providing participants with *ownership of their products and outcomes.*

Another basic element in our educational model is connected to the *encompassing nature of creativity.* That is, creativity is possible for all students, regardless of their school achievements as measured according to the traditional standards. In this sense, all students are given an equal chance to express their strong points and talents through creativity, a chance they were never provided through traditional methods and standardized education. Hence, the creativity workshops attracted both outstanding students and those who were considered "weak" based on conventional measures of school achievement. Indeed, the workshop content was adapted to each student, regardless of their "achievements" in the regular classes, under the project slogan *"Every Child Can."*

In this context, it is worth noting that during a systematic observation I conducted at the Manshiat Zabda Elementary School, the principal invited me to see a mixed creativity workshop attended by both special education and regular students. The instructor (who was trained through INSANN's creativity project) gave the students the freedom to plan their own activities as they wished. Some were busily engaged in creative writing, others expressed themselves through drama, and still others used the medium of drawing and painting. One of the most interesting conversations I had was with a special education student who was busily engaged in drawing. I asked the teacher whether the student's enthusiasm was typical or whether he was doing something exceptional. She did not answer, but rather smiled and asked me to follow her to the student who was immersed in his drawing. She asked him: "Tell me, Hussein, do you like the creativity workshop?" He immediately answered: "Yes, very much." The teacher asked: "Why is that?" Hussein enthusiastically replied: *"In the regular classes we do what the teacher wants, in the creativity workshop we do what we want."*

Obstacles and Lessons To Be Learned from INSAAN's Experience

This chapter has traced the experience of INSANN over nearly three decades by discussing a number of nationwide projects in the areas of community empowerment, school development, and social change. Due to space limitations, I focused only on two major projects: the Mobile Community Center, which was operated in non-recognized and remote Arab villages in the northern, central, and southern regions of the country, and the creativity project, which was implemented in dozens of Arab schools across the country. These pioneering projects represent an outstanding attempt to enhance alternative empowering education and social change among the Palestinian Arabs in Israel through a civil society organization. Despite harsh conditions, financial constraints, and many other barriers related to state policy and local hamula-related conservation factors, these initiatives sought to give hope and contest the status quo among the most disadvantaged sectors of the Palestinian community, while providing an alternative model for Arab schools that is based on *transformative and critical empowering education.*

Nevertheless, INSANN faced a number of impediments and limitations. In the next sections, I briefly outline the main problems and difficulties faced by INSANN and the major lessons to be learned from this experience.

One of the major obstacles we faced stemmed from the Palestinian Arab community's limited experience with nationwide civil society organizations. As mentioned earlier, the Palestinians in Israel lagged almost two decades behind the Jewish population in terms of development of civil society organizations. Moreover, political and religious organizations emerged in Arab society long before general educational organizations. Indeed, independent, nationwide, nonpartisan, and nonreligious civil society organizations only began to emerge in the Palestinian Arab community in the late 1990s. Upon its establishment in 1991, INSANN was the first comprehensive and nationwide Palestinian Arab educational NGO in Israel. While this fact has been quite inspiring, it also proved to be a serious disadvantage since we had no role model to follow and no experience on which we could build and use to draw conclusions.

The second obstacle, which to a great extent is related to the first, was the *sense of powerlessness* among the Arab schools, and specifically among teachers. This sense of powerlessness was the result of a long-lasting official policy of control over the Arab population, and especially over the education system, as discussed throughout this book. Hence, it took us a while to convince Arab teachers and school principals that an Arab NGO is capable of making a difference. At first, many teachers had trouble accepting our message that they can become educational leaders and initiators in the school. Overall, the teachers' attitudes reflected their deeply entrenched sense of helplessness. Never before had they felt they were real partners, leading to their strong belief that they were outsiders and that any likely change in the school system would come from the *top down* rather than from the *bottom up*.

A significant barrier to INSANN's activities was related to the tribal hamula-based structure of the Arab community. INSANN's experience demonstrates that the rural structure of the Palestinian community that is dominated by local kinship groups and other local solidarities constitutes a serious barrier to the formation and functioning of civil society organizations. Indeed, in many cases support from local authorities for schools within their jurisdictions or the appointment of project instructors involved local political considerations. In some cases, local political conflicts penetrated the school system and restricted our efforts to form a network for cooperation between schools and parents' committees.

The obstacles placed by state authorities were no less difficult. At first, INSANN's activities in many Arab schools were met with a great deal of suspicion and lack of cooperation on the part of some school superintendents, who demanded formal permission to allow us to work in these schools. If we were unable to obtain this official permission, we had to search for creative ways to enter the schools. We also utilized practical lessons from our study on the status and conditions of Arab teachers (chapter 5) to pave our way into the school system. As mentioned earlier, one of the central conclusions of that study was that principals' authority in the school system is on the rise. In fact, in the eyes of the teachers, the principals have much more power than the superintendents. Hence, after the first year of activity, all our contacts began with principals. This proved very effective once the principals realized that cooperating with our projects would be fruitful and advantageous for them and their school and would improve their image among the parents and the community at large. We also built a strategic coalition with a number of parties who saw cooperation with us as a win-win situation. Central among these were the National Association of Teachers in Israel, local and national Associations of Arab Parents, academic institutions (mainly the University of Haifa), and the Follow-Up Committee on Arab Education in Israel. This coalition enabled us to expand our activities in Arab schools and obtain wide cooperation from both principals and teachers.

Our activities in the non-recognized villages faced many other obstacles connected to the lack of schools and the problematic infrastructure and conditions in most of these villages. Yet the most difficult barriers were placed by formal Israeli authorities. At first, state authorities, especially those involved in the national Judaization of the Galilee project, made every effort to block these activities. For example, in one of the villages that had no school or appropriate building for running the Mobile Community Center activities and workshops, we built a large tent for this purpose. When the Green Patrol saw this tent, they issued us a warning and eventually demolished the tent. Note that the Green Patrol was established in 1976 with the declared goal of preserving state lands as part of the government's Judaization project (see chapter 2). We eventually rented a large mobile van for these activities. In some villages, such as in Kammaneh (which served as our case study in this chapter), we ran our activities in a large room donated by the parents of E'id Sawaed, chair of the local village committee.

One of the main pillars of our empowerment strategy was working with and through the local leadership. Hence, in most of the non-recognized villages, the local leaders became our natural partners. Indeed, they gained a sense of ownership over the project that was extremely helpful in ensuring its success. In addition, as mentioned earlier, as part of INSANN's community empowerment model for the non-recognized villages we organized public events and mass cultural festivals. Arab leaders from across the political spectrum participated in these events, including Knesset members, the head of the Supreme Follow-Up Committee of the Arab Population in Israel, mayors, academics, and cultural icons from across the country. As indicated in the Kammaneh case study, these activities played a major role in connecting the local residents with the outside world, lifting their morale, enhancing their persistence, and eventually accelerating official recognition of these villages. At the same time, these activities laid the groundwork for establishing permanent educational and cultural institutions and eventually reinforced trust between INSANN and the local residents.

Notwithstanding the above-mentioned successful strategy, funding and financial constraints constituted a major obstacle for INSANN. Like civil society organizations in general, and Palestinian Arab organizations in Israel in particular, INSANN was completely dependent on fundraising and external resources. The funding resources of Arab NGOs are limited and largely dependent on private foundations from the US and Canada and on European resources, mainly from EU and German political foundations. Some of these foundations have their own agendas, which do not always go hand in hand with the orientation and goals of authentic Palestinian civil society organizations. Moreover, some of the donors have created an exclusive circle of NGOs that they have supported continuously for many years, thus closing their doors and in essence blocking the possibility of developing or expanding new initiatives.

Conclusion

This monograph has provided a detailed analysis of the education system among indigenous Palestinian Arabs in Israel over seven decades, from the establishment of Israel until the present period, with a short background on the pre-state period. It traced the main developments in Arab education at the different levels, from early childhood through elementary and high school and up to higher education. It offered an in-depth analysis of the changes in educational structure, formal educational policies, and educational goals, as well as the main trends in educational attainment, school curriculum, teachers' status, and socioeconomic returns from education. It concluded with a discussion of self-empowerment strategies among Palestinian Arabs by drawing on the case study of INSANN, the first nationwide Arab NGO in the field of education and culture.

Based on a broad variety of quantitative and qualitative methods, the monograph addressed a number of widely debated theoretical questions pertaining to the role of education among minorities and disadvantaged groups in deeply divided societies. More specifically, it discussed this topic in the context of social change, ethnic inequalities, critical multiculturalism, cultural hegemony, and strategies for self-empowerment by exploring the following questions:

Is education a catalyst for social change and minority empowerment? Or is it rather a mechanism of social control and cultural hegemony manipulated by the dominant group? Is education a *great equalizer* that overcomes ethnic stratification and contributes to socioeconomic mobility among minorities and disadvantaged groups? Or is it rather a *major stabilizer* in that it constitutes a mechanism for reproducing the social and economic inequalities used by the majority group to maintain its socioeconomic dominance? How do ongoing conflicts affect educational content and school curricula? Is the majority's use of the school curriculum as an instrument for promoting patriotism and national ethos compatible with the development of inclusive multicultural democracy and peace education? Or rather does this use perpetuate cultural hegemony and exacerbate oppositional identity and alienation among minority groups? What strategies for positive change can minorities adopt in order to transition from powerlessness to self-empowerment? More specifically, how can civil society organizations be utilized as counter-hegemonic forces?

The monograph considered these questions through a comparative perspective that systematically juxtaposed the Arab and Hebrew education systems. It delineated the contradictory educational expectations of Israel's state authorities and those of indigenous Palestinian Arabs. It analyzed educational developments in conjunction with economic, demographic, and sociopolitical changes in broader Arab society that are characterized by economic dependency accompanied by social and political localization (see chapter 2). Contextual regional developments and trends in the Israeli-Palestinian conflict were also considered. The terms Palestinian Arabs in Israel, Palestinian Arabs, the Palestinian/Arab minority, Arabs, and Arab population were used interchangeably throughout the monograph.

From the outset, the education system in Israel in general and education for Arabs in particular were designed as central components of the state's nationalization project. This project is defined exclusively in terms of ethnonational-Jewish-Zionist characteristics that serve to actualize the affiliation between the state and the Jewish core nation. This affiliation finds expression through a militaristic culture and emergency procedures deriving from the notion that the state faces ongoing existential threats. It consequently excludes Arabs, who are considered not only a barrier to this project but also a security risk and a cultural and demographic threat to its realization (see chapter 2).

The consequence of the aforementioned factors is that official policy toward Arab education has been based on three main pillars: controlled segregation, securitization, and homogenization. First, in the absence of a democratic secular orientation to Israeli citizenship and based on the fact that Israeli identity was strongly interwoven with Jewish-Zionist symbols, Arabs have been excluded from any type of multicultural citizenship. Under the auspices of the ethnonational definition of the state, the Arabs have been treated as a linguistic-religious-cultural minority rather than as a national minority or as an indigenous people deserving of differentiated group rights. Furthermore, official state rejection of any Arab claim for recognition as a "unique minority" has been coupled with treatment of the Arabs as a "mixture of tiny minorities" (see Smooha 1980) based on religion (Muslims, Christians, and Druze) or on geo-cultural characteristics (Bedouins). Hence, the prevailing policy regarding Arab education has been one of *controlled segregation*, such that the Arab schools are both separate from the Jewish education system and totally controlled by the state. Consequently, the Ministry of Education's Division for Arab Education was treated as a separate, though not unique, unit in which Arabic was the medium of instruction. Nevertheless, this unit was given no educational autonomy or collective rights of any sort that would give Arabs a say over their own educational administration, curriculum, and content.

Second, the policy toward education for Arabs has been placed under the rubric of *securitization* rather than *democratization*, with security considerations as the cornerstone of the formal policy determining educational structure, administration, and goals (see Ben-Or 1951, 8). Accordingly, education for Arabs was designed in advance to achieve the twin goals of educating the younger generations of Arabs to be loyal to the State of Israel and preventing them from developing any sense of national identity that might pose a danger to Israel's security or challenge its cultural hegemony.

Third, education has been assigned the role of ideological homogenization as an integral part of building the Israeli nation-state. As such, it has been used as a central element in shaping the majority's exclusive Jewish-Zionist narrative and national ethos and in fostering its cultural dominance over the Palestinian minority. Concurrently, Arab education has been denationalized in order to obliterate the Palestinian narrative and perpetuate a form of coexistence in which the minority rationalizes its inferior status and accepts the ethnonational definition of the state provided by the majority.

To facilitate implementation of the aforementioned policy, Israeli authorities totally dismantled the structure, content, and administration of the pre-state Palestinian education system. Under the auspices of this policy, the state put an end to the developing seeds of educational autonomy in the Christian and Muslim communities, merging both these systems into a centralized Israeli public educational system and thus abolishing any kind of autonomous educational administration or content. Under pressure from Western countries, Israeli authorities subsequently recognized the Christian schools while retaining total control of their educational curriculum and content. Muslims, in contrast, were not allowed to keep their autonomous educational and religious institutions (Layish 1966; Al-Haj 2006). Unlike the case of Arab education, the state officially recognized the autonomous educational systems of various Jewish ideological streams, including the national religious and ultra-Orthodox streams, even at the expense of the state's original secular character (Lehmann 2012).

In the absence of multicultural democracy in Israel, negotiations between the Arabs and the state regarding educational and cultural rights have been extremely cumbersome and complicated, especially on issues related to curriculum, content, narratives, educational autonomy, and self-administration. State authorities have often deflected these negotiations toward issues of educational access, funding, construction, and material resources, while completely overlooking other claims concerning collective rights (see also Al-Haj 1995a, 2006). Therefore, not only has educational expansion among the Palestinian Arabs in Israel been severed from their authentic knowledge, culture, and experience, but it has been also accompanied by intensive state efforts to suppress their Palestinian narrative, collective memory, and identity.

Research shows that many indigenous and national minorities have made a good deal of progress in achieving institutional autonomy and group-differentiated rights on issues such as autonomy, land, language, culture, and education (see, for example, Burger 2019; Aikman and King 2012; Lightfoot 2010; Kymlicka 2007b, 2018). In contrast, my analysis shows that the struggle of the Palestinian Arabs in Israel has yielded very little in terms of self-determination and collective rights. Furthermore, unlike other Western democracies that have exhibited a tendency toward accepting the legitimacy of minority nationalism (see Kymlicka 2007b, 2018), Israeli authorities have classified Arab nationalism under the securitization rubric. Thus, they have responded by applying oppressive means and expanding the nationalization of the state, further strengthening its ethnonational Jewish-Zionist character and marginalizing the Palestinian Arabs (see Ghanem and Khatib 2017). In fact, recognition of Arabic as an official language—the only collective right granted to the Arabs in Israel—was abolished by the 2018 Nationality Law that declared Hebrew to be Israel's only official language (see Al-Haj 2019).

The above analysis provides important background for understanding the wide gap between *quantitative* and *qualitative* changes in Arab education. The quantitative changes are manifested in access to education, educational expansion, and a rise in the level of teachers' formal education. The qualitative changes find expression in school achievements and outcomes, school curriculum and content, criteria for admission to academic institutions (especially to universities and prestigious tracks of study), and socioeconomic returns for higher education.

Our examination of the formal education system among Arabs since the establishment of the State of Israel from elementary through the end of secondary school (see chapter 3) revealed impressive quantitative changes and educational expansion, with the exception of early childhood education. These changes are reflected in the convergence between Arabs and Jews in terms of school attendance at the primary, intermediate, and secondary levels. The expansion of education for women has been a very essential part of this change.

Yet whereas the quantitative discrepancies between Arabs and Jews have narrowed in terms of educational access, the qualitative differences in educational outcomes and school achievements have persisted, and in some cases even widened. This gap is reflected by every qualitative educational measure in Israel, including the Meitzav achievement test scores in the primary and middle schools and every criterion connected with the matriculation exams in the secondary schools. It is also reflected by scores on international tests: PISA tests of reading literacy for 15-year-olds and TIMSS mathematics and science assessments in fourth through eighth grades. On all these tests, the achievements of Jewish students are significantly higher than those of Arab students. That is to say, in terms of quantitative measures the Arab schools are approaching the standard in the Jewish schools and those in most developed industrialized countries. Yet in terms of qualitative measures the Arab schools are still positioned at the bottom of third world countries. Indeed, a gap of nearly 20 years separates the quantitative and qualitative educational developments among Arabs. In other words, the Jewish schools are twenty years ahead of the Arab schools on qualitative measures.

The above discrepancy between the quantity and quality of educational achievements among the Arabs also applies to higher education. Our findings show that higher education among the Arab population has expanded considerably over time, as reflected in a rise in the absolute number of Arab students as well as in their relative percentage at academic institutions in Israel. In addition, the number of Arab women in higher education has risen significantly so that by 2017/18 women constituted the majority of Arab students at both the undergraduate and the graduate levels.

At the same time, my analysis shows that higher education in Israel replicates the nationwide stratification system and reflects the cultural hegemony of broader society. In this context, the culturally biased Psychometric Entrance Test (PET) serves as a gatekeeper that considerably reduces Arab students' access to higher education institutions in Israel, especially to universities and prestigious areas of study. In fact, the PET reflects a colonial practice that exists elsewhere in which the achievements of indigenous students are often evaluated by non-indigenous standards and Western culturally biased contents that ultimately discriminate against indigenous students and offer a flawed picture of their skills and capabilities (see Aitken and Radford 2018). Al-Haj's Committee, which was empowered by the Council for Higher Education to deal with various aspects of higher education among Arabs, clearly pointed out this fact. As noted in chapter 6, Al-Haj's Committee declared that the PET discriminates against Arab students and constitutes a "main gatekeeper that hampers their access to higher education" because it was constructed and designed "mainly for students with a Western cultural background" (CHE and PBC 2001, 7).

Moreover, both the written and the hidden curricula at Israeli higher education institutions, as reflected in the atmosphere on campus, are controlled by the Jewish-dominant group and serve as a mechanism for perpetuating its cultural hegemony. Similar to colonial settings elsewhere (see Adam 2019), this Hebrew/Western cultural hegemony with its total absence of Arab culture constitutes a typical form of *epistemological colonization* (see Quijano 2007; Mbembe 2016). Indeed, it signals to Arab students that their culture is inferior to the superior culture of the Jewish majority, in which Western culture constitutes a central component (see also Halabi 2016; Mahajne and Bar-on 2022). A student in a previous study published elsewhere aptly stated: "During my first year at the university I was totally confused: I had to read in English, think in Arabic and speak in Hebrew. Over time this confusion diminished a bit since I continued to read in English but began to think and also speak in Hebrew" (Al-Haj 2003, 361). The above confession perfectly reflects the notion of *coloniality of the mind*, that is, a situation in which indigenous students and those who belong to dominated groups are cut off from their own culture and become completely submerged within the dominant culture. As described by Quijano (2007), this hegemonic relationship consists "in the first place, of a colonization of the imagination of the dominated; that is, it acts in the interior of that imagination, in a sense, it is a part of it" (169).

In light of the colonial-oriented reality described above, no policy for enhancing diversity and cultural competence has been developed in Israeli academia—either for Palestinian students or for the benefit of the system as a whole. Unlike in other countries that have recognized the collective rights and unique cultural needs of indigenous students (e.g., Sonn, Bishop, and Humphries 2000; Dietz 2019; Coates, Trudgett, and Page 2020), Israeli academic institutions have never treated Palestinian Arab students as an indigenous or unique group that deserves recognition within a context of multiculturalism or diversity. Hence, no effort has been made to decolonize and indigenize the curriculum and atmosphere at these institutions in order to create an inclusive space that respects Arab students and embraces their culture and identity.

The above discussion raises the following question: Where should Israel be positioned along Goastellec's *fairness in access* chronology of higher education? According to my analysis, Israel's higher education policy is based on three main characteristics typical of Goastellec's second period (1990s): First, the requirements for admission to higher education in Israel are socially biased, culturally dependent, and positively correlated with national and socioeconomic inequalities. Second, similar to the situation in the United States during the 1990s, Israel has implemented the principle of *separate but equal* through geographic decentralization and diversification of higher education (for the US, see Goastellec 2008, 74; for Israel, see Swirski and Swirski 1997; Ayalon and Yogev 2006; Caplan et al. 2009). That is, formal equality is achieved through a policy based solely on quantitative expansion of higher education among peripheral groups. Under this policy, most students from disadvantaged backgrounds, including Arabs, are directed to second-tier and usually less selective public colleges. Third, the strategy for minimizing unfairness and promoting equal access to higher education in Israel is still based on affirmative action and on quotas for specific disadvantaged groups. In other words, Israel lags more than two decades behind the international trend toward enhancing fair access to higher education that began toward the end of the 1990s.

My analysis of employment opportunities among Arab university graduates reiterates the findings of earlier studies pointing to Arabs' limited chances of translating higher education into suitable lucrative jobs. In this context, the Arab labor force has been absorbed only at the margins of the labor market, with most of the jobs going to the Jewish majority. Positions that are more prestigious and rewarding are for the most part closed to Arabs due to so-called security issues. Indeed, many jobs are dependent upon past military service. Moreover, most Arabs reside in peripheral areas and start from a much weaker point when competing with Jews for prestigious and rewarding positions. In fact, my analysis demonstrates *significant occupational segregation* between Arabs and Jews such that Arabs are excluded from high-ranked positions and mainly concentrated in low-status occupations. In this regard, as Arabs become more educated their chances for integration into the wider Jewish labor market decrease (see Al-Haj 2003; Semyonov and Lewin-Epstein 2011; Yonay and Kraus 2018; Yaish and Gabay-Egozi 2021).

My findings also shed light on the theoretical debate regarding the relationship between the expansion of higher education and socioeconomic mobility among disadvantaged groups and minorities. Despite widespread educational expansion among Arabs, my analysis shows that cumulative and persistent inequalities between Arabs and Jews still remain. These inequalities, which apply to both Arab men and women, find expression in the uneven odds of being accepted to prestigious areas of study and the unequal possibilities for translating academic success into socioeconomic mobility. That is to say, despite higher education's great potential to serve as a channel for upward mobility, the broad quantitative expansion of education has failed to alter the marginal status of the Arab population in Israel or to bridge the wide socioeconomic gap and other inequalities between Jews and Arabs. This leads me to conclude that when multicultural democracy is lacking and a policy of control prevails, education becomes a *great stabilizer* rather than a *great equalizer*.

The above conclusion negates arguments based upon neoliberal ideology, which sees formal education as a *genuine meritocratic system* and contends that higher education is a key engine for upward mobility, independent of social background (see review by Bodovski, Chykina, and Khavenson 2019, 393–94; Hout 1988, 2012). In contrast, taking into consideration the persistent inequalities in higher educational attainment and quality over time, my analysis shows that for the Arabs in Israel education serves as a mechanism of social reproduction. This disadvantaged reproduction is also reflected in the ways in which one generation's economic capital is transferred to the next (for socioeconomic reproduction, see Lucas 2001, 2009; Apple 2006; Semyonov and Lewin-Epstein 2011; Gabay-Egozi and Yaish 2021).

Cultural hegemony over Arab education is also evident in the school curriculum. My examination of the history curriculum in Arab and Jewish schools over a period of 70 years (1950–2020) reveals that despite some changes over time, no considerable steps have been taken toward education for multiculturalism in Israel. In particular, no alternative narrative has been introduced, either to Jewish or to Arab students. Jewish students are still taught a predominantly Jewish-Zionist ethnonational and particularistic narrative, while Arab students continue to be deprived of any independent Palestinian narrative (see also Shemesh 2009; Kizel 2008; Abu-Sa'ad 2007; Hourani 2010; Al-Haj 2021).

These findings lead to the conclusion that the school system in Israel and the history curriculum in particular reflect the existing gap between the social structure and the political culture of Israeli society. As noted in chapter 4, although Israeli society comprises a multiplicity of cultures, Israel's official political culture has remained strictly ethnonational, with no formal recognition of the nation's social and cultural diversity. In addition, the content of the history curricula in the Arab and Hebrew schools reflects the asymmetric Jewish-Arab relations and the peripheral political and cultural status of the Palestinian Arabs. In this context, the *controlled segregation strategy* that has been systematically implemented in Arab education throughout the different periods has yielded a dual system of *hegemonic curriculum segregation*. This curriculum segregation has enabled the dominant group to build a separate, though subordinate, curriculum for the minority aimed at preserving the cultural and political dominance of the majority and securing the minority's loyalty to the state, while continuing to practice a form of controlled multiculturalism under the misnomer of multicultural education. Such a structure does not fit any definition of education for multiculturalism. Indeed, this form of multiculturalism is totally controlled by the state and is imposed upon the minority, which is excluded from the decision-making apparatus. Moreover, it is oriented toward perpetuating a form of coexistence in which the minority rationalizes its inferior status and accepts the majority's definition of the character and exclusive identity of the state.

Furthermore, the history curriculum reflects a systematic policy of *ideological assimilation* imposed on Arab schools. Indeed, from the outset and for various reasons, state authorities abandoned the option of *linguistic assimilation* of Arabs (see chapter 3). In contrast, intensive efforts were devoted toward *ideological assimilation*, especially in subject areas related to shaping students' identity and attitudes. This has led to official homogenization of the history curriculum, which is based on *one narrative, one national ethos, and one historical truth*—that of the Jewish-Zionist collective.

This situation is especially problematic for Palestinian Arab students, who perceive a wide discrepancy between the formal history taught in schools and the informal history and narrative they absorb through their own experiences and other informal socialization agents. Hence, the hegemonic culture that Arab students are taught at school, which is devoted to imbuing them with a sense of self-denial and national inferiority, totally contradicts their perceptions of their own status and expectations as an indigenous group and *a minority with a sense of majority* (see chapter 2).

Focusing on indigenous groups in Canada, Mullen (2020) asserts that the omission of indigenous content from the curriculum is part of a neocolonial policy. She emphasizes that for the good of society as a whole, a number of changes should be implemented in order to decolonize the Canadian education system. These include a holistic plan for restructuring education and replacing the homogenized colonial structures and

Eurocentric curriculum by a new indigenized system that fits the needs, culture, aspirations, and identity of indigenous students (672). Aronowitz and Giroux (1993) also contend that depriving minority students of their historical narrative through the official curriculum creates continuing tension between the hegemonic discourses comprising the official curriculum and the discourses of subordinate groups as "they might appear in 'forgotten' or 'erased' histories" (128).

Indeed, my analysis shows that the education system in Israel is not—and in its current form cannot be—a resource for peace and reconciliation between Jews and Palestinian Arabs. On the contrary, the way history is conveyed to Jewish students perpetuates the conflict and reinforces their sense of "us—Jews" against "them—Palestinian Arabs." On the other hand, the history taught to Arab students, which denies their collective Palestinian narrative, reinforces their sense of alienation from school and from the State of Israel. Moreover, this curriculum precludes any possibility of developing an all-inclusive form of citizenship to be shared by Arabs and Jews (see Al-Haj 2021).

The state has also exercised control over Arab education by controlling teachers. The Ministry of Education has effectively used the matter of security clearance in hiring and firing teachers and as a means of selecting specific types of teachers who comply with the official policy and discouraging those who show resistance to this policy. From the outset, this reality instilled a *culture of silence* among Arab teachers. It still constitutes a central factor that prevents Arab teachers from assuming the role of educational leaders and ultimately enhances their sense of helplessness and burnout. This culture of silence is also maintained through a hidden curriculum that finds expression in blocking actual issues from being discussed at school and in promoting a nondemocratic school climate that marginalizes the role and status of these teachers. The unprofessional considerations that permeate the school system through local hamula politics only exacerbate this culture of silence and increase the distress, burnout rates, and marginal status of Arab teachers (see chapter 5).

It should be noted that Arab education is subject to a dual system of control: that of the state and that of the Arab local authority, which is motivated by hamula-based politics. Each system has its own interests and expectations, which are not always identical. Yet both share the same goal of using education as a mechanism of control and domination (Al-Haj 1995c). This dual system of control, or *dual system of oppression* (as framed by Freire 1998b), further limits the role of education as a catalyst of social change. Nevertheless, state control remains much more powerful and comprehensive, ultimately determining the structure, administration, content, and outcomes of education.

In the absence of any sort of cultural-educational autonomy and considering the wide gap between school and society, matters related to collective cultural and national identity among Palestinian Arabs have been relegated to informal local sources of knowledge, such as the family, political parties, religious movements, parents' committees, civil society organizations, social networks, and others.

This conclusion concerning the development of alternative unofficial knowledge prompted an in-depth discussion of the role of civil society organizations in promoting self-empowerment and reconstruction of indigenous culture and identity. The following section outlines some important insights and lessons emerging from my analysis of INSANN, the first nationwide Palestinian civil society organization in Israel in the field of education and culture, which was established in 1991.

Notwithstanding the many obstacles and limitations, the INSANN venture serves as a concrete example of Gramscian theory, according to which civil society organizations are counter-hegemonic forces that continuously challenge the hegemonic political society and state control over education (see chapter 7; see also review of Gramscian theory, Ransome 1992, 132). Moreover, INSANN realizes the International Human Rights-Based Approach to Education, which includes two basic principles: participation and inclusion together with empowerment (UNICEF and UNESCO 2007, chap. 1, 10–11). INSANN's experience also highlights the significance of civil society organizations in creating alternative models of empowering, decolonizing, and indigenizing education. These models provide indigenous students the tools to shift from being passive listeners and knowledge consumers to assuming their natural role as active partners and knowledge producers, a role in which their experience and their individual and collective identities and authentic culture are given a voice (for more on transformative education, see Freire 1973, 1998a; also see chapter 1). Indeed, as shown in the analysis (chapter 7), INSANN's activities brought a new spirit of pride and hope to Arab schools across the country and among the Palestinian Arabs living in non-recognized villages, remote communities, and other Arab towns and villages.

Needless to say, civil society organizations in general, and those among indigenous and disadvantaged groups in particular, are limited in terms of power and resources and hence in their ability to bring about a comprehensive change in society at large (see Gellman and Bellino 2019, 19). Yet the significance of the role of NGOs lies in their ability to inspire the community, to create a discourse that challenges the status quo, and to set up successful models for empowerment that contain the seeds for social change (see Gellman and Bellino 2019; Gramsci 1971, 35–36).

One of the main questions addressed throughout this monograph concerns the relationship between education and social change. More specifically, whether education is a catalyst for empowerment and social change among minority groups or whether it is a mechanism of control used by the majority. I discussed this point in my previous work in the 1990s, where I came to the conclusion that empowerment and control through education are two sides of the same coin. Whereas minorities and disadvantaged groups perceive education as an important asset for empowerment and social change, dominant groups manipulate education as a mechanism for control and cultural hegemony and systematically use it as a reproduction system to maintain the status quo and perpetuate their socioeconomic dominance (see Al-Haj 1995a, 1996).

The current study reiterates the aforementioned conclusion, as demonstrated throughout these chapters and as briefly discussed in these concluding remarks. The *empowerment/control formula* is still prevalent, and most likely will continue to remain at the center of Arab-Jewish relationships, reflecting the contradictory educational expectations of the state and those of the Palestinian Arabs. In fact, this is a universal formula that characterizes the relationships between dominant and subordinated groups as far as education is concerned. Nevertheless, my longitudinal research, which provided an important opportunity to examine trends with the added perspective afforded by the passage of time, leads to the conclusion that the policy of control and the state's hegemony over Arab education have *become deeper and more salient over time,* despite some minor changes introduced to create a sense of acquiescence among the Palestinian community and alleviate their responses to the state's hegemony. Hence, the state's increasing policy of control strongly challenges the counter-hegemonic forces that have in the meantime developed in the Palestinian community. In what follows, I briefly address the factors behind this conclusion.

As mentioned, since the early 1980s, the education systems in various countries, including Israel, have been subject to neoliberal reforms. Despite being marked by decentralization and privatization policies, these reforms in fact have been accompanied by neoconservative values and a tightening of state control over educational goals and content, with the aim of intensifying ideological homogenization (in the global context, see Apple 2006b; Giroux 2010; Perryman et al. 2011; in the Israeli context, see Yonah, Dahan, and Markovich 2008; Agbaria 2018).

Indeed, the changes brought by these reforms have further weakened Arab education and widened the gap between schools and society (see chapter 5). No less significant, together with the imposed standardization and comprehensive system of national and international assessment of scholastic achievements, these reforms have assigned a negative label to Arab education and intensified the prevailing sense of helplessness in the school system (for the impact of these standardized tests on the Israeli education system, see Feniger, Israeli, and Yehuda 2016; Feniger 2020). Furthermore, media representation of the scores on these tests (see chapter 3) has reinforced stereotyped perceptions of Arab schools and society and distorted the discourse regarding social inequality. Stakeholders have also used these test scores to shift responsibility from the state to teachers, parents, and the Arab community at large (see chapter 3). In accordance with Gramscian theory (Gramsci 1971, 325–26), these tests have created a new common sense among large segments of Arab teachers, principals, and parents regarding their view of educational problems, outcomes, and solutions.

Indeed, neoliberal-neoconservative reforms and the standardization of education have ultimately diverted public interest toward numbers and statistics and overshadowed the genuine discourse regarding state domination and social inequalities. Equally important, Arab parents and the Arab community at large have placed tremendous pressure on Arab schools, and in particular on Arab teachers. Moreover, the reported high rate of failure among Arab students has had a negative impact on the self-efficacy perceptions of Arab teachers, resulting in rising burnout rates. In brief, these reforms have been extremely destructive to teachers' status and conduct and have further widened the gap between Arab schools and society (see chapter 5; for a discussion of the major reforms in Israeli schools, see also Tamir and Shaked 2016; Arar, Tamir, and Abu-Hussain 2019).

In the past two decades, and especially since 2009, the above neoliberal reforms have been coupled with political radicalization among the Jewish population, demonstrated in particular by the rising power of religious Zionist and ultra-Orthodox parties. This combination has paved the way for nongovernmental stakeholders and organizations affiliated with the Jewish extreme right to penetrate the education system and exert a massive influence on the state's education policy. Consequently, there has been a growing trend toward imposing more Jewish-Zionist content on Arab schools. At the same time, any demand for educational autonomy on the part of the Arab population has been rejected, and content with the potential to foster a collective national identity among Arab students has been suppressed. This trend is likely to grow in the wake of the recent elections (November 1, 2022), which led to the formation of the most extremist government in Israel's history (see chapter 2).

Notwithstanding the deepening hegemonic policy toward Arab education, various changes in the Palestinian Arab population since the 1990s have continuously challenged the state's policy of control and have produced and further reinforced counter-hegemonic forces among the Palestinian Arab community. These changes include the growth of human capital throughout all segments of the Arab population, the increasing availability and dissemination of informal knowledge through social technologies and informal learning contexts, intensive politicization and nationalization processes, the rising activity of civil society organizations, and the intensification of the Arabs' campaign on behalf of their citizenship and group-differentiated rights, including their educational and cultural rights as indigenous peoples (see chapters 2 and 7). We are also witnessing the development of a new coping strategy among Arab teachers, through initiatives to counterbalance the formal policy of preventing actual issues connected to national identity and citizenship rights from being discussed in Arab schools (see chapter 5). Although still in its infancy, and even though most Arab teachers still manifest a *culture of silence*, this new coping strategy represents the seeds of the creation of counter-hegemonic forces within the school system, in coordination with parents and civil society organizations. Nevertheless, the following questions remain open: Can counter-hegemonic forces outside and inside the school system unite to bridge the gap between school and society? Or rather will this gap become unbridgeable in light of the tightening policy of control and the state's hegemony over Arab education, thus creating the perception among indigenous Palestinians that formal education in its current form is a barrier rather than an asset for empowerment and social change.

References

Abu Ghazaleh, Adnan. 1972. "Arab Cultural Nationalism in Palestine During the British Mandate." *Journal of Palestine Studies* 1, no. 3 (Spring): 37–63. https://doi.org/10.2307/2535866.

Abu-Kaf, Sarah, and Enas Khalaf. 2020. "Acculturative Stress among Arab Students in Israel: The Roles of Sense of Coherence and Coping Strategies." *International Journal of Environmental Research and Public Health* 17:1–19.

Abu-Kishk, Bakir. 1981. "Arab Land and Israeli Policy." *Journal of Palestine Studies* 7 (3): 31–54.

Abu-Sa'ad, Ismael. 2004. "Separate and Unequal: The Consequences of Racism and Discrimination Against Palestinian Arabs in the Educational System in Israel." *Social Identities* 10 (2): 101–27. https://doi.org/10.1080/135046304 2000191010.

———. 2007. "The Portrayal of Arabs in Textbooks in the Jewish School System in Israel." *Arab Studies Quarterly* 29 (1): 21–38.

———. 2008. "Present Absentees: The Arab School Curriculum in Israel as a Tool for De-Educating Indigenous Palestinians." *Holy Land Studies* 7 (1): 17–43.

———. 2016. "Access to Higher Education and its Socio-Economic Impact among Bedouin Arabs in Southern Israel." *International Journal of Educational Research* 76:96–103.

———. 2019. "Palestinian Education in the Israeli Settler State: Divide, Rule and Control." *Settler Colonial Studies* 9 (1): 96–116. https://doi.org/10.1080/22 01473X.2018.1487125.

Abu Samah, Asnarulkhadi, and Fariborz Aref. 2009. "Empowerment as an Approach for Community Development in Malaysia." *World Rural Observations* 1 (2): 63–68.

Acuña, Felipe. 2023. "Governing Teachers' Subjectivity in Neoliberal Times: The Fabrication of the Bonsai Teacher." *Journal of Education Policy*, 1–20. https://doi.org/10.1080/02680939.2023.2196954.

Adalah. 2007. "The Democratic Constitution." Adalah: The Legal Center for Arab Minority Rights in Israel. Haifa. https://www.adalah.org/uploads/oldfiles/Public/files/democratic_constitution-english.pdf.

Adam, Taskeen. 2019. "Digital Neocolonialism and Massive Open Online Courses (MOOCS): Colonial Pasts and Neoliberal Futures." *Learning, Media and Technology* 44 (3): 365–80. https://doi.org/10.1080/17439884.2019.1640740.

Agbaria, Ayman K. 1995. "The Mobile Matnass: Does Not Stop in Red." [In Hebrew.] Mobile Cultural Center. *Bamatnassim* (October): 18–19.

———. 2015. "Arab Civil Society and Education in Israel: The Arab Pedagogical Council as a Contentious Performance to Achieve National Recognition." *Race Ethnicity and Education* 18 (5): 675–95. https://doi.org/10.1080/1361 3324.2012.759930.

———. 2018. "The 'Right' Education in Israel: Segregation, Religious Ethnonationalism, and Depoliticized Professionalism." *Critical Studies in Education* 59 (1): 18–34. https://doi.org/10.1080/17508487.2016.1185642.

Agbaria, Ayman K., and Muhanad Mustafa. 2014. "The Case of Palestinian Civil Society in Israel: Islam, Civil Society, and Educational Activism." *Critical Studies in Education* 55 (1): 44–57. https://doi.org/10.1080/17508487.2014.857360.

Agbaria, Ayman K., Muhanad Mustafa, and Y. T. Jabareen. 2015. " 'In Your Face' Democracy: Education for Belonging and Its Challenges in Israel." *British Educational Research Journal* 41 (1): 143–75.

Agbaria, Ayman K., and Halleli Pinson. 2019. "Navigating Israeli Citizenship: How Do Arab-Palestinian Teachers Civicize their Pupils?" *Race Ethnicity and Education* 22 (3): 391–409. https://doi.org/10.1080/13613324.2018.1511527.

Agbaria, Ayman K., and Hazar Obeid Shehadeh. 2022. " 'Minority within Minority' or a 'Minority of Two Majorities': Religious Education and the Making of Christian Identity in Israel." *British Journal of Religious Education* 44 (3): 256–70. https://doi.org/10.1080/01416200.2021.2021504.

Ahonen, S. 2001. "Politics of Identity through History Curriculum: Narratives of the Past for Social Exclusion—or Inclusion?" *Journal of Curriculum Studies* 33 (2): 179–94. https://doi.org/10.1080/00220270010011202.

Aikman, Sheila, and Linda King. 2012. "Indigenous Knowledges and Education." *Compare: A Journal of Comparative and International Education* 42 (5): 673–81. https://doi.org/10.1080/03057925.2012.706450.

Aitken, A., and L. Radford. 2018. "Learning to Teach for Reconciliation in Canada: Potential, Resistance and Stumbling Forward." *Teaching and Teacher Education* 75:40–48. https://doi.org/10.1016/j.tate.2018.05.014.

Al-Abbasi, Mahmoud. 1997. "Motifs, Themes and Foci in the Fourth Book of 'Kalat Lia Alriahin.' " Revised ed. [In Arabic.] *Al-Sinnarah*, December 12, 1997.

Alafenish, Salim. 1987. "Processes of Change and Continuity in Kinship System and Family Ideology in Bedouin Society." *Sociologia Ruralis* 27 (4): 323–40.

Alayan, Samira. 2012. "Arab Education in Israel: Lessons from Positive Learning Experiences of Palestinian-Israelis." *Diaspora, Indigenous, and Minority Education* 6 (4): 214–29. https://doi.org/10.1080/15595692.2012.715104.

Al-Haj, Majid. 1987. *Social Change and Family Processes: Arab Communities in Shefar-Am*. Boulder, CO: Westview Press.

———. 1988a. "The Arab Internal Refugees in Israel: The Emergence of a Minority Within the Minority." *Immigrants and Minorities* 7 (2): 149–65.

———. 1988b. "The Changing Arab Kinship Structure: The Effect of Modernization in an Urban Community." *Economic Development and Cultural Change* 36, no. 2 (January): 237–58.

———. 1988c. "Arab Graduates in Israel: Main Characteristics, Potential of Graduates, and Employment Situation." [In Hebrew.] In *Employment Difficulties for Arab Graduates in Israel*, edited by Al-Haj Majid, 9–22. Haifa: Jewish-Arab Center, University of Haifa.

———. 1989a. "Social Research on Family Lifestyles among Arabs in Israel." *Journal of Comparative Family Studies* 20 (2): 176–95.

———. 1989b. "The Arabs in Israel in the Shadow of the Intifada: Standing on the Green Line." [In Hebrew.] *HETZ: A Quarterly for Education* 2:19–21.

———. 1993. "The Impact of the Intifada on the Orientation of the Arabs in Israel: The Case of a Double Periphery." In *Framing the Intifada: Media and People*, edited by Akiba Cohen and Gadi Wolsfeld, 64–75. Norwood, NJ: Ablex Publishing.

———. 1995a. *Education, Empowerment and Control: The Case of the Arabs in Israel*. Albany: State University of New York Press.

———. 1995b. *The Arab Teacher in Israel: Status, Questions, and Expectations*. [In Hebrew.] Research Report. Haifa: Center for the Study of Arab Education, University of Haifa.

———. 1995c. "Kinship and Modernization in Developing Societies: The Emergence of Instrumentalized Kinship." *Journal of Comparative Family Studies* 26 (3): 311–28.

———. 1996a. *Education of Arabs in Israel: Control and Social Change*. [In Hebrew.] Jerusalem: Magnes Press.

———. 1996b. "The Political Organization of the Arab Population in Israel: The Development of a Center Within the Periphery." [In Hebrew.] In *Israel Towards the Year 2000, Society and Culture*, edited by Moshe Lissak and Baruch Kane Paz, 90–102. Jerusalem: Magnes Press.

———. 1997. "Identity and Political Orientation among the Arabs in Israel: The Status of a Double Periphery." [In Hebrew.] *Medina Mimshal Viahasim Benleumiyyim* 41/42:103–22.

———. 1999. "Higher Education among the Arabs in Israel: Condition, Needs, and Recommendations." [In Hebrew.] Position paper submitted to the Council for Higher Education in Israel. Jerusalem.

———. 2002. "Multiculturalism in Deeply Divided Societies: The Israeli Case." *International Journal of Intercultural Relations* 26:169–83.

———. 2003. "Higher Education among the Arabs in Israel: Formal Policy between Empowerment and Control." *Higher Education Policy* 16:351–68.

———. 2004. *Identity and Creativity: Analysis of the Annual Books of Children's Works, 1993–1998*. Revised ed. [In Arabic]. Shefa-'Amr: INSANN.

———. 2005a. "Whither the Green Line? Trends in the Orientation of the Palestinians in Israel and the Territories." *Israel Affairs* 11 (1): 183–206. https://doi.org/10.1080/1353712042000324517.

———. 2005b. "National Ethos, Multicultural Education, and the New History Textbooks." *Curriculum Inquiry* 35:47–71. https://doi.org/10.1111/j.1467-873X.2005.00315.x.

———. 2006. *Education of the Palestinian in Israel: Between Control and the Culture of Silence*. Revised ed. [In Arabic]. Beirut: Center for the Study of Arab Unity.

———. 2019. *The Russian Immigrants in Israel: A New Ethnic Group in a Tribal Society*. New York: Routledge.

———. 2021. "Rival Histories in a Deeply Divided Society: The Israeli Case." In *Israel-Palestine: Lands and People*, edited by Omer Bartov, 239–62. New York: Berghahn Books.

Al-Haj, Majid, Elihu Katz, and Samuel Shai. 1993. "Arab and Jewish Attitudes towards a Palestinian State." *Journal of Conflict Resolution* 37 (4): 619–32.

Al-Haj, Majid, and Henry Rosenfeld. 1989. "The Emergence of an Indigenous Political Framework in Israel: The National Committee of Chairmen of Arab Local Authorities." *Asian and African Studies* 23:205–44.

———. 1990. *Arab Local Government in Israel*. Boulder, CO: Westview Press.

Al-Haj, Majid, and Avner Yaniv. 1983. "Uniformity or Diversity: A Reappraisal of the Voting Behavior of the Arab Minority in Israel." In *The Elections in Israel 1981*, edited by A. Arian, 139–64. New Brunswick, NJ: Transaction.

Alizadeh, Somayeh, and Meena Chavan. 2016. "Cultural Competence Dimensions and Outcomes: A Systematic Review of the Literature." *Health and Social Care in the Community* 24 (6): e117–e130.

Al-Krenawi, Alean, and John R. Graham. 1998. "Divorce Among Muslim Arab Women in Israel." *Journal of Divorce & Remarriage* 29 (3–4): 103–19. https://doi.org/10.1300/J087v29n03_07.

A'mal, Iskander. 1996. "INSANN Continues the Journey of Creativity." [In Arabic.] *Al-Ittihad* (Haifa), January 3, 1996.

Amara, Muhammad. 2016. "Language, Identity and Conflict: Examining Collective Identity Through the Labels of the Palestinians in Israel." *Journal of Holy Land and Palestine Studies* 15 (2): 203–23.

———. 2019. "Arabisation, Globalisation, and Hebraisation Reflexes in Shop Names in the Palestinian Arab linguistic Landscape in Israel." *Language and Intercultural Communication* 19 (3): 272–88. https://doi.org/10.1080/14708477.2018.1556676.

Amara, Muhammad, and Izhak Schnell. 2004. "Identity Repertoires among Arabs in Israel." *Journal of Ethnic and Migration Studies* 30 (1): 175–93. https://doi.org/10.1080/1369183032000170222.

Amiel, May, and Miri Yemini. 2023. "Who Takes I? The Rise of Education Policy Networks and the Shifting Balance of Initiative-taking amongst Education Stakeholders in Israel." *Journal of Education Policy* 38 (4): 586–606. https://doi.org/10.1080/02680939.2022.2130996.

Anaya, S. J. 2008. "The Right of Indigenous Peoples to Self-Determination in the Post Declaration Era." *Journal of Indigenous People's Rights* 2: 47–57.

Antoniou, A. S., F. Polychroni, and C. Kotroni. 2009. "Working with Students with Special Educational Needs in Greece: Teachers' Stressors and Coping Strategies." *International Journal of Special Education* 24 (1): 100–111.

Apple, Michael W. 1979. *Ideology and Curriculum*. New York: Routledge and Kegan Paul.

———. 1982. *Education and Power*. London: Routledge and Kegan Paul.

———. 1999. *Power, Meaning and Identity*. New York: Peter Lang.

———. 2000. *Official Knowledge*. 2nd ed. New York: Routledge.

———. 2004. *Ideology and Curriculum*. New York: Routledge Falmer.

———. 2006a. *Educating the 'Right' Way: Markets, Standards, God, and Inequality*. New York: Routledge.

———. 2006b. "Understanding and Interrupting Neoliberalism and Neoconservatism in Education." *Pedagogies* 1 (1): 21–26. https://doi.org/10.1207/s15544818ped0101_4.

———. 2013. *Knowledge, Power, and Education: The Selected Works of Michael W. Apple*. New York: Routledge.

Arar, Khalid. 2011. "'Trapped between Two Worlds'—Muslim Palestinian Women from Israel in Jordanian Universities: New Identity and the Price It Demands." *Social Identities* 17:625–42. http://dx.doi.org/10.1080/13504630.2011.595205.

———. 2019. "Arab Principals' and Teachers' Perceptions of Trust and Regulation and Their Contribution to School Processes." *Leadership and Policy in Schools* 18 (4): 648–63. https://doi.org/10.1080/15700763.2018.1475576.

———. 2022. "Understanding the Educational Administrator's Role in a Turbulent Ethnic Education System." *Leadership and Policy in Schools* 21 (2): 222–37. https://doi.org/10.1080/15700763.2020.1757723.

Arar, Khalid, and Khaled Abu-Asbah. 2013. "Not Just Location: Attitudes and Perceptions of Education System Administrators in Local Arab Governments in Israel." *International Journal of Educational Management* 27 (1): 54–73.

Arar, Khalid, and Yonis Abu El-Hija. 2018. "A University for the Arab Minority in Israel: Stake Holders' Perceptions and Proposed Models." *Higher Education Policy* 31:75–96.

Arar, Khalid, and Fadia Ibrahim. 2016. "Education for National Identity: Arab Schools Principals and Teachers' Dilemmas and Coping Strategies." *Journal of Education Policy* 31 (6): 681–93. https://doi.org/10.1080/02680939.2016.1182647.

Arar, Khalid, and Kussai Haj-Yehia. 2010. "Emigration for Higher Education: The Case of Palestinians Living in Israel Studying in Jordan." *Journal of Higher Education Policy* 23 (3): 358–80.

———. 2013. "Higher Education Abroad: Palestinian Students from Israel Studying in Jordanian Universities." *Journal of Applied Research in Higher Education* 5 (1): 95–112.

———. 2016. *Higher Education and the Palestinian Arab Minority in Israel*. New York: Palgrave.

Arar, Khaled, and Asmahan Massry-Herzallah. 2016. "Motivation to Teach: The Case of Arab Teachers in Israel." *Educational Studies* 42 (1): 19–35. https://doi.org/10.1080/03055698.2015.1127136.

Arar, Khalid, Asmahan Masry-Harzalla, and Kussai Haj-Yehia. 2013. "Higher Education for Palestinian Muslim Female Students in Israel and Jordan: Migration and Identity Formation." *Cambridge Journal of Education* 43 (1): 51–67. https://doi.org/10.1080/0305764X.2012.749391.

Arar, Khalid, and Muhanad Mustafa. 2011. "Access to Higher Education for Palestinians in Israel." *Education, Business and Society: Contemporary Middle Eastern Issues* 4 (3): 207–28.

Arar, Khalid, Emanuel Tamir, and Jamal Abu-Hussain. 2019. "Understanding Reforms, School Reactions to Major Changes: The Case of Israel." *Journal of Educational Administration and History* 51 (4): 402–18. https://doi.org/10.1080/00220620.2019.1624511.

Arian, Asher. 2002. "Israeli Public Opinion on National Security." Memorandum No. 61. Tel Aviv: Jaffee Center for Strategic Studies, Tel Aviv University.

Arieli, Shaul. 2016. "Geographical, Historical and Political Aspects in Determining Political Border in Intra-state Conflicts: The Israeli-Palestinian Case." PhD diss., Faculty of Social Sciences, University of Haifa.

Arlozorov, Merav. 2013. "It Is Easier for Arabs to Study Medicine than Engineering: The Success of Israeli Arabs in Medicine is Sectoral and Limited." [In Hebrew.] *The Marker*, June 20, 2013. https://www.themarker.com/career/1.2051003.

Aronowitz, S., and H. A. Giroux. 1993. *Education: Still Under Siege*. 2nd ed. Westport, CT: Bergin and Garvey.

Aronson, Brittany, and Judson Laughter. 2020. "The Theory and Practice of Culturally Relevant Education: Expanding the Conversation to Include Gender and Sexuality Equity." *Gender and Education* 32 (2): 262–79. https://doi.org/10.1080/09540253.2018.1496231.

Association of Civil Rights in Israel. 2004. "Abolition of the Method of 'Aggregation' in Admission to Universities." [In Hebrew.] Updated February 13, 2008. https://law.acri.org.il/he/1693.

Atkins, Danielle N., Angela R. Fertig, and Vicky M. Wilkins. 2014. "Connectedness and Expectations: How Minority Teachers Can Improve Educational Outcomes for Minority Students." *Public Management Review* 16 (4): 503–26. https://doi.org/10.1080/14719037.2013.841981.

Aurell, Jaume. 2006. "Autobiography as Unconventional History: Constructing the Author." *Rethinking History* 10 (3): 433–49. https://doi.org/10.1080/13642520600816213.

Avger, Ido. 2015. *Academic Institutes for Minority Groups: A Comparative Overview.* [In Hebrew.] Jerusalem: Israeli Knesset, Information and Research Center. https://www.knesset.gov.il/ mmm/data/pdf/m03050.pdf.

Avigur-Eshel, Amit, and Izhak Berkovich. 2017. "Who 'Likes' Public Education: Social Media, Activism, Middle-Class Parents, and Education Policy in Israel." *British Journal of Sociology of Education* 39 (6): 844–59. https://doi.org/10.1080/01425692.2017.1418294.

Avraham, Ada. 1986. "The Teacher in the Mirror of Group and Self." *Psychology and Counseling in Education*, 139–70.

Awawdeh, Wadi'. 1995. "The Winds of Change Are Blowing in Arab Schools." [In Arabic.] *Kul el-Arab*, November 24, 1995.

———. 1997. "INSANN Works in Unrecognized Villages to Compensate Their Children for What the State has Deprived Them of." [In Arabic.] *Kul el-Arab*, November 21, 1997.

Ayalon, Hanna, Nachum Blass, Yariv Feniger, and Yossi Shavit. 2019. *Educational Inequality in Israel: From Research to Policy.* [In Hebrew.] Jerusalem: Taub Center for Social Policy Studies in Israel.

Ayalon, Hanna, and A. Yogev. 2006. "Stratification and Diversity in the Expanded System of Higher Education in Israel." *Higher Education Policy* 19:187–203.

Badran, N. 1969. *Education and Modernization in Palestine 1918–1948.* Palestine Monograph, No. 63. Beirut: Palestine Liberation Organization Research Center.

Ball, Stephen J. 2016. "Subjectivity as a Site of Struggle: Refusing Neoliberalism?" *British Journal of Sociology of Education* 37 (8): 1129–46. https://doi.org/10.1080/01425692.2015.1044072.

Ball, A. F., and C. A. Tyson. 2011. "Preparing Teachers for Diversity in the Twenty-First Century." In *Studying Diversity in Teacher Education*, edited by A. F. Ball and C. A. Tyson, 399–416. Lanham, MD: Rowman and Littlefield.

Baltodano, Marta. 2012. "Neoliberalism and the Demise of Public Education: the Corporatization of Schools of Education." *International Journal of Qualitative Studies in Education* 25 (4): 487–507. https://doi.org/10.1080/09518398.2012.673025.

Bamberger, Annette, and Min Ji Kim. 2022. "The OECD's Influence on National Higher Education Policies: Internationalisation in Israel and South Korea." *Comparative Education*, 1–18. https://doi.org/10.1080/03050068.2022.2147635.

The Bank of Israel. 2020. *Economic Aspects of the Arab Society Before and After the Corona*. [In Hebrew.] Jerusalem. https://www.boi.org.il/publications/press releases.

———. 2021. *A New Research: The Arab Population in the High-tech Sector in Israel*. [In Hebrew.] Public Relations and Economic Advocacy, Jerusalem, October 4, 2021. https://www.boi.org.il/publications/pressreleases.

Banks, James. 1981. *Multiethnic Education: Theory and Practice*. Boston: Allyn and Bacon.

———. 1996. *Multicultural Education, Transformative Knowledge, and Action*: *Historical and Contemporary Perspectives*. New York: Teachers College Press.

———. 2001a. *Cultural Diversity and Education*: *Foundation, Curriculum, and Teaching*. Boston: Allyn and Bacon.

———. 2001b. "Multicultural Education: Characteristics and Goals." In *Multicultural Education*: *Issues and Perspectives*, edited by James A. Banks and Cherry A. McGee Banks, 3–30. New York: John Wiley and Sons.

———. 2004. "Multicultural Education: Historical Development, Dimensions, and Practice." In *Handbook of Research on Multicultural Education*, edited by J. A. Banks and C. A. McGee Banks, 2nd ed., 3–29. San Francisco: Jossey-Bass.

———. 2006. *Race, Culture and Education: The Selected Works of James A. Banks*. London: Routledge.

———. 2017. "Failed Citizenship and Transformative Civic Education." *Educational Researcher* 46 (7): 366–77.

Banks, James A., and Cherry A. McGee Banks, editors. 2001. *Multicultural Education: Issues and Perspectives*. 4th ed. Boston: Allyn and Bacon.

Banting, Keith, and Will Kymlicka, editors. 2006. *Multiculturalism and the Welfare State: Recognition and Redistribution in Contemporary Democracies*. Oxford: Oxford University Press.

Baran, G., M. Y. Bıçakçı, F. İnci, M. Öngör, A. Ceran, and G. Atar. 2010. "Analysis of Burnout Levels of Teacher." *Procedia: Social and Behavioral Sciences* 9:975–80. https://doi.org/10.1016/j.sbspro.2010.12.270.

Bar-Gefen, Linoi. 2001. "The Law of Abolishment of the Psychometric Test Passed a Preliminary Reading." [In Hebrew.] *Ynet*, March 21, 2001. https://www.ynet.co.il/articles/0,7340,L-613769,00.html.

Barghouti, Sai'd. 1991. "The New History Curriculum for Arab Schools." Revised ed. In *Education for the Arab Minority in Israel: Issues, Problems and Demands*, edited by Mohammed Habib-Allah and Attallah Kupty, 114–23. [In Arabic.] Haifa: al-Karmah.

Barghouti, Sai'd. 1998. *The Modern History of the Middle East, part 2*. [In Arabic.] Jerusalem: Ministry of Education.

Bar-Navi, Eli, and Ayal Naveh. 1999. *Modern Times. Part 1, 1870–1920; part 2, 1920–2000*. [In Hebrew.] Tel Aviv: Tel Aviv Books.

Barsh, R. L. 1996. "Indigenous Peoples and the UN Commission on Human Rights: A Case of the Immovable Object and the Irresistible Force." *Human Rights Quarterly* 18:782–813.

Bar-Tal, Daniel. 1996. *The Rocky Road toward Peace: Societal Beliefs in Times of Intractable Conflict—The Israeli Case.* [In Hebrew.] Jerusalem: Hebrew University of Jerusalem, Institute for Research and Development in Education.

———. 1999. "The Arab-Israel Conflict as an Intractable Conflict and its Reflection in Israeli Text-Books." [In Hebrew.] *Megamot* 29 (4): 445–91.

Barzilai, Gad. 1992. *A Democracy in Wartime: Conflict and Consensus in Israel.* [In Hebrew.] Tel Aviv: Sfriyat Poalim.

Bashi, Joseph, Sorel Kahan, and Daniel Davis. 1981. *The Academic Achievements of the Arab Primary School in Israel.* [In Hebrew.] Jerusalem: School of Education, Hebrew University.

Bauer, Yehuda. 2023. "On Israeli Democracy." *Israel Journal of Foreign Affairs*, 1–5. https://doi.org/10.1080/23739770.2023.2187164.

Beller, Michal. 1994. "Psychometric and Social Issues in Admissions to Israeli Universities." *Educational Measurement: Issues and Practice* 13 (2): 12–20.

———. 2001. "Admission to Higher Education in Israel and the Role of the Psychometric Entrance Test: Educational and Political Dilemmas." *Assessment in Education: Principles, Policy & Practice* 8 (3): 315–37. https://doi.org/10.1080/09695940120089125.

Bellier, Irène, and Martin Préaud. 2012. "Emerging Issues in Indigenous Rights: Transformative Effects of the Recognition of Indigenous Peoples." *The International Journal of Human Rights* 16 (3): 474–88. https://doi.org/10.1080/1364298 7.2011.574616.

Bellino, Michelle J. 2015. "The Risks We are Willing to Take: Youth Civic Development in 'Postwar' Guatemala." *Harvard Educational Review* 85 (4): 537–61. https://doi.org/10.17763/0017-8055.85.4.537.

Bellino, Michelle J., Julia Paulson, and Elizabeth Anderson Worden. 2017. "Working through Difficult Pasts: Toward Thick Democracy and Transitional Justice in Education." *Comparative Education* 53 (3): 313–32. https://doi.org/10.1080/03050068.2017.1337956.

Ben-Amos, Avner, and Ilana Bet-El. 2003. "Militaristic Education and Commemoration: Nationalistic Memorial Ceremonies in Israeli Schools." [In Hebrew.] In *In the Name of Security: The Sociology of Peace and War in Israel in Changing Times*, edited by Majid Al-Haj and Uri Ben-Eliezer, 369–400. Haifa: Haifa University Press and Pardes Publishers.

Ben-Artzi, Yosef. 1980. Residential Patterns and Intra-Urban Migration of Arabs in Haifa. Occasional Papers on the Middle East (New Series) No. 1. [In Hebrew.] Haifa: Jewish-Arab Center, University of Haifa.

Ben-Eliezer, Uri. 1998. *The Making of Israeli Militarism.* Bloomington: Indiana University Press.

———. 2003. "Civil Society and Military Society in Israel: Neo-Militarism and Anti-Militarism in the Post Hegemonic Era." [In Hebrew.] In *In the Name of Security: The Sociology of Peace and War in Israel in Changing Times*, edited by Majid Al-Haj and Uri Ben-Eliezer, 29–76. Haifa: Haifa University Press and Pardes Publishers.

———. 2019. *War Over Peace: One Hundred Years of Israel's Militaristic Nationalism*. Oakland: University of California Press.

Ben-Gurion, David. 1971. *Uniqueness and Destiny. Issues About Israel's Security*. [In Hebrew.] Tel Aviv: Ministry of Defense, Maa'rachot Publishing.

Ben-Gurion University and Negev Center for Sustainability. 2020. *Online Data Base on the Bedouin Society in Negev*. [In Hebrew.] https://in.bgu.ac.il/humsos/negevSus/SYBSN/Pages/demographics.aspx.

Ben-Hanania. 1947. "The Arab Kindergarten." [In Hebrew.] *Hed Hakhinukh* 21:32–33.

Ben-Or, Yehuda. 1950. "Arab Education in Israel." *Middle Eastern Affairs* 1, no. 8–9 (August–September): 224–29.

———. 1951. "The Arab Education in Israel." [In Hebrew.] *Hamizrach Hehadash* 31 (9): 1–8.

Ben-Porat, G. 2013. *Between State and Synagogue: The Secularization of Contemporary Israel*. Vol. 42. Cambridge: Cambridge University Press.

Ben-Porat, Ido. 2019. "Nationality Law Inters the Curriculum." [In Hebrew.] *Arutz 7*, August 15, 2019. https://www.inn.co.il/news/410257.

Ben-Rafael, Eliezer, Julius H. Schoeps, Yitzhak Sternberg, and Olaf Glockner, editors. 2016. *Handbook of Israel: Major Debates*. Oldenbourg: De Gruyter.

Ben-Rafael, Eliezer, and Yitzhak Sternberg, editors. 2009. *Transnationalism, Diasporas and the Advent of a New (Dis) Order*. Leiden, Neth.: Brill.

Ben-Shakhar, G., I. Kiderman, and M. Beller. 1996. "Comparing the Utility of Two Procedures for Admitting Students to Liberal Arts: An Application of Decision-Theoretic Models." *Educational and Psychological Measurement* 56, 90–107.

Berkovich, I., and V. J. Foldes. 2012. "Third Sector Involvement in Public Education: The Israeli Case." *Journal of Educational Administration* 50 (2): 173–87.

Bilton, Chris, and Gonzalo Soltero. 2020. "Cultural Policy as Mythical Narrative." *International Journal of Cultural Policy* 26 (5): 681–96. https://doi.org/10.1080/10286632.2019.1624736.

Bitton, Y. 2012. "Finally Our Own Brown!" *Israel Law Review* 45 (2): 267–89.

Bligh, Alexander. 2013. "Political Trends in the Israeli Arab Population and its Vote in Parliamentary Elections." *Israel Affairs* 19 (1): 21–50. https://doi.org/10.1080/13537121.2013.748286.

Blumenfeld, Emily R. 2010. "Reflections on Student Journals and Teaching about Inequality." *Journal of Poetry Therapy* 23 (2): 101–6. https://doi.org/10.1080/08893675.2010.482812.

Bodovski, Katerina, Volha Chykina, and Tatiana Khavenson. 2019. "Do Human and Cultural Capital Lenses Contribute to Our Understanding of Academic Success in Russia." *British Journal of Sociology of Education* 40 (3): 393–409. https://doi.org/10.1080/01425692.2018.1552844.

Boneh, Moran Zadok, Rinat Feniger-Schaal, Tali Aviram Bivas, and Alexandra Danial-Saad. 2021. "Teachers Under Stress During the COVID-19: Cultural Differences." *Teachers and Teaching* 28 (2): 164–87. https://doi.org/10.1080/13540602.2021.2017275.

Bourdieu, Pierre, and J. C. Passeron. 1990. *Reproduction in Education, Society and Culture*. London: Sage.

Brady, David. 2004. "Why Public Sociology May Fail?" *Social Forces* 82:1629–38.

Bremner, N. 2019. "From Learner-Centred to Learning-Centred: Becoming a 'Hybrid' Practitioner." *International Journal of Educational Research* 97:53–64.

Brown, Laura M. 2021. "The Impact of Student-Centered Learning through Use of Peer Feedback in the Dance Technique Classroom." *Journal of Dance Education*, 1–11. https://doi.org/10.1080/15290824.2021.1932911.

Brubaker, Rogers. 1996. *Nationalism Reframed: Nationhood and the National Question in the New Europe*. Cambridge: Cambridge University Press.

———. 2011. "Nationalizing States Revisited: Projects and Processes of Nationalization in Post-Soviet States." *Ethnic and Racial Studies* 34 (11): 1785–1814. https://doi.org/10.1080/01419870.2011.579137.

Burawoy, Michael. 2004. "Public Sociologies: Contradictions, Dilemmas, and Possibilities." *Social Forces* 82:1603–18.

Burger, Julian. 2019. "After the Declaration: Next Steps for the Protection of Indigenous Peoples' Rights." *The International Journal of Human Rights* 23 (1–2): 22–33. https://doi.org/10.1080/13642987.2018.1562916.

Buunk, Abraham P., Jose Maria Peíró, Isabel Rodríguez, and M. Jesus Bravo. 2007. "A Loss of Status and a Sense of Defeat: An Evolutionary Perspective on Professional Burnout." *European Journal of Personality* 21:471–85. https://doi.org/10.1002/per.627.

Bystrov, Evgenia, and Arnon Soffer. 2013. *Israel: Demography 2013–2034*. [In Hebrew.] Mount Carmel: Reuven Chaikin Chair in Geostrategy, University of Haifa.

Calvo-Armengol, A., and M. O. Jackson. 2004. "The Effects of Social Networks on Employment and Inequality." *American Economic Review* 94 (3): 426–54.

Caplan, Tom, Orly Furman, Dmitri Romanov, and Noam Zussman. 2009. "The Quality of Israeli Academic Institutions: What the Wages of Graduates Tell About It?" [In Hebrew.] Working Paper, No. 42. Jerusalem: Central Bureau of Statistics, Chief Scientist Department and Bank of Israel, Research Department.

Carmi, Shulamit, and Henry Rosenfeld. 1989. *Changes in Class-National Relations in Palestine-Israel: A Political Economy Perspective*. Tel Aviv: International Center for Peace in the Middle East.

Carnevale, A. P., M. Van Der Werf, M. C. Quinn, J. Strohl, and D. Repnikov. 2018. *Our Separate and Unequal Public Colleges: How Public Colleges Reinforce White Racial Privilege and Marginalize Black and Latino Students.* Center on Education and the Workforce, Georgetown University. https://cew.georgetown.edu/cew-reports/sustates/.

Caspit, Ben. 2023. "State Education has Become an Excess Burden that Everyone Abuses." [In Hebrew.] *Ma'ariv*, August 25, 2023. https://www.maariv.co.il/journalists/Article-1032964.

CBS (Central Bureau of Statistics). 1983. *Population and Housing Census.* [In Hebrew.] Jerusalem: Central Bureau of Statistics.

———. 1995. *Monthly Bulletin of Statistics.* [In Hebrew.] Central Bureau of Statistics, 71.

———. 2017. *A Press Release.* [In Hebrew.] Central Bureau of Statistics, September 6, 2017.

———. 2020a. *Christmas 2020: Christians in Israel.* [In Hebrew.] Jerusalem: Central Bureau of Statistics. https://www.cbs.gov.il/he/mediarelease/DocLib/2020/419/11_20_419e.pdf.

———. 2020b. *Characterization and Classification of Geographical Units by the Socio-Economic Level of the Population 2017.* [In Hebrew.] Press Release, December 15, 2020. https://www.cbs.gov.il/he/mediarelease/DocLib/2020/403/24_20_403b.pdf.

———. 2022. *Gaps between Jews and Arabs, 2020–2021.* [In Hebrew.] Selected data from the Society in Israel Report, No. 14. https://www.cbs.gov.il/he/mediarelease/DocLib/2023/192/33_23_192b.pdf.

Central Bureau of Statistics, Ministry of Education and Culture, and Planning and Budgeting Committee. 1996. *Admission of Matriculation Certificate Holders to First-Degree Studies in Universities, Cohorts of 1983/84–1988/89: Follow-up until 1994/95.* [In Hebrew.] Current Statistics No. 36, Jerusalem.

Central Bureau of Statistics and Planning and Budgeting Committee. 1995. *Candidates for First-Degree Studies, Demographic Characteristics and District of Residence, 1992/93, Monthly Bulletin of Statistics.* [In Hebrew.] Supplement No. 4. *Statistical Pamphlets on Education and Culture*, No. 229, Jerusalem.

CHE and PBC (Council for Higher Education and Planning and Budgeting Committee). 1997. *Annual Report No. 23, 1995/96.* [In Hebrew]. Jerusalem.

———. 1998. *Annual Report No. 24, 1996/97.* [In Hebrew]. Jerusalem.

———. 2001. *Report of the Committee for the Advancement of Higher Education among the Arabs in Israel* (Al-Haj's Committee). [In Hebrew.] Mimeographed. Jerusalem, December 12, 2001.

———. 2018. *Growth in the Number of Arab Students: A Report.* [In Hebrew.] Jerusalem.

Chen, Peiying. 2012. "Empowering Identity Reconstruction of Indigenous College Students through Transformative Learning." *Educational Review* 64 (2): 161–80. https://doi.org/10.1080/00131911.2011.592574.

Chiang, H. S., M. A. Clark, and S. McConnell. 2017. "Supplying Disadvantaged Schools with Effective Teachers: Experimental Evidence on Secondary Math Teachers from Teach for America." *Journal of Policy Analysis and Management* 36 (1): 97–125. https://doi.org/10.1002/pam.21958.

Chin, Rita. 2017. *The Crisis of Multiculturalism in Europe: A History.* Princeton, NJ: Princeton University Press. Reviewed by Nedjib Sidi Moussa. 2018. *Journal of Contemporary European Studies.* https://doi.org/10.1080/14782804.2018.142 9226.

Chomsky, Noam. 1987 (1967). "The Responsibility of Intellectuals." In *The Chomsky Reader*, edited by J. Peck, 61–82. New York: Random House.

Cinamon, Rachel Gali. 2009. "Role Salience, Social Support, and Work-Family Conflict Among Jewish and Arab Female Teachers in Israel." *Journal of Career Development* 36:139–58. http://dx.doi.org/10.1177/0894845309345849.

Cinamon, Rachel Gali, Halah Habayib, and Margalit Ziv. 2016. "The Conception of Work and Higher Education among Israeli Arab Women." *International Journal of Educational Research* 76:129–40.

Clegg, P. 2008. "Creativity and Critical Thinking in the Globablised University." *Innovations in Education and Teaching International* 45:219–26.

Clennon, Ornette D. 2020. "Scholar Activism as a Nexus between Research Community Activism and Civil Rights Via the Use of Participatory Arts." *The International Journal of Human Rights* 24 (1): 46–61. https://doi.org/10.108 0/13642987.2019.1624535.

Cnaan, R. 1988. "Social Services for the Enemy? Education for Social Work and the Arab Sector in Israel." *International Social Work* 31:33–43.

Coates, S. K., M. Trudgett, and S. Page. 2020. "Indigenous Higher Education Sector: The Evolution of Recognized Indigenous Leaders Within Australian Universities." *Australian Journal of Indigenous Education*, 1–7. https://doi. org/10.1017/jie.2019.30.

Cobo, José R. Martinez. 1986. *Study of the Problem of Discrimination Against Indigenous Populations: Conclusions, Proposals and Recommendations.* New York: United Nations, Sales No. E.86.XIV.3.

Cohen, Aharon. 1951. "Problems of Education for Arab Children in Israel." [In Hebrew.] *Megamot* 2, no. 2 (January): 126–37.

Cohen, Asher, and Bernard Susser. 2009. "Jews and Others: Non-Jewish Jews in Israel." *Israel Affairs* 15 (1): 52–65.

Cohen-Kovach, G., and N. Kasir. 2020. "Trends in Integrating Arab Society in Israel in the Field of High-Tech." [In Hebrew.] Jerusalem: Ministry of Labor, Welfare and Social Services.

Cohron, Madalyn. 2015. "The Continuing Digital Divide in the United States." *Serials Librarian* 69 (1): 77–86. https://doi.org/10.1080/0361526X.2015.1036195.

Conversi, Daniele. 2012. "Majoritarian Democracy and Globalization Versus Ethnic Diversity?" *Democratization* 19 (4): 789–811. https://doi.org/10.1080/1351 0347.2011.626947.

Copty, Makram, I. 1990. "Knowledge and Power in Education: The Making of Israeli Arab Educational System." PhD diss., University of Texas.

Crossley, M., and L. Tikly. 2004. "Postcolonial Perspectives and Comparative and International Research in Education: A Critical Introduction." *Comparative Education* 40 (2): 147–56.

Danahar, Paul. 2015. *The New Middle East: The World after the Arab Spring*. Edinburgh: Bloomsbury.

Degani, Arnon Yehuda. 2015. "The Decline and Fall of the Israeli Military Government, 1948–1966: A Case of Settler-Colonial Consolidation?" *Settler Colonial Studies* 5 (1): 84–99. https://doi.org/10.1080/2201473X.2014.905236.

Degani, Arnon. 2018. "Both Arab and Israeli: The Subordinate Integration of the Palestinian Arabs into Israeli Society, 1948–1967." PhD diss., UCLA.

Dewey, John. 1915. *The School and Society*. Chicago: University of Chicago Press.

Dietz, Gunther. 2019. "Multiculturalism, Indigenism and New Universities in Mexico: A Case of Intercultural Multilateralities." *Journal of Multicultural Discourses* 14 (1): 29–45. https://doi.org/10.1080/17447143.2018.1563608.

Doherty, Robert A. 2007. "Education, Neoliberalism and the Consumer Citizen: After the Golden Age of Egalitarian Reform." *Critical Studies in Education* 48 (2): 269–88. https://doi.org/10.1080/17508480701494275.

Donnelly, Michael J. 2021. "Discrimination and Multiculturalism in Canada: Exceptional or Incoherent Public Attitudes?" *American Review of Canadian Studies* 51 (1): 166–88. https://doi.org/10.1080/02722011.2021.1893052.

Drudy, Sheelagh. 2008. "Gender Balance/Gender Bias: The Teaching Profession and the Impact of Feminisation." *Gender and Education* 20 (4): 309–23. https://doi.org/10.1080/09540250802190156.

Dumitru, Ion, and Ioan Talpos. 2012. "Stress Factors in the Professional Activities of Romanian Teachers." *Procedia: Social and Behavioral Sciences* 55:887–93. https://doi.org/10.1016/j.sbspro.2012.09.577.

Dunham, J. 1984. *Stress in Teaching*. London: Croom Helm.

Durkheim, Emile. 1984. *The Division of Labor in Society*. Translated by W. D. Halls. *Glencoe:* Free Press

Dustmann, C. A. Glitz, U. Schönberg, and H. Brücker. 2016. "Referral-Based Job Search Networks." *Review of Economic Studies* 83 (2): 514–46.

Dvir, Noam (Dvol). 2022. "State Comptroller's Report: Negative Score Regarding Dropout in the Education System." [In Hebrew.] *Yisrael Hayoum*, July 4, 2022. https://www.israelhayom.co.il/news/education/article/12032728.

Dynarski, S. M. 2017. "Online Schooling: Who Is Harmed and Who Is Helped?" *Brookings Institution Report*. https://www. brookings.edu/research/who-should-take-online-courses/.

Eduah, D. K. 2019. "Using Innovation in Organisation as a Survival Strategy in a Highly Competitive Telecommunication Industry of Ghana: Prospects and Challenges: The Case of Vodafone Ghana Limited." *Texila International Journal of Management* 5 (1): 251–62.

Emery, D. W., and B. Vandenberg. 2010. "Special Education Teacher Burnout and Act." *International Journal of Special Education* 25 (3): 119–31.

Enteman, Shifra, and Aryeh Shirom. 1987. "On Organizational, Employment and Personal Influences on Burnout of Secondary-School Teachers." [In Hebrew.] *Megamot* 30 (3): 349–61.

Entwistle, Harold. 1979. *Antonio Gramsci: Conservative Schooling for Radical Politics.* London: Routledge and Kegan Paul.

Erdreich, Lauren. 2006. "Instructive Ritual: The Arab Student and the Communitas of the Palestinian Israel Education." *Social Analysis* 50:127–45.

Erdreich, Lauren, Julia Lerner, and Tamar Rapoport. 2005. "Reproducing Nation, Redesigning Positioning: Russian and Palestinian Students Interpret University Knowledge." *Identities: Global Studies in Culture and Power* 12 (4): 539–62. https://doi.org/10.1080/10702890500332709.

Erez, Oded, and Arnon Yehuda Degani. 2021. "Songs of Subordinate Integration: Music Education and the Palestinian Arab Citizens of Israel During the Mapai Era." *Ethnic and Racial Studies* 44 (6): 1008–29. https://doi.org/10.1080/01419870.2021.1877764.

Erichsen, Jakob, and Florian Waldow. 2020. "Fragile Legitimacy: Exclusive Boarding Schools between the Meritocratic Norm and Their Clientele's Desire for a Competitive Advantage." *European Education* 52 (2): 102–16. https://doi.org/10.1080/10564934.2020.1723420.

Estrada, Kelly, and Peter McLaren. 1993. "A Dialogue on Multiculturalism and Democratic Culture." *Educational Researcher* (April): 27–33.

Evans, R. J. 2003. "Introduction Redesigning the Past: History in Political Transitions." *Journal of Contemporary History* 38 (1): 5–12.

Falah, Ghazi. 1989. "Israeli State Policy Toward Bedouin Sedentarization in the Negev." *Journal of Palestine Studies* 18, no. 2 (Winter): 71–91.

Falah, Salman. 1974. *The History of the Druze in Israel.* [In Hebrew.] Jerusalem: Prime Minister's Office.

———. 1977. "Education among the Druze in Israel." [In Hebrew.] *Ma'alot* (June): 3–9.

Farber, B. A., and J. Miller. 1981. "Teacher Burnout: A Psychoeducational Perspective." *Teachers' College Record* 83:235–44.

Feishbin, Yael. 1988. "A Complex Business." [In Hebrew.] *Davar.* January 21, 1988.

Feniger, Yariv. 2020. "Evidence-Based Decision Making or a Tunnel Vision Effect?: TIMSS, Problem Definition and Policy Change in Israeli Mathematics Education." *Critical Studies in Education* 61 (3): 363–79. https://doi.org/10.1080/17508487.2018.1448877.

Feniger, Yariv, and Hanna Ayalon. 2016. "English as a Gatekeeper: Inequality between Jews and Arabs in Access to Higher Education in Israel." *International Journal of Educational Research* 76:104–11.

Feniger, Yariv, Mirit Israeli, and Smadar Yehuda. 2016. "The Power of Numbers: The Adoption and Consequences of National Low-Stakes Standardised Tests in Israel." *Globalisation, Societies and Education* 14 (2): 183–202. https://doi.org/10.1080/14767724.2015.1010438.

Feniger, Yariv, Idit Livneh, and Abraham Yogev. 2012. "Globalisation and the Politics of International Tests: The Case of Israel." *Comparative Education* 48 (3): 323–35. https://doi.org/10.1080/03050068.2011.622539.

Feniger, Yariv, Oded Mcdossi, and Hanna Ayalon. 2014. "Ethno-Religious Differences in Israeli Higher Education: Vertical and Horizontal Dimensions." *European Sociological Review*, 1–14.

Fierro, Jaime. 2020. "Indigenous People, Recognition, and Democracy in Latin America." *Ethnic and Racial Studies* 43 (15): 2746–65. https://doi.org/10.1080/01419870.2019.1691740.

Fischer, C. S., and Michael Hout. 2006. *Century of Difference: How America Changed in the Last 100 Years*. New York: Russell Sage Found.

Flores, Maria Assunção. 2020. "Surviving, Being Resilient and Resisting: Teachers' Experiences in Adverse Times." *Cambridge Journal of Education* 50 (2): 219–40. https://doi.org/10.1080/0305764X.2019.1664399.

Follow-Up Committee on Arab Education. 1991. "A Position Paper on the Failure of Arab Schools." [In Hebrew.] January 23, 1991. Shefa-A'mr: Follow-Up Committee on Arab Education.

———. 2020. "The Arab Education in Israel: Needs and Problems that Require Immediate Response towards the Opening of the 2020/21 School Year." [In Hebrew.] Nazareth: Follow-Up Committee on Arab Education.

Forman, Geremy. 2006. "Military Rule, Political Manipulation, and Jewish Settlement: Israeli Mechanisms for Controlling Nazareth in the 1950s." *Journal of Israeli History* 25 (2): 335–59. https://doi.org/10.1080/13531040600810292.

Frambach, Janneke, Erik Driessen, Philip Beh, and Cees P. M. van der Vleuten. 2014. "Quiet or Questioning? Students' Discussion Behaviors in Student-Centered Education Across Cultures." *Studies in Higher Education* 39 (6): 1001–21. https://doi.org/10.1080/03075079.2012.754865.

Franke, Mark F. N. 2007. "Self-Determination Versus the Determination of Self: A Critical Reading of the Colonial Ethics Inherent to the United Nations Declaration on the Rights of Indigenous Peoples." *Journal of Global Ethics* 3 (3): 359–79. https://doi.org/10.1080/17449620701728063.

Freire, Paulo. 1972. *Pedagogy of the Oppressed*. Translated by Myra Bergman Ramos. New York: Hender and Hender.

———. 1973. *Education for Critical Consciousness*. London: Sheed and Ward.

———. 1985. *The Politics of Education: Culture, Power and Liberation*. S. Hadley, MA: Bergin and Garvey.

———. 1998a. *Pedagogy of Hope: Reliving Pedagogy of the Oppressed*. New York: Continuum International.

———. 1998b. "Cultural Action for Freedom." *Harvard Education Review* 68 (4): 476–521.

Freudenberger, H. J. 1974. "Staff Burnout." *Journal of Social Issues* 30 (1): 159–65.

Friedman, Milton. 1955. "The Role of Government in Education." In *Economics and the Public Interest*, edited by R. A. Solo. New Brunswick, NJ: Rutgers University Press.

———. 1997. "Public Schools: Make Them Private." *Education Economics* 5 (3): 341–44. https://doi.org/10.1080/09645299700000026.

Friedman, Yitzhak, 1991. "Student Behavior that Creates Pressure: The Psycho-Social Aspect of Teacher Burnout." *Educational Organization and Administration* 17:155–74.

———. 1992a. "Burnout in Teaching: The Concept and its Particular Components." [In Hebrew.] *Megamot* 24 (2): 248–61.

———. 1992b. "What Burns Out Teachers." [In Hebrew.] *Hed Hahinnukh* 11–12:5–7.

———. 2000. "Burnout: Shattered Dreams of Impeccable Professional Performance." *Journal of Clinical Psychology* 56:595–606.

Friedman, Yitzhak, and Barry A. Farber. 1992. *The Professional Image of the Teacher and Burnout*. [In Hebrew.] Jerusalem: Henrietta Szold Institute.

Friedman, Yitzhak, and Ayala Lotan. 1987. "The World of Teachers Who Foresee Their Own Emotional Burnout." [In Hebrew.] *Megamot* 20:417–34.

———. 1993. *Pressure and Burnout in Teaching: Causes and Ways of Prevention*. Jerusalem: Henrietta Szold Institute.

Furrer, C., and E. Skinner. 2003. "Sense of Relatedness as a Factor in Children's Academic Engagement and Performance." *Journal of Educational Psychology* 95 (1): 148–62. https://doi.org/10.1037/ 0022-0663.95.1.148.

Gabay-Egozi, Limor, and Meir Yaish. 2021. "Trends in Intergenerational Educational Mobility in Israel: 1983–2008." *British Journal of Sociology of Education* 42 (5–6): 752–74. https://doi.org/10.1080/01425692.2021.1894548.

Gamliel, A., and S. Kahan. 2004. "Lack of Fairness in University Acceptance: The Modern Version of the Fable, 'The Poor Man's Lamb.' " [In Hebrew.] *Megamot* 33 (3): 433–45.

Gavish, B., and I. A. Friedman. 2010. "Novice Teachers' Experience of Teaching: A Dynamic Aspect of Burnout." *Social Psychology of Education* 13:141–67. https://doi.org/10.1007/s11218-009-9108-0.

Gay, G. 1983. "Multiethnic Education: Historical Developments and Future Prospects." *Phi Delta Kappan* 64:560–63.

Geertz, Clifford. 1995. *After the Fact: Two Countries, Four Decades, One Anthropologist*. Cambridge, MA: Harvard University Press.

Gellman, Mneesha, and Michelle Bellino. 2019. "Fighting Invisibility: Indigenous Citizens and History Education in El Salvador and Guatemala." *Latin American and Caribbean Ethnic Studies* 14 (1): 1–23. https://doi.org/10.1080/17 442222.2018.1457006.

Ghanem, As'ad. 2016. "Understanding the Divide: Arabs and Jews in Israel." In Ben-Rafael et al., *Handbook of Israel: Major Debates*, 779–93. Oldenbourg: De Gruyter.

Ghanem, As'ad, and Sarah Ozacky-Lazar. 1999. *The Arab Vote for the Fifteenth Knesset*. [In Hebrew.] Givat Haviva: Arab-Jewish Center for Peace.

Ghanem, As'ad, and Ibrahim Khatib. 2017. "The Nationalisation of the Israeli Ethnocratic Regime and the Palestinian Minority's Shrinking Citizenship." *Citizenship Studies* 21 (8): 889–902. https://doi.org/10.1080/13621025.2017.1380651.

Giancola, J., and R. D. Kahlenberg. 2016. *True Merit: Ensuring Our Brightest Students Have Access to Our Best Colleges and Universities*. Lansdowne, VA: Jack Kent Cooke Foundation.

Gibson, Melissa Leigh, and Carl A. Grant. 2012. "Toward a '*Paideia* of the Soul': Education to Enrich America's Multicultural Democracy." *Intercultural Education* 23 (4): 313–24. https://doi.org/10.1080/14675986.2012.716723.

Gidron, B., M. Bar, and H. Katz. 2004. *The Israeli Third Sector: Between Welfare State and Civil Society*. New York: Kluwer.

Gilbar, Gadi. 1989. *Trends in the Demographic Development of the Palestinians, 1870–1987*. [In Hebrew.] Mimeographed. Tel Aviv: Moshe Dayan Center for Middle Eastern and African Studies.

Gindi, Shahar, and Rakefet Erlich-Ron. 2019. "Bargaining with the System: A Mixed-Methods Study of Arab Teachers in Israel." *International Journal of Intercultural Relations* 69:44–53. https://doi.org/10.1016/j.ijintrel.2018.12.004.

Giroux, Henry A. 1985. Introduction to *The Politics of Education: Culture, Power and Liberation*, x–xix. By Paulo Freire, translated by Donaldo Macedo. S. Hadley, MA: Bergin and Garvey.

———. 1987. "Literacy and the Pedagogy of Political Empowerment." In *Literacy: Reading the Word and the World*, edited by Paulo Freire and Donaldo Macedo, 1–28. London: Routledge and Kegan Paul.

———. 1992. *Border Crossing: Cultural Workers and the Politics of Education*. New York: Routledge.

———. 1997. *Pedagogy and the Politics of Hope. Theory, Culture and Schooling*. Boulder, CO: Westview Press.

———. 2001. *Theory and Resistance in Education: Towards a Pedagogy for the Opposition*. Westport, CT: Bergin and Garvey.

———. 2010. "In Defense of Public-School Teachers in a Time of Crisis." *Policy Futures in Education* 8 (6): 709–14. http://dx.doi.org/10.2304/pfie.2010.8.6.709.

Giroux, Henry A., and R. I. Simon, editors. 1989. *Popular Culture, Schooling and Everyday Life*. S. Hadley, MA: Bergin and Garvey.

Goastellec, Gaële. 2008. "Globalization and Implementation of an Equity Norm in Higher Education: Admission Processes and Funding Framework Under

Scrutiny." *Peabody Journal of Education* 83 (1): 71–85. https://doi.org/10.1080/01619560701649174.

Goldscheider, Calvin. 1995. "Population, Ethnicity and Nation-Building: Themes, Issues and Guidelines." In *Population, Ethnicity and Nation-building*, edited by Calvin Goldsheider, 1–17. Boulder, CO: Westview Press.

———. 2002. *Israel's Changing Society: Population, Ethnicity, and Development*. Boulder, CO: Westview Press.

———. 2006. "Religion, Family and Fertility: What Do We Know Historically and Comparatively?" In *Religion and the Decline of Fertility in the Western World*, edited by R. Derosas and F. van Poppel, 41–57. Dordrecht, Neth.: Springer.

———. 2015. *Israeli Society in the Twenty-first Century: Immigration, Inequality and Religious Conflict*. Boston: Brandeis University Press.

Goldscheider, C., and P. R. Uhlenberg. 1969. "Minority Group Status and Fertility." *American Journal of Sociology* 74 (4): 361–72.

Goldschmidt, Marlen, Franz-Josef Scharfenberg, and Franz X. Bogner. 2016. "Instructional Efficiency of Different Discussion Approaches in an Outreach Laboratory: Teacher-Guided Versus Student-Centered." *Journal of Educational Research* 109 (1): 27–36. https://doi.org/10.1080/00220671.2014.91760.

Goodstein, Lynne. 1994. "Achieving Multicultural Curriculum: Conceptual, Pedagogical and Structural Issues." *Journal of General Education* 43 (2): 102–16. https://www.jstor.org/stable/27797217.

Gordon, Heather Sauyaq Jean, and Ranjan Datta. 2021. "Indigenous Communities Defining and Utilizing Self-Determination as an Individual and Collective Capability." *Journal of Human Development and Capabilities* 23 (2): 182–295. https://doi.org/10.1080/19452829.2021.1966613.

Government Yearbook. 1953. Government Year Book. [In Hebrew.] Jerusalem: Government's Printer.

———. 1961. Government Year Book. [In Hebrew.] Jerusalem: Government's Printer.

———. 1972. Government Year Book. [In Hebrew.] Jerusalem: Government's Printer.

———. 1975. Government Year Book. [In Hebrew.] Jerusalem: Government's Printer.

Gramsci, Antonio. 1971. *Selections from the Prison Notebooks of Antonio Gramsci*. Edited and Translated by Quintin Hoare and Geoffrey Nowell Smith. London: Lawrence and Wishart.

Greenhow, Christine, Cathy Lewin, and K. Bret Staudt Willet. 2021. "The Educational Response to Covid-19 Across Two Countries: A Critical Examination of Initial Digital Pedagogy Adoption." *Technology, Pedagogy and Education* 30 (1): 7–25. https://doi.org/10.1080/1475939X.2020.1866654.

Grek, S. 2009. "Governing by Numbers: The PISA 'Effect' in Europe." *Journal of Education Policy* 24 (1): 23–37.

Gross, M., and L. Terra. 2018. "What Makes Difficult History Difficult?" *Kapan* (May): 51–56.

Grossman, Herbert. 1995. *Teaching in a Diverse Society*. Boston: Ally and Bacon.

Grubbs, Samuel Jacob. 2020. "Does Cooling Out Still Apply? Community Colleges and Educational Expectations." *Community College Journal of Research and Practice* 44 (10–12): 819–34. https://doi.org/10.1080/10668926.2020.172 4573.

Guri-Rosenblit, S. 1999. "Changing Boundaries in Israeli Higher Education." *Mediterranean Journal of Educational Studies* 4:91–114.

Gutierrez, L., R. J. Parsons, and E. O. Cox. 1998. *Empowerment Social Work Practice: A Source Book*. Pacific Grove, CA: Brooks/Cole.

Gutierrez, Rhoda Rae, and Pauline Lipman. 2016. "Toward Social Movement Activist Research." *International Journal of Qualitative Studies in Education* 29 (10): 1241–54. https://doi.org/10.1080/09518398.2016.1192696.

Guttman, Emanuel, and Davis Hes. 1960. "The Four Arab Villages." *Public Administration in Israel and Abroad* 1: 83–90. Jerusalem: Hebrew University.

Habiballah, Muhammad. 1984. "Elementary Education: Level and Curricula." In *The Arab Education in Israel: Issues and Demands*, 21–35. [In Arabic.] A Conference Report. The National Committee of the Heads of Arab Local Authorities and Directors of Education Departments. Nazareth: Dar el-Nahdah.

Habiballah, Muhammad, and Atallah Copti, editors. 1991. *Education and the Arab Minority in Israel: Situation, Problems, and Needs*. [In Arabic.] Haifa: al-Karmeh.

Haddad Haj-Yahia, Nasreen, and Arik Rudentzky. 2018. "The Arab Education System in Israel: Situation and Future Challenges." [In Hebrew.] Jerusalem: Israeli Democracy Institute.

Hager, Tamar, and Yousef Jabareen. 2016. "From Marginalisation to Integration: Arab-Palestinians in Israeli Academia." *International Journal of Inclusive Education* 20 (5): 455–73. https://doi.org/10.1080/13603116.2015.1090488.

Haimovich, Talia, and G. Ben-Shakhar. 2004. "Matriculation Certificate (Bagrut) Grades and Psychometric Entrance Test (PET) Scores as Predictors of Graduation and Attrition." [In Hebrew.] *Megamot* 33 (3): 446–70.

Haj-Yahia, Muhammad, and Dorit Roer-Strier. 1999. "On the Encounter between Jewish Supervisees in Israel." *Clinical Supervisor* 18 (2): 17–37.

Haj-Yahia, Nasreen, and Yoav Lavee. 2018. "Division of Labor and Decision-Making in Arab Families in Israel: Processes of Change and Preservation." *Marriage and Family Review* 54 (1): 15–33. https://doi.org/10.1080/01494929.2017.1283384.

Haj-Yehia, Kussai. 2013. "Higher Education among Arab Students from Israel: The Dilemma of Studying in an Israeli University or Abroad." *Romanian Journal of Society and Politics* 8 (1): 37–54.

Haj-Yehia, Kussai, and Khaled Arar. 2016. "Palestinian Students from Israel Studying at a Palestinian University in West Bank-Palestine." *Journal of Applied Research in Higher Education* 8 (4): 504–21.

———. 2022. "The Global Mobility of Palestinian Arab Students: Current Trends and Flows." *Higher Education Governance and Policy* 3 (2): 89–101.

Haklai, Oded. 2009. "State Mutability and Ethnic Civil Society: The Palestinian Arab Minority in Israel." *Ethnic and Racial Studies* 32 (5): 864–82. https://doi.org/10.1080/01419870802270917.

Halabi, Rabah. 2016. "Arab Students in a Hebrew University—Existing but Unnoticed." *Intercultural Education* 27 (6): 560–76. https://doi.org/10.1080/14675986.2016.1262131.

Hall, Caroline, Martin Lundin, and Kristina Sibbmark. 2020. "Strengthening Teachers in Disadvantaged Schools: Evidence from an Intervention in Sweden's Poorest City Districts." *Scandinavian Journal of Educational Research* 66 (2): 208–24. https://doi.org/10.1080/00313831.2020.1788154.

Hanna, Ilham. 1997. "The Mobile Community Center Provides its Services to Villages Rich in their Children's Skills." [In Arabic.] *Al-Sinnara*, November 21, 1997.

Harpaz, Yossi, and Ikhlas Nassar. 2021. "Crossing Borders, Choosing Identity: Strategic Self-Presentation among Palestinian-Israelis Travelling Abroad." *Ethnic and Racial Studies* 45 (12): 2340–61. https://doi.org/10.1080/01419870.2021.2008465.

Hassanin, Sai'd. 2003. "INSANN's Festival for Creativity." [In Arabic.] *Kul el-Arab*, May 30, 2003.

Hassib, Khair el-Din. 2013. *The Arab Spring: Critical Analysis*. Beirut: Center for Arab Unity and Routledge.

Hatzikidi, Katerina, Corinne Lennox, and Alexandra Xanthaki. 2021. "Cultural and Language Rights of Minorities and Indigenous Peoples." *The International Journal of Human Rights* 25 (5): 743–51. https://doi.org/10.1080/13642987.2020.1859487.

Hayes, Aneta, Kathy Luckett, and Greg Misiaszek. 2021. "Possibilities and Complexities of Decolonising Higher Education: Critical Perspectives on Praxis." *Teaching in Higher Education* 26 (7–8): 887–901. https://doi.org/10.1080/13562517.2021.1971384.

Heath, Anthony, and Neli Demireva. 2014. "Has Multiculturalism Failed in Britain?" *Ethnic and Racial Studies* 37 (1): 161–80. https://doi.org/10.1080/01419870.2013.808754.

Hermessi, Tarek. 2022. "Motivation for Learning EFL in Tunisia: An Eclectic Theoretical Approach and a Structural Equation Modeling Approach." *Innovation in Language Learning and Teaching* 17 (2): 1–19. https://doi.org/10.1080/17501229.2021.2012477.

Hitman, Gadi. 2021. "Together We Stand, Divided We Fall: The Arab Minority in Israel's General Elections, 2019–20." *Israel Affairs* 27 (2): 284–99. https://doi.org/10.1080/13537121.2021.1891502.

Hourani, B. R. 2010. *What Palestine Do We Teach? The History Curriculum for Palestinian Arabs, 1961–1999*. Saarbrucken: Lap Lambert Academic Publishing.

Hout, Michael. 1988. "More Universalism, Less Structural Mobility: The American Occupational Structure in the 1980s." *American Journal of Sociology* 93 (6): 1358–1400.

———. 2012. "Social and Economic Returns to College Education in the United States." *Annual Review of Sociology* 38:379–400.

Howe, Lori, and Ann Van Wig. 2017. "Metacognition via Creative Writing: Dynamic Theories of Learning Support Habits of the Mind in 21st Century Classrooms." *Journal of Poetry Therapy* 30 (3): 139–52. https://doi.org/10.1080/08893675.2017.1328830.

Hussein, Rashid. 1957. "The Arab School in Israel." *New Outlook* 5 (November–December): 44–48.

INSANN–Association for Education and Culture. 1992. *The First Annual Report.* [In Arabic.] Shefa-'Amr: Elmashreq Publishing House.

———. 1993. *The Second Annual Report.* [In Arabic.] Shefa-'Amr: Elmashreq Publishing House.

Ismailova, Baktygul. 2004. "Curriculum Reform in Post-Soviet Kyrgyzstan: Indigenization of the History Curriculum." *Curriculum Journal* 15, no. 3 (Autumn): 247–64. https://doi-org.ezproxy.haifa.ac.il/10.1080/09585170412331311501.

Israel Government, Civil Service Commission. 2021. *Report for 2021.* [In Hebrew.] Jerusalem.

Israel Medical Association. 2016. "A Shortage of Physicians." [In Hebrew.] https://www.ima.org.il/heskem/ViewCategory.aspx?CategoryId=5505.

Israel, National Insurance Institute. 2018. *Annual Report on Poverty.* [In Hebrew.] Jerusalem: National Insurance Institute.

Jabareen, Yehia A. 2019. "Dr. Sharaf Hassan Speaking to 'Bokra' On Preparations Towards the School Year." *Bokra*, August 27, 2019. https://www.bokra.net/Article-1418570.

Jabareen, Yousef T., and Ayman K. Agbaria. 2017. "Minority Educational Autonomy Rights: The Case of Arab-Palestinian in Israel." *Virginia Journal of Social Policy and the Law* 24 (1): 26–55.

Jackson, S. E., Richard L. Schwab, and Randall S. Schuler. 1986. "Toward an Understanding of the Burnout Phenomenon." *Journal of Applied Psychology* 71 (4): 630–40.

Jansen, Jonathan D., editor. 2019. *Decolonisation in Universities: The Politics of Knowledge.* Johannesburg, SA: Wits University Press.

Jenks, Charles, James O. Lee, and Barry Kanpol. 2001. "Approaches to Multicultural Education in Preservice Teacher Education: Philosophical Frameworks and Models for Teaching." *The Urban Review* 33 (2): 87–105.

Jennings, L. B., D. M. Parra-Medina, D. K. H. Messias, and K. McLoughlin. 2006. "Toward a Critical Social Theory of Youth Empowerment." *Journal of Community Practice* 14:31–55.

Jiryis, Sabri. 1976. *The Arabs in Israel.* New York: Monthly Review Press.

Johnston, Bill. 1985. "Organizational Structure and Ideology in Schooling." *Educational Theory* 35:333–43.

Jones, Steve. 2006. *Antonio Gramsci.* Oxford: Routledge. Created from Haifa University Library, July 10, 2023. http://ebookcentral.proquest.com/lib/haifa/detail.action?docID=292760.

Joppke, C. 2004. "The Retreat of Multiculturalism in the Liberal State: Theory and Policy." *British Journal of Sociology* 55 (2): 237–57.

Jorgensen, S. L. 2015. "The History We Need: Strategies of Citizen Formation in the Danish History Curriculum." *Scandinavian Journal of Educational Research* 59 (4): 443–60. https://doi.org/10.1080/00313831.2014.907200.

Joseph, Rigaud. 2020. "The Theory of Empowerment: A Critical Analysis with the Theory Evaluation Scale." *Journal of Human Behavior in the Social Environment* 30 (2): 138–57. https://doi.org/10.1080/10911359.2019.1660294.

Kaldor, Mary. 2003. "Civil Society and Accountability." *Journal of Human Development* 4 (1): 5–27. https://doi.org/10.1080/1464988032000051469.

Kanaana, Sharif. 1975. *Survival Strategies of Arabs in Israel.* Birzeit: Birzeit University Publications.

Karpat, Kemal. 1988. "The Ottoman Ethnic and Confessional Legacy in the Middle East." In *Ethnicity, Pluralism and State in the Middle East,* edited by Milton Esman and Itamar Rabinovich. Ithaca, NY: Cornell University Press.

Karppinen, Kari, Hallvard Moe, and Jakob Svensson. 2008. "Habermas, Mouffe and Political Communication." *Javnost: The Public* 15 (3): 5–21. https://doi.org/10.1080/13183222.2008.11008973.

Katz, Yaacov J. 1999. "The Development of State Religious Education in Israel." *Paedagogica Historica* 35 (suppl. 1): 369–77. https://doi.org/10.1080/00309230.1999.11434950.

Kenneth Cohen, T. 2001. *Differential Prediction and Differential Validity of the University Admission System According to the Socio-Economic Status of the Candidates* (Report No. 285). [In Hebrew.] Jerusalem: National Center for Examinations and Assessment.

Kenneth Cohen, T., S. Bronner, and C. Oren. 1999. "The Predictive Validity of the Components of the Process of Selection of Candidates for Higher Education in Israel." [In Hebrew.] *Megamot* 40:54–71.

Khaizran, Yusri. 2020. "Arab Society in Israel and the 'Arab Spring.'" *Journal of Muslim Minority Affairs* 40 (2): 284–301. https://doi.org/10.1080/13602004.2020.1777664.

Khalaily, Muhammed, and As'ad Ghanem. 2023. "The Politics of Faith among the Palestinian-Arab Minority in Israel: Increasing Human Capital and Public Engagement." *Middle East Critique.* https://doi.org/10.1080/19436149.2023.2226887.

Khalidi, Rashid. 1997. *Palestinian Identity.* New York: Colombia University Press.

Khanolainen, Daria, Yulia Nesterova, and Elena Semenova. 2020. "Indigenous Education in Russia: Opportunities for Healing and Revival of the Mari and Karelian Indigenous Groups?" *Compare: A Journal of Comparative and International Education* 25 (5): 768–85. https://doi.org/10.1080/03057925. 2020.1834350.

Kim, Youb, Jennifer D. Turner, and Pamela A. Mason. 2015. "Getting into the Zone: Cases of Student-Centered Multicultural Literacy Teacher Education." *Action in Teacher Education* 37 (2): 102–19. https://doi.org/10.1080/01626 620.2015.1013162.

Kimhi, Ayal. 2010. "Jewish Households, Arab Households, and Income Inequality in Rural Israel: Ramifications for the Israeli-Arab Conflict." *Defense and Peace Economics* 21 (4): 381–94. https://doi.org/10.1080/10242694.2010.491717.

Kimmerling, Baruch. 1998. "The New Israelis: Multiple Cultures with No Multi-culturalism." [In Hebrew.] *Alpayim* 16: 264–308..

———. 2001. *The Invention and Decline of Israeliness: State, Society and Military.* Berkeley: University of California Press.

———. 2004. *Immigrants, Settlers, Natives: The State and Society between Cultural Pluralism and Cultural Wars.* [In Hebrew.] Tel Aviv: Am Oved.

———. 2016. "Patterns of Militarism in Israel." In Ben-Rafael et al., *Handbook of Israel: Major Debates*, 609–35.

Kincheloe, J. L. 2007. "Critical Pedagogy in the Twenty-First Century: Evolution for Survival." In *Critical Pedagogy: Where Are We Now?*, edited by P. McLaren and J. L. Kincheloe, 9–42. New York: Peter Lang.

Kizel, A. 2008. *Subservient History: A Critical Analysis of History Curricula and Textbooks in Israel, 1948–2006.* [In Hebrew.] Tel Aviv: Mofet Institute Press.

Kleibl, Tanja, and Ronaldo Munck. 2017. "Civil Society in Mozambique: NGOs, Religion, Politics and Witchcraft." *Third World Quarterly* 38 (1): 203–18. https://doi.org/10.1080/01436597.2016.1217738.

Knesset. 2018. "The Nationality Law Has Been Finally Approved." [In Hebrew.] Press Release, July 19, 2018. https://main.knesset.gov.il/News/PressReleases/Pages/press19.07.18.aspx.

Kosko, Stacy J. 2013. "Agency Vulnerability, Participation, and the Self-Determination of Indigenous Peoples." *Journal of Global Ethics* 9 (3): 293–310. https://doi.org/10.1080/17449626.2013.818385.

Kremnitzer, Mordechai, and Amir Fuchs. 2016. "The Non-Separation of Religion and State in Israel: Does It Support the Racism and Nationalism Wave?" In Ben-Rafael et al., *Handbook of Israel: Major Debates*, 181–95.

Kupileivitch, Emanuel. 1973. "Education in the Arab Sector: Facts and Problems." [In Hebrew.] In *The Education in Israel*, edited by Haim Urimian. Jerusalem: Ministry of Education and Culture.

Kymlicka, Will. 1995. *Multicultural Citizenship.* Oxford: Clarendon Press.

———. 2007a. *Multicultural Odysseys: Navigating the New International Politics of Diversity*. Oxford: Oxford University Press.

———. 2007b. "The New Debate on Minority Rights (and Postscript)." In *Multiculturalism and Political Theory*, edited by Anthony Simon Laden and David Owen, 25–59. New York: Cambridge University Press.

———. 2010. "Testing the Liberal Multiculturalist Hypothesis: Normative Theories and Social Science." *Canadian Journal of Political Science* 43 (2): 257–71.

———. 2018. "The Rise and Fall of Multiculturalism? New Debates on Inclusion and Accommodation in Diverse Societies." *International Social Science Journal* 68 (227–28): 133–48.

Kyriacou, C. 1981. "Social Support and Occupational Stress among School Teachers." *Educational Studies* 7:55–60.

———. 1987. "Teacher Stress and Burnout: An International Review." *Educational Research* (2): 146–52.

Ladegaard, Hans J., and Alison Phipps. 2020. "Intercultural Research and Social Activism." *Language and Intercultural Communication* 20 (2): 67–80. https://doi.org/10.1080/14708477.2020.1729786.

Lavian, Rivka Hillel. 2012. "The Impact of Organizational Climate on Burnout among Homeroom Teachers and Special Education Teachers (Full Classes/Individual Pupils) in Mainstream Schools." *Teachers and Teaching* 18 (2): 233–47. https://doi.org/10.1080/13540602.2012.632272.

Lave, J., and E. Wenger. 1991. *Situated Learning: Legitimate Peripheral Participation*. Cambridge, MA: Cambridge University Press.

Lavy, Victor. 1998. "Disparities between Arabs and Jews in School Resources and Student Achievement in Israel." *Economic Development and Cultural Change* 47 (1): 175–92.

Law, Ian. 2014. "Theories of Multiculturalism: An Introduction; A Book Review." *Ethnic and Racial Studies* 37 (10): 1963–66. https://doi.org/10.1080/01419870.2014.911348.

Layish, Aharon. 1966. "The Muslim Waqf in Israel." *Asian and African Studies* 2, 41–76.

Lehmann, David. 2012. "Israel: State Management of Religion or Religious Management of the State?" *Citizenship Studies* 16 (8): 1029–43. https://doi.org/10.1080/13621025.2012.735027.

Leiter, M. P., and C. Maslach. 1988. "The Impact of Interpersonal Environment on Burnout and Organizational Commitment." *Journal of Organizational Behavior* 9 (4): 297–308. https://doi.org/10.1002/ job.4030090402.

Levinson, M. 2012. *No Citizen Left Behind*. Cambridge, MA: Harvard University Press.

Lewin-Epstein, Noah. 1990. "The Arab Economy in Israel: Growing Population, Jobs Mismatch." Discussion Paper No. 14, 90. Tel Aviv: Pinhas Sapir Center for Development, Tel Aviv University.

Lewin-Epstein, Noah, Majid Al-Haj, and Moshe Semyonov. 1994. *Arabs in Israel in the Labor Market*. [In Hebrew.] Jerusalem: Floersheimer Institute for Policy Studies.

Lewin-Epstein, Noah, and Moshe Semyonov. 1986. "Ethnic Group Mobility in the Israeli Labor Market." *American Sociological Review* 51 (June): 342–51.

———. 1993. *The Arab Minority in Israel's Economy: Patterns of Ethnic Inequality*. Boulder, CO: Westview Press.

Lightfoot, Sheryl R. 2010. "Emerging International Indigenous Rights Norms and 'Over-Compliance' in New Zealand and Canada." *Political Science* 62 (1): 84–104. https://doi.org/10.1177/0032318710370584.

Liebskind, Kalman. 2015. "The Ministry of Education Should Present a Clear Position: If We Had Not Won That War, We Would Not Be Here Today." [In Hebrew.] *Ma'ariv*, March 28, 2015. https://www.maariv.co.il/journalists/journalists/Article-469831.

Lim, Leonel. 2016. "Analysing Meritocratic (In)Equality in Singapore: Ideology, Curriculum and Reproduction." *Critical Studies in Education* 57 (2): 160–74. https://doi.org/10.1080/17508487.2015.1055777.

Lim, Leonel, and Michael Tan. 2020. "Meritocracy, Policy and Pedagogy: Culture and the Politics of Recognition and Redistribution in Singapore." *Critical Studies in Education* 61 (3): 279–95. https://doi.org/10.1080/17508487.2018.1450769.

Litosseliti, Lia. 2003. *Using Focus Groups in Research*. London: Continuum.

Livnat, Ofer. 2019. "The Gaps between the Jewish and Arab Students: The Ministry of Education Was Surprised How Deep Was the Crisis." [In Hebrew.] *Ma'ariv*, December 3, 2019. https://maariv.co.il/news/Education/Article-733142.

Lorenz, Dalia. 2020. "My Unique Poem Is Me: Our Poems Are Universal; A Creative Interactive Poetry Therapy Inquiry." *Journal of Poetry Therapy* 33 (4): 252–64. https://doi.org/10.1080/08893675.2020.1803617.

Loury, L. D. 2006. "Some Contacts Are More Equal Than Others: Informal Networks, Job Tenure, and Wages." *Journal of Labor Economics* 24:299–318.

Lucas, Samuel R. 2001. "Effectively Maintained Inequality: Education Transitions, Track Mobility and Social Background Effects." *American Journal of Sociology* 106 (6): 1642–90. https://doi.org/10.1086/321300.

———. 2009. "Stratification Theory, Socioeconomic Background, and Educational Attainment: A Formal Analysis." *Rationality and Society* 21:459–511.

Luleci, C., and A. Coruk. 2018. "The Relationship between Morale and Job Satisfaction of Teachers in Elementary and Secondary Schools." *Educational Policy Analysis and Strategic Research* 13 (1): 45–70. https://doi.org/10.29329/epasr.2018.137.3.

Lustick, Ian. 1980. *Arabs in the Jewish State: Israel's Control of a National Minority*. Austin: University of Texas Press.

Macklem, Patrick. 2008. "Indigenous Recognition in International Law: Theoretical Observations." *Michigan Journal of International Law* 30:177, 207.

Mada al-Carmel. 2007. The Haifa Declaration. Haifa. https://mada-research.org/storage/uploads/2020/06/haifaenglish.pdf.

Maeroff, Gene I. 1988. *The Empowerment of Teachers: Overcoming the Crisis of Confidence.* New York: Teachers College Press.

Magal, Tamir, Daniel Bar-Tal, and Eran Halperin. 2016. "Why Is It So Difficult to Resolve the Israeli-Palestinian Conflict by Israeli Jews? A Socio-Psychological Approach." In Ben-Rafael et al., *Handbook of Israel: Major Debates*, 1211–39.

Magaldi, Danielle Timothy Conway, and Leora Trub. 2018. "I Am Here for a Reason: Minority Teachers Bridging Many Divides in Urban Education." *Race Ethnicity and Education* 21 (3): 306–18. https://doi.org/10.1080/13613324.2016.1248822.

Mahajne, Ibrahim, and Arnon Bar-on. 2022. "Arabization of Social Work in Israel's Native Arab Minority: Potential and Obstacles." *Social Work Education* 41 (6): 1109–22. https://doi.org/10.1080/02615479.2021.1933930.

Makransky, Guido, Philip Havmose, Maria Louison Vang, Tonny Elmose Andersen, and Tine Nielsen. 2017. "The Predictive Validity of Using Admissions Testing and Multiple Mini-Interviews in Undergraduate University Admissions." *Higher Education Research Development* 36 (5): 1003–16. https://doi.org/10.1080/07294360.2016.1263832.

Maldonado-Torres, Nelson. 2007. "On the Coloniality of Being." *Cultural Studies* 21 (2–3): 240–70.

Mangum, Maruice, and Ray Block Jr. 2021. "Perceived Racial Discrimination, Racial Resentment, and Support for Affirmative Action and Preferential Hiring and Promotion: A Multi-Racial Analysis." *Politics, Groups, and Identities* 10 (4): 674–95. https://doi.org/10.1080/21565503.2021.1892781.

Mardones, Juan Gallegos, and Nelyda Campos-Requena. 2021. "Can Higher Education Admission be More Equitable? Evidence Supporting the Inclusion of Relative Ranking in the Process." *Economic Research-Ekonomska Istraživanja* 34 (1): 2539–54. https://doi.org/10.1080/1331677X.2020.1833745.

Margalioth, Sharon Rabin. 2004. "Labor Market Discrimination Against Arab Israeli Citizens: Can Something Be Done?" *New York University Journal of International Law and Politics* 36 (4): 845–84. https://www.nyujilp.org/print-edition/volumes-40-31/.

Margolis, Eric, and Mary Romero. 1998. "The Department is Very Male, Very White, Very Old, and Very Conservative: The Functioning of the Hidden Curriculum in Graduate Sociology Departments." *Harvard Educational Review* 68 (1): 1–33.

Mari, Mariam. 1988. "The Arab School and Actual Issues." [In Arabic.] In *Identity, Co-Existence and Contents of Education*, 95–103. A report of a Study Day conducted on August 22, 1988. Haifa: National Committee for Heads of Arab Local Authorities and the Follow-Up Committee on Arab Education.

Mari, Sami. 1974. "The School and Society in the Arab Village in Israel." [In Hebrew.] *Iyonim Bahinukh* 4 (June): 85–104.

———. 1978. *Arab Education in Israel.* Syracuse, NY: Syracuse University Press.

Marri, A. R. 2003. "Multicultural Democracy: Toward a Better Democracy." *International Education* 14 (3): 263–77. https://doi.org/10.1080/1467598032000117060.

Martin, Todd Forrest. 2020. "Toward a Theory of Fertility and Ethnic Social Capital." *Marriage and Family Review* 56 (1): 1–19. https://doi.org/10.1080/01494929.2019.1630046.

Maslach, C., and S. F. Jackson. 1981. "The Measurement of Experienced Burnout." *Journal of Occupational Behavior* 2:99–113.

Maslach, C., S. E. Jackson, and M. P. Leiter. 2018. *Maslach Burnout Inventory: Manual.* 4th ed. Menlo Park, CA: Mind Garden.

Maslach, C., and M. P. Leiter. 2016. "Understanding the Burnout Experience: Recent Research and Its Implications for Psychiatry." *World Psychiatry* 15 (2): 103–11. https://doi.org/10.1002/wps.20311.

Maslach, C., W. B. Schaufeli, and M. P. Leiter. 2001. "Job Burnout." *Annual Review of Psychology* 52:397–422.

Matar, Midhat. 2016. *The Arab Spring: Reality vs. Imagination.* [In Arabic.] Amman: Jordan, Dorub Thakafya.

May, Paul. 2021. "Canada: The Standard Bearer of Multiculturalism in the World? An Analysis of the Canadian Public Debate on Multiculturalism (2010–2020)." *Ethnic and Racial Studies* 45 (10): 1939–60. https://doi.org/10.1080/01419870.2021.1977366.

Mazawi, Andre. 1994. "Palestinian Arabs in Israel: Educational Expansion, Social Mobility and Political Control." *Compare* 24 (3): 277–84.

Mazza, Nicholas. 2012. "Poetry/Creative Writing for an Arts and Athletics Community Outreach Program for At-Risk Youth." *Journal of Poetry Therapy* 25 (4): 225–31. https://doi.org/10.1080/08893675.2012.73849.

Mazuz-Harpaz, Y., and Z. Krill. 2016. "The High-Tech Leap." [In Hebrew.] Chief Economist Division. Jerusalem: Ministry of Finance.

Mbembe, Achille. 2016. "Decolonising the University: New Directions." *Arts and Humanities in Higher Education* 15 (1): 29–45.

McGrath, K. F., and P. van Bergen. 2015. "Who, When, Why and to What End? Students at Risk of Negative Student-Teacher Relationships and Their Outcomes." *Educational Research Review* 14:1–17. https://doi.org/10.1016/j.edurev.2014.12.001.

McKenzie, Kirsten, and Robert Schweitzer. 2001. "Who Succeeds at University? Factors Predicting Academic Performance in First Year Australian University Students." *Higher Education Research and Development* 20 (1): 21–33. https://doi.org/10.1080/07924360120043621.

McLaren, Peter. 2000. *Che Guevara, Paulo Freire, and the Pedagogy of Revolution*. Boulder, CO: Rowman and Littlefield.

McNamee, S. J., and R. K. Miller. 2018. *The Meritocracy Myth*. 4th ed. Lanham, MD: Rowman and Littlefield.

Meir, Abinoam, and Dov Barnia. 1987. "Spatial Aspects and Structural Changes in the Educational System of the Bedouins in the Negev." [In Hebrew.] *Hivra Verivaha* 2:157–67.

Meoded Karabanov, Galia, Merav Asaf, Margalit Ziv, and Dorit Aram. 2021. "Parental Behaviors and Involvement in Children's Digital Activities among Israeli Jewish and Arab Families during the COVID-19 Lockdown." *Early Education and Development* 32 (6): 881–902. https://doi.org/10.1080/1040 9289.2021.1882810.

Mignolo, Walter D. 2007. "Introduction." *Cultural Studies* 21 (2–3): 155–67. https://doi.org/10.1080/09502380601162498.

Ministry of Education and Culture. 1975. *Report of the Arab Education Team*. [In Hebrew.] Mimeographed. Jerusalem: Planning Project of Education in the Eighties, Ministry of Education and Culture.

———. 1977. *Director General's Circular*. [In Hebrew.] Mimeographed. Jerusalem: Ministry of Education and Culture.

———. 1982. *The Curriculum of Teaching History in the Arab High Schools*. [In Arabic.] Jerusalem: Center for School Curricula, Ministry of Education and Culture.

———. 1983. *Director General's Circular 1983*. [In Hebrew.] Jerusalem: Ministry of Education and Culture.

———. 1985. *Report of the Committee for the Examination of the Arab Education*. [In Hebrew.] Mimeographed. Committee of the Directors Generals for Educational Alternatives. Jerusalem: Ministry of Education and Culture.

———. 1987. *The System of Education and Culture for Druze*. [In Hebrew.] Mimeographed. Jerusalem: Ministry of Education and Culture.

———. 1988. *How Can We Deal with the Actual Issues? Ministry of Education, The Unit for Democracy and Coexistence*. [In Hebrew and Arabic.] Mimeographed. Jerusalem: Ministry of Education and Culture.

———. 1997. *Matriculation Exam Data 1995/96, 1996/97*. [In Hebrew.] Pedagogical Administration Examinations Division and Systems Information Management Department. Jerusalem: Ministry of Education.

———. 1998. *History Curriculum for Grades Seven to Nine in the State Stream*. [In Hebrew.] 2nd revised ed. Jerusalem: Ministry of Education and Culture, Pedagogic Secretariat.

———. 1999a. *History for Senior High School (Grades 10–12) in Arab Schools*. [In Hebrew.] Jerusalem: Ministry of Education, Culture, and Sport.

———. 1999b. *Senior High School History Curriculum Committee of the Ministry of Education*. [In Hebrew.] Jerusalem: Ministry of Education, Culture, and Sport.

Ministry of Education. 2000. *Director General's Circular.* [In Hebrew.] October 2, 2000. Jerusalem: Ministry of Education.

———. 2024. *The Site of Druze and Circassian Education.* [In Hebrew.] https://edu.gov.il/mazhap/DruzeCircassianEdu/Pages/hp.aspx.

———. 2012. *Director-General's Circular.* [In Hebrew.] November 1, 2012. Jerusalem: Ministry of Education.

Ministry of Education and Shkifut Bachinch. 2022. Facts and Statistics. Jerusalem: Ministry of Education. [In Hebrew.] https://shkifut.education.gov.il/national.

Ministry of Minorities. 1949. *Report on the Minorities Ministry Activities.* [In Hebrew.] Mimeographed. May 1948–January 1949. Jerusalem: Ministry of Minorities.

MK Jabareen, Yousef. 2019. "Minister Bennett Distorts History in the Civics Textbook." *Bokra.* [In Arabic.] January 31, 2019. https://www.bokra.net/Article-1404911.

Moore, W. 2006. *Behind the Open Door: Racism and Other Contradictions in the Community College.* Victoria, BC: Trafford.

Morgan, David. 1998. *The Focus Group Guidebook.* Thousand Oaks, CA: Sage.

Mountford-Zimdars, Anna, and Joanne Moore. 2020. "Identifying Merit and Potential Beyond Grades: Opportunities and Challenges in Using Contextual Data in Undergraduate Admissions at Nine Highly Selective English Universities." *Oxford Review of Education* 46 (6): 752–69. https://doi.org/10.1080/03054985.2020.1785413.

Moussa Sidi, Nedjib. 2018. "The Crisis of Multiculturalism in Europe—A History." *Journal of Contemporary European Studies* 26 (1): 136–37. https://doi.org/10.1080/14782804.2018.1429226.

Mullen, Carol A. 2020. "De/colonization: Perspectives on/by Indigenous Populations in Global Canadian Contexts." *International Journal of Leadership in Education* 23 (6): 671–90. https://doi.org/10.1080/13603124.2019.1631986.

Murphy, Michael. 2014. "Self-Determination as a Collective Capability: The Case of Indigenous Peoples." *Journal of Human Development and Capabilities* 15 (4): 320–34. https://doi.org/10.1080/19452829.2013.878320.

Muslih, Muhammad. 1993. "Palestinian Civil Society." *Middle East Journal* 47, no. 2 (Spring): 258–74. https://www.jstor.org/stable/4328571.

Mustafa, Muhanad. 2009. *Psychometric Exam: Barrier to University Entrance for Arab Citizens of Israel.* Nazareth: Dirasat, Arab Center for Law and Policy and the Follow-Up Committee on Arab Education. English summary.

Nagayoshi, Kikuko. 2011. "Support of Multiculturalism, but for Whom? Effects of Ethno-National Identity on the Endorsement of Multiculturalism in Japan." *Journal of Ethnic and Migration Studies* 37 (4): 561–78. https://doi.org/10.1080/1369183X.2011.545272.

Nakhleh, Emile. 1977. *The Arabs in Israel and Their Role in a Future Arab-Israeli Conflict: A Perception Study.* Mimeographed. Alexandria, VA: Abott Association.

Nakhleh, Khalil. 1975. "Cultural Determinants of Palestinian Collective Identity: The Case of the Arabs in Israel." *New Outlook* 18, no. 7 (October/November): 31–40.

Nardi, Noah. 1945. *Education in Palestine 1920–1945*. New York: Zionist Organization of America.

Näring, G., M. Briët, and A. Brouwers. 2006. "Beyond Demand–Control: Emotional Labour and Symptoms of Burnout in Teachers." *Work & Stress* 20 (4): 303–15. https://doi.org/10.1080/ 02678370601065182.

Nash, June. 2006. "Towards Pluricultural States." *Latin American and Caribbean Ethnic Studies* 1 (1): 125–40. https://doi.org/10.1080/17486830500510042.

National Committee for the Heads of the Arab Local Authorities. 2006. *The Future Vision of the Palestinian Arabs in Israel*. Nazareth. https://www.adalah.org/uploads/oldfiles/newsletter/eng/dec06/tasawor-mostaqbali.pdf.

National Committee for the Heads of the Arab Local Authorities and Committee for Directors of Education Departments. 1984. *The Arab Education in Israel: Issues and Demands*. [In Arabic.] Nazareth: Dar al-Nahdha.

National Committee for the Heads of the Arab Local Authorities and the Follow-Up Committee on Arab Education. 1986. *A Memorandum to the Minister of Education about Arab Education in Israel*. [In Hebrew.] Shefa-'Amr, January 1986.

———. 1989. *A Memorandum to the Minister of Education about Administration of Arab Education in Israel*. [In Hebrew.] Shefa-'Amr, August 1989.

Nesterova, Yulia. 2019. "Multiculturalism and Multicultural Education Approaches to Indigenous People's Education in Taiwan." *Multicultural Education Review* 11 (4): 253–70.

Nielson, Kai. 1995. "Reconceptualising Civil Society for Now: Some Somewhat Gramscian Turnings." In *Towards a Global Civil Society*, edited by Michael Walzer, 41–67. Providence, RI: Berghahn Books.

Nieto, Sonia. 2000. *Affirming Diversity: The Sociopolitical Context of Multicultural Education*. 3rd ed. New York: Longman.

Nieto, Sonia, and Patty Bode. 2008. *Affirming Diversity: The Sociopolitical Context of Multicultural Education*. 3rd ed. Boston: Pearson Education.

NITE (National Institute for Testing and Evaluation). 2001. *Multiyear Report, 2001 (1991–2000)*. [In Hebrew.] Jerusalem. https://www.nite.org.il/research-and-publications/statistical-data/.

NITE. 2005. *Annual Report 2005 (for 2004)*. [In Hebrew.] Jerusalem. https://www.nite.org.il/research-and-publications/statistical-data/.

NITE. 2013. *Annual Report 2013*. [In Hebrew.] Jerusalem. https://www.nite.org.il/research-and-publications/statistical-data/.

NITE. 2020. *Multiyear Report, 2020; Statistical Reports for 2006–2020*. [In Hebrew.] Jerusalem. https://www.nite.org.il/research-and-publications/statistical-data/.

Nóvoa, A., and T. Yariv-Mashal. 2003. "Comparative Research in Education: A Mode of Governance or a Historical Journey." *Comparative Education* 39 (4): 423–38.

Odello, Marco. 2012. "Indigenous Peoples' Rights and Cultural Identity in the Inter-American Context." *The International Journal of Human Rights* 16(1): 25–50. https://doi.org/10.1080/13642987.2011.597747

OECD (Organization for Economic Cooperation and Development). 2005. *Teachers Matter: Attracting, Developing, and Retaining Effective Teachers.* Paris: OECD, Centre for Educational Research and Innovation. https://doi.org/10.1787/9789264018044-en.

———. 2011. *Higher Education in Regional and City Development: The Galilee, Israel.* Paris: Centre for Educational Research and Innovation. https://doi.org/10.1787/9789264088986-en.

———. 2013. *Education at a Glance.* London: OECD Publications.

———. 2016. *Innovating Education and Educating for Innovation: The Power of Digital Technologies and Skills.* Paris: OECD Publishing. http://dx.doi.org/10.1787/9789264265097-en.

———. 2018. *OECD Economic Survey of Israel: Towards a More Inclusive Society.* Jerusalem, March 11, 2018. https://www.oecd.org/economy/surveys/Towards-a-more-inclusive-society-OECD-economic-survey-Israel-2018.pdf.

Offer, Shira, and Michal Sabah. 2011. "Individual and Familial Determinants of Married Arab Israeli Women's Labor Force Participation: Trends of Change and Stability." *Marriage and Family Review* 47 (5): 326–43. https://doi.org/10.1080/01494929.2011.594214.

Ogbu, John U. 1991. "Immigrant and Involuntary Minorities in Comparative Perspective." In *Minority Status and Schooling: A Comparative Study of Immigrant and Involuntary Minorities,* edited by Margaret A. Gibson and John U. Ogbu, 3–33. New York: Garland Publishing.

Ojong, Nathanael. 2020. "Indigenous Land Rights: Where Are We Today and Where Should the Research Go in the Future?" *Settler Colonial Studies* 10 (2): 193–15. https://doi.org/10.1080/2201473X.2020.1726149.

Olneck, Michael R. 1990. "The Recurring Dream: Symbolism and Ideology in Intercultural and Multicultural Education." *American Journal of Education* 98 (2): 147–74.

Oppenheimer, Jonathan. 1978. "The Druze in Israel as Arabs and Non-Arabs: An Essay on the Manipulation of Categories of Identity in a Non-Civil State." *Cambridge Anthropology* 4 (2): 23–44.

Ozacky-Lazar, Sarah. 1996. "The Crystallization of Mutual Relations between Jews and Arabs in the State of Israel: The First Decade, 1948–1958." PhD diss., University of Haifa.

———. 2002. "Military Government as a Control Apparatus of Arab Citizens." [In Hebrew.] *Hamizrah Hehadash* 43:104–32.

Pagano, Riccardo. 2017. "Culture, Education and Political Leadership in Gramsci's Thought." In *Antonio Gramsci: A Pedagogy to Change the World,* edited by Nicola Pizzolato and John D. Holst, 49–66. New York: Springer. https://link.springer.com/book/10.1007/978-3-319-40449-3.

Page, Nanette, and Cheryl E. Czuba. 1999. "Empowerment: What Is It?" *Journal of Extension* 37, no. 5 (October). https://archives.joe.org/joe/1999october/index.php.

Parker, W. 1996. "Curriculum for Democracy." In *Democracy, Education, and the Schools*, edited by Roger Soder, 182–210. San Francisco: Jossey-Bass.

Pavlidou, Kyriaki, Anastasia Alevriadou, and Alexander-Stamatios Antoniou. 2022. "Professional Burnout in General and Special Education Teachers: The Role of Interpersonal Coping Strategies." *European Journal of Special Needs Education* 37 (2): 191–205. https://doi.org/10.1080/08856257.2020.1857931.

Pearrow, Melissa M., and Stanley Pollack. 2009. "Youth Empowerment in Oppressive Systems: Opportunities for School Consultants." *Journal of Educational and Psychological Consultation* 19 (1): 45–60. https://doi.org/10.1080/10474410802494911.

Peres, Y., A. Erlich, and N. Yuval-Davis. 1968. "National Education for Arab Youth in Israel: A Comparative Analysis of Curricula." [In Hebrew.] *Megamot* 17 (1): 26–36.

Peres, Y., and N. Yuval-Davis. 1969. "Some Observations on the National Identity of the Israeli-Arab." *Human Relations* 22:219–33.

Perryman, Jane, Stephen Ball, Meg Maguire, and Annette Braun. 2011. "Life in the Pressure Cooker—School League Tables and English and Mathematics Teachers' Responses to Accountability in a Results-driven Era." *British Journal of Educational Studies* 59 (2): 179–95. https://doi.org/10.1080/00071005.2011.578568.

Phillips, Evelyn Newman. 1995. "Multicultural Education Beyond the Classroom." In *Multicultural Education, Critical Pedagogy, and the Politics of Difference*, edited by Christine Sleeter and Peter McLaren, 371–98. Albany: State University of New York Press.

Piketty, Thomas. 2020. *Capital and Ideology*. Cambridge, MA: Harvard University Press.

Pinson, Halleli. 2022. "Neo Zionist Right-Wing Populist Discourse and Activism in the Israel Education System." *Globalization, Societies and Education* 20 (2): 124–37. https://doi.org/10.1080/14767724.2021.1872372.

Presentense. 2020. *Main Findings: Survey of Arab Society on Entrepreneurship in Israel*. Presentense (Organization). https://presentense.org/2020-survey/.

Prime Minister's Office. 1955. *Report on Arab Education in Israel*. [In Arabic.] Jerusalem.

Quijano, Aníbal. 2007. "Coloniality and Modernity/Rationality." *Cultural Studies* 21 (2–3): 168–78. https://doi.org/10.1080/09502380601164353.

RAMA, Ministry of Education. 2018. *Meitzav, 2018: Efficiency and School Growth Indicators*. [In Hebrew.] Ramat Gan: RAMA.

———. 2019. *PISA 2018: Literacy among 15-Year Old Students in Reading, Math, and Sciences; Israeli View*. [In Hebrew.] December 2019. Ramat Gan: RAMA. https://meyda.education.gov.il/files/Rama/PISA_2018_Report.pdf.

———. 2020a. *Meitzav, 2018: Selected Findings*. [In Hebrew.] Ramat Gan: RAMA.

———. 2020b. *The Main Findings of the TIMMS Study, 2019: Achievements in Mathematics and Sciences of 8th Grades in Israel and Their Attitudes Towards Fields of Knowledge*. [Hebrew summary.] December 8, 2020. Ramat Gan: RAMA. https://meyda.education.gov.il/files/Rama/timss/TIMSS_2019_SUMMARY.pdf.

———. 2020c. *Remote Learning and Teaching: Insights from the Period of Closure in the Wake of the Corona Crisis*. [In Hebrew.] Ramat Gan: RAMA.

———. 2021. *Remote Learning and Teaching: Insights from the Period of Closure in the Wake of the Corona Crisis; Second Phase: A Parents' Survey, January–February 2021*. [In Hebrew.] Ramat Gan: RAMA.

Ransome, Paul. 1992. *Antonio Gramsci*: A New Introduction. New York: Harvester Wheatsheaf.

Rappaport, J. 1981. "In Praise of Paradox: A Social Policy of Empowerment Over Prevention." *American Journal of Community Psychology* 9:1–25.

———. 1984. "Studies in Empowerment: Introduction to the Issue." *Prevention in Human Services* 3:1–7.

Rebhun, Uzi, and Gilad Malach. 2012. "Demography, Social Prosperity, and the Future of Sovereign Israel." *Israel Affairs* 18 (2): 177–200. https://doi.org10. 1080/13537121.2012.659075.

Regmi, Kapil Dev. 2023. "Decolonising Meritocratic Higher Education: Key Challenges and Directions for Change." *Globalisation, Societies and Education*, 1–18. https://doi.org/10.1080/14767724.2023.2210516.

Reiter, Yitzhak. 2009. *National Minority, Regional Majority: Palestinian Arabs Versus Jews in Israel*. Syracuse, NY: Syracuse University Press. Reviewed by Paul Bera. 2011. *Shofar: An Interdisciplinary Journal of Jewish Studies* 29 (2): 198–200.

———. 2022. "No Need to Evacuate any Bedouin: The Solution is Different." [In Hebrew.] *Ynet*, January 19, 2022. https://www.ynet.co.il/news/article/syby184pf#autoplay.

Rekhess, Eli. 1973. *Survey of Minority Graduates of Higher Education Institutes*. [In Hebrew.] Tel Aviv: Sheluah Institute for the Research of the Middle East and Africa, Tel Aviv University.

———. 1976. "The Israeli Arabs After 1967: The Sharpening of the Orientation Problem." [In Hebrew.] In *Skerot*, 11–55. Sheluah Institute for the Research of the Middle East and Africa. Tel Aviv: Tel Aviv University.

———. 1977. *The Israeli Arabs and the Land Confiscations in the Galilee: Background, Events and Repercussions, 1975–1977*. [In Hebrew.] Tel Aviv: Sheluah Institute for the Research of the Middle East and Africa. Tel Aviv: Tel Aviv University.

———. 1988. "Socio-Political Implications of the Employment of Arab University Graduates." [In Hebrew.] In *The Employment Distress of Arab University Graduates in Israel*, edited by Majid Al-Haj, 49–55. Haifa: Jewish-Arab Center, University of Haifa.

———. 1989. "The Arabs in Israel and the Arabs in the Territories: A Political Linkage and National Solidarity (1967–1988)." [In Hebrew.] *Hamizrah Hehadash*, special issue, edited by Aharon Layish, 165–91.

———. 2002. "The Arabs of Israel After Oslo: Localization of the National Struggle." *Israel Studies* 7, no. 3 (Fall): 1–44.

———. 2007. "The Arab Minority and the 17th Knesset Elections: The Beginning of a New Era?" [In Hebrew.] In *The Arab Minority and the 17th Knesset Elections*, edited by Eli Rekhess, 57–72. Tel Aviv: Tel Aviv University.

Resnik, Julia. 1999. "Particularistic vis Universalistic Content in the Israeli Education System." *Curriculum Inquiry* 29 (4): 486–511.

———. 2006. "Alternative Identities in Multicultural Schools in Israel: Emancipatory Identity, Mixed Identity and Transnational Identity." *British Journal of Sociology of Education* 27 (5): 585–601. https://doi.org/10.1080/014256906009587.

Rissel, C. 1994. "Empowerment: The Holy Grail of Health Promotion." *Health Promotion International* 9 (1):39–47.

Roer-Strier, Dorit, and Muhammad M. Haj-Yahia. 1998. "Arab Students of Social Work in Israel: Adjustment Difficulties and Coping Strategies." *Social Work Education* 17 (4): 449–67. https://doi.org/10.1080/02615479811220431.

Rosenfeld, Henry. 1964. *They Were Peasants*. [In Hebrew.] Tel Aviv: Hakebbutz Hameuahad.

———. 1978. "The Class Situation of the Arab National Minority in Israel." *Comparative Studies in Society and History* 20(3): 374–407.

———. 1980. "Men and Women in Arab Peasant to Proletariat Transformation." In *Theory and Practice*, edited by Stanley Diamond, 195–219. The Hague: Mouton.

Rosenthal, A., and G. Ben-Shakhar. 1990. "The Validity of Annual Grades and Matriculation Exam Scores in Predicting Achievements at the Hebrew University of Jerusalem." [In Hebrew.] *Megamot* 32:416–83.

Rotem, Michal, and Neve Gordon. 2017. "Bedouin Sumud and the Struggle for Education." *Journal of Palestine Studies* 46 (4): 7–21. https://doi.org/10.1525/jps.2017.46.4.7.

Rouhana, Nadim. 1989. "The Political Transformation of the Palestinians in Israel: From Acquiescence to Challenge." *Journal of Palestine Studies* 18, no. 3 (Spring): 38–59.

———. 1997. *Identities in Conflict: Palestinian Citizens in an Ethnic Jewish State*. New Haven, CT: Yale University Press.

Rudge, David. 1993. "Bridging the Gaps in Arab Education." *The Jerusalem Post*, March 31, 1993.

Rudnitzky, Arik. 2016. "Back to the Knesset? Israeli Arab Vote in the 20th Knesset Elections." *Israel Affairs* 22 (3–4): 683–96. https://doi.org/10.1080/13537121.2016.1174384.

———. 2021. *The Voting of the Arab Citizens in the 24th Knesset Elections, March 2021*. Jerusalem: Israel Democracy Institute, April 4, 2021. https://www.idi.org.il/articles/34241.

Ryan, M. 2014. "Reflexivity and Aesthetic Inquiry: Building Dialogues between the Arts and Literacy." *English Teaching: Practice and Critique* 13:5–18.

Ryan, P. 2010. *Multicultiphobia*. Toronto: University of Toronto Press.

Sa'ar, Raley. 2001. "Instead of Psychometric Test, Weighting of Three Matriculation Scores: From Next Year, Admission to Universities Will be Possible Even Without a Psychometric." [In Hebrew.] *Haaretz*, January 25, 2001. https://www.haaretz.co.il/misc/2001-09-25/ty-article/0000017f-e6db-d97e-a37f-f7ffa7650000.

———. 2003. "Universities Return to Aptitude Exams to Keep Arabs Out." [In Hebrew.] *Haaretz*, November 27, 2003.

Saabneh, Ameed. 2019. "Displaced and Segregated: The Socio-economic Status of the Second Generation of Internally Displaced Palestinians in Israel." *Population Studies* 73 (1): 19–35. https://doi.org/10.1080/00324728.2018.1544658.

Saaresranta, Tiina. 2014. "Education in Pursuit of the Development Dream? Effects of Schooling on Indigenous Development and Rights in Bolivia." *Nordic Journal of Human Rights* 32 (4): 352–71. https://doi.org/10.1080/18918131.2015.957464.

Sabbagh, Clara, and Nura Resh. 2018. "World Culture and Social Justice in a Divided Society: Evaluations of Israeli Jewish and Arab Teachers and Students." *Globalisation, Societies and Education* 16 (4): 494–514. https://doi.org/10.1080/14767724.2018.1512046.

Sadeghi, Karim, and Sima Khezrlou. 2014. "Burnout among English Language Teachers in Iran: Do Socio-Demographic Characteristics Matter?" *Procedia: Social and Behavioral Sciences* 98:1590–98. https://doi.org/10.1016/j.sbspro.2014.03.582.

Sagi, Avi. 2016. "Religion and State in Israel." In Ben-Rafael et al., *Handbook of Israel: Major Debates*, 166–80.

SAI (Statistical Abstract of Israel). SAI 1972, no. 23; 1977, no. 28; 1981, no. 32; 1982, no. 33; 1984, no. 35; 1985, no. 36; 1986, no. 37; 1989, no. 40; 1990, no. 41; 1991, no. 42; 1995, no. 46; 1996, no. 47; 1997, no. 48; 2000, no. 51; 2007, no. 58; 2010, no. 61; 2018, no. 69; 2019, no. 70; 2020, no. 71; 2021, no. 72; 2022, no. 73.

Saito, Eisuke. 2023. "Collateral Damage in Education: Implications for the Time of COVID-19." *Discourse: Studies in the Cultural Politics of Education* 44 (1): 45–60. https://doi.org/10.1080/01596306.2021.1953443.

Salameh, George. 2009. *The Modern History of the Middle East*. [In Arabic.] Revised ed. Haifa: al-Karmah.

Salinas, Moises, and Johanna Garr. 2009. "Effect of Learner-Centered Education on the Academic Outcomes of Minority Groups." *Journal of Instructional Psychology* 36 (3): 226–37.

Sargent, Sarah. 2012. "Transnational Networks and United Nations Human Rights Structural Change: The Future of Indigenous and Minority Rights." *The International Journal of Human Rights* 16 (1): 123–51. https://doi.org/10.1080/13642987.2011.622126.

Sarid, Ariel, Kussai Haj-Yehia, Hait Shaham, and Amihai Rigbi. 2022. "Linking Demographic Variables to Motivation: Investigating the Motivation to Choose Teaching among Arab and Jewish Students in Israel." *European Journal of Teacher Education* 45 (1): 5–25. https://doi.org/10.1080/02619768.2020.1793945.

Sass, T. R., J. Hannaway, Z. Xu, D. N. Figlio, and L. Feng. 2012. "Value Added of Teachers in High-Poverty Schools and Lower Poverty Schools." *Journal of Urban Economics* 72 (2–3): 104–22. https://doi.org/10.1016/j.jue.2012.04.004.

Schaufeli, Wilmar B., and Bram P. Buunk. 2003. "Burnout: An Overview of 25 Years of Research and Theorizing." In *The Handbook of Work and Health Psychology*, edited by Marc J. Schabracq, Jacques A. M. Winnubst, and Cary L. Cooper, 383–425. Chichester, UK: Wiley.

Schleicher, A. 2018. *World Class: How to Build a 21st-Century School System*. Paris: OECD Publishing. https://doi.org/10.1787/9789264300002-en.

Schnell, Izhak, and Nasreen Haj-Yahya. 2014. "Arab Integration in Jewish-Israeli Social Space: Does Commuting Make a Difference?" *Urban Geography* 35 (7): 1084–1104. https://doi.org/10.1080/02723638.2014.929257.

Schultz, T. W. 1977. "Investment in Human Capital." In *Power and Ideology in Education*, edited by J. Karabel and A. H. Halsy, 313–24. New York: Oxford University Press.

Schwab, R. L., and S. F. Iwanicki. 1982. "Who Are Our Burnout Teachers?" *Educational Research Quarterly* 7:5–17.

Semyonov, M., and Andrea Tyree. 1981. "Community Segregation and the Costs of Ethnic Subordination." *Social Forces* 59 (3): 649–66.

Semyonov, Moshe, and Ephraim Yuchtman-Yaar. 1988. "Ethnicity, Education and Occupational Inequality: Jews and Arabs in Israel." [In Hebrew.] Discussion Paper No. 16–88. Tel Aviv: Pinhas Sapir Center for Development, Tel Aviv University.

Semyonov, Moshe, and Noah Lewin-Epstein. 2011. "Wealth Inequality: Ethnic Disparities in Israeli Society." *Social Forces* 89 (3): 935–59.

Shahar, Ilan. 2020. "How Much is Invested in Your Children's Education? Depends Where You Live." [In Hebrew.] *Hashomrim*, August 31, 2020. https://www.hashomrim.org/hebrew/336.

Shaik, Daphna. 2003. *Matriculation Exams: Review of the Changes that Have Taken Place in the Matriculation Exams Over the Years and a Discussion of Their Goals*. [In Hebrew.] Jerusalem: Knesset Research Center.

Shaked, Haim. 2020. "This Is How the Corona Deepens the Gaps in the Education System." [In Hebrew.] *Globes*, September 14, 2020. https://www.globes.co.il/news/article.aspx?did=1001342636.

Shdema, Ilan, Hisham M. Abu-Rayya, and Izhak Schnell. 2019. "The Interconnections between Socio-Spatial Factors and Labour Market Integration Among Arabs in Israel." *Papers in Regional Science* 98 (1): 497–514.

Sheffer, Gabriel, and Oren Barak. 2016. "Militaristic and Civil-Military Relations in Israel: A New Approach." In Ben-Rafael et al., *Handbook of Israel: Major Debates*, 590–608.

Shemesh, (Rash) Hana. 2009. "Shaping the Past in History Textbooks in Arab Schools in Israel (1948–2008)." [In Hebrew.] PhD diss, Hebrew University of Jerusalem.

Shor, Ira. 1992. *Empowering Education*. Chicago: University of Chicago Press.

Shwed, U., and Yossi Shavit. 2006. "Occupational and Economic Attainments of College and University Graduates in Israel." *European Sociological Review* 22:431–42. https://doi.org/10.1093/esr/jcl006.

Sieder, Rachel, and Anna Barrera Vivero. 2017. "Legalizing Indigenous Self-Determination: Autonomy and Buen Vivir in Latin America." *Journal of Latin American and Caribbean Anthropology* 22 (1): 9–26.

Sleeter, Christine E. 1992. *Keepers of the American Dream*. London: Falmer Press.

———. 1996. *Multicultural Education as Social Activism*. Albany: State University of New York Press.

Sleeter, Christine. E., and Carl A. Grant. 1993. *Making Choices for Multicultural Education: Five Approaches to Race, Class, and Gender*. New York: Macmillan.

———. 2001. "Race, Class, Gender, Language, Disability and Classroom Life: Approaches to Multicultural Education." In James A. Banks and Cherry A. McGee Banks, *Multicultural Education: Issues and Perspectives*, 1:59–81.

Sleeter, Christine. E., and Dolores Delgado Bernal. 2004. "Critical Pedagogy, Critical Race Theory, and Antiracist Education: Implications for Multicultural Education." In James A. Banks and Cherry A. McGee Banks, *Handbook of Research on Multicultural Education*, 240–60.

Sleeter, Christine, and Peter McLaren. 1995. "Introduction: Exploring Connections to Build a Critical Multiculturalism." In Sleeter and McLaren, *Multicultural Education, Critical Pedagogy, and the Politics of Difference*, 5–32.

Smith, Anthony D. 1981. "War and Ethnicity: The Role of Warfare in the Formation, Self-Images and Cohesion of Ethnic Communities." *Ethnic and Racial Studies* 4 (4): 375–97.

Smooha, Sammy. 1980. "The Control of Minorities in Israel and Northern Ireland." *Comparative Studies in Society and History* 22, no. 2 (April): 256–80.

———. 1989. *Arabs and Jews in Israel: Conflicting and Shared Attitudes in a Divided Society*. Vol. 1. Boulder, CO: Westview Press.

———. 2004. *Index of Arab–Jewish Relations 2004*. Haifa: Jewish-Arab Center, University of Haifa.

———. 2007. "Multiculturalism in Israeli Society." [In Hebrew.] *Zman Yihudi Hadash* 4:221–28.

———. 2010. *Arab–Jewish Relations in Israel: Alienation and Rapprochement*. Washington, DC: United States Institute of Peace.

———. 2016. "Israeli Democracy: Civic and Ethnonational Components." In Ben-Rafael et al., *Handbook of Israel: Major Debates*, 672–90.

Soffer, Arnon. 1988. *On the Demographic and Geographic Situation in Eretz Yisrael: Is It the End of the Zionist Vision?* [In Hebrew.] Haifa: Gistlet.

———. 2016. *Israel's Challenges–2016: Recommendations for National Priorities*. [In Hebrew.] Haifa: Reuven Chaikin Chair in Geostrategy, University of Haifa.

Sommer, Carol A., Nadezda Kholomeydek, Paul Meacham Jr., Zaducka Thomas, Morgan L. Bryant, and Emily C. Derrick. 2012. "The Supervisee with a Thousand Faces: Using Stories to Enhance Supervision." *Journal of Poetry Therapy* 25 (3): 151–63. https://doi.org/10.1080/08893675.2012.709716.

Sonn, Christopher, Brian Bishop, and Ross Humphries. 2000. "Encounters with the Dominant Culture: Voices of Indigenous Students in Mainstream Higher Education." *Australian Psychologist* 35 (2): 128–35. https://doi.org/10.1080/00050060008260334.

Sparks, D. 1983. "Practical Solutions for Teacher Stress." *Theory Into Practice* 22:33–42.

Squillaci, Myriam. 2020. "Analysis of the Burnout Levels of Special Education Teachers in Switzerland in Link with a Reform Implementation." *European Journal of Special Needs Education* 36 (5): 844–53. https://doi.org/10.1080/08856257.2020.1809802.

Standel, Ori. 1973. *The Minorities in Israel: Trends in the Development of Arab and Druze Communities, 1948–1973*. Jerusalem: Israel Economist.

Stanley, W. B. 2007. "Democratic Realism, Neoliberalism, Conservatism, and Tragic Sense of Education." In McLaren and Kincheloe, *Critical Pedagogy: Where Are We Now?*, 371–89.

State Archives (SA). The Arab Minority. Files No. 1351/1616/GL; 145/1223/GL; 1528/1621/GI; 145/1292/GL; 145/1733/G; 145/1293/GL; 25/2402/Foreign Ministry; 3822/1631/GL.

Stavenhagen, Rodolfo. 2009. "Indigenous Peoples as New Citizens of the World." *Latin American and Caribbean Ethnic Studies* 4 (1): 1–15. https://doi.org/10.1080/17442220802681373.

Steinmetz, Moshe, and Eli Ashkenazi. 2015. "An Agreement Was Reached: Thirty-Three Thousand Students of Christian Schools Will Return to Studies." [In Hebrew.] *Walla*, September 28, 2015. https://news.walla.co.il/item/2892866.

Stevens, M. 2007. *Creating a Class*. Cambridge, MA: Harvard University Press.

Sulphey, M. M., Nasser Saad Al-Kahtani, and Abdul Malik Syed. 2018. "Relationship between Admission Grades and Academic Achievement." *Entrepreneurship and Sustainability Issues* 5, no. 3 (March): 648–58. http://doi.org/10.9770/jesi.2018.5.3(17).

Swartz, David. 1997. *Culture and Power: The Sociology of Pierre Bourdieu*. Chicago: University of Chicago Press.

Swift, A. 2003. *How Not to Be a Hypocrite: School Choice for the Morally Perplexed Parent*. London: Routledge.

Swirski, Shlomo, and B. Swirski. 1997. *Higher Education in Israel*. [In Hebrew.] Tel Aviv: Adva Center Series on Equality No. 8.

Tadajewski, Mark. 2016. "Focus Groups: History, Epistemology and Nonindividualistic Consumer Research." *Consumption Markets and Culture* 19 (4): 319–45. https://doi.org/10.1080/10253866.2015.1104038.

Tamimi, A. 2001. *Rachid Ghannouchi: A Democrat within Islamism.* Oxford: Oxford University Press.

Tamir, Emauel, and Khaled Arar. 2019. "High School Principal's Resources Allocation in an Era of Reforms." *International Journal of Educational Management* 33 (5): 15–32.

Tamir, Emanuel, and Lea Shaked. 2016. "What to Do with the Bounty? Organizational Patterns for the Implementation of Resources Allocated by the 'Courage to Change' Reform (Oz Letmura) Reform." *Leadership and Policy in Schools* 15 (4): 567–97. https://doi.org/10.1080/15700763.2016.1181190.

Tan, K. P. 2008. "Meritocracy and Elitism in a Global City: Ideological Shifts in Singapore." *International Political Science Review* 29 (1): 7–27.

Tannenbaum, Michal. 2009. "What's in a Language? Language as a Core Value of Minorities in Israel." *Journal of Ethnic and Migration Studies* 35 (6): 977–95.

Tarlau, Rebecca. 2017. "Gramsci as Theory, Pedagogy, and Strategy: Educational Lessons from the Brazilian Landless Workers Movement." In Pizzolato and Holst, *Antonio Gramsci: A Pedagogy to Change the World*, 107–26.

Thomas, Norma D., and Raina J. León. 2012. "Breaking Barriers: Using Poetry as a Tool to Enhance Diversity Understanding with Youth and Adults." *Journal of Poetry Therapy* 25 (2): 83–93. https://doi.org/10.1080/08893675.2012.680721.

Tibawi, Abd-al-Latif. 1956. *Arab Education in Mandatory Palestine: A Study of Three Decades of British Administration.* London: Luzac.

Tomic, Welko, and Elvira Tomic. 2008. "Existential Fulfillment and Burnout among Principals and Teachers." *Journal of Beliefs and Values* 29 (1): 11–27. https://doi.org/10.1080/13617670801928191.

Torche, F. 2011. "Is a College Degree Still the Great Equalizer? Intergenerational Mobility Across Levels of Schooling in the US." *American Journal of Sociology* 117 (3): 763–807. https://www.jstor.org/stable/10.1086/661904.

Tsofen. 2020. *Policy Paper: Promotion and Construction of High-Tech and Innovation in Arab Society.* [In Hebrew.] Mimeographed. Nazareth: Tsofen.

Tzartzur, Sa'ad. 1981. "Arab Education in a Jewish State: Central Dilemmas." [In Hebrew.] In *One of Every Six Israelis: Mutual Relations between the Arab Minority and the Jewish Majority*, edited by Alouf Hare'evn, 113–31. Jerusalem: Van Leer Institute.

Tzischinsky, O., and I. Haimov. 2017. "Comparative Study Shows Differences in Screen Exposure, Sleep Patterns and Sleep Disturbances between Jewish and Muslim Children in Israel." *Acta Paediatrica* 106 (10): 1642–50. https://doi.org/10.1111/apa.13961.

UNESCO (United Nations Educational, Scientific and Cultural Organization). 1998. *World Declaration on Higher Education for the Twenty-First Century: Vision and*

Action. Paris, World Conference on Higher Education, October 9, 1998. https://en.wikipedia.org/wiki/World_Declaration_on_Higher_Education#cite_note-1.

UNESCO. 2012. "Global Flow of Tertiary-Level Students." Montreal: Institute for Statistics, Scientific and Cultural Organization. https://www.uis.unesco.org/Education/Pages/international-student-flow-viz.aspx.

UNICEF and UNESCO. 2007. A Human Rights-Based Approach to Education for All: A Framework for the Realization of Children's Right to Education and Rights within Education. New York: UNESCO Digital Library. https://unesdoc.unesco.org/ark:/48223/pf0000154861.

UNDRIP (United Nations Declaration on the Rights of Indigenous Peoples). 2007. *The United Nations Declaration on the Rights of Indigenous Peoples*. New York: UN, September 13, 2007. https://www.un.org/development/desa/indigenous-peoples/wp-content/uploads/sites/19/2018/11/UNDRIP_E_web.pdf.

Valeeva Roza, A., and Ilshat R. Gafurov. 2017. "Initial Teacher Education in Russia: Connecting Theory, Practice and Research." *European Journal of Teacher Education* 40 (3): 342–60. https://doi.org/10.1080/02619768.2017.1326480.

Van Horn, J. E., W. B. Schaufeli, and D. Enzmann. 1999. "Teacher Burnout and Lack of Reciprocity." *Journal of Applied Social Psychology* 29:91–108. https://doi.org/10.1111/j.1559-1816.1999.tb01376.x.

Venne, Sharon H. 2011. "The Road to the United Nations and Rights of Indigenous Peoples." *Griffith Law Review* 20 (3): 557–77. https://doi.org/10.1080/10383441.2011.10854710.

Vergen, Yuval, and Orly Lutan. 2007. *Education System in the Bedouin Sector in the Negev: Situation in a Number of Central Aspects*. Prepared for the Knesset's Committee for Education and Culture. [In Hebrew.] Jerusalem: The Israeli Knesset.

Vurgan, Y. 2012. *Israeli Arab Students' Education in the Fields of Education and Teaching in Higher Education Institutions in the Palestinian Authority*. [In Hebrew.] Jerusalem: The Israeli Knesset, Information and Research Center. https://main.knesset.gov.il/Activity/Info/Research/Pages/incident.aspx?docid=175c6b58-e9f7-e411-80c8-00155d010977.

Waschitz, Joseph. 1957. "The Education of Arab Children in Israel." [In Hebrew.] *Ofakim* 11, no. 3 (39): 26–73.

Waterman, Stanley. 1987. "Partitioned State." *Political Geography Quarterly* 6:151–70.

Weber, Max. 1946. "Power." In *From Max Weber: Essays in Sociology*, translated, edited, and introduction by H. H. Gerth and C. W. Mills, 159–71. New York: Oxford University Press.

Webster, Edward. 2008. "Sociologist Unbound: A Celebration of the Work of Jacklyn Cock." *South African Review of Sociology* 39 (2): 175–82. https://doi.org/10.1080/21528586.2008.10425084.

Weiner, Eric J. 2007. "Critical Pedagogy and the Crisis of Imagination." In Peter McLaren and Joe L. Kincheloe, *Critical Pedagogy: Where Are We Now?*, 57–77.

Weiss, Mark. 2022. "Change Coalition Collapse: Bennett, Lapid Send Israel to 5th Elections." *The Jerusalem Post*, June 30, 2022. https://www.jpost.com/jerusalem-report/article-710818.

Weisblai, Iti. 2017. *Church Schools: State of Affairs*. [In Hebrew.] Jerusalem: Knesset Center for Research and Information.

Weisblai, Iti, and Assaf Venger. 2015. *The Education System in Israel*. [In Hebrew.] Submitted to the Knesset Committee for Education, Culture and Sport. Jerusalem: Knesset Center for Research and Information. https://fs.knesset.gov.il/globaldocs/MMM/f7536b58-e9f7-e411-80c8-00155d010977/2_f7536b58-e9f7-e411-80c8-00155d010977_11_10259.pdf.

Wergift, Nurit. 1989. "A School for Discrimination." [In Hebrew.] *Kul Hair* (Jerusalem), June 2, 1989.

Wiggan, Greg, and Marcia J. Watson-Vandiver. 2019. "Pedagogy of Empowerment: Student Perspectives on Critical Multicultural Education at a High-Performing African American School." *Race Ethnicity and Education*, 22 (6): 767–87. https://doi.org/10.1080/13613324.2017.1395328.

Wilkinson, Sue. 1998. "Focus Group Methodology: A Review." *International Journal of Social Research Methodology* 1 (3): 181–203. https://doi.org/10.1080/13645579.1998.10846874.

Williams, Raymond. 1976. "Base and Superstructure in Marxist Cultural Theory." In *Schooling and Capitalism*, edited by R. Dale, G. Esland, and M. MacDonald, 202–10. Boston: Routledge and Kegan Paul.

The World Bank. 2023. *Indigenous Peoples*. https://www.worldbank.org/en/topic/indigenouspeoples.

World Economic Forum. 2018. "Who and What Is Civil Society?" *World Economic Forum* (website). https://www.weforum.org/agenda/2018/04/what-is-civil-society/#.

Yaish, Meir, and Limor Gabay-Egozi. 2021. "Cumulative Disadvantage Dynamics for Palestinian Israeli Arabs in Israel's Economy." *Sociology* 55 (5): 906–26. https://journals.sagepub.com/doi/full/10.1177/0038038520988220.

Yanko, Adir. 2019a. "Drop in Grades, Huge Gaps between Jewish and Arab Students: PISA Exam Data." [In Hebrew.] *Ynet*, December 3, 2019. https://www.ynet.co.il/articles/0,7340,L-5636364,00.html.

———. 2019b. "Without 'Al Quds' and 'Palestine': The Storm of the Citizenship Book for the Arab Sector." [In Hebrew.] *Ynet*, January 31, 2019. https://www.ynet.co.il/articles/0,7340,L-5455308,00.html.

Yashar, Deborah J. 1999. "Democracy, Indigenous Movements, and Postliberal Challenge in Latin America." *World Politics* 52 (1): 76–104.

Yemini, M., and A. Fulop. 2015. "The International, Global and Intercultural Dimensions in Schools: An Analysis of Four Internationalised Israeli Schools." *Globalisation, Societies and Education* 13 (4): 528–52. https://doi.org/10.1080/14767724.2014.967185.

Yemini, M., and Y. Bronshtein. 2016. "The Global–Local Negotiation: Between the Official and the Implemented History Curriculum in Israeli Classrooms." *Globalisation, Societies and Education* 14 (3): 345–57. https://doi.org/10.108 0/14767724.2015.1123086.

Yiftachel, Oren. 2016. "'Ethnocracy': The Politics of Judaizing Israel/Palestine." In Ben-Rafael et al., *Handbook of Israel: Major Debates*, 643–71.

Yonay, Yuval, and Vered Kraus. 2018. *Facing Barriers: Palestinian Women in a Jewish-Dominated Labor Market*. Cambridge: Cambridge University Press.

Yonah, Yossi, Yossi Dahan, and Dalya Markovich. 2008. "Neo-Liberal Reforms in Israel's Education System: The Dialectics of the State." *International Studies in Sociology of Education* 18 (3–4): 199–217. https://doi.org/10.1080/ 09620210802492799.

Young, Iris Marion. 2009. "Two Concepts of Self-Determination." In *Ethnicity, Nationalism and Minority Rights*, edited by Stephen May, Tariq Modood, and Judith Squire, 176–95. Cambridge: Cambridge University Press. https://www-cambridge-org.ezproxy.haifa.ac.il/core/books/ethnicity-nationalism-and-minority-rights/7 4A7A1823C17C475121BC96D3532E4AA.

Yuval, Yoram. 2017. "After a Hundred Years of Zionist Success Story, We Are Allowed to Be Free Also from Fear: On the Decision Not to Sing the National Anthem at the Hebrew University." [In Hebrew.] *Ynet*, May 19, 2017.

Zembylas, Michalinos. 2023. "A Decolonial Approach to AI in Higher Education Teaching and Learning: Strategies for Undoing the Ethics of Digital Neocolonialism." *Learning, Media and Technology* 48 (1): 25–37. https://doi.org/1 0.1080/17439884.2021.2010094.

Zhou, Xiang. 2019. "Equalization or Selection? Reassessing the 'Meritocratic Power' of a College Degree in Intergenerational Income Mobility." *American Sociological Review* 84 (3): 459–85. https://www.jstor.org/stable/10.2307/48595 774.

Zimmerman, Marc A. 1995. "Psychological Empowerment: Issues and Illustrations." *American Journal of Community Psychology* 23 (5): 581–99.

———. 2000. "Empowerment Theory: Psychological, Organizational and Community Levels of Analysis." In *Handbook of Community Psychology*, edited by J. Rappaport and E. Seidman, 43–63. Boston: Springer.

Zimmerman, Aaron S. 2018. "Democratic Teacher Education: Preserving Public Education as a Public Good in an Era of Neoliberalism." *The Educational Forum* 82 (3): 351–68. https://doi.org/10.1080/00131725.2018.1458358.

Zinsser, Judith P. 2004. "A New Partnership: Indigenous Peoples and the United Nations System." *Museum International* 56 (4): 76–88. https://doi.org/10.1111/ j.1468-0033.2004.00053.x.

Zlikovich, Moran. 2006. "Sarid: Abolishment of the Psychometric is a Right Step." [In Hebrew.] *Ynet*, May 23, 2006. https://www.ynet.co.il/articles/0,7340, L-3253903,00.html.

Zwick, Rebecca. 2019. "Assessment in American Higher Education: The Role of Admission Tests." *Annals of the American Academy of Political and Social Science* 683 (1): 130–48. https://doi.org/10.1177/0002716219843469.

Zwick, Rebecca, Andrew Blatter, Lei Ye, and Steven Isham. 2021. "Using an Index of Admission Obstacles with Constrained Optimization to Increase the Diversity of College Classes." *Educational Assessment* 26 (1): 20–34. https://doi.org/10.1080/10627197.2020.1841626.

Index